THE SURGERY BOOK

THE SURGERY BOOK

An Illustrated Guide to 73 of the Most Common Operations

By Robert Youngson, M.D.
and The Diagram Group

St. Martin's Press
New York

Author Dr. Robert Youngson

The Diagram Group
Project coordinator Jane Robertson
Editor Margaret Doyle
Copy editor Mike Darton
Designer Richard Hummerstone
Production Chapman Bounford & Associates, T. J. Graphics
Artists James Dallas, Brian Hewson, Kyri Kyriacou,
Lee Lawrence, Ali Marshall

Library of Congress Cataloging-in-Publication Data

Youngson, R.M.
    The surgery book/Robert M Youngson, with The Diagram
    Group.
        p. cm.
    ISBN 0-312-09398-5
1. Surgery–Popular works.   2. Surgery–Atlases.
    I. Diagram Group. II. Title.
RD31.3.Y67 1993   93-20759
617–dc20   CIP

Note to the reader:
It is essential that any reader who has reason to suspect that
he or she suffers from any of the diseases or physical/
mental ailments discussed in this book contact a physician
and/or surgeon promptly. Neither this nor any other book
should be used as a substitute for professional medical care,
diagnosis, or treatment.

Hospital practices and surgical techniques vary widely and
must often be altered to meet the specific needs of each
individual patient. The procedures outlined in this book are
not to be assumed to be the best or only procedures, nor
should it be concluded that a particular surgeon is
necessarily deviating from good surgical practice if he or she
does not use the same methods described in this book. This
book attempts to present a general description of standard
surgical practice, current as of the time of initial publication.

First Edition: October 1993
10 9 8 7 6 5 4 3 2 1

Foreword

Having an operation can be one of the most traumatic—and least understood—events in our lives. Many of us undergo surgical procedures without a firm grasp of what is being done and, often more important, how it will affect our lives. **The Surgery Book** is designed to address that gap in our knowledge by setting out, in accessible, jargon-free language and easy-to-follow illustrations, exactly what is done and how in more than 70 of the most commonly performed operations.

How is the decision to operate made? What happens when you are admitted to the hospital? These and other questions are typical of those asked by patients facing the prospect of surgery. Whatever the procedure being considered, however minor or major, all potential patients will benefit from the detailed overview of the hospital provided by the first four chapters of **The Surgery Book**. Chapter 1 describes general hospital procedures, including how operations are classified by urgency. The different types of anesthesia available are explained, and common fears about anesthesia are addressed. Chapter 2 is a thorough look at the various diagnostic tests that may be carried out before your operation, including biopsies and scans, to provide more information on your condition and overall health. Chapter 3 explains the complexities of blood: how it is typed, how transfusions work, and what special concerns are involved, including what modern measures are taken to prevent spread of human immunodeficiency virus (HIV). The latest developments in transplants—of bone marrow, tissues, and organs—are also featured in this chapter, as are the options available for replacing parts of the body with mechanical or prosthetic devices. Chapter 4 concludes the introductory section with an overview of the operating room: what it looks like, who does what, and what equipment may be used. Knowing what to expect will go a long way toward relieving your apprehension about a hospital stay.

Chapters 5 through 13 describe the specific surgical procedures. Each procedure is organized clearly and concisely in the form of answers to commonly asked questions, ranging from Why have the operation? to How does it feel immediately following the procedure? The text takes the reader through a step-by-step description of how the procedure is performed, explaining alternative methods or techniques where they apply. Each procedure is illustrated with simple but accurate diagrams labeled for easy reference. To help address what are often patients' most pressing concerns, the procedures each conclude with descriptions of how you will feel immediately after surgery and of any longterm effects.

The Surgery Book also includes an extensive glossary of surgery-related terms, not only those used within the book but also others you might come across. Each term is explained in simple, concise language.

Written by an experienced surgeon and approved by a panel of medical experts, **The Surgery Book** can be trusted to provide you with accurate details about the latest surgical techniques and developments. Whether it is used to help you overcome fear of an upcoming procedure, or to provide better support for a friend or loved one having an operation, **The Surgery Book** will provide the answers you need to better understand modern surgery.

Contents

CHAPTER 6 · **SURGERY TO THE HEAD**

CHAPTER 7 · **NECK SURGERY**

CHAPTER 8 · **ARM AND LEG SURGERY**

CHAPTER 9 · **HEART SURGERY**

CHAPTER 10 · **SURGERY TO THE CHEST**

CHAPTER 11 · **ABDOMINAL AND LOWER BACK SURGERY**

CHAPTER 12 · **THE REPRODUCTIVE SYSTEM**

CHAPTER 13 · **COSMETIC SURGERY**

CHAPTER 1
HOSPITAL PROCEDURES

BEFORE, DURING, AND AFTER SURGERY

Facing a surgical operation is a daunting experience we would all like to avoid. Since you are reading this book, the chances are that you are scheduled for surgery. And however courageous you may be, it would be unusual if you were not feeling anxious, perhaps even fearful. You are likely to be wondering how you can get out of this unpleasant situation, and how necessary your operation really is.

That is not always an easy question to answer and your surgeon may not have had much time to discuss it with you. You may have misunderstood something that was said to you and it's possible that the proposed operation is not as essential as you think. Yet your operation may be more critical to your health than you realize. However worried you are, it is always better to know the facts so that you can clearly understand what you are facing. Truth may be unpleasant, but it is something most people can face up to and cope with. The real problem is what to do about the unknown. So to help you get some realistic answers to the questions that may be troubling you, let's start by taking a look at the different categories of surgery.

CATEGORIES OF SURGERY

There are five categories. In order of increasing urgency they are:
- optional
- elective
- necessary
- essential
- emergency

You should certainly be aware of which category you are in. If you are in any doubt, ask your surgeon. But first, read on.

Optional surgery. This is surgery that you decide you want to have, not because it is necessary or even conducive to health, but because you want it. In general, optional surgery is done for cosmetic reasons and there should never be any pressure on you, either from the surgeon or from anyone else, to have it done. Occasionally, you may come across a surgeon who leans on you to have a cosmetic procedure. Unless the surgeon is an exceptional person with a high, disinterested regard for your psychological well-being, chances are he or she is thinking of a higher bank balance. This is acceptable if the surgery is something you deeply desire. But beware the surgeon who tries to persuade you, against your inclinations, that you need a nose job or breast reduction or any other form of optional surgery.

This is not to imply that all cosmetic surgery is optional. The removal of blemishes that are a serious disadvantage, socially, commercially, or psychologically, might well fall into the elective or even the necessary category.

Elective surgery. Here again there is an element of choice, but less than in the optional category. Elective procedures include correction of conditions that, realistically, should be operated upon but that, if left alone, would not cause any worsening in your condition or give rise later to any complications or hazards. If you elect not to have such surgery, things will probably stay as they are and you will have to live with the problem. Some elective procedures, such as vasectomy or laparoscopic sterilization, may confer some advantage but are not essential to your health. Other procedures aim to correct conditions that are obviously to your disadvantage and that most people would think should be corrected. Some of these are conditions of mainly cosmetic concern.

Necessary surgery. When surgery is deemed "necessary," it is right and proper—in fact mandatory—for doctors to try to persuade you to have it. Surgeons who do not do so, or who do not ensure that you are fully aware of the implications of refusing surgery, would be failing in their duties. It is, however, important for you to understand that no one can compel you to have surgery if you have decided that you don't want it. A surgeon who insists on and actually carries out an operation against your will would be guilty of an actionable assault.

In this category there is not usually any great urgency, although delay may sometimes lead to a worsening of your condition. Usually you will have time for discussion and mature consideration. There is a large range of conditions for which surgery is necessary. Indeed, most operations performed fall into this category.

Essential surgery. Essential surgery is often also urgent. Unless it is performed, your condition is likely to go downhill fairly quickly. Alternatively, you may remain liable to a sudden deterioration or even to sudden death. Surgery in this category is not a matter for argument or even discussion. A positive diagnosis has been made and the consequences of your failing to get effective surgical treatment are not in dispute. You really have little or no choice and, although you retain a legal right to refuse surgery, you would be ill advised to decide against it.

There is a gray area between this and the highest category—emergency surgery. Some essential operations come very close to being emergency procedures; others may fall into either category depending on the degree of severity.

Emergency surgery. Emergency surgery is always urgent, sometimes critically urgent, and is usually necessary to save life. It is needed when vital functions are threatened by disorders affecting the heart, circula-

Categories of surgery

Examples of operations performed under each of the five classes of surgery. Note: certain operations may fall into more than one class.

Optional surgery

- *excess fat removal (suction lipectomy)*
- *breast implant (augmentation mammoplasty)*
- *wart, mole, or tattoo removal*
- *face lift (rhytidectomy)*
- *nose reshaping (rhinoplasty)*

Elective surgery

- *correction of long-term squint (strabismus) in adults*
- *removal of bunions*
- *enhancement of unsightly teeth*
- *correction of long-standing contractions of the limbs or hands*
- *removal of a cataract in one eye*
- *removal of or disguise of conspicuous birthmarks (port-wine marks and cavernous hemangiomas)*
- *circumcision*
- *vasectomy*
- *laparoscopic sterilization*

Necessary surgery

- *removal of torn knee cartilage (meniscectomy)*
- *hip or knee replacement (prosthetic arthroplasty)*
- *cataract surgery when both eyes are affected*
- *hernia repair*
- *gallbladder removal (cholecystectomy)*
- *operations for longterm sinusitis*
- *prostate surgery without obstruction (prostatectomy)*
- *reduction of a hiatus hernia*
- *correction of squint in a young child*
- *breast lump diagnosis (breast biopsy)*

Essential surgery

- *removal of a brain tumor*
- *coronary artery bypass*
- *heart valve replacement*
- *pacemaker implantation*
- *prostate surgery with obstruction (prostatectomy)*
- *appendectomy*
- *removal of a malignant melanoma*
- *kidney or heart transplant*
- *operations for cancer of the lung or colon*
- *removal of malignant breast lump (lumpectomy)*
- *removal of the womb (hysterectomy) for cancer*

Emergency surgery

- *treatment for any life-threatening condition*

tion, and brain, or when there is a risk of overwhelming infection or bacterial or other poisoning (toxemia).

Severe bleeding, either from injury or disease, is a common indication for emergency surgery. This may occur from a ruptured spleen, from damage to any of the large arteries in the trunk or limbs, or from varicose veins that have formed in the lower end of the esophagus (gullet) as a result of cirrhosis of the liver. Bleeding within the skull (epidural, subdural, or subarachnoid hemorrhage) is particularly dangerous and often calls for urgent emergency surgery to relieve the pressure before the brain stem is forced fatally downward. Other conditions that may call for emergency surgery include imminent rupture of an inflamed appendix or the resulting widespread abdominal infection (peritonitis); repair of massive ballooning, with threatened rupture, of the largest artery in the body (an aortic aneurysm); repair of stab wounds of the heart; and removal of a loop of gangrenous intestine caused by twisting (volvulus) or compression in an abdominal wall orifice (strangulated hernia).

By now you will probably have decided into which category your operation falls. Remember that your surgeon almost certainly knows a great deal more about your condition than you do, and that the surgeon's advice is based on detailed knowledge of the condition you are suffering from and of what will probably happen if you don't have the operation. Don't hesitate to change your mind if you are clearly in the optional and elective categories. But think very seriously and take careful advice if you are in the other categories.

BEFORE YOUR OPERATION
It is very helpful to know what to expect when you go into the hospital for your operation. Of course, different hospitals have different routines, but there are certain broad principles that apply to all, and an understanding of these, and of the reasons behind them, may go a long way to relieving your anxiety.

Medical records. Medical records are important, sometimes critically important, and one of the first things that happens to you when you go into the hospital for an operation is the preparation or updating of your records. The surgeon will already know a great deal about you from earlier consultations, but after you enter the hospital the existing records must be filled out and updated. This will probably be done by an intern, but you are likely also to be questioned by a nurse. The anesthetist, too, will add to the notes, as we shall see.

Don't be surprised, or annoyed, if you find a young doctor asking you many questions that you have already answered. The medical history is usually the most important part of the investigation and it's often valuable for more than one person to take the details. Different people have different experience and can direct questions differently. It is impossible for your doctors to know too much about you.

You will be asked about:

- the history of your present complaint and whether there has been any recent change
- your previous medical history—anything that has happened to you might be relevant—especially major illnesses or persistent problems, even if they seem unconnected with the immediate disorder
- your general health—your standard of fitness, any tendency to breathlessness, palpitations, ankle swelling, or any persistent cough
- your eating habits and bowel action, urinary difficulty or incontinence, whether you get up at night to empty your bladder, and whether you have any sleeping problems
- your family history—the age, state of health or cause of death of close relatives. Disorders often run in families, even without an obvious genetic basis. The doctor will be especially interested in any family history of coronary heart disease, high blood pressure, or diabetes.
- your occupation or lifestyle. Many jobs involve subtle hazards to health. Even work undertaken many years before could have relevance to current disease. If, for example, you have a persistent cough and breathlessness, previous employment in an asbestos-processing plant could be highly relevant. Or if you are in the hospital for an examination under anesthesia to investigate the cause of blood in your urine, the fact that you used to work in the rubber industry could be of major importance. Antioxidants used in rubber manufacture can cause cancer of the bladder. Many industrial processes are now known to be hazardous and to have a longterm adverse effect on health.
- any allergies you might have, or if you have ever had a reaction to any medication or other substance
- your smoking and drinking habits. Try to be honest, especially about the latter. There is a strong tendency to underreport our alcohol intake, even to ourselves. The doctor is interested in doing what's best for you, not in expressing a critical attitude about drinking, and an accurate knowledge of alcohol consumption can be important.
- overseas travel. Many conditions, rare in the United States, may be acquired abroad. Some of these cause real diagnostic puzzles and often the symptoms don't make sense until you mention that you have been out of the country.

Medication while in the hospital. On your admission, the nurses will want to know about any medication you are taking, and you should tell them about any supplies you have with you. During your hospital stay, all necessary medication will be arranged and will be given at set times.

Naturally, you must not take any of your own medication in addition—this could lead to overdosage or could interfere with prescribed treatment. As long as the medical staff know all about you and your medical needs, you can safely leave all questions of medication to them. Any longterm treatment you need will be added to the list of prescribed treatments and will be given to you on the routine drug rounds. If you are an insulin-dependent diabetic, the staff will take responsibility for your control and are likely to perform independent checks on your blood sugar. The anesthetist will be especially interested in your blood sugar situation, and is likely to set up an intravenous catheter before your operation, even if you don't need this for other reasons. The main concern, during the period you are anesthetized, will be the possibility of a critical drop in your blood sugar (hypoglycemia), and the anesthetist will take steps to avoid this.

Routine checks. At regular intervals your temperature, pulse rate, and blood pressure will be checked and recorded. You may also be weighed. It is customary to do certain routine tests on all patients, regardless of the reason for their admission. You can read all about medical tests and diagnostic procedures in the next chapter, but, at the least, you are likely to have some blood taken for tests of your hemoglobin level and red and white blood cell counts. You are also likely to be asked to give a urine specimen for routine urinalysis.

Preoperative examination. This is second in importance only to your medical history. The doctor may:
- check your pulse and blood pressure
- check the color of your skin for jaundice
- look at the insides of your lower eyelids for anemia
- look in your mouth and check the state of your teeth and tongue
- examine the state of the lymph nodes in your neck, armpits, groin, and elsewhere
- examine your chest, tapping it to check for normal resonance and listening to your heart and breath sounds with a stethoscope
- test your tendon jerk reflexes

Depending on the reason for your admission, your doctor will then carry out a more specific examination directed at the current state of your particular surgical problem. Whatever part is affected will be closely scrutinized and, if appropriate, carefully palpated. If you have an abdominal problem, the doctor will carefully press all over with the flat of his or her hand, feeling for tenderness or masses, and may do so by feeling, on either side, between both hands. In many cases a rectal examination is essential. If you have already had this done, you will know that it is nothing to worry about. The doctor wears disposable plastic gloves and uses a gel lubricant. The procedure is completely painless, but some people find it a little embarrassing. Just remember that the doctor has done this often and is interested solely in what can be found out from the examination—and that is often a great deal.

If you are a woman with a pelvic or gynecological problem, a vaginal examination is also likely to be essential. This may be distasteful for you but, for the doctor, it is a daily routine.

The day before your operation

For many routine procedures, outpatient surgery can be arranged. In this case, if your operation is to be in the morning, you will be told about the importance of not eating or drinking anything after midnight on the previous day. But if you have been admitted to the hospital before the day of your operation, preparations will begin the evening before surgery.

Food. For safety, it is usual for the staff to hang a notice over your bed that states NOTHING BY MOUTH. This prohibition applies for about six hours before you have an anesthetic. It is instituted because if there is anything in your stomach when you are given a general anesthetic, there is a definite risk that, when all your muscles have relaxed, the stomach contents may well up into your throat. Because your gag reflex has been temporarily nullified, you may inhale the strongly acidic material into your lungs. This can lead to a particularly severe and damaging form of pneumonia. So if, for any reason, you have broken the rules, it is vitally important for you to say so before you have the anesthetic.

Marking the skin. The intern will probably check the notes and, having confirmed the type and site of the operation to be done, will mark your skin with a felt pen, making an arrow or other mark to ensure that the right operation is done in the right place. It is very rare for mistakes to happen, and they are unpardonable. Marking helps to avoid such misfortunes. Marking is also sometimes used to indicate the exact location of a lump or other abnormality, or to show the surgeon where the incisions should be made. Plastic and cosmetic surgeons are particularly liable to draw a map of the operation on you the day before. These marks are not easy to wash off, but then there is no reason for you to try; they are an aid to your surgeon.

Shaving the skin. It may be necessary for a nurse to shave your skin at and around the site of the operation. There are differences of opinion about the value of shaving and it seems likely that it does not in fact reduce bacterial skin contamination. Long skin hair can, however, be a nuisance to the surgeon, especially when stitching up an incision, and many surgeons prefer the area to be shaved.

Nasogastric intubation. For some procedures it is necessary to pass a fine, soft-plastic tube down into the stomach before surgery in order to suck out the contents and keep it empty. This is not a complicated procedure. The tube passes along the floor of your nose and down the back of your throat and esophagus (gullet). At first you may have a continuous feeling that you want to swallow, but this will pass and soon you will hardly notice the tube.

Urethral catheterization. It is sometimes necessary to ensure that the bladder is kept empty, so a blunt-nosed rubber or plastic tube—a catheter—may be inserted inside the urine outlet tube (the urethra) and into the bladder. Catheters are fitted with a push-in stopper or are connected to a disposable plastic bag. If your bowels are operating satisfactorily, well and good, but if you are constipated, an enema might be recommended.

Blood transfusions. Many operations inevitably involve substantial loss of blood, however careful the surgeon may be to tie off and control bleeding vessels. Surgical shock, in which the available blood volume may, for various reasons, be inadequate to maintain proper circulation, is also an ever-present risk. For these reasons it is often routine to start an intravenous fluid infusion before the operation and to convert this to a blood transfusion during the operation as the need arises. The blood transfusion may be continued for a day or two afterward. In anticipation of this, your blood type (A, B, O, rhesus, Kell, etc.) will be carefully checked and a quantity of donated blood will be set aside for your exclusive use. This blood will be cross-matched with your own blood to ensure that both are completely compatible and that the transfusion will be safe. All donated blood is carefully tested for AIDS and hepatitis so that the risk of infection during a transfusion is very low. Some hospitals will store several pints of the patient's own blood taken in several sessions up to three days prior to surgery.

The visit from the anesthetist. It is usual for the anesthetist to visit you on the day or evening before the operation. The first concern is to ensure that you are fit for surgery and that the anesthetic is going to be safe. The anesthetist will not take chances and, if doubtful, will postpone the operation, even at the risk of annoying the surgeon. He or she will be especially interested in whether you have any signs of a chest infection and whether your blood pressure is satisfactory. Also, the anesthetist will read your records and may query a few points with you, especially about your general health, as well as about allergies and any family history of anesthetic problems.

After listening carefully to your heart and lungs the anesthetist is likely to have a look at the shape of your neck and then look in your mouth to check whether you have any loose teeth. He or she is also likely to ask if you have any crowned teeth. The reason for all this is that after you are asleep the anesthetist will probably be passing a tube down your throat and between your vocal cords into your trachea (windpipe). This can be easy or difficult, depending on the shape of your neck. The anesthetist is also concerned to ensure that no loose teeth

© DIAGRAM

get knocked out in the process, which involves the use of an instrument called a laryngoscope. A tooth that comes adrift and passes down is no joke for anyone.

Finally, your anesthetist is likely to discuss the question of premedication. From your point of view, this is a major issue because it can make a great difference to your state of mind as the time for the operation approaches. Suitable "premed" can produce a calm, relaxed, even pleasurable attitude both before and after the operation. It is quite likely that you will wake up after your operation with no recollection of having being taken to the operating room.

It's normal to experience anxiety as you settle down to try to sleep the night before your operation. Your room may be perfectly quiet, and you may have complete confidence in your anesthetist and surgeon, but you are still going to worry. So if the nurse asks you if you would like a pill to help you to sleep, don't hesitate. This is one occasion when a sleeping pill is eminently justified.

ANESTHESIA

Fear of the anesthetic. Some people may be almost as apprehensive about the anesthetic as about the surgery. But cases in which things go wrong with a general anesthetic get into the media only because they are uncommon and exceptional. In fact, millions of people have anesthetics every year. Today, general anesthesia is safer than it has ever been, mainly because of improved standards of anesthetic training and discipline, but also because modern anesthetic methods allow the use of small doses of anesthetic agents: you are never allowed to go into really deep anesthesia. So there is no risk of your coming to harm from anesthetic overdose. Also, the monitoring equipment that continuously checks your condition, and especially the level of oxygen in your blood, provides better and more reliable surveillance than ever before. A great deal of attention has rightly been given in recent years to improving the routine safety of general anesthesia.

Talking in your sleep. Maybe, like many people, you are worried that you might talk during anesthesia and give away your innermost secrets. Certainly, very lightly anesthetized people do, occasionally, mutter some meaningless sounds, but with general anesthesia, rarely is this recognizable speech. Comments on the operation by the patient, however uninformative, are a signal to the anesthetist that the level of anesthesia is a little too shallow and that a slightly larger dose of one of the anesthetic agents is needed.

Waking up too soon. Many people are terrified at the possibility that they may wake up during the operation. Surprisingly, in view of the light anesthesia used nowadays, this does not seem to be a problem. Even patients who move a little during the operation—and this is quite common—do not appear to have any recollection of doing so or of being conscious. Again, it is possible for a patient who has been deliberately paralyzed by muscle relaxants such as curare to approach consciousness, but this cannot happen without an observable change occurring in the monitoring equipment so that the anesthetist is prompted to deepen the level a little. It would be extremely rare for a patient to complain of awareness during an operation, and even very lightly anesthetized patients never experience any pain.

The pulse oximeter. The one thing that really matters during an anesthetic is whether your brain is getting enough oxygen. Methods are now available for continuous monitoring of the oxygen level in the blood. So, whatever happens—even if the oxygen tube somehow becomes disconnected, or the cylinder of oxygen runs out—the blood oxygen monitor can immediately inform everyone in the operating room (OR) that something has happened and appropriate action can immediately be taken. It is the pulse oximeter, a small device that clips onto your fingertip or earlobe or may, perhaps, be taped to your forehead, that achieves this remarkable standard of safety. As long as the device is in place and your blood oxygen is up to 95 percent, a regular beep occurs and everyone in the OR knows that you are OK. But if the oxygen level drops by only 5 percent, the beep will change. And, of course, if the oximeter head drops off, this will be apparent at once.

Blood oxygen is not the only parameter that is monitored. Your heart rate and electrocardiogram tracing (ECG), your blood pressure, your breathing rate, even the volume of gases you are breathing per minute, all are continuously displayed and, often, recorded.

For these and other reasons, anesthetics have never been safer. They are now given routinely and safely to patients who would, not so many years ago, have been thought too seriously ill or frail to be given an anesthetic at all.

Modern anesthetic methods
General anesthesia. Years ago it was necessary to give large doses of anesthetic drugs to achieve the deep level of muscle relaxation required for surgery. Modern anesthetic methods work differently. The current aim is to keep you quietly asleep, quite near to the level of consciousness, and to use other nonanesthetic drugs to take away all pain and other sensation, to relax your muscles, and to keep you from surgical shock.

Induction of anesthesia with a mask and anesthetic gas or vapor is rare these days, although vapors can be used that are pleasant to inhale and rapid in their action. But mostly the anesthetist puts you to sleep (if you are not already asleep from the preoperative injection) by giving you a small injection of a rapidly acting and powerful drug. Modern induction agents work so quickly and efficiently that, from your

© DIAGRAM

point of view, the injection has no sooner started than you are waking up in the recovery room, or back in bed, astonished to find it is all over.

Local anesthesia. Methods of removing all pain sensation from limited areas of the body have improved so much in recent years that many operations, formerly possible only under general anesthesia, can now be done using some form of local anesthesia or regional nerve block. There is no loss of consciousness with local anesthesia, although sometimes the method is combined with a sedative such as diazepam so that you can be thoroughly relaxed. Patients under local anesthesia are able to talk to their surgeon, and some may even watch the operation taking place by means of a video monitor above the operating table.

The idea, in giving a local anesthetic, is to prevent the passage of nerve impulses along the nerves that carry pain messages to the brain. This is done by injecting cocainelike drugs that act on the nerves to prevent them temporarily from working. Actual cocaine is never given by injection. Most local anesthetic drugs are synthetic substances similar in structure to cocaine. There is no question of addiction.

The injection may be given:

● into the area in which the surgeon is working
● around the main trunks of the nerves carrying sensation
● around the part of the spinal cord carrying pain fibers up to the brain

In each case, the effect is the same. As long as all the nerves carrying pain messages from the operation site are prevented from conducting impulses, nothing will be felt. It doesn't matter how far away the injection is from the operation site.

Injections into the spine. Because the nerves relaying sensation to the brain are all packed closely together as they enter the spinal cord, a small injection in this area can cause temporary anesthesia over a wide area of the body below the point of the injection. In epidural anesthesia—which is widely used in childbirth—and spinal block anesthesia, the anesthetic drug is concentrated in the region of the back part of the lower end of the spinal cord. These methods are used mainly for surgery on the legs and lower abdomen.

Surface anesthesia. Surface anesthesia can be used in parts of the body that are able to absorb local anesthetic drugs, by spraying or by applying it as a cream.

Depending on the procedure you are to have, one or other of these methods of local anesthesia may be used. None of them involves significant pain, and few cause any adverse reactions as long as the dosages used are moderate and the drug is not absorbed directly into the bloodstream. In the event of rapid absorption you may feel dizzy. With epidural and spinal blocks faintness can occur because of a drop in blood pressure from interference with the nerves of the sympathetic

Surface anesthesia
Forms of surface anesthesia and examples of use

Creams
Any injection can be made painless by first rubbing an anesthetic cream into the skin.

Gels
The urinary passage (urethra) can be numbed with an anesthetic gel before a catheter is passed or a cystoscope is pushed through it for examination of the inside of the bladder. The gel is squeezed in from a tube through a blunt applicator.

Lozenges
Lozenges containing the anesthetic drug benzocaine can be sucked to numb the mouth and throat.

Sprays
The throat, the larynx (voice box), the trachea (windpipe), and the larger breathing tubes (bronchi) can be sprayed before passing down a bronchoscope.

Suppositories
Anesthetic ointments or suppositories can be used to relieve the pain of hemorrhoids (piles) or fissures around the anus.

nervous system. The alert anesthetist knows how to deal with this complication. A spinal anesthetic may be followed by a fairly severe headache, but this can be relieved by lying flat or through other measures.

AFTER YOUR OPERATION
Your condition and state of mind. After your operation you may feel perfectly OK—or you may experience bouncing euphoria or extreme debility and wretchedness. The outcome depends on many factors, including the condition for which you have been treated, your general state of health, and the events in the OR. Although modern anesthetics produce none of the sickness and depression formerly associated with ether and other agents, a major operation can be a debilitating and depressing experience, especially if you lose a lot of blood. So don't be surprised, or too disappointed, if you feel less than 100 percent afterward.

© DIAGRAM

Nausea. After an abdominal operation you may experience quite a lot of nausea as a result of the handling your stomach or intestines have undergone. Sometimes the stomach loses its normal tension and balloons out with fluid. This is called dilatation, and it can cause considerable nausea. In this event a fine tube is carefully passed down into the stomach, and the stomach contents are sucked out via a plastic syringe. After this you will feel a lot better.

Colic. Another common postoperative symptom is colic from internal gas production, which may be sufficient to cause distention of the abdomen. Gas can cause severe discomfort or even pain, and may sometimes endanger the success of the operation. The answer is a fairly wide tube passed into the rectum to let out the gas during the first day or two. Don't let this embarrass you; it's just another common medical routine.

Pain. Postoperative pain should never be a major problem. It is part of the duty of your anesthetist to ensure that pain after the operation is adequately controlled. Modern anesthetists are experts at this. They know, for instance, that the old idea of not giving painkillers until the pain becomes severe is quite wrong, and that drugs such as morphine are far more effective when given in small doses at frequent intervals than given in larger doses only when the patient is in agony. They also know that the use of major narcotics is commonly justified, and that the risk of addiction when they are given for pain over the course of a few days is negligible. Narcotics, such as morphine, not only relieve pain but also produce a serene state of mind that can be invaluable for a short period after a major operation.

There is even a method by which the patient decides when he or she needs more pain relief and receives a small dose of a drug such as papaveretum (a mixture of opium alkaloids) simply by pressing a button on a device strapped to the forearm. This requires a saline infusion to be running continuously, and the system monitors the dosage so that it is impossible to take too much.

The importance of movement. You will be urged to move about in bed, and even to get up, long before you feel ready for it, and you may well find yourself alarmingly weak and shaky. You may also find movement painful. Try not to let these things discourage you from a positive attitude and a determination to recover as soon as possible. You will soon make up lost blood and, with an effort, recover your fitness. Your attitude will have a major effect on your rate of recovery.

But there is another very important reason for maintaining as near a normal degree of movement as possible. People who lie quietly in bed for some considerable time after an operation are liable to develop long, snaky blood clots in the veins of their legs. These clots are attached at one end and can grow to a considerable size. If such a clot breaks loose from the wall of the vein it may be carried up to the right side of the heart and pumped from there to the lungs, where it may completely block the major vessels carrying blood to the lungs. This is called a pulmonary embolism, and a major one is nearly always fatal.

Movement also helps you to breathe deeply and so avoid stagnation pneumonia. It helps to keep your circulation going more briskly, and it is good for your morale to be able to do things for yourself, such as going to the toilet. You may well feel you have excellent reasons to feel sorry for yourself and just want to lie there and be pampered. It is certainly possible you have good reasons to pity yourself, but such an attitude is negative and unproductive. Movement is life.

Some procedures make it impossible for you to get out of bed for many days after surgery. In such a case, regular movement of at least your legs is vital.

Many people find it difficult to use a bedpan, mainly out of embarrassment. As a result, postoperative constipation is common. If you mobilize early and are able to make your own way to the toilet, don't worry about a few days' constipation. This can do no harm. Ask for a gentle laxative, such as lactulose, and wait patiently. If you are confined to bed, the time may come when you need an enema. This is a simple matter, nowadays, using the small, modern, plastic, disposable type of enema with a short nozzle and a squeezable bulb containing the fluid.

Stitch removal. Stitches (sutures) often don't have to be removed these days. It is quite common for surgeons to use absorbable stitches, and these are simply left alone. If there are exposed knots, these eventually drop off—or you can simply pick them out after a couple of weeks.

If your surgeon has used nonabsorbable stitches or skin clips or even staples, there is no need to be nervous about removal. This is usually done five to ten days after the operation. Sometimes the smaller stitches are removed in the first session, and a number of larger tension sutures are left to take the strain of the wound for a few days longer. Stitches are cut with pointed scissors or with a special curved scalpel blade, and this, of course, is entirely painless. Each stitch is cut flush with the skin, and you may then feel a little discomfort or tugging as the cut stitch is pulled through the deeper tissues and out, with tweezerlike forceps.

Probably the worst aspect of stitch removal is when the stitches have become matted with dried serum or discharge, and have stuck together or to adjacent hairs. If this happens and it causes pain, ask the nurse to apply a pad of gauze soaked in saline to free the stitches. Sometimes the hair has to be cut, but this is of little consequence.

Skin clips and staples are removed with an instrument that bends them backward so that the pointed ends separate and swing out.

GOING HOME

The length of time you spend in the hospital depends on the procedure you have had, your response to it, and the rate of your recovery. Complications may set you back and delay your discharge. In general, however, you will be deemed fit to go home when:

 you are past the stage at which complications are likely to occur

 you are safely mobile

 you are reasonably free of pain

 the function of your digestive system has returned to normal

 the operation wound is secured and all drains are removed

 there is no sign of infection or fever

 the results of all tests are satisfactory

Later in the book you will find details of the average length of stay for most of the operations described.

When you are given a date for discharge you can start arranging for transportation, and for your clothes to be brought in. If you need any medication, this, or a prescription, will be provided, and you will be given a letter for your own physician so that he or she can be adequately informed about what has happened to you. Arrangements are also likely to be made for your progress to be followed up by your surgeon in the office or in the outpatient clinic. However well you may feel, don't consider driving yourself home. Get a relative or friend to pick you up, or take a taxi.

But before you go, how about a word of thanks to the dedicated nurses and doctors who have looked after you so well?

OUTPATIENT SURGERY

For various reasons, mostly financial, much minor surgery is performed without an overnight stay in the hospital. This can save you, or your insurance company, quite a lot of money and, as long as commercial motives do not override medical discretion, outpatient surgery is usually safe. Other plus points include less domestic disturbance, a much shorter time away from home, the comforts of home convalescence, and often a quicker return to work. All the preliminary studies and checks can be done on an outpatient basis.

For outpatient surgery under general anesthesia you must, of course, have consumed nothing to eat or drink from the previous midnight (see above for reasons), and you will probably have to report to the clinic or hospital at a very early hour in the morning. When you arrive you will change into a hospital gown and settle down in bed, where you will be seen by your surgeon and anesthetist.

Outpatient surgery under local anesthesia offers no real problem, but if you are having general anesthesia, the staff will have to be assured that you make a full recovery before they let you go home. There is no question of your making your way home by yourself, however fully you may seem to have recovered. This would be asking for trouble. So it is essential that arrangements should be made, beforehand, for you to be accompanied by a relative or friend.

For outpatient surgery, anesthetists use drugs that clear rapidly from your body, and you may feel OK, but it would be very unwise, and indeed dangerous, for you to drive until at least the following day. If anything went wrong, you could be liable to a charge of driving under the influence of drugs.

CHAPTER 2
EXAMINING THE BODY

One of the few basic principles in medicine is that you try to find out what is wrong before you do anything about it. In medical jargon, diagnosis should always, when possible, precede therapy. Of course there are occasions when something has to be done at once without waiting to find out the cause. It would be unthinkable to deny a patient available relief of severe pain simply because the cause was unknown. But doctors in this situation are always very uneasy and try to get to a diagnosis as soon as possible. Treating without a diagnosis is called symptomatic treatment. To do this routinely is very bad medicine and is rightly condemned by scientific doctors.

In general, surgical conditions—disorders that are corrected by an operation—tend to be easier to diagnose than medical conditions—those treated purely by drugs. In many surgical conditions the diagnosis is fairly obvious from the outset. Sometimes, however, it is necessary to operate simply to find out what is causing the trouble. Surgery of this kind is most commonly necessary within the abdominal cavity, in which case the operation is called an exploratory laparotomy, and the access and information it provides often allow the surgeon to proceed immediately to curative intervention. Laparotomies are also sometimes done not because there is doubt as to the diagnosis, but in order to find out how far a disease has already progressed and whether it can be corrected during the exploratory procedure.

It isn't often necessary to resort to exploratory surgery. In the great majority of cases the facts can be established by less invasive methods. In this chapter we look at some of the ways in which the modern surgeon is able to reach a diagnosis, including:

- X-ray examination, including angiography
- scanning, including CT scanning, magnetic resonance imaging (MRI), PET scanning, ultrasound and radionuclide scanning
- endoscopy—a process that uses various optical devices for viewing the interior of the body
- examination using microscopes
- electrical tests, including EEGs and ECGs
- laboratory tests, including those carried out on blood, urine, and other fluids
- biopsies—microscopic examination of tissue samples

X RAYS

X rays can provide photographic images of the inside of the body. They have a shorter wavelength than light and so can pass through material opaque to light. The degree to which X rays can penetrate depends on the density of the material concerned. The lower the density, the more transparent it is to the rays. Soft tissues, such as skin and muscle, are thus more transparent to X rays than bone or dense objects such as kidney stones and bullets.

Phosphor screens
Phosphor screens can be used with X rays to show a moving image of what is happening inside the body. They are used:
- to guide wires into arteries to direct catheters
- to ensure that metal pins, or nails, being driven down the center of bones get to the right place
- to follow the progress down the alimentary canal of a barium "meal" swallowed by the patient, to observe the state of the coronary arteries during angiography, and for many other purposes

Contrast media
X-ray examination may be supplemented and made more versatile by the use of a range of substances that to one degree or another block out the rays and that can be introduced into the various systems of the body to outline the interior structure. These are called contrast media. They include barium sulfate, which can be swallowed or used as an enema for the examination of the digestive system, and various iodine solutions, which can be used in the blood (see p.30 under angiography) and the urinary system. The use of contrast media, when appropriate, can provide far more information than simple X rays. A deep ulcer on the lining of the stomach, for instance, will fill with barium and show on the film as a conspicuous "button" projecting outward from the outline of the rest of the barium. An abnormal mass within an organ, such as a cancer, will, on the other hand, show as an area in which the barium is absent. This is called a filling defect.

Dangers of X rays
Rightly, people are now much more concerned about unnecessary exposure to radiation than they used to be. This is because we now know a lot more about the way X rays and other radiation can damage us. We know that high doses of radiation can cause mutations in DNA that can in turn lead to cancer. The risk in radiotherapy depends on the dose and on the number of exposures, and the tissues most sensitive to radiation are those that reproduce most rapidly, such as:
- the blood-forming cells
- the cells lining the intestines
- the sperm- and ovum-forming cells
- hair-forming cells
- the cells of a newly conceived embryo or a young fetus

Around 90 percent of the total dose of artificial ionizing radiation received by people comes from diagnostic X rays.

Having an X ray

When you go for an X ray you will be asked to take off enough clothing to expose the part being examined. You will also be asked to remove any metal articles, jewelry, hairpins, or other things that would show up on the film and obscure the detail. Your name and personal particulars, the date, and a "right" or "left" marker are automatically printed on the corner of each film so that there is no possibility that your films will be confused with those of any other patient.

To obtain the right aspect on film you may have to be placed in what seems to be a very awkward position. Positioning is an important part of the skill of the X-ray technician: it is necessary to ensure that the part of the body the surgeon is interested in shows up properly and is not obscured by bone. If you are in pain or severe discomfort, this may be a bit of an ordeal and it may not be possible for you to get into the ideal position.

It is almost always necessary to take views from different angles—front-to-back as well as side-to-side. If it is difficult for you to move, perhaps because you have a fracture, it is often possible to move the X-ray tube instead of you. When all is ready, the technician will go behind a screen to press the button that makes the exposure. He or she will tell you when to hold still. Try not to move during the actual taking of the picture, in order to avoid a blurred image and perhaps repeat X rays. Don't worry about a slight tremor—just avoid obvious movement for the second or two of the exposure.

Today, doctors don't request X rays casually; they always balance the risk, small though it may be, against the necessity to gain information. They are especially concerned not to x-ray pregnant women. If you are a woman and there is any chance you might be pregnant, you should avoid having X rays. It shouldn't matter, however, during the first ten days after the start of a menstrual period, and the risk to a newly fertilized egg is, for its first two or three weeks, in any case very small. Damage to the fetus is much more likely in the period from the fourth to the eighth week of pregnancy, when the organs are first being formed. If you have missed a period or if your period is overdue, you should not have X rays to your lower abdomen, or nearby areas, unless they are considered essential by your physician.

Looking at the arteries—angiography

This is a special kind of X-ray examination that shows up the blood in arteries and thus reveals the state of the interior of these vessels. The method is to inject into the bloodstream a liquid that is opaque to X rays (a contrast medium), and then to take the pictures or do the screening. Angiography does not show the vessels themselves, but outlines the

X-RAY PROCESS FOR THE HAND
a *The hand on X-ray plate*
b *The hand is x-rayed*
c *The developed X-ray photographic plate*

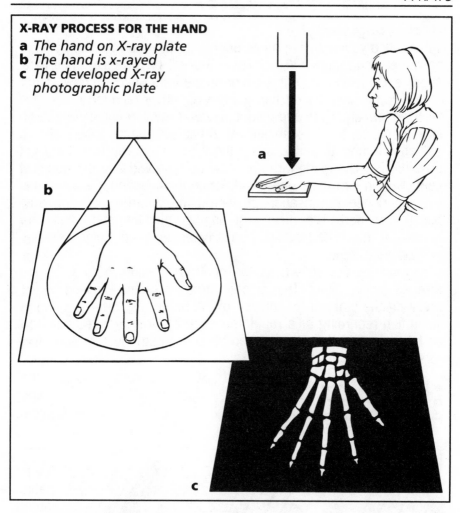

shape of the column of blood within them. It can show:
- a vessel blocked by an obstruction (embolism, shown as the column of blood coming to an abrupt halt)
- a vessel partly blocked by an obstruction such as a blood clot (thrombosis, shown as a column of blood abruptly thinning)
- an artery ballooning (aneurysm, shown as a column of blood grotesquely widening)
- clumps of abnormal vessels, suggesting congenital abnormalities or tumors
- the presence and degree of diseases such as atherosclerosis, which damage and thicken a vessel's lining (shown as a thin, attenuated column of blood)

Angiography is indispensable in investigating the state of the coronary arteries that supply the muscle of the heart and of the major arteries that run up the neck and form a network supplying the brain.

Having angiography

You will find yourself lying on an operating table surrounded by X-ray equipment and large TV monitors. You will be given a small local anesthetic injection in your groin or on the front of your elbow. Under sterile conditions, a long thin guide-wire with a rounded tip is then inserted into an artery and guided, under X-ray screening control, up into the vessel to be examined (**a**). A fine soft-plastic tube, called a catheter, is now threaded along the wire until its tip is in the right position (**b**). The guide-wire can now be removed and the contrast fluid injected into the catheter (**c**). When the injection is started you will experience a sensation of warmth most strongly in the area being examined. The design of angiography catheters has now reached a fine art and many different types are used. Guide-wires are not always essential.

The view on the screen as the contrast medium permeates the arteries is dramatic. The arterial "tree" suddenly flushes white, revealing the state of the interior of the branching vessels. Either a video film recording or a rapid sequence of X-ray pictures can now be taken so that the situation can be studied at length by your doctors.

a *Guide-wire inserted in artery*
b *Catheter inserted*
c *Contrast medium being injected through catheter*

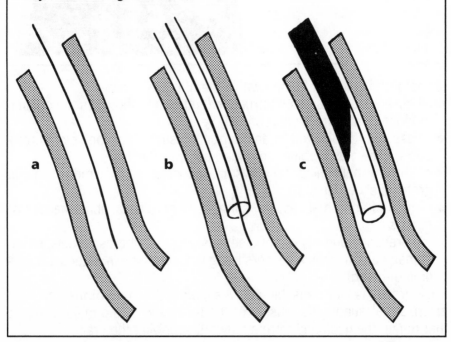

Without angiography beforehand, it would be impractical and unsafe to plan an artery-widening procedure by balloon angioplasty or a coronary artery bypass operation. In people threatened by stroke, angiography can often reveal the cause and can sometimes indicate the feasibility of surgery to remove the causal obstruction in the neck arteries.

Angiography without catheters—digital subtraction angiography

One refinement in angiographic technique is called digital subtraction angiography. Two X rays are taken, one after the other, of the area to be examined. These are electronically processed into digital form and one is turned into a negative. If the two are now combined, all detail will be canceled on a uniformly gray picture and nothing will show. But if, between the two exposures, a quantity of contrast medium is injected into the bloodstream, the only thing that will show up is that medium in the blood vessels. All other detail, including obscuring bone, will be gray. The big advantage of this method is that the injection of the contrast medium can be given directly into a vein instead of into an artery and a catheter need not be used. With normal angiography, if contrast medium were injected into a vein it would immediately become too greatly diluted to show up sufficiently. But in this method, only the contrast medium appears on the final image, and because the image is digitized it can also be electronically enhanced.

Passing tubes into the heart—cardiac catheterization

Catheters are used not only for angiography and for the investigation of the state of the coronary arteries but also for the diagnosis of a wide range of heart conditions in people of all ages, from newborn babies to the elderly. The use of catheters:

- allows blood samples to be taken from the different chambers of the heart for blood gas analysis, thus providing vital information about the state of the overall circulation
- allows contrast medium to be injected into the heart chambers so that accurate pictures can be taken of its internal structures (especially valuable in congenital heart disease)
- permits the efficiency of the heart valves to be investigated by taking measurements of the blood pressure on either side of them
- allows biopsy specimens to be taken of the muscle on the inside of the heart
- makes possible the deliberate widening of narrowed arteries by internal pressure (balloon angioplasty)
- allows drugs that can dissolve clots (thrombolytic agents) to be carried to the place where they can act most effectively

© DIAGRAM

SCANNING
Seeing with sound—ultrasonic imaging

How it works. Ultrasound works on the same principle as marine sonar. A beam of sound at a frequency many times higher than can possibly be heard is projected into the body from a small vibrating crystal in a hand-held scanner head. When the beam meets a surface between tissues of different density, echoes are sent back again, which are picked up by the same crystal. The time between sending the sound and receiving back the echo depends on the distance between the crystal and the reflecting surface. This time is recorded.

Sound waves can be focused into a narrow parallel beam that is scanned from side to side. The returning echoes are correlated, in a computer, with the corresponding angle of the beam, and this enables a two-dimensional picture to be built up. From a sequence of such "slices," taken at different levels, three-dimensional reality can be visualized.

Why it is used. Although the resolution of the image is not as good as that of some other scanning methods, ultrasound imaging is suitable for:

- examining fluid-filled organs such as a pregnant womb, the gallbladder, and soft solid structures such as the liver
- revealing the sex of a baby in the womb, or certain fetal abnormalities
- heart imaging
- checking the inside of an eyeball
- examining the kidneys and the bile duct system of the liver

An advanced form of ultrasound investigation, called Doppler ultrasound, is routinely used by surgeons to investigate the rate of blood flow through arteries. This is often critically important in deciding whether arterial surgery is needed.

Ultrasound imaging is completely safe. This is why it is so widely used to examine pregnant women to confirm that all is well with the baby. No risk to the growing fetus is involved.

Computerized tomographic scanning (CT scanning)

How it works. X rays are very helpful in diagnosing bone problems and show up almost any bone defect excellently, but they are much less useful for investigating soft tissue changes. To a large extent, CT scanning overcomes this problem. Instead of using a film, the machine has an array of X-ray detectors, arranged in an arc, that view "slices" of the body. With a computer this data can be used to produce pictures of slices of the body in any desired plane. By comparing views showing different planes, the surgeon gets a three-dimensional view of the situation.

Having an ultrasound scan

When having an ultrasound scan, normally you will be lying down and the area to be examined will be exposed. Usually a contact gel is used between the scanner head and your skin. Then the smooth, flat scanner head will be pressed against the body surface nearest the part the doctors are interested in and moved about. As this is done, the internal image appears on a screen.

a *Scanner*
b *Echo returned by body organ*
c *An internal organ of the body*
d *Beam of sound sent from scanner*
e *Body surface*

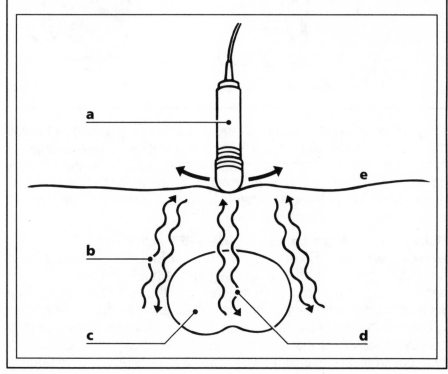

© DIAGRAM

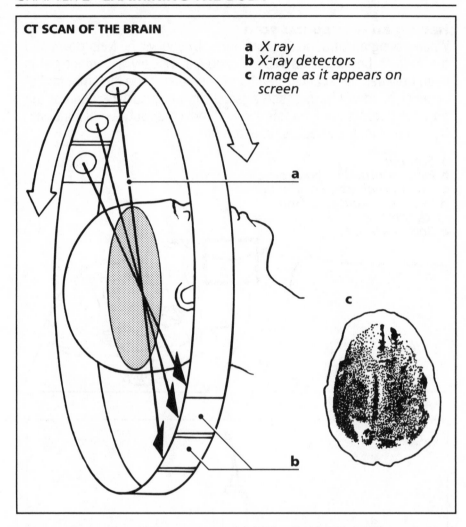

CT SCAN OF THE BRAIN

a *X ray*
b *X-ray detectors*
c *Image as it appears on screen*

Why it is used. CT scanning shows far better resolution of detail than normal X-ray pictures. It can, for instance, easily distinguish between the white matter and the gray matter of the brain and can pick up quite tiny tumors only a millimeter or two across. The ability to detect and stop potentially dangerous disease processes at such an early stage is often life-saving.

Using anti-matter to see inside—PET scanning

How it works. PET stands for Positron Emission Tomography, a technique used most often to investigate the brain. Positively charged particles, called positrons, are injected into the patient's bloodstream via a radioactive isotope that has been created in a lab.

Once inside the body, the isotope is taken up in greater concentration by tissue areas that are more active metabolically. There, short-lived positrons are released and in turn release photons. By detecting

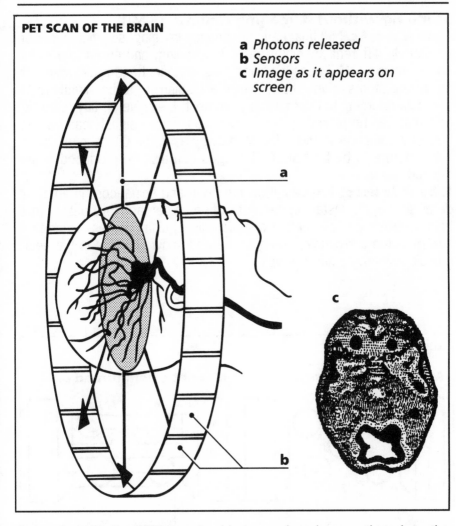

PET SCAN OF THE BRAIN

a *Photons released*
b *Sensors*
c *Image as it appears on screen*

a

c

b

those photons, the PET scan is able to produce images that show the tissue's metabolic and chemical activity. PET scans show what is actually happening in the body rather than what has happened. They can, for instance, provide an accurate indication of the consumption of oxygen in any tissue. This gives invaluable information on the state of vitality and metabolic activity. Areas that have been deprived of their blood supply and are dying for lack of nutrition, or areas that have already died, can readily be detected.

Because of the sophisticated equipment required, such as cyclotrons to make the isotopes, PET scans are expensive and can be performed only in hospitals with immediate access to a cyclotron.

Why it is used. PET scans are useful for detecting tumors and for investigating stroke damage to the brain, Parkinson's disease and other movement disorders, epilepsy, and mental illness.

Scanning without damaging radiation—MRI

How it works. MRI (Magnetic Resonance Imaging) scanners work on an entirely different principle from CT scanning, and no nuclear radiation is involved. MRI uses a strong magnetic field and radio waves to cause the atoms in your body, which are spinning, to be slightly reoriented. In returning to their former alignment, they give off tiny radio signals that can be picked up by nearby coils. These signals can be analyzed by computer in much the same way as in the CT scanner, allowing a picture to be built up. MRI images can also be produced in any desired plane.

Why it is used. MRI can show the brain and spinal cord in amazing detail so that, for instance, the areas of nerve damage (plaques) of multiple sclerosis can be seen. It can also distinguish patches of dead tissue from the surrounding living tissue and show changes in the heart muscle following a heart attack.

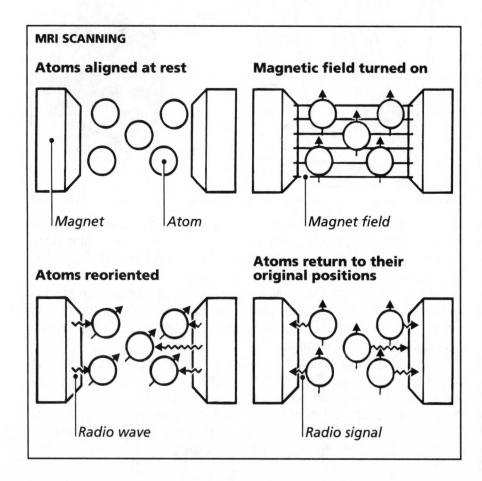

MRI SCANNING

Atoms aligned at rest

Magnet   *Atom*

Magnetic field turned on

Magnet field

Atoms reoriented

Radio wave

Atoms return to their original positions

Radio signal

Having a CT, MRI, or PET scan

The patient's experience of these three methods of scanning—CT, MRI, and PET scanning—are all much the same. The technician will ensure that you have no metal or other solid objects on your body and you will be asked to lie down on a rather narrow padded board and to keep your arms by your sides. The board will then move longitudinally so that your head, or your whole body, passes through a circular opening into the operating part of the machine. You will feel nothing while the scan is in progress. Some people find the experience a bit claustrophobic but there is really no need for concern. You remain at all times under the eyes of the technician at the console where the images are being displayed on the screens.

Keeping still is important and the technician will brief you on that. Although both CT and PET scanning involve radiation, the amount involved is no greater than that of a conventional X ray. MRI involves very strong magnetic fields and radio waves. Although radiation is again involved, it is not of the dangerous ionizing kind.

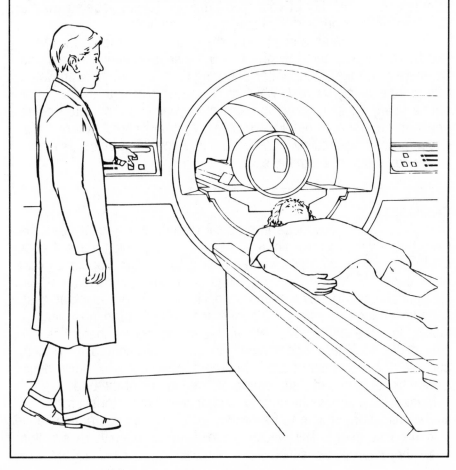

© DIAGRAM

Radionuclide scanning

Why it is used. This scanning method is used for special purposes such as:

- studying the function of the thyroid gland
- checking the healing of bone fractures
- assessing damage to the heart after coronary episodes
- locating tumors or the spread of primary tumors to other parts of the body (secondary cancer)

How it works. The radionuclide scanner, called a gamma camera, measures radiation given off by low-level radioactive isotopes introduced into the body and converts it to an image.

Having a radionuclide scan

To have a radionuclide scan you first must have an injection of a liquid containing radioactive isotopes with a low level of radiation output. The substances used are selected for their properties of concentrating in the area of interest, or of concentrating in tumors. Sometimes a quantity of your blood may be taken, "labeled" with a radioactive isotope, and then reinjected into a vein.

The gamma camera starts to form an image of the inside of the body. This is a rather slow process and a session under the gamma camera may take an uncomfortably long time. Usually you can watch the image being formed, which is fascinating. If you are having a bone scan, for instance, you can watch your entire skeleton being built up on a screen before your eyes. Any "hot spots" where a disease process or healing of a fracture is going on appears as a conspicuous patch of brightness.

ENDOSCOPY

One of the major advances in medical diagnosis in recent years has been the development of fiberoptic endoscopes, which make it possible to look inside the body without having to cut large openings or, in many cases, without making openings at all. Fixed endoscopes—simple optical tubes to look into various parts of the body—such as cystoscopes for looking into the bladder and straight bronchoscopes for looking into the lungs, have been in use for decades. Fiberoptics, bundles of flexible glass fibers made up into sophisticated instruments capable of being steered around corners, have brought a new dimension of access to, and visualization of, the interior of the body.

Modern endoscopes have several important characteristics:

- They allow bright light to be conducted along one fiberoptic channel in the instrument. This, in turn, allows for a magnified view along another fiberoptic channel.

TYPES OF ENDOSCOPES
Illustrated here are various types of endoscopes. Some of the organs examined through each type of endoscope are shown in brackets.

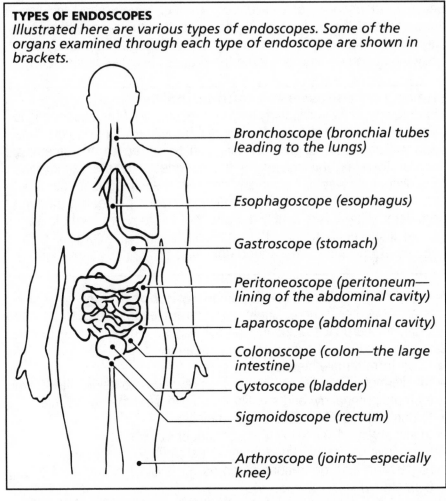

Bronchoscope (bronchial tubes leading to the lungs)

Esophagoscope (esophagus)

Gastroscope (stomach)

Peritoneoscope (peritoneum— lining of the abdominal cavity)

Laparoscope (abdominal cavity)

Colonoscope (colon—the large intestine)

Cystoscope (bladder)

Sigmoidoscope (rectum)

Arthroscope (joints—especially knee)

- They have spare channels down which a range of instruments, including lasers, can be passed.
- They are steerable. By rotating large knobs at the end near the eyepiece the surgeon can cause the last few inches of the instrument to turn in any direction.
- They have channels through which fluids can be injected to wash obscured areas and through which harmless gas can be pumped to inflate cavities and improve visualization.

The combination of illumination, viewing, and steerability allows the surgeon to maneuver the end of the instrument around corners within the body and to look in any desired direction.

Doctors have found endoscopy to be so useful in examining the inside of the intestines (from either the mouth or the anus) and in examining the inside of the air passages that they have become impatient with the limitations of using only the natural orifices of the body.

Because endoscopes can be passed through a very short incision in the surface of the body, it has become routine to do so, when necessary, to allow access for examination of other parts of the body, especially the abdomen, in which case the process is called laparoscopy.

Having an endoscopic examination

Endoscopy is not particularly pleasant, especially if the endoscope is passed in through the mouth. You will be asked to lie on your side and will probably be given an injection of diazepam or something similar to relax you and make the experience less of an ordeal. Endoscopy by way of the anus is done after ensuring that your bowels are empty. So, although you may experience the feeling that you are defecating, this is simply the effect of the movement of the lubricated instrument through the anal canal. Having a surgical endoscopic examination is described opposite.

Surgery by endoscope—laparoscopic operating

It is also becoming increasingly common for endoscopes to be used not only for purposes of inspection but also as a means of performing surgical operations. Laparoscopy has been used:

- to perform female sterilization
- to diagnose conditions such as pregnancy outside the womb (ectopic pregnancy) and sterility from Fallopian tube obstruction
- to confirm doubtful cases of appendicitis
- to investigate diseases of the gallbladder or liver
- to remove the gallbladder (cholecystectomy)
- to perform lung operations, such as removal of one lobe of a lung (lobectomy)

No doubt the next edition of this book will describe a wide range of operations done in this way.

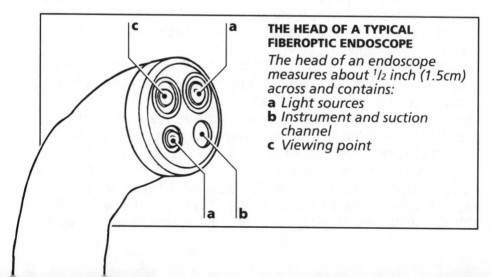

THE HEAD OF A TYPICAL FIBEROPTIC ENDOSCOPE

The head of an endoscope measures about ¹/₂ inch (1.5cm) across and contains:
a *Light sources*
b *Instrument and suction channel*
c *Viewing point*

Having a laparoscopy

Laparoscopy is usually performed under general anesthesia. The harmless gas carbon dioxide (injected through a needle in the abdominal wall or passed through the endoscope) is used to inflate the potential space in the abdomen and move the intestines out of the way. The endoscope is then inserted through a small incision, and various instruments are then passed through it.

- Tissues can be vaporized using a laser and cut without bleeding using an endoscopic wire loop cautery device.
- Patches of diseased tissue can be destroyed using a laser or wire loop cautery.
- Biopsies can be taken from any organ, including the liver, using biopsy forceps, which pinch out a minute piece of organ tissue.

You may find that the pressure of the gas causes discomfort for a day or two, but it will soon be absorbed by the body.

In videolaparoscopy a video camera is attached to the laparoscope and the interior of the abdomen is viewed on a TV monitor. This allows the surgeon to carry out the procedure while watching the screen—a much more comfortable way of operating than looking through a small eyepiece for long periods. The method also allows videotape recordings to be made for research and teaching purposes.

These are some of the attachments the surgeon may use during a laparoscopic examination. Each instrument, when closed, measures approximately ¹/₄ inch (0.5cm) in diameter. The instruments are shown here much larger than their actual size.

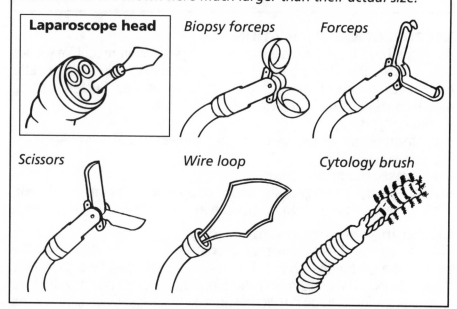

Laparoscope head

Biopsy forceps

Forceps

Scissors

Wire loop

Cytology brush

© DIAGRAM

Cystoscopy

If you have a problem with your bladder, such as persistent infection, bladder stones, polyps, or possible cancer, you will certainly have to undergo cystoscopy. This is a method of illuminating and inspecting the inside of the bladder by means of a narrow, straight, optical instrument that is passed in via the narrow passage by which the urine reaches the exterior (the urethra). This is much longer in the male than in the female, and a general anesthetic is usually needed for men. In women—who, incidentally, require the examination far less often than men—cystoscopy can usually be performed under local anesthesia.

Cystoscopy permits:

- local diagnosis
- retrograde urography whereby fine catheters are inserted into the tubes leading to the kidneys (the ureters) so that contrast medium can be injected for X-ray studies of the urine drainage system
- crushing of bladder stones using strong forceps passed through the cystoscope
- the taking of biopsies (see p.50)

Having a cystoscopic examination

The cystoscope is lubricated and passed fairly easily into the bladder. Once the end is in place, the surgeon runs in enough sterile water through the instrument to fill the bladder. This expands the membranous lining of the bladder so that the whole of the inner surface can be examined. By moving the cystoscope about, the surgeon can observe almost the whole of the inside of the bladder.

MICROSCOPIC EXAMINATION

Surgeons have turned increasingly to microscopes in recent years not only to assist them in delicate operations but also to help them to get a more detailed view of what is happening to the tissues. Surgeons using microscopes for examination include:

- gynecologists
- ophthalmologists, who use slit-lamp biomicroscopes for diagnosis (see next page)
- ear, nose, and throat surgeons
- artery (vascular) surgeons who can now examine the inside of living blood vessels under high magnification

Examining the cervix—colposcopy

This means the direct microscopic examination of the surface of the neck of the womb (the cervix). The vagina is held open by a stretching device called a speculum and the binocular microscope used has a long enough focus to be positioned outside the vulva. Colposcopy gives

---

Having a colposcopy examination

Colposcopy is usually carried out in the gynecologist's office. You will be asked to lie at the foot of the table, with your legs in stirrups. The gynecologist directs the colposcope at the cervix, through a speculum. The field of vision is illuminated by a powerful light. This shows up abnormal tissues, which turn white, and makes clearer the pattern of capillaries on the surface. Next, the cervix is painted with iodine. This may sting for a moment.

Iodine stains normal cells brown; enlarged or abnormal ones do not change color. If a punch biopsy is performed, you may be given a local anesthetic. Still using the colposcope, the gynecologist snips tiny fragments out of the cervix with a special forceps, moving around the lesion. These will be examined under the microscope to make sure the cells beneath the surface of the cervix are normal. When the colposcopy is finished, you may experience some light bleeding after the biopsy.

---

the specialist an excellent close-up view of the surface lining of the cervix and reveals any suspicious areas from which samples can be taken for pathology examination. Colposcopy is the ideal follow-up routine when a Pap test (a cervical smear test) has shown any significant abnormality. Experts state that every patient with surface cancer of the cervix (intra-epithelial neoplasia) should be examined by colposcopy prior to treatment. The microscope also allows local treatment to be carried out under direct visual control with magnification so that the risk of incomplete treatment is reduced.

Examining the eyes—slit-lamp microscopy

The slit-lamp microscope is a binocular instrument for examining the eye, coupled to an intensely bright light source that moves with the microscope so that the area being examined remains well illuminated. The light can be reduced to a narrow slit that can be projected into the eye, illuminating a narrow cross-section of the transparent parts, similar to what is seen by a pathologist examining a section of tissue on a slide.

A slit-lamp examination is the standard method of ophthalmic examination of the eye. It is used to diagnose diseases such as conjunctivitis, inflammation of the white of the eye (scleritis and episcleritis), corneal ulcer, corneal inflammation and injury, pterygium, inflammation of the iris and ciliary body (uveitis), tumors of the iris, iris degeneration, cataracts of all kinds, various disorders of the vitreous gel, and a wide range of retinal diseases. Minor operations—such as to remove corneal foreign bodies—are often performed with a slit lamp.

© DIAGRAM

Having a slit-lamp examination

If you are having a slit-lamp examination you will be asked to put your chin on a rest on one side of the instrument and to rest your forehead firmly against a curved plastic strap. This will ensure that you do not move backward and go out of focus. Although the light is very bright, the beam is so narrow that you will not be uncomfortable. You may, however, see a tree-like image of the branching blood vessels inside your eye.

To examine your retina with the slit lamp, the surgeon will put a drop of local anesthetic on your cornea—this will sting momentarily—and will then put a thick contact lens on your cornea to reduce its optical power so that the surgeon can focus through to the back. As long as you relax and try not to shut your eyelid you will feel nothing.

The examination will usually include a check of the pressure within your eyes using a tonometer. This, too, is done after an anesthetic drop has been used. All you will be aware of is a bright blue light coming ever closer to you until, for a moment, you can see nothing else. Again, if you keep your eye open you will feel nothing.

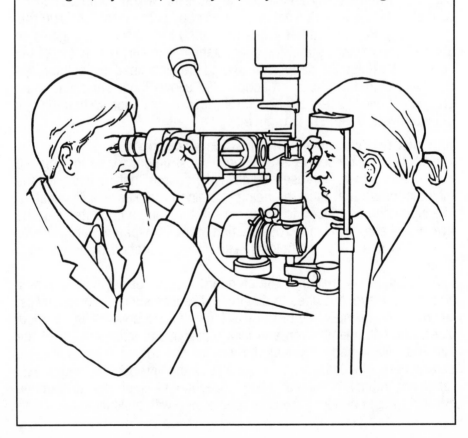

SAMPLING THE CEREBROSPINAL FLUID—LUMBAR PUNCTURE

Lumbar puncture is a procedure for obtaining some of the cerebrospinal fluid that bathes the brain and spinal cord. The procedure also:

- allows drugs, such as antibiotics, to be injected into the cerebrospinal fluid
- allows fluids opaque to X rays to be run in for X-ray examination of the spinal canal

The procedure is used to help in the diagnosis of all forms of meningitis—spinal or otherwise—including bacterial, tubercular, and viral; poliomyelitis; multiple sclerosis; and neurosyphilis, among others.

Having a lumbar puncture

If you are having a lumbar puncture you will be asked to lie on one side with your head and shoulders bent forward and your knees drawn up. This curves your spine sharply so that the vertebrae are pulled as widely apart as they will go. Your skin will then be painted with an antiseptic solution and a small injection of local anesthetic given. The doctor will now feel for the space between two of the lowest bones and will carefully insert a long needle between the bones. You will feel nothing. There is no risk of damage to your spinal cord because the needle is put in below the bottom end of the cord. The needle has a wire stylet within it and when it has entered the spinal canal the stylet is removed and the cerebrospinal fluid runs through and is collected in a tube. Only a little fluid is taken—enough to allow tests that can help to establish the cause of the trouble. You will be asked to remain lying flat for 24 hours. This reduces the risk of leakage of fluid and of a severe headache.

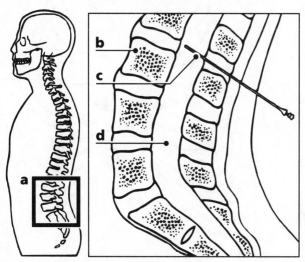

a *Site for lumbar puncture*
b *Vertebrae of the lower back*
c *Lumbar puncture needle*
d *Cerebrospinal fluid*

ELECTRICAL TESTS
Recording the heart action—the electrocardiogram (ECG)
How it works. Every time your heart beats, rapidly varying electric currents are formed and these can be detected by metal contacts made at different points on the surface of your body. These currents are very small, and special amplifiers are needed to distinguish them. Five standard connections are made, one from each limb and one from various positions on the front and side of your chest. Electrodes are attached to these points, and wires (leads) are taken from them to a machine called an electrocardiograph (ECG) which writes the varying trace on a moving strip of calibrated paper.

This tracing is called an electrocardiogram (also ECG); doctors can recognize the normal tracing and the many variations of it characteristic of disease or defective action of the heart.
Why it is used. The ECG can reveal:
- abnormalities of rhythm
- changes in the strength of beat
- enlargement of the chambers
- blockages in the conduction of the controlling impulses that pass throughout the heart muscle

An ECG taken during exercise—as on a treadmill—will often show up latent problems that are not revealed on the resting tracing.

ECGs can be interpreted by a computer with a memory store of most of the recognized patterns of heart disease.

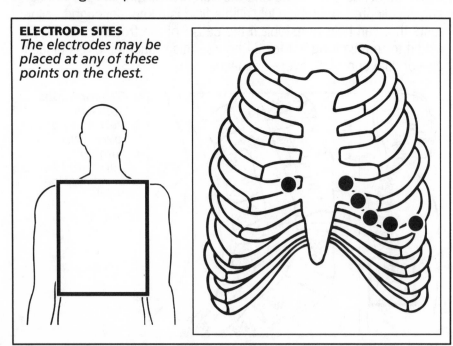

ELECTRODE SITES
The electrodes may be placed at any of these points on the chest.

Patterns of the brain—electroencephalogram (EEG)

How it works. This is a multiple tracing of the electrical activity of the brain, derived from the constantly varying voltage differences that occur between pairs of points on the surface of the head. Currents are picked up by pairs of silver electrodes glued to the scalp. The machine works in a similar manner to the ECG but simultaneously records six to twelve separate channels, each supplied by a separate pair of leads from the scalp.

It would be a mistake to think that the electroencephalogram (EEG) does for the brain what the ECG does for the heart. EEG diagnosis is much less precise, mainly because of the impossibility of sorting out the mass of superimposed electrical activity going on in the brain, and it merely provides supportive rather than positive evidence. The method can, however, pick up a range of characteristic rhythms—called alpha, beta, theta, and delta (see next page)—and demonstrate their disturbances in various conditions.

Why it is used. Patterns of tracings can indicate:
- various forms of epilepsy
- brain tumor or brain injury
- concussion
- internal bleeding
- brain inflammation (encephalitis)
- hyperventilation
- effects of various drugs
- certain psychiatric disorders

The EEG is especially helpful in the diagnosis of brain death and is important in helping to make decisions about taking organs for transplantation. A straight-line EEG is not, however, a certain indication of brain death, and other criteria must also be considered.

DETECTING BRAIN WAVES

1 Electrical signals ripple across the brain as millions of brain cells fire repeatedly.

2 Electrodes at intervals along the head reveal a set of brain wave traces.

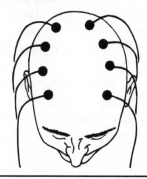

© DIAGRAM

TYPES OF WAVE

The four types of brain wave are named after Greek letters.

δ **Delta waves**: *due to brain tumors. Also found in sleep and early infancy*

θ **Theta waves**: *dominant at ages 2–5 and in psychopaths, or evoked by frustration*

α **Alpha waves**: *prominent in adults with eyes closed and the mind at rest*

β **Beta waves**: *mainly seen in adults. Related to the brain's sensor and motor areas*

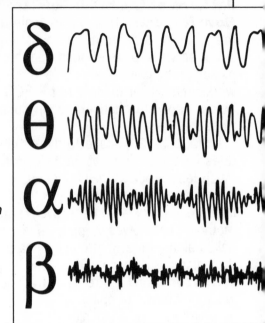

LABORATORY TESTS

The results of laboratory tests are often of the first importance in diagnosis and in assessing a patient's progress under treatment. It would be impossible to conduct the work of a modern hospital without the assistance of the pathology laboratory. Now, most labs are completely automated; large multichannel, computer-controlled machines are fed with endless small containers of blood and other body fluids and the results automatically printed out so that they can be readily incorporated into patients' case notes.

Blood tests

The blood and its varying components are so central to health that a major section of any pathology laboratory is concerned with carrying out tests of the blood and its functions. The number of possible blood tests may surprise you. There are literally hundreds, but they can be divided into two broad groups:

1 tests of whether there are any changes in the normal constituents of the blood

2 tests of whether the blood contains any abnormal constituents

Among the most commonly performed tests are those to check:

- the number of red and white blood cells and the proportions of the different types of white cells (differential count)
- the size, shape, and hemoglobin content of the red cells
- the antibodies to any particular diseases present in the blood

- whether the levels of these antibodies are rising, as in the case of a current infection
- the proportions of the electrolytes in the blood—sodium, potassium, phosphate, magnesium, calcium, and so on
- the clotting power of the blood
- the presence of any enzymes of the kind released when tissues such as heart muscle or liver are damaged by disease

Most of these tests require a larger sample of blood than can be provided by pricking a finger or earlobe, and the sample will almost always be taken from a vein using a needle and a syringe. If you are having many tests you will soon become accustomed to this mildly unpleasant experience. The main discomfort is not from the prick in the skin but from the passage of the needle through the vein wall.

Urine and stool tests

Urine tests can reveal abnormalities such as the presence of glucose, protein, cells, kidney-tubule casts, crystals, and others. Stool tests may reveal dangerous organisms, worm eggs, abnormally unsplit dietary constituents (especially fat), and so on.

Bacterial culture

Another very common group of laboratory tests are those for the presence of bacteria that cause disease. For example, sputum tests reveal bacteria, such as *Mycobacterium tuberculosos*, abnormal cells, bronchial casts, and others. To perform these tests, swabs of cloth, sponge, or gauze must first be used to collect sample cells:

- of the throat
- of wounds or of the skin
- of blood or other body fluids

Once taken, the samples are sent to the laboratory. Specimens thought to contain bacteria may be smeared on a gel of agar in shallow, circular glass or plastic dishes, or may be inoculated into small containers of broth or other material in which they will grow rapidly. The dishes or culture vials are then placed in incubators where they are kept at the exact temperature of the inside of the body (98.6°F/37°C). This is the temperature at which organisms causing disease reproduce best. The process is called bacterial culture.

Bacteria taken from a patient in one of these ways and cultured in an incubator can produce visible colonies on agar plates overnight and these can then be identified by various tests, thereby determining the exact cause of the infection. The colonies can also be picked up with a sterile wire loop, replated, and grown again on agar containing a range of antibiotics to check which are most effective in preventing their reproduction. In this way, the best treatment can be established.

Microscopic examination of tissue samples

A complete diagnosis that includes the precise nature of the disease process causing the problem can often be made only when a small sample of the diseased tissue is taken for microscopic and other examination in a laboratory. Both the process and the specimen are called a biopsy.

Biopsies can be taken from any tissue in the body—even the brain—and can be taken during an operation or as a separate procedure. They can be taken directly from the skin under local anesthesia, or using a fiberoptic endoscope (see p.38). Breast biopsies following the discovery of a lump are routine and often essential. It is not necessary to take a large quantity of tissue. A biopsy can be sucked through a needle, and this is commonly done in cases of suspicious breast lumps. The Pap smear test on the lining of the neck of the womb (the cervix), in which a few cells are scraped off with a small plastic spatula, is a biopsy.

Biopsy tissue consisting of separate cells is spread on a glass slide, stained, and examined under a microscope. Solid tissue is soaked in molten paraffin wax, allowed to harden into a block, and then cut into very thin slices. These are spread on slides, stained, and examined. If there is a great hurry—as when the result is needed during an operation—the block can be frozen, sliced, and examined—either in a room adjoining the OR or in a lab, from which the results are phoned to the OR. This is called a "frozen section" and it allows the surgeon to proceed with vital information about the nature of the problem. Frozen sections often save the patient a second operation.

Biopsies are examined by experts, called histopathologists, who are experienced in the interpretation of disease processes in tissues. In most cases, the pathologist can state with certainty exactly what is going on—whether the process is:
- a simple degeneration
- an inflammation
- an atrophy (wasting away caused by lack of use or poor circulation)
- a nonmalignant increase in cell size (hypertrophy)
- a simple increase in cell numbers (hyperplasia)
- a benign tumor or a cancer

The histopathologist is skilled in recognizing the specific patterns in diseased tissue representative of particular types of disease and, in conjunction with other laboratory tests, almost always arrives at a precise diagnosis.

Checking compatibility—tissue typing

Every cell in the body carries on its surface chemical markers called antigens. These antigens are unique to the individual but fall into one of a number of distinct categories, in a manner similar to the blood groups, but called HLA (Human Leukocyte Antigen) groups or tissue types. No two people, except identical twins, have HLA groups that are exactly the same, but broad groupings may be shared. Close blood relatives tend to share these broad groups. If there is a question of organ transplantation, the tissue groups of the donor and the recipient become very important, and these must be matched as closely as possible in order to minimize the risk of problems. The immunological response to these antigens is the cause of most graft rejection.

A test involving HLA groups is being increasingly done in hospital laboratories. Antigens can readily be identified by observing their reaction with known antibodies. The development of the techniques of producing large quantities of pure monoclonal antibodies (artificial antibodies used to diagnose and treat some cancers) has made it a routine laboratory task to identify antigens, including the HLA group. The HLA test involves the collection of a small sample of blood by pricking an earlobe and drawing a drop or two into a fine tube. White cells in the blood in contact with a solution containing the right antibody will clump visibly together or will take up, and remove from the solution, an easily detectable protein called complement. In either event, the antigen is identified so that the best donor can be matched to the person requiring the transplant.

CHAPTER 3
SPARE PARTS AND REPLACEMENTS

Among the most impressive areas of surgical advance in recent years have been tissue and organ transplantation and the use of artificial body parts. Advances in transplantation surgery have been made possible by increased understanding of the processes by which transplanted parts, if not initially tissue-typed properly, are rejected by the body. Recent years have additionally seen an explosion in our knowledge of the complex processes of immunology, and with this understanding scientists have been able to develop methods to defeat the natural rejection processes.

Cooperation among surgeons, mechanical engineers, and materials scientists has led to notable successes in the design of internal functional parts such as artificial joints, arteries, heart valves, heart pacemakers, ligaments, and eye lenses. There have also been substantial

BLOOD COMPONENTS AND BLOOD CELLS

Components
a *Red blood cells*
b *White blood cells (leukocytes and platelets)*
c *Plasma (serum plus coagulation agents)*

Cells
d *Leukocytes (white blood cells)*
e *Platelets (white blood cells)*
f *Red blood cells*

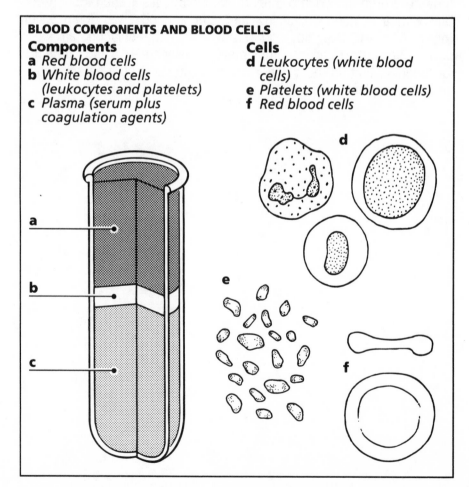

advances in the design of external appliances, such as artificial limbs, artificial eyes, external bone fixators, and various cosmetic devices such as breast and chin implants. Regrettably, a practical artificial heart remains a dream for the future. Devices to assist the action of a failing heart have, however, been successfully developed.

Let's look first at the transplantation of human material. One particular form of transplant of tissue between individuals—blood transfusion—has been practiced for many years. A consideration of transfusion and how it may affect you makes a convenient introduction for it shares some of the problems encountered in the transplantation of other tissues and organs.

3

BLOOD TRANSFUSION
Most surgical practice involves blood transfusion, and much surgery would be impracticable or dangerous without it. Before many operations it is necessary to ensure that an adequate quantity of blood is immediately available for the patient, and it is common for a transfusion to be set up during the operation. The blood to be used has to be of the right group, and ensuring this involves some careful preliminary work.

Blood typing
The ABO system. All the cells of the body carry surface markers called antigens. The red blood cells are no exception. There are four major blood groups: A, B, AB, and O. These arbitrary names refer to the particular antigens on the walls of the red blood cells. Group AB blood cells have both A and B antigens and group O blood has neither. In the liquid part of the blood, the serum, group A people have antibodies to B antigens, Group B people have antibodies to A antigens, Group AB people have no antibodies, and group O people have both A and B antibodies.

Notice that no one has antibodies of the same letter as their anti-

ANTIGENS AND ANTIBODIES		
Blood group	**Agglutinogen**[1]	**Agglutinin**[2]
A	A	b
B	B	a
AB	A and B	None
O	None	a and b

[1] Antigen that stimulates the production of an agglutinin
[2] Antibody that causes blood cells to stick together in lumps

© DIAGRAM

BLOOD GROUP COMPATIBILITY

Donor blood group	Recipient blood group			
	A	**B**	**AB**	**O**
A	Yes	No	No	Yes
B	No	Yes	No	Yes
AB	Yes	Yes	Yes	Yes
O	No	No	No	Yes

gens. Antibodies and antigens of the same type immediately combine and cause the red blood cells to clump together into massive and dangerous lumps. This is what would happen if we had antibodies in our serum corresponding to the antigens on our cells, and this is what happens when someone is given a transfusion of blood of the wrong group.

To prevent this disaster we must know the group of the blood to be transfused and also the group of the person who is to have the transfusion. But the matter is so important that hospital staff don't just rely on what it says on the blood pack. They do a final check called a cross-match in which a little of the serum from the donor is mixed, in a hollow in a white plastic plate, with a little of the blood from the prospective recipient. If the groups are the same nothing happens. But if the bloods are incompatible, the red cells stick together (agglutinate) in lumps that are easily seen with the naked eye.

The rhesus factor. The ABO system is not the only classification of blood groups, but it is the most important. The rhesus factor is an antigen present in the blood of about 85 percent of people, and this factor must also be matched if blood is to be transfused. The rhesus factor is of special importance in pregnancy. If a rhesus-negative woman has a baby by a rhesus-positive man, the baby has a high chance of being rhesus positive. In this case, during pregnancy the baby's blood will cause the mother to produce antibodies against it. There are not usually enough of these antigens produced in the first pregnancy to damage the baby, but in later pregnancies the levels of antibodies rise rapidly and cause serious or even fatal effects on the baby. If the problem is recognized—and today this should always be the case—the baby's blood can be exchanged as soon as it is born or even, in some cases, before it is born. Blood exchange is necessary even after birth because a rhesus baby's red cells continue to break down, releasing bilirubin that damages the brain.

Plasma

Plasma is the yellowish fluid in which blood cells—red and white—are suspended, together with proteins and coagulation agents. A transfusion of plasma can be valuable in many cases to make up lost blood volume and to thicken the blood. Plasma contains many substances essential to life and has a high protein content. The soluble plasma proteins, albumin and globulins, are important in retaining water in the blood and preventing it from accumulating in the tissues (edema). The globulins are mainly antibodies. Plasma also has the advantage that it can be dried and stored for long periods and reconstituted with sterile water when required.

Having a blood transfusion

From your point of view there is really no difference between having a blood transfusion and having an intravenous infusion of any other kind of fluid. They all go in the same way. The most easily accessible veins are at the front of the elbow, but the use of these for transfusion limits elbow movement, and they are usually avoided. A vein in the left forearm or on the back of the hand is selected more often, but any reasonably large vein will do. At the end of the device used to get into the vein is a very sharp hollow needle completely covered, except at the point, by a plastic sheath called a cannula. The other end of the cannula is shaped to fit on the end of a syringe and has a locking device.

A tourniquet is put on your upper arm to make the veins stand out, and the skin at the selected site is thoroughly cleaned with alcohol. The sheathed needle is now pushed through your skin and laid alongside the vein. This is not particularly painful, but if you are squeamish, don't look. The doctor now tilts the needle so that it slides through the wall of the vein and pushes it onward until the sheath covering it is well up the vein. You may feel a dull pain as the vein is entered. The doctor checks that the blood is running back freely through the needle into the syringe and then removes the needle, leaving the cannula in the vein. The doctor then straps it firmly to your skin with adhesive tape.

The end of the cannula can now be connected to the tube from the collapsible plastic bottle of blood. The doctor is careful to ensure that no air can get into the tube or the bottle. The rate of flow of the blood into the vein is adjusted by means of a plastic device that partly compresses the tube from the blood bottle: the effect of this can be judged by watching the blood dropping through a widened portion of the tube called a drip chamber. The more urgently you need blood, the faster the rate of flow set. In an emergency, two or three separate transfusions may be set up, and pressure may even be applied to the blood bottles to get the blood in faster. This is rare, however, and blood is normally run in slowly enough for the separate drops to be seen and, if necessary, counted.

© DIAGRAM

It is fairly common for people to have minor reactions to blood trans-fusions, but this does not necessarily mean that anything serious is happening. A touch of fever, perhaps an episode of shivering, may be triggered by substances in the blood called pyrogens. Any such reactions should, of course, be monitored by the doctor and will be carefully evaluated. Major reactions are rare. Nevertheless, blood is never given without good reason, and some doctors believe that a transfusion of just a single unit of blood (500 ml) is not justified.

If the patient is not anemic and more than one unit of blood is needed, it is sometimes possible to set up an autologous transfusion, in which the patient donates blood before an operation, to be used as needed later. Another option that may be available is to filter and re-transfuse the patient's own blood during an operation.

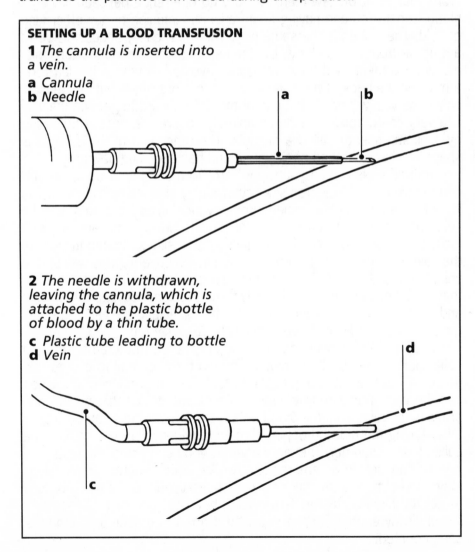

SETTING UP A BLOOD TRANSFUSION

1 *The cannula is inserted into a vein.*
a *Cannula*
b *Needle*

2 *The needle is withdrawn, leaving the cannula, which is attached to the plastic bottle of blood by a thin tube.*
c *Plastic tube leading to bottle*
d *Vein*

TISSUE AND ORGAN TRANSPLANTATION

Organs and tissues can be transplanted—or "grafted"—from one individual to another or from one site to another within the same person. Transplantation of the cornea of the eye was the first repeatable and successful exchange of tissue from one individual to another. Surprisingly, many functioning corneal grafts were achieved even before the immunological principles were understood. The reason for this is simple. In order to remain transparent, corneas have no blood vessels. So although a transplanted corneal disk is actually foreign tissue that would normally be rejected by the body, the cells and the antibodies that cause rejection cannot reach the donor tissue because they could get there only by way of the bloodstream.

Unfortunately, apart from cartilage that is not often needed, no other tissue or organ that we might wish to transplant enjoys this advantage. To prevent the destruction and rejection of transplanted kidneys, hearts, lungs, livers, pancreases, or bone marrow it is necessary to interfere with the normal action of the immune system.

COMMON TISSUE GRAFTS
a Hair
b Fetal brain cells
c Lens; cornea
d Bones and bone marrow
e Heart valve
f Blood, blood vessels, and nerves
g Skin

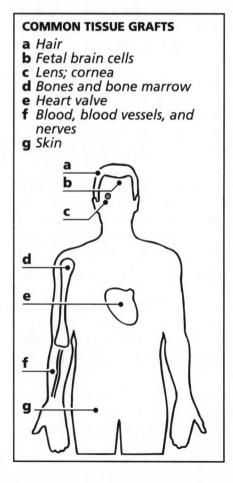

ORGAN TRANSPLANTS
a Lungs
b Liver
c Kidneys
d Heart
e Pancreas

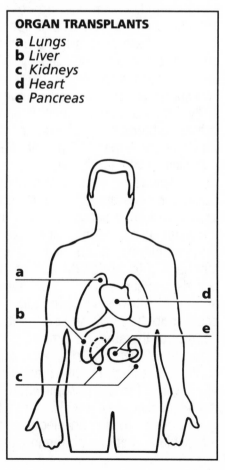

© DIAGRAM

This is, of course, a dangerous game because we depend on the immune system for protection against infection and, to a lesser extent, cancer. Also, some of the drugs used to suppress the action of the immune system can interfere with wound healing. Fortunately, as knowledge has grown, it has proved possible to develop drugs with a selective action that can prevent rejection without causing dangerous immune deficiency.

When a person's own tissue is moved from one part of the body to another, the question of rejection does not arise because the body recognizes the tissue as "self." All that is necessary for success is that the tissue should, in its new location, have an adequate blood supply. So let's start by looking at one of the most common transplant procedures of all—skin grafting.

Skin grafting
Skin from a donor can be useful as a temporary dressing or cover for large areas of burns or skin loss, but will not be successful permanently. So skin grafting really means the transfer of a piece of a person's own skin from one area of the body to another. This is done to provide cover for an area that, for some reason, has lost its normal skin cover. If a bare area is not grafted over, it will usually heal eventually, but it does so accompanied by the formation of ugly and functionally unsatisfactory scar tissue. Large areas of scar tissue tend to tighten and shrink, which may cause severe contractures and disability, especially if they are near a joint. Common indications for skin grafting are extensive burns, large ulcers, and surgical operations for skin cancer in which safety demands removal of a wide area of skin around the tumor.

A skin graft may be either of partial or, if small, of full thickness, which includes deeper layers of skin and requires stitches to close. Cover for large areas is usually provided by what are called split skin grafts cut from a suitable area of the body, such as the front or side of the thigh, using a long-bladed, very sharp knife called a dermatome. Cutting split skin grafts by hand is something of an art. With an assistant helping to stretch the skin of the donor site tightly between two flat boards, the surgeon presses the well-lubricated knife flat on the surface and cuts with a sawing motion, removing a thin, almost transparent sheet, hopefully with no holes in it. It is not easy to cut at just the right depth, but the surgeon aims to go just deep enough to cause multiple pinpoints of bleeding to appear, arising from the thousands of tiny skin papillae that push up into the surface layers from the deeper tissues. The level of the cut is somewhere between one-third and two-thirds of the full thickness of the skin—less than one millimeter thick. Some surgeons prefer to use an electric dermatome (skin-cutting knife) with a rotary blade that can do the job just as well.

USING A DERMATOME
a *Dermatome*

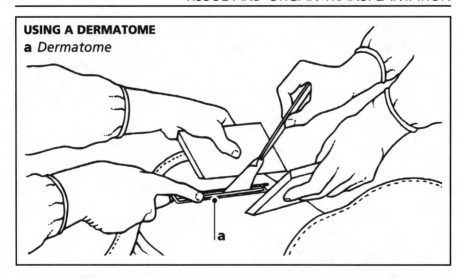

a

The graft is carefully spread on the bare area to be covered, and is held in place either by gentle pressure from a well-padded dressing or by a few small stitches. The raw donor area is covered with a sterile, nonadherent dressing for a couple of days to protect it from infection. There is quite a lot of oozing of serum at first, but this soon stops and the area can then be exposed in order to dry up and heal. A new outer layer of skin regenerates from the deeper layer in about two weeks. Sometimes the need for skin is so great, and the healthy area so limited, that the same donor area has to be harvested repeatedly.

Skin becomes a precious commodity when large areas have to be covered, as in extensive burns, and there are various methods for making a small amount of skin cover a wider area:

Meshing and stretching a piece of skin by putting it through rollers in the same way that metal sheets are expanded to form grills. This can make up the difference needed to achieve full coverage, but the final appearance is not as good as a graft with unmeshed skin.

Seeding out the area to be covered with large numbers of small "pinch" grafts cut from healthy skin and pressed into place on the new site. Pinch grafts are produced by picking up small cones of skin and cutting them off with scissors. Although new skin will grow out from the pinch grafts to cover the bare areas between them, the final appearance is very irregular and far from natural.

Using full-thickness skin grafts. These are limited in size because the donor site cannot regenerate and must be closed by undermining the edges and bringing them together. Also, full-thickness grafts are more likely to fail because of the problem of tying in a blood supply. For this reason full-thickness grafts cannot be larger than an inch or two wide.

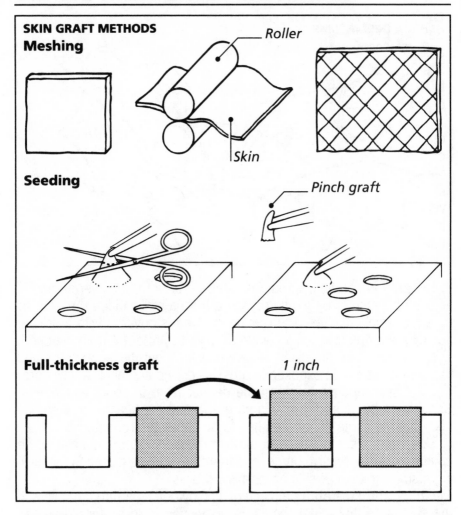

SKIN GRAFT METHODS
Meshing
Roller
Skin

Seeding
Pinch graft

Full-thickness graft
1 inch

Full-thickness grafts are commonly used on the face, but in spite of careful selection of the donor site it is difficult to achieve a good match in thickness, color, and texture, and patients may be disappointed at the final appearance. Full-thickness grafts for the face are commonly taken from behind the ear. Such grafts require good surgical and sterile techniques and must be stitched securely in place. Great care is taken to avoid the development of blood clots (hematomas) under them. A hematoma or any infection is likely to lead to loss of the graft, which simply turns black and shrivels.

To overcome the size limitation with full-thickness grafts, surgeons are now sometimes taking larger grafts with muscle attached to them and with a fair-sized artery and vein running through them. These vessels are connected, by microsurgery, to vessels at the new site so that the graft has a full blood supply and will heal well in the new position.

Organ transplantation

Before organs can be successfully transplanted from one person to another, two completely different sets of problems have to be solved. The first is the problem of joining the blood circulation of the recipient to that of the organ so that the organ receives an adequate flowthrough of blood carrying oxygen and nutrients.

This requirement has now been fully met by wonderful refinements of operating methods (microsurgical techniques) and by the development of miniature operating instruments and extremely sharp and tiny needles connected to hairlike but strong stitch material (sutures). Using a microscope, the surgeon is now able to link up quite small arteries and veins, making leakproof connections with those of the donated organ. In most cases, the organs concerned—especially the kidney and the heart—have arteries and veins of such a size that end-to-end or end-to-side connections are not too difficult to make.

The second set of problems concerns immunological rejection of the donated part. As we have seen, although remarkable advances have been made, the problem of rejection has not been entirely solved. When any foreign tissue enters the body it is at once inspected by cells of the immune system and its surface markers (antigens) are checked to see whether they correspond to those on the body's own cells. If they do not match, the immune system immediately mounts a concerted attack on the foreign tissue. Millions of white blood cells concentrate around the foreign tissue, attacking it with poisonous substances and trying to absorb it. In these circumstances, a graft becomes intensely inflamed and is soon severely damaged and then killed. This was what happened to all the grafts (except those between identical twins) that were tried before the action of the immune system was understood.

Tissue typing for organ transplants

Now that we know about tissue types, we are able to select donors whose organs are less likely to be rejected. The group of antigen markers on cells, called the major histocompatibility complex (HLA group), is inherited through genes in each cell nucleus on chromosome #6. This means that when an organ is donated by a parent to a child there is a fifty-fifty chance that the match will be good. When organs are transplanted between brothers and sisters, there is a one-in-four chance that the antigens will be largely the same. Transplants between HLA-matched brothers and sisters, or parents and children, give results almost as good as those between identical twins.

Unfortunately, there will never be enough living donors to provide the numbers required, and it is therefore necessary to rely on unrelated donors who have recently died, usually from severe injury. This is where sophisticated techniques of tissue typing must be applied. When people

TIMES WITHIN WHICH DONOR ORGANS MUST BE USED		
Organ	**Time**	**Conditions**
Kidney	48 hours	if stored cold
Pancreas	48 hours	if stored cold
Heart	4 hours	if stored cool
Liver	4 hours	if stored cool
Heart–lung	immediately	donor and recipient operated on at same time
Cornea	several days	if stored at 39°F

are identified as needing organ transplants, their profile of tissue types is determined and the data is fed into a national computer, which also receives information from current possible donor sources. There are four major subgroups of tissue types—A, B, C, and D. Compatibility in all four gives the best chance of success but, in practice, it is usually sufficient to match the HLA groups A, B, and C as closely as possible. In addition to tissue matching, it is essential that donors and recipients have compatible A, B, AB, or O blood groups.

Only by using a computer can adequate matching be achieved between suitable donors and recipients. Even so, this takes time, and there is often a frantic rush to get a donated organ to the patient and his or her transplantation surgeons in time. Organs must be used within hours of the death of the donor. Using special preservation methods, kidneys and pancreases can be used within 48 hours if stored cold. Hearts and livers must be used within about four hours. Heart–lung transplants require that both the donor and the recipient be in the same operating room at the same time. Two operating teams are needed.

Immunosuppression
The second line of attack against rejection is the use of drugs that suppress the action of the immune system in attacking foreign tissue. Corticosteroid drugs, commonly known as steroids, have this effect, but are not sufficient on their own to prevent rejection. Other drugs have been developed that prevent the massive increase in the number of immune cells necessary to cause the rejection process. The first drug to be used with high success in this way was azathioprine. This drug blocks the synthesis of DNA. Other important drugs are cyclophosphamide and, especially, cyclosporin A. The latter drug has a

selective action against the cells (lymphocytes) that are mainly responsible for rejection. These drugs are toxic and have to be used with care, but they have greatly improved the success rate in grafting.

Immunosuppressive treatment may in some patients cause one or more side effects:
- infection (occurs in about 40 percent of patients)
- inflammation of the pancreas (pancreatitis)
- stomach duodenal ulcer
- diabetes
- damage to kidneys or liver
- osteoporosis
- tumors of the lymphoid system (lymphomas)

The science of immunosuppression is still in its infancy. With future advances a radical rethink of surgery and of the treatment of many serious conditions may become necessary. In time, we may come to consider it a routine matter to treat diabetes by pancreas transplants, bowel cancer by intestinal transplants, and serious injury by limb transplants. It may even be possible to treat infertility by ovarian or testicular transplants.

Selection of nonrelated donors
Unless donor selection is made by national computer, it is the responsibility of the surgeon in charge of the case to identify suitable organ donors and to confirm, in consultation with colleagues, the diagnosis of brain death. Relatives will have to be approached, at a time when their distress is at a peak, and asked to agree to the removal of organs. Donors are normally:
- healthy people who have been killed in accidents in which they have suffered head injury
- people who have had sudden bleeding inside the head (subarachnoid hemorrhage)
- people who have died from cardiac or respiratory arrest

Some people are unsuitable donors—for example, people who have died from infections, cancer, high blood pressure, or kidney disease are, generally, unsuitable as organ donors. There are certain upper age limits for hearts, heart–lungs, and livers. These are not suitable if the prospective donor is much over age 50. Kidneys may be taken from donors up to age 70 if there is no history of kidney disease. Donors must be screened for HIV and hepatitis B. Corneas, on the other hand, can be used from almost anyone, provided that the eyes were healthy.

MECHANICAL AND PROSTHETIC PARTS

For most people there are no rejection problems with implanting synthetic mechanical parts such as artificial hip joints, knee joints, heart valves, and so on, but that does not mean that they can be made of any material. The body is highly intolerant of many metals and other substances, and materials to be implanted must be carefully chosen. Iron or normal steels, for instance, would excite a severe reaction as soluble salts are formed by the action of the body fluids. Copper and several other metals also cause severe reactions.

Mechanical parts can be manufactured from:
- metal—usually high-strength stainless steels
- metal alloy—usually alloys of cobalt, chromium, and molybdenum
- ceramics
- plastics

Today there is an adequate range of safe materials from which mechanical parts can be manufactured.

Some plastics are particularly well suited for implantation. Silicone rubber (silastic), for instance, is relatively inert in the body and has the additional advantage of being permeable to oxygen so that it does not interfere with local oxygen supply. It can be used anywhere in the body where structural support or bulking is needed. It is, for instance, used for repairing facial fractures, such as the loss of the floor of an eye socket, and for cosmetic breast implants. For the latter purpose it is often formed into a bag containing silicone oil. (For further information, see p.428.)

The waxy plastic polytetrafluoroethylene (PTFE), familiar as the lining of frying pans, and the plastic textile polyethylene terephthalate are ideal for making artificial arteries. For this purpose they are made into fibers that are used to form woven or knitted tubes. These are presoaked in blood, and the openings soon fill up with clot, which is gradually changed into fibrous tissue. Such arterial grafts link up well with the natural arteries and soon come to resemble them. Artery grafts woven in these materials have been extensively used to repair dangerous bulging of the largest arteries in the body or to replace lengths of artery destroyed by injury. Many lives have been saved by this procedure. Plastic arterial grafts can also be used to bypass lengths of artery that are completely blocked.

Artificial hip joints

Hip replacement has been one of the triumphs of modern spare-part surgery (see p.194). Millions of people severely disabled by arthritis have been restored to painless mobility by this operation. Millions more, devastated by fractures of the neck of the thighbone involving loss of the blood supply to the head of the bone, have been able to resume normal living after a total hip joint replacement.

One of the main difficulties is to ensure the longterm integrity of the connection between prosthesis and bone. The socket of the artificial hip must be secured in the hollow in the side of the pelvis. Because of the smooth, low-friction connection between the high-density polyethylene socket and the spherical steel or ceramic head, there is no great tendency for the artificial socket to become displaced but, in some cases, loosening has been a problem.

The arm of the ball section of the prosthesis, made of cobalt, chrome alloy, or stainless steel, must be firmly fixed into the hollow shaft of the thighbone (femur), and this itself may cause problems. Unfortunately, the osteoporosis (brittleness of bone) that is such a common feature of elderly people, especially women, often leads to weakening of the bone around the long arm of the ball section so that, after a number of years, even the polymethyl methacrylate cement that is normally used may be unable to keep it secure. Undue elasticity in the metal is another important cause of loosening: the metal titanium is being used to try to reduce this. Research is continuing, and knowledge is increasing.

Artificial knee and finger joints

Knee joint technology has lagged somewhat behind hip developments. This is partly because it was not at first appreciated that the knee joint is a much more complex joint than the hip. The hip joint is a simple ball-and-socket joint allowing freedom of movement in all directions. The knee joint is not a simple hinge, as was first thought, but involves an element of sliding, and this must be allowed for in the design of artificial joints. Many different designs have been evolved and tried, and the artificial joint is gradually being improved. Artificial finger joints have also been developed to deal with disablement from arthritic and stiffened fingers.

Artificial ligaments

This development has excited less publicity than joint replacement but has been of great value to many patients. The application of carbon fiber technology to the surgical problems posed by torn or stretched ligaments has been highly successful. Surgeons have been provided with remarkably strong and flexible artificial ligaments that can be used in many different sites, often being secured in place by means of holes drilled in the bone. Lax joints, in particular, can now be restored to normal stability. Wobbly ankles with a constant tendency to "turn over," or knees that bend sideways, can now be tightened up using artificial ligaments.

Intraocular lens replacement

A cataract is an opacity in the internal lens of the eye, immediately behind the iris. Opacities cannot be removed, so the whole lens has to be taken out. The effect of this is to defocus the eye to a serious

ARTIFICIAL AIDS

1 Hair
2 Hearing aid
3 Teeth
4 Drain for excess brain fluid
5 Shoulder joint
6 Breast
7 Elbow joint
8 Hip joint
9 Knuckle joint
10 Testicles
11 Knee joint
12 Supportive plate
13 Radioactive implant
14 Protective plate
15 Eye
16 Ear
17 Jaw
18 Larynx
19 Heart valve
20 Pacemaker
21 Pacemaker battery
22 Major blood vessel
23 Arm
24 Hormonal implant
25 Bladder simulator
26 Hand
27 Penile implant
28 Leg

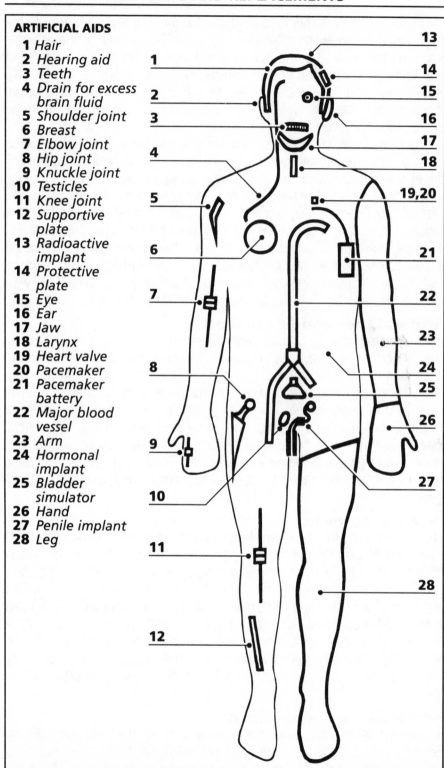

degree. Formerly, the only way to see clearly after a cataract operation was to wear thick, strong, and heavy glasses, which caused magnification and distortion. The trend today is to replace the removed lens with a tiny plastic lens—an intraocular lens implant. Modern intraocular lenses are little miracles of optical perfection and design. They are so small and light that even the delicate internal tissues of the eye can tolerate them and the delicate plastic loops by which they are supported and centered. Almost anyone who has cataract surgery can now have a lens implant, performed as part of the same operation. (For further information, see p.94.) It is even possible, in some cases, for people who have previously had cataract removal without implant to have this done as a secondary procedure. The safety of this depends on how much trauma and cell loss has already been sustained by the inner lining of the cornea of the eye. These cells do not regenerate and are damaged by any operative procedure that involves opening the eye.

Artificial heart

At the time of publication no practical artificial heart has been produced, although many attempts have been made and a number of optimistic reports have been published. This may surprise you, for it may seem that it would be a simple matter to produce a compact yet powerful pump that could keep the blood circulating throughout the body. Unfortunately, there is rather more to it than this. It is a fairly simple matter to construct a pump that can maintain the circulation for a matter of hours—as is done in the heart–lung machine used during open-heart surgery or heart transplantation. Even so, such a pump needs a power supply that makes a self-contained device impracticable.

This apart, one of the chief problems is the tendency for such a pump, used longterm, to produce clotting in the blood and to throw off blood-clot emboli that immediately plug important arteries in the brain and elsewhere. Other problems include surgical failure at the connection between the device and the patient's blood vessels, causing massive internal bleeding, infection, and kidney failure. So far, of the few people who have been kept alive for more than a few months with artificial hearts, such as the Jarvik models, almost all have died or become severely incapacitated from stroke caused by these emboli.

There can be no progress, however, without experimentation, and the quest for the successful artificial heart continues. Recent advances in artificial heart design have been encouraging. Although up to now people using them have had to remain permanently connected to a console, there are signs that portable battery packs carried on the body may be feasible for short-term use away from the console. The electrical power can be transmitted through the skin by means of an implanted induction coil and an external coil supplied by the batteries.

© DIAGRAM

No physical connection is needed. The problem of clotting has also been tackled. One promising approach has been actually to encourage clotting on the inside of the artificial heart by deliberately making it rough so that a layer of firmly adherent clot develops. The kind of lining formed seems to prevent further clot formation, and some patients have been able to do without anticoagulant treatment. This lining is the subject of intense research.

Currently, there seems to be a place for artificial hearts in keeping people alive long enough to have a heart transplant, but most informed medical opinion is, at present, against attempts to employ them on a permanent basis. A device known as the "intra-aortic balloon pump," which supplements the power of a failing heart, has been in use for many years. The balloon lies within the main artery of the body and inflates automatically between each heartbeat, providing extra force to the circulation. This can be a great help, especially in improving the flow through the coronary arteries so that the heart muscle gets a better blood supply and can function more vigorously. The extra force applied to the circulation also relieves the strain on the heart.

Doctors now appreciate, partly through experience with artificial hearts, that there is more to heart action than simple pumping. Many other factors are involved, including elaborate feedback control mechanisms and poorly understood biochemical processes. It may be that the production of a truly satisfactory artificial heart will have to wait for the solution of more than purely technological problems.

BONE MARROW TRANSPLANTS
Bone marrow is a liquid resembling blood and is the source of all blood cells, both red and white, including those of the immune system. The majority of bone marrow transplants are not, in fact, transplantations, but are autografts—grafts of the patient's own bone marrow. Described here are both procedures.

Transplants
Bone marrow transplants—that is, transplants using bone marrow taken from a donor—are experimental and have not yet been perfected. However, they have aroused much interest and many clinical trials are under way. They are currently used for various purposes including the improvement in acceptance of kidney, heart, and other organ grafts.

If bone marrow transplants are to be successful, an accurate tissue match is necessary between the donor and the recipient, and it is unusual to find such a satisfactory match from an unrelated donor. As a rule, donors are parents or brothers or sisters. Identical twins are ideal. When a good match cannot be obtained the recipient must be given a large dose of radiation to all lymphoid tissue in the body, to prevent the

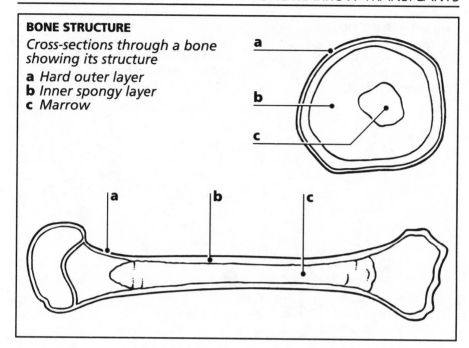

BONE STRUCTURE

Cross-sections through a bone showing its structure

a *Hard outer layer*
b *Inner spongy layer*
c *Marrow*

newly introduced foreign bone marrow from being destroyed by the patient's own immune system.

While the radiation treatment is being given, the patient's bones that contain blood-forming marrow—the skull, ribs, and pelvis—are shielded. This prevents the existing marrow contained within them from being affected by the radiation. Both the donor cells and the recipient's own cells then populate the body, and for reasons still not understood, this seems to allow the body to tolerate grafted organs.

Bone marrow autografts

Autografts are used to treat bone marrow failure. Bone marrow failure may occur for a variety of reasons. For example, the high-dose radiation and chemotherapy used to treat conditions such as cancer often leads to severe anemia, bleeding disorders, infection from immune deficiency, and even total failure of the bone marrow to produce cells. Leukemia—a kind of cancer of the cell-producing marrow cells—can also result in bone marrow failure. To circumvent these problems a sample of marrow may be taken from a patient prior to radiation or chemotherapy treatment, or from a leukemia patient in remission, and later replaced. Autografts have been used successfully in the treatment of:

• leukemia
• non-Hodgkin's and Burkitt's lymphomas
• some cases of ovarian cancer
• some cases of malignant melanoma

© DIAGRAM

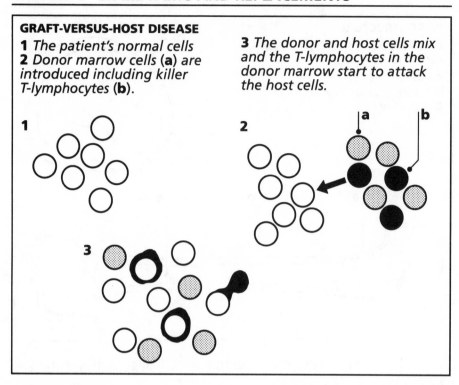

GRAFT-VERSUS-HOST DISEASE
1 *The patient's normal cells*
2 *Donor marrow cells (**a**) are introduced including killer T-lymphocytes (**b**).*

3 *The donor and host cells mix and the T-lymphocytes in the donor marrow start to attack the host cells.*

Complications

Immune deficiency that persists (until the bone has been able to produce the normal number of immune system white cells) increases the risk of infection. For this reason it is usually necessary to maintain strict isolation for four to six weeks after the bone marrow graft. When the graft has been taken from another donor (transplantation), graft-versus-host disease may occur. To reduce the risk of this disease, the bone marrow is often "laundered" (the T-lymphocyctes are removed). T-lymphocytes can be removed using antibodies or by passing the marrow through columns containing soya bean lectins, proteins with a high affinity for a particular sugar. Immunosuppressant drugs, such as cyclosporin and corticosteroids, also help to prevent and treat rejection of this kind.

Procedure for an autograft

Marrow is usually taken from the breastbone, the crest of the pelvis, or the side of the tibia. After an injection of local anesthetic, a short, stout needle with a metal handle and stylet is forced through the bone and into the marrow cavity, with a screwing motion. When the tip of the needle reaches the marrow, the stylet and handle are removed and a syringe is attached. A quantity of marrow is then sucked out into the syringe. After the needle is removed, firm pressure is applied for a few minutes and then the site of the prick is covered with a Band-Aid®.

The marrow is mixed with a preservative and frozen in stages to -190°F, after which it may be stored indefinitely until needed. Once the marrow sample is held, a patient with leukemia or one of various other forms of cancer can be given a dose of radiation or chemotherapy that destroys the cancer and remaining marrow. The patient is nursed in an isolation room to minimize the risk of infection (not having the immune cell-making bone marrow).

The preserved marrow is later thawed and simply injected into a vein. Once inside the body, it is capable of reconstituting the blood-forming system: some of the special cell-making marrow cells (known as "stem" cells) settle in the spongy center of flat bones and start to reproduce. Stem cells occur in about 1 in every 250 marrow cells and are capable of rapid division: they are able to divide themselves into red cells, immune cells, and blood-clotting platelets.

Fortunately, as the preserved marrow is the patient's own, no immunological rejection occurs. The success of the procedure depends entirely on whether the radiation or chemotherapy treatment for the cancer has entirely destroyed the disease and on whether a high enough proportion of stem cells has survived to start up blood cell production.

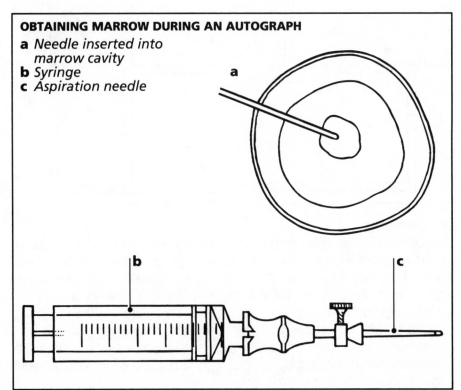

OBTAINING MARROW DURING AN AUTOGRAPH
a *Needle inserted into marrow cavity*
b *Syringe*
c *Aspiration needle*

© DIAGRAM

CHAPTER 4
OPERATING ROOM AND STAFF

THE OPERATING ROOM (OR)

Large hospitals must have large suites of operating rooms. In well-designed units, these are grouped conveniently in relation to the surgical wards. Each group may contain up to six or eight separate ORs, usually sharing central facilities, such as sterilizing equipment, rest rooms, and so on. It will be convenient to look at these from the point of view of the surgeon coming to work, noting what the surgeon sees and does before getting on with an operating list. Of course, no two operating suites are exactly alike, but all of them share the features described below.

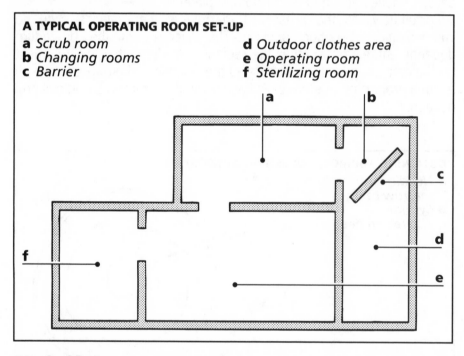

A TYPICAL OPERATING ROOM SET-UP

a *Scrub room*
b *Changing rooms*
c *Barrier*

d *Outdoor clothes area*
e *Operating room*
f *Sterilizing room*

OR clothing

Your access to the operating room is invariably by way of double swing or sliding doors wide enough to allow passage for a bed or wide patient trolley. The surgeon and other staff members, however, enter by a separate normal-sized door, probably marked "Private." This door leads to a restricted "outdoor clothes" area where staff entering the OR must remove all outdoor clothing, shoes, watches, rings, and jewelry, and change into fresh suits of cotton slacks and loose shirts. These are commonly colored pale blue or green. Hair is bundled into disposable caps so that none of it is exposed.

OR clothing, donned in the changing rooms, is not sterile but has been freshly laundered and is worn for one session only. It is then thrown into a bin to be laundered again. Before entering the OR proper, the surgeon, who has changed and has walked through from the changing room in socks, now goes to a barrier to put on a pair of short white rubber boots. Some surgeons prefer clogs or other forms of footwear. Boots probably have the surgeon's name marked on them with black felt-tip pen, and so identifying them from among other pairs laid out in rows may require some hunting. Crossing the barrier, the surgeon now enters the OR. No one, not even the patient, wears normal outdoor clothing in this area.

4

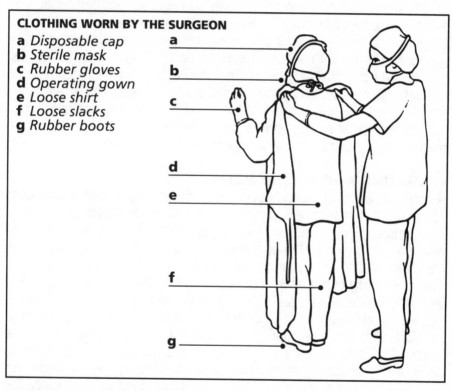

CLOTHING WORN BY THE SURGEON

a *Disposable cap*
b *Sterile mask*
c *Rubber gloves*
d *Operating gown*
e *Loose shirt*
f *Loose slacks*
g *Rubber boots*

Avoidance of infection

From the description of the trouble taken with clothing, and from what follows, you will appreciate that the first consideration, in the design and organization of an OR, is the avoidance of infection of the open surgical wound. To this end, the operating environment is kept as free from bacteria as possible. Obviously, there is no practical way in which the whole environment can be kept sterile. But much can be done to keep the bacterial count low. Floors, walls, tables, and major items of equipment are all designed to be easily washed down each day. Walls are tiled and floors covered with smooth washable material.

Lightboxes for viewing X-ray and CT scan films are built flush to the walls and their exposed surfaces are washable. To check the efficiency of these measures, bacterial culture plates are regularly exposed open in various locations in the OR and are then sent to the laboratory to be incubated. If more than a very few colonies of bacteria grow, or if there is a higher than acceptable incidence of wound infection, the cause of the contamination is investigated and corrected.

The surgeon does not immediately enter the room where the operation is to be carried out and where several other members of staff are waiting. The first stop is a scrub annex fitted with a row of elbow-operated faucets. There the surgeon and assistants meticulously clean and scrub their hands and arms, using nail brushes and antiseptic fluid and working carefully over the whole surface of the exposed skin. This takes at least five minutes and when they are finished they dry their hands and arms with sterile towels before putting on sterile gowns, masks, and thin rubber gloves. The scrub nurses have already gone through this routine. From now on, the surgeon keeps his or her hands together, held high up in front of the chest, and is very careful to touch nothing except sterilized towels and instruments. The surgeon is now ready to start operating and goes into the operating room.

OPERATING ROOM EQUIPMENT

A large operating lamp, specially designed to produce shadowless illumination, is suspended from the ceiling on a substantial hinged arm. This lamp can be moved and tilted so as to direct its beam almost anywhere in the region of the operating table that lies under it. There may be other supplementary lamps, on mobile floor stands, near the table.

The operating table itself is of heavy construction and very rigid. It is generally made of stainless steel and is covered with a thick slab of conductive rubber for your comfort and protection—at least for your comfort after the operation, if not during it. A hard table can cause severe aches and pains in the postoperative period. The table is designed to be easily raised and lowered, tilted in any direction and bent up or down at each end. Some of these controls, especially the height control, are operated by pedals so that the table can be adjusted by the surgeon. Others are hand-operated and have to be worked by a circulating nurse or orderly who is not wearing sterile gloves and clothing.

The anesthetic trolley is situated near the operating table and is easily recognized by the cylinders of oxygen and anesthetic gases fixed to it and by the valves and gauges for controlling the flow rate of gases. It also carries a mechanical respirator with its corrugated flexible tubes, and various monitoring devices. Many hospitals do not use gas cylinders in the OR but maintain large cylinders centrally and convey the gases to all parts through permanently installed piping. In such cases, there are convenient outlets in all ORs, in anesthetic rooms, and in convey rooms, at which tubes can be connected to carry gases to the patient. In hospitals that do not use this system, the anesthetic trolleys are so designed that they can be connected to the patient in the anesthetic room and wheeled into the OR alongside the patient's trolley. Recovery rooms have separate oxygen cylinders on stands with reducing valves, pressure gauges, pipes, and masks.

Instrument tables. Surrounding the operating table are several stainless steel wheeled tables covered with sterile towels on which sterile instruments have been laid out under the supervision of the scrub nurse. There are always more instruments than seem necessary, and usually more than are necessary. Surgeons expect everything they need in the course of an operation to be immediately available, and are likely to become impolite if kept waiting for some instrument to be put through the sterilizer (autoclave). So the chief nurse usually advises the supply nurse to err on the side of generosity in the choice of instruments. The supply nurse has formal lists for each procedure but regularly lays out larger numbers of items than are stipulated.

Plastic waste buckets in steel frames can be wheeled about by the scrub nurse.

Sterile basins contain sterile saline or other solutions in which packs can be soaked by the scrub nurse.

A suction machine with large glass reservoirs will be situated near the operating table. Suction is an important facility during operations and may be used to remove blood and other fluids so as to improve surgical visibility. The plastic tubes used to connect the metal sucker cannulas used by surgical assistants or the surgeon are sterilized, but are connected to the machine by a circulating nurse or orderly who touches only the end near the machine.

A high-frequency electrical diathermy machine, used by the surgeon to seal off bleeding points or to make bloodless cuts, is standing by, as is a range of other equipment, which may include:
- various imaging devices
- fiberoptic endoscopes
- heart–lung machines
- electromagnets for the removal of metallic foreign bodies
- special frames for the support of the patient

Sterilizing
Adjoining the OR is the sterilizing room, where the large, compressed-steam autoclaves are installed, and where most of the operating instruments are stored on shelves, often sealed up, presterilized, in transparent or labeled packages for quick identification.

© DIAGRAM

Autoclaving is still the main method of sterilizing instruments, swabs, packs of surgical towels, operating gowns, and draping sheets. The machine works on the principle of the pressure cooker. If water is boiled in a strong, closed chamber so that the steam is not allowed to escape, the pressure rises and this causes the boiling point to rise well above the normal 100°C (212°F). Some organisms can form spores which resist heating to 100°C (212°F), but the moist heat temperatures reached in an autoclave—around 127°C (260°F) at 20 pounds pressure per square inch—will kill them all.

Other sterilizing methods commonly used include:

- soakage in chemical sterilizing solutions (sometimes damaging to instruments)
- dry heat in an oven
- irradiation with gamma rays from a cobalt bomb

Central sterilization of large quantities of material can often be most efficiently achieved by irradiation. Material is cleaned and then sealed in airtight polythene bags inside outer wrappings. These are then put on a conveyor belt, which carries them through a heavily shielded barrier and past a Cobalt-60 radioactive source. Within seconds, all living organisms in the material are destroyed. Gamma irradiation cannot cause material to become radioactive. Because the surgical material is sealed in bags, new germs cannot get in, and because the wrappings are doubled, the bags can be opened by people not wearing sterile clothing and gloves without contaminating the contents.

Surgical instruments

Hemostats. The instrument present in greatest numbers is the hemostat or artery forceps. Hemostats are like scissors with flat, serrated jaws instead of blades, and usually have a ratchet catch so that they stay closed when tightened. They are used to grab cut arteries and stop the bleeding until the artery can be tied off with a ligature of catgut. Quite a lot of time is spent doing this during an operation, and it is common at an early stage in surgery to see the incision festooned with a couple of dozen hemostats. Arteries secured in hemostats can also be sealed by touching the hemostat with a diathermy probe. This causes heat coagulation of the cut end of the artery and is quicker than using ties.

Forceps and clamps. Other kinds of forceps are also much in evidence. These are used mainly for tissue holding and dissection. Some of them have fairly fierce-looking teeth at the tip that interlock, one into two, or two into three. Non-toothed forceps almost always have serrated jaws. Smooth tips would not hold slippery tissue. Forceps should be distinguished from clamps. The latter usually have long jaws and are usually smooth. Often the jaws are covered with rubber sheaths so that they do not damage the tissue they are holding. Clamps are used to secure and prevent leakage from large blood vessels, intestines, and various organs. Accordingly, they come in a wide range of sizes.

Knives and scissors. Only a few different kinds of surgical knives (scalpels) are used. The most common type consists of a nondisposable handle to which can be fixed one of a range of disposable, and very sharp, blades. The Bard-Parker system is the most widely used. Bard-Parker blades are supplied presterilized, in separate, sealed packets that can be peeled open to release the blade onto the instrument table. The blades are discarded after being used once.

Scissors of various kinds and sizes are widely used in surgery, and are used with as much care as are the knives. Most of them have rounded, blunt tips and either straight or curved blades. The curve may be "on the flat" or "on the edge." Scissors are also widely used for what is called "blunt dissection," in circumstances in which cutting might be dangerous. The method is to push the tip of the closed scissors into the tissues and then open the blade. This is done repeatedly and causes the tissues to split open, often along natural planes of cleavage, and without endangering important structures such as blood vessels or nerves.

Swabs. On one corner of the instrument trolley are bundles of square, folded gauze swabs or sponges. These are used to mop up blood so that the surgeon can see the work area. Large numbers are used. Discarded swabs are not thrown away but are hung up on a spike rack to be counted and to provide an indication of blood loss. Before the wound is closed the senior nurse present supervises a swab count to ensure that it tallies with the number taken from the packets. Surgeons don't like having to explain to patients that they must go in again to retrieve a swab left behind.

Swabs are mostly held in the fingers but it is often necessary for them to be held in long-nosed forceps specially designed for the purpose. These are called sponge-holding or swab-holding forceps.

Needles and sutures. Surgical needles come in all sizes, straight and curved, and usually have a thread of some kind swaged to them. The thread, or the combination of a needle and its thread, is called a suture. The days when surgical needles had eyes, and nurses were kept busy threading them, have long since gone. The possible permutations of needles and sutures are enormous and ORs have to hold large stocks. Surgical needles and sutures are always presterilized and are contained in individual double coverings and packed in plastic boxes. One wall of an OR storeroom may be completely covered with these boxes, labeled on their ends with the contents. The instrument trolley will certainly carry a selection of sutures.

© DIAGRAM

Sutures of different material and different gauge are used for different purposes, such as sewing up cut organs, membranes, blood vessels, and skin. Many sutures are made of absorbable material such as catgut or collagen. These are inserted and left. Some sutures are non-absorbable and are made of plastic material. These are used for skin and for securing vital structures like heart valves that must not come adrift. Many suture needles are too small to be held in the fingers and are gripped in special needle holders. These, too, come in a range of

INSTRUMENTS

Illustrated here are some of the instruments required for the average abdominal operation.

a *Scalpel*
b *Forceps*
c *Hemostat*
d *Suture clamp*
e *Wound clip*
f *Cutting scissors*
g *Blunt scissors*
h *Needle*
i *Swabs*
j *Needle holder*

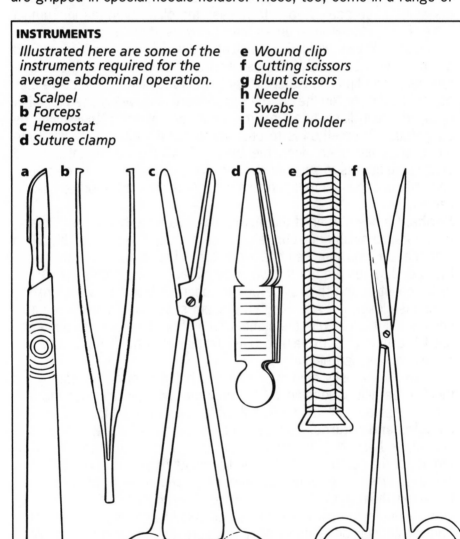

sizes. Needle holders resemble hemostats but are mostly of stouter construction.

Sutures are not the only means of surgical closure. Increasingly, surgeons are using metal clips or staples applied with special forceps or staple guns. Clips are commonly used to close the skin incision. Staples are not confined to the skin but are also sometimes used internally, on the intestines and elsewhere.

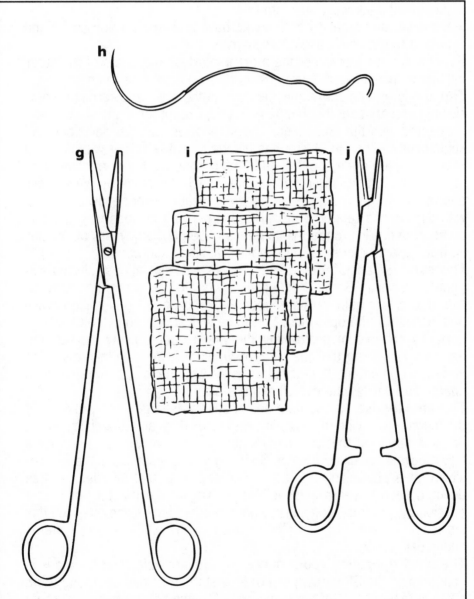

OPERATING ROOM STAFF

The surgeon can function only with the support of a considerable staff of people. Indeed, when working in the OR, the surgeon is at the apex of a large pyramid of people all of whom contribute to the success of the operation. Many of these have already played their part:

- the office and outpatient staff
- the radiographers and radiologists
- the technicians operating the scanners
- the pathology laboratory staff
- the hospital administrative staff
- the junior nurses and doctors who have looked after you so far and helped to get your case notes in order

But now we must consider the more immediate members of the surgical hierarchy—those actually engaged in the operating room.

The surgeon. The surgeon is the boss of the team and carries responsibility for everything that happens to you, except for matters expressly connected with the anesthetic. The surgeon makes the decisions and implements them. He or she has decided what is wrong with you and what should be done about it, and then carries out the corrective operation. The surgeon is qualified to make such decisions by the acquisition of formal qualifications and a great deal of experience in dealing with similar and related surgical problems, and in observing the outcome of decisions made. All surgeons undergo many years of specialist training and apprenticeship under practicing surgeons.

The surgical assistants. Surgical assistants are almost always surgeons in training. Some are beginners who do little more than hang on to retractors to hold incisions open and who do not otherwise participate actively in the operation. Some are well advanced in their training, perfectly capable of performing the whole operation by themselves, and usually wishing that the surgeon would ask them to take over. But however competent the assistant may be, the surgeon remains in charge and carries the overall responsibility.

The anesthetist. At one time anesthetics was largely the province of the nurse. But with the growth in knowledge and specialization it became apparent that anesthetics had become very much a job for a fully medically qualified person. So today your anesthesia is the responsibility of a physician who, after receiving a normal MD degree, has devoted several years of specialist training to the mastery of all the physiology, pharmacology, instrumentation, and medicine on which this discipline is based. The anesthetist is an expert in life-support systems and in pain control.

The chief operating room nurse. This responsible senior nurse is in charge of all the OR nursing and orderly staff. The chief operating room nurse is responsible for the standards of training of the operating room nursing staff and may also be engaged in training. This person has administrative as well as clinical duties. The chief operating room nurse studies the operating lists, allocates staff to particular surgeons, and ensures a fair distribution of duty. Other responsibilities include maintaining duty rosters and organizing overtime arrangements, staff vacations, and sickness reliefs.

The surgical supply nurse. It is a long-established rule that surgeons must never be kept waiting for the materials they need—surgical towels and drapes, skin-cleaning fluids, gloves, masks, caps, and operating gowns. It is the job of the surgical supply nurse to ensure that, at all times, adequate stocks of all these things, and many others, are maintained in the OR so that they are immediately available for use.

Space is at a premium so the surgical supply nurse cannot simply order large quantities of everything. Stocks must be continuously reviewed and replacements must be ordered in good time from medical stores.

The scrub nurses (suture nurses). The scrub nurse does not actually participate in the operation, but is situated close by, standing at one or more trolleys covered with sterile drapes on which all the necessary instruments and supplies have been laid out in accordance with lists drawn up before the actual operation. The scrub nurse must know exactly what is going on at all times and be thoroughly conversant with the routine of each operation so as to anticipate the surgeon's needs. The scrub nurse watches carefully, keeps the surgeon provided with plenty of swabs, opens suture and other packs in good time, and hands the surgeon all necessary instruments, usually without prompting. The scrub nurse is often asked to use the sucker to keep the wound dry.

The circulating nurses. In spite of the best organization, it often happens that equipment or instruments are needed that have not already been laid out. In addition, operations sometimes take longer than anticipated and consume more supplies than normal. So it is essential to have someone standing by to attend to these special needs. This is the function of a circulating nurse. This person does not wear a sterile gown or gloves but, because of the routine of the operating room, is never actually involved with any surgical procedure.

The operating room orderlies. Orderlies are needed to take over, from the outside porters, the trolley on which you are lying, move you over onto an OR trolley, wheel you into the anesthetic room and, after you are asleep, move you into the OR and position you on the table. They are also needed to move heavy equipment in and out of the OR, clear the OR of all mobile equipment after an operating list, and wash down the walls and floors.

CHAPTER 5
SURGERY INSIDE THE SKULL

Removal of a brain tumor or blood clot

Why have the operation?

Anything that causes pressure within the tissues of the brain—a tumor, a blood clot in or at the side of the brain—may lead to damage to brain cells, often with potentially dangerous results that may include loss of voluntary movement, loss of speech and understanding, and even (if treatment is withheld) loss of life. For these reasons, surgery on the brain is both corrective, to relieve the pressure and restore normal brain function; and often preventive, to avoid even worse damage.

CEREBRAL THROMBOSIS

A blood clot (thrombus) (a) forms in a cerebral blood vessel (b), impairing the flow of blood to the brain. The area supplied by the blocked vessel is deprived of oxygen and glucose, resulting in the death (necrosis) of some brain tissue.

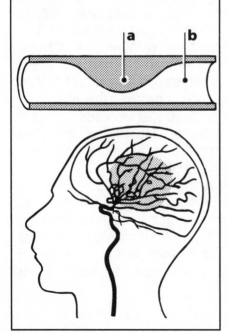

CEREBRAL EMBOLISM

A small but solid mass of organic material (an embolus) (a)—perhaps a piece of a blood clot from elsewhere in the body—blocks an artery (b) that supplies blood to the brain. Again brain cells are deprived of oxygen and glucose, and die.

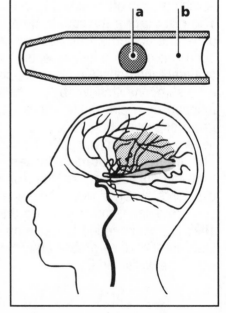

What is the physical cause of the problem?

Not all brain tumors are malignant. Anything growing within the tight confines of the skull, however—whether malignant or benign—is dangerous because it increases pressure there. About half of all tumors in the brain arise in tissues that help to supply and support the brain rather than in the brain cells themselves: most of such tumors are malignant. Others include tumors of the pituitary gland, of blood vessels, of the nerves to and from the ears, or of other parts of the body that have spread through the bloodstream to the brain. A different type of tumor altogether grows on the membranes that are not actually part of the brain but that cover and protect it. Such tumors are called meningiomas and are never malignant; they account for around 20 percent of all brain tumors and are more responsive to treatment than are many other forms of brain tumor.

5

MENINGIOMA

A tumor in the membranes that enclose and protect the brain (the meninges) increases in thickness and presses on the brain. Pressure on the left temporal lobe (as shown here) would tend to result in impaired speech and understanding.

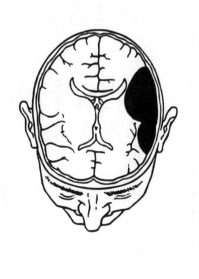

CEREBRAL HEMORRHAGE

*A weak area (**a**) in a blood vessel's wall (**b**) swells and ruptures (an aneurysm). Blood floods from the vessel into surrounding brain tissue, and clots. Emergency surgery may stanch the flow—but the clots may have to be removed by the surgery described here.*

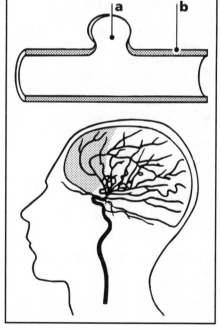

© DIAGRAM

What is the specific goal of surgery?

The goal of the surgeon in the case of a brain tumor is to remove the tumor and all associated cells so that it will not recur. In the case of a blood clot, the aim is to relieve the pressure, remove the blood clot, and drain any excess blood and cerebrospinal fluid that may have contributed to the trauma. Not all of these objectives are attainable in every case. Removal of tumors located deep within the brain—such as tumors of the connective tissue of the nervous system (gliomas)—may involve so much damage to other essential structures that the patient's condition may be made fundamentally worse. Modern imaging techniques can accurately pinpoint tumors and, as often as possible, total removal is attempted. But the surgeon has to make an individual assessment in every case, balancing probable advantages against risks. When total removal is not feasible—perhaps because a malignant tumor has spread destructively throughout the brain tissue in many directions—a palliative operation, to relieve the symptoms, is com-

---

THE TISSUE LAYERS

Between the brain and the outside air are six layers of tissue, some protective, some supportive:
a *Skin of the scalp, with hair, fat and other tissues*
b *Periosteum: a thin membrane covering the skull*
c *The skull, housing the brain; its fused bones and domed shape give it tensile strength disproportionate to its average thickness*
d *The dura mater, the tough, inelastic outer membrane immediately within the skull*
e *The arachnoid: an elastic "skin" attached to the dura mater*
f *Blood vessels*
g *Subarachnoid space*
h *The pia mater, a thin "skin" on top of the irregular surface of the brain itself*
i *Brain tissue*

The dura mater, arachnoid and pia mater membranes are together known as the meninges.

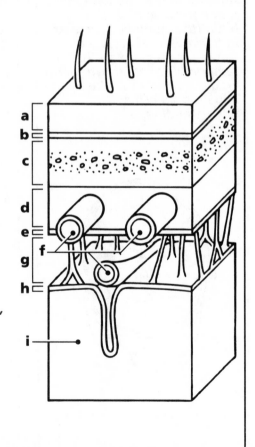

monly performed. Part of the tumor may be removed, or the tumor may be reduced in size by radiotherapy. In either case, the damaging pressure within the skull is relieved. Surgery to drain excess fluid and drug therapy with steroids to reduce fluid within the tissues are alternative methods for relieving the pressure. At the very least, such measures may afford a patient who has an inoperable brain tumor significant relief of symptoms and an extended period of relatively normal life (a remission).

Exactly what is involved in the surgical operation?

The operation to remove a meningioma—a nonmalignant tumor in the membranes that cover and protect the brain—is classic for the type of surgery that aims at the removal of cancer or a blood clot. The tumor is relatively accessible, well defined, slow growing and rounded, usually embedded in the outer surface of the brain but not actually penetrating it; removal is unlikely to cause further damage to brain nerve cells.

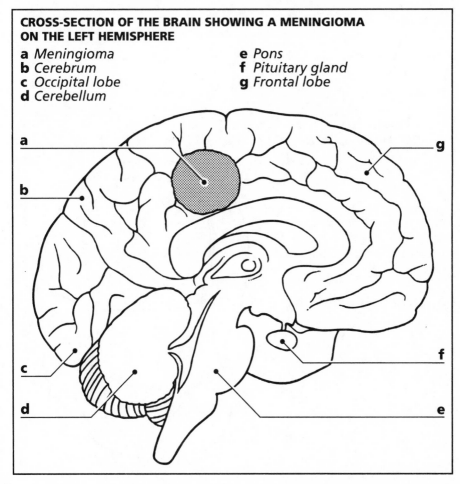

CROSS-SECTION OF THE BRAIN SHOWING A MENINGIOMA ON THE LEFT HEMISPHERE

a *Meningioma*
b *Cerebrum*
c *Occipital lobe*
d *Cerebellum*

e *Pons*
f *Pituitary gland*
g *Frontal lobe*

© DIAGRAM

Preliminary steps. Careful evaluation and CT scanning (p.32) or MRI studies (p.36) determine the probable type of the tumor and its precise location. Shortly before going to the OR, your head will be shaved. Then the anesthetist will induce general anesthesia.

Step-by-step surgical procedure. With a felt pen the surgeon has marked out a large square flap on the scalp covering the area over the tumor (**a**). Following this mark, the surgeon first cuts through the skin tissues as far as the periosteum, the thin membrane covering the skull bone. The scalp has a good blood supply and bleeds readily, so many small bleeding arteries will have to be picked up with artery forceps and

PROCEDURE FOR THE REMOVAL OF A MENINGIOMA

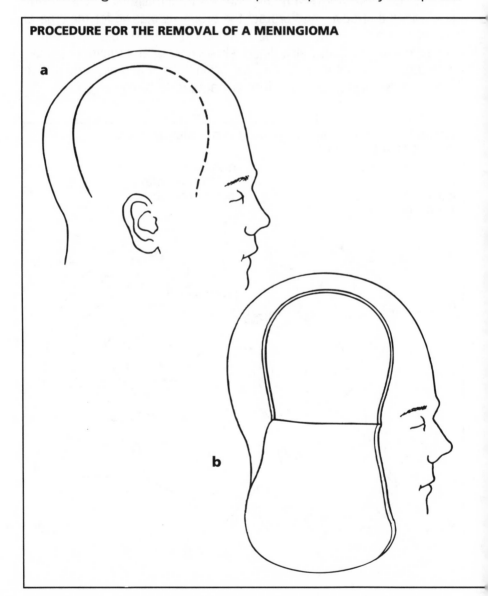

sealed with a high-frequency electric diathermy. The scalp flap is then folded back, and the bone exposed (**b**). The periosteum must also be cut through and elevated. A circle of holes is now made in the skull itself (**c**) with a burr drill, and a soft metal guide is passed under the bone (but not as far as the dura mater, the tough membrane immediately within the skull) from one hole to the next. A fine wire saw—a Gigli saw—is then passed along the guide channel under the bone between adjacent holes. The ends of the saw are then attached to handles (**d**). The surgeon saws through the bone by grasping these handles and alternating pulls at each end until the flap of bone is free and can be

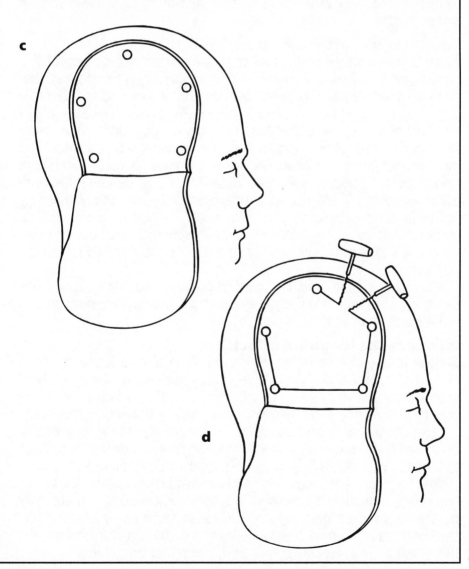

© DIAGRAM

hinged back or lifted clear altogether. This exposes the dura mater, a flap of which is cut away using scissors (**e**).

The other membranes covering the brain—the pia mater and arachnoid—are now visible. The tumor should also be seen, pressed into the brain itself. Before attempting to remove the tumor, however, the surgeon identifies the fairly numerous blood vessels supplying blood to the meningioma and ties them off. All bleeding must be controlled: continued hemorrhage within the skull is dangerous. Finally, the tumor may be carefully shelled out of its bed using a dissector with a blunt edge.

The surgeon now stitches the layer of dura mater covering the brain. Replacing the bone flap, the surgeon secures it with a few twisted pieces of fine, soft wire (**f**). The scalp incision is closed with catgut stitches (**g**).

What is it like after the operation?
Every patient's speed and extent of recovery following surgery of this type depends individually on the severity of the surgery performed and on factors such as overall health and age. But in general, and certainly in the case of a meningioma operation, healing is rapid because of the excellent blood supply to the area. Recovery is quick, and you are likely to be out of bed within a day or two, and at home within a week. You must expect to have a headache for a few days, perhaps with some pain from the scalp wound—but these can easily be controlled with painkilling drugs. If you have a bandage around your head, it may feel hot and uncomfortable as your hair begins to regrow underneath it: medical staff will change the bandage at appropriate times. The soft wires used to reattach the skull bone are permanent and cause no discomfort.

If pressure on the brain had caused problems such as poor coordination in movement or defective eyesight, these may have disappeared or be much improved.

What are the longterm effects?
Serious longterm effects following total removal of a tumor or blood clot are uncommon. Following a cerebral hemorrhage, however, some brain damage is likely to have occurred. The effects in the meantime may be those of general tiredness and volatility of temper, with some impairment in speech and understanding, gradually improving over several months. In rare cases, specific movements or activities may have to be relearned, possibly with the help of specialized therapists.

When surgery has been for cerebral hemorrhage, thrombosis, or embolism, outpatient examinations over the succeeding months may be needed to investigate any specific cause (such as high blood pressure or deep-vein thrombosis in the legs) with the aim of minimizing the risk of future emergencies by physical, dietary, or drug therapy.

PROCEDURE FOR THE REMOVAL OF A MENINGIOMA (continued)

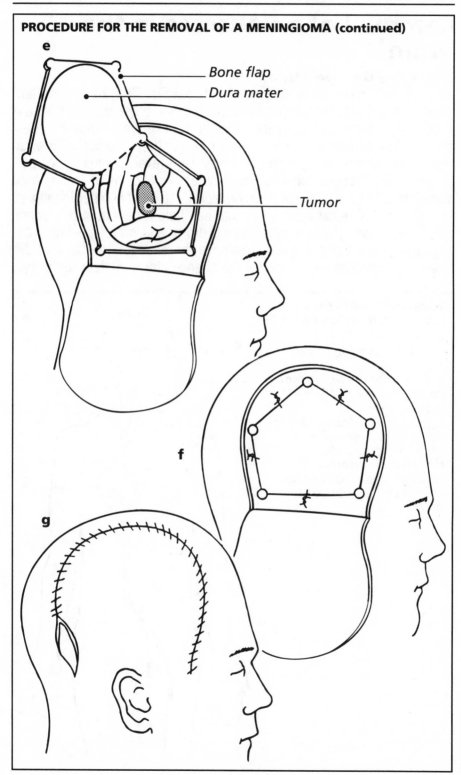

e

Bone flap

Dura mater

Tumor

f

g

Removal of an abscess in the brain

Why have the operation?

An abscess in the brain is dangerous in two ways. First, by forming and growing it causes pressure on the brain tissue—pressure which in turn causes symptoms that correspond to the part of the brain being pressurized. The effects may be severe, ranging from headache, drowsiness, and vomiting to epileptic seizures, high fever, confusion, or partial paralysis. Second, an abscess is infective and, as it grows, may spread to other areas of the brain or reproduce itself in other locations. There are nonsurgical treatments that can help a patient in this condition—particularly the use of antibiotic drugs and steroids—but if deterioration continues, surgery to remove the abscess is vital, and the earlier it is undertaken, the better the chances for complete recovery.

SOURCES OF INFECTION RESULTING IN BRAIN ABSCESS

a *Direct penetration through a wound in the skull*
b *Spread of bacteria from an abscess in an infected ear*
c *Spread of infection from the nasal sinuses after a cold, influenza, etc.*
d *Spread of infection through the bloodstream from a distant part of the body*

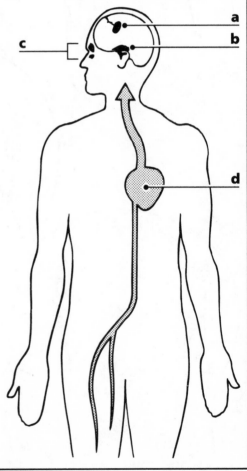

What is the physical cause of the problem?

Brain abscess is nearly always caused by infective organisms that spread to the brain. The affected brain tissue first becomes inflamed and then begins to be pushed outward as pus accumulates at the center. The tissues in contact with the pus harden and become fibrous—and may do so progressively, so that the abscess in effect acts like a growing tumor—also making it difficult for antibiotic drugs to reach, and deal with, the infective organisms in the abscess. This is why antibiotic therapy, given at the same time as surgery, generally involves unusually high dosages.

What is the specific goal of surgery?

Once an abscess has formed, the prime objective is to minimize damage to the brain. Surgery must preserve intact as much brain tissue as possible while ensuring that all traces of infective material are removed.

Exactly what is involved in the surgical operation?

Before surgery, you will undergo extensive tests and scanning to pinpoint the precise location of the abscess. Knowing this, the surgeon can determine the optimum site of surgical access—whether a small burr-hole (about ⅜ inch in diameter) drilled in the skull is sufficient (if the abscess is still localized) or whether the skull opening will have to be more extensive. This will determine whether all, or only a small area, of your scalp should be shaved clean.

Preliminary steps. As with most operations involving general anesthesia, you will be given a preoperative injection about an hour before surgery to dry up internal fluids and to encourage drowsiness. (Technically, the operation can be—and occasionally is—performed under local anesthetic, for the brain itself is entirely insensitive to pain and the only tissue that has to be anesthetized is that of the scalp.)

Step-by-step surgical procedure. Once you are fully anesthetized, the surgeon makes an incision directly over the location of the abscess (so that access is achieved with minimum disturbance of healthy brain tissue). If the incision is to be near the temples or at the back of the head, however, the local muscles must first be anesthetized, severed, and held apart with retractors. Incisions around the top of the head—where there are no muscles—are easier: the incision is made directly down to the bone surface of the skull, and the skin edges kept apart by retractors. Either way, the bone is reached and an area of the thin membrane covering the skull (the periosteum) is scraped away and is then ready for the drill.

A burr-hole in the skull is all that is necessary for most abscesses, and is quickly made using a special power-tool designed for surgery. Less commonly, a hand-operated brace-and-bit drill may be used. The brace is exactly like a standard carpenter's brace, but a little smaller

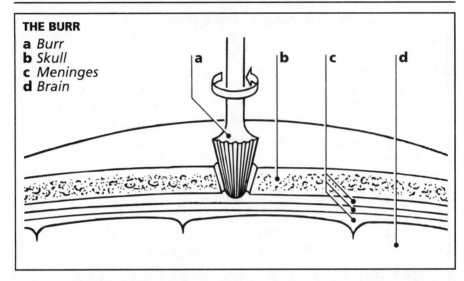

THE BURR
a *Burr*
b *Skull*
c *Meninges*
d *Brain*

and all metal. The burr bit fits into a chuck. The hole is then smoothed off with a burr bit. In this way, a small, circular area of bone is lost. Underneath is the triple membrane (the meninges) that protects the brain. The three membranes that make up the meninges are the dura mater, arachnoid, and pia mater. The dura mater is gently lifted up through the hole with a hook and snipped twice to make a cross-shaped opening through which other instruments may pass into the brain itself. (Less commonly, several holes are drilled and a flap of the skull bone is then opened to attain a much greater area of access inside. In such cases, a portion of the fibrosed tissue surrounding the abscess may also be cut out.)

A hollow needle with a wide bore can now be pushed into the abscess, and through it pus and dead brain tissue can be sucked out by a vacuum machine. Afterward, a soft plastic catheter replaces the hollow needle and is left in the wound, its end in the abscess cavity, so that when the surgical part of the operation is over, antibiotic drugs may be administered directly to the seat of the problem. The catheter is taped to the scalp and the edges of the incision are allowed to close around it. Aseptic dressings and bandages complete the operation.

What is it like immediately after the operation?
You will wake up in the intensive care unit (ICU), where your condition can be closely watched by specially trained staff. For the next ten days antibiotics will be administered through the catheter into your brain at regular intervals, and the effect of the operation (in particular whether any infective material, which could cause new inflammation, remains in the brain) will be monitored by frequent CT scans. You may not be too aware of your surroundings at first, although removal of the abscess should increase your overall alertness from its presurgery level. Pain

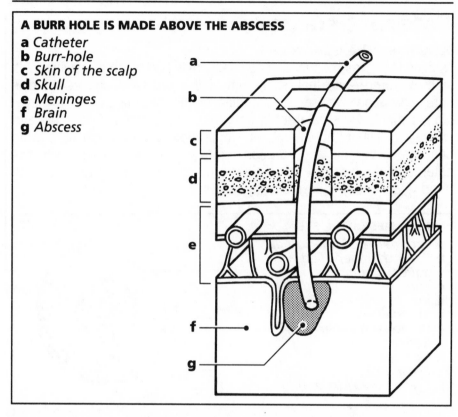

A BURR HOLE IS MADE ABOVE THE ABSCESS
a *Catheter*
b *Burr-hole*
c *Skin of the scalp*
d *Skull*
e *Meninges*
f *Brain*
g *Abscess*

should not be a problem (and can be dealt with through the use of painkilling drugs), although there may be recurrent headache.

The length of your stay in the hospital depends on the severity of your original condition and on how much it is improved by the operation. You may, for instance, need physical therapy or speech therapy or other forms of assistance not necessarily available at home.

What are the longterm effects?

The major longterm effect is survival. However, depending on where in the brain the abscess was situated and on how destructive the abscess had become, you may have lost some mental or physical ability. Lost brain tissue does not regenerate and if brain tissue affecting movement, sensation, speech, verbal comprehension, vision, etc., is destroyed by the abscess, the function concerned cannot be restored. One fairly common side effect of brain abscess surgery is epilepsy (experienced by 50 percent of patients), and you may be prescribed anticonvulsant drugs on a regular basis for the rest of your life as a precaution—and may therefore be prohibited from driving motor vehicles by some authorities.

Regular monitoring of your brain by CT or other scanning methods is advisable.

© DIAGRAM

Cataract surgery

Why have the operation?

Nothing improves the morale and quality of life so much as having one's sight restored—and that is the aim of this relatively simple, but delicate, operation. Cataract is clouding of the internal lens of the eye. Many patients have cataract in both eyes and suffer considerable and increasing visual impairment. The operation is performed usually on one eye at a time: the surgeon removes the internal lens with the cataract and replaces it with a clear synthetic lens. In nearly all patients good visual acuity is permanently restored.

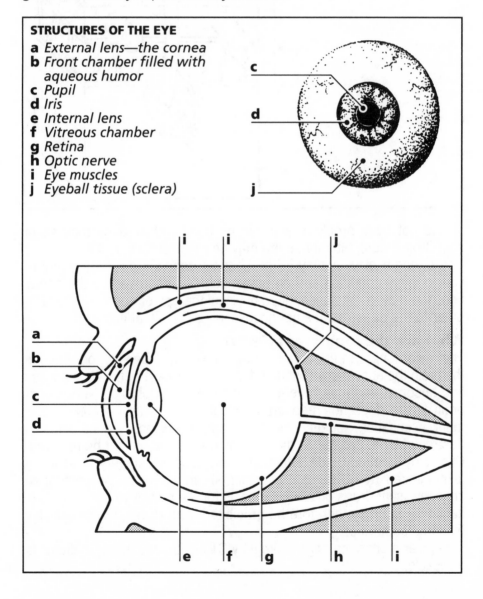

STRUCTURES OF THE EYE

a *External lens—the cornea*
b *Front chamber filled with aqueous humor*
c *Pupil*
d *Iris*
e *Internal lens*
f *Vitreous chamber*
g *Retina*
h *Optic nerve*
i *Eye muscles*
j *Eyeball tissue (sclera)*

What is the physical cause of the problem?

The opacity in the lens of the eye results from changes in the structure and alignment of the protein fibers that make up the lens. Such changes may be due to:

- the normal effect of aging. Most cataract patients are in their 60s or older.
- rubella virus infection in the womb during gestation
- various genetic conditions
- direct injury to the eye

For most patients, the gradual loss of transparency in the natural lens causes progressive but painless blurring of vision, reduction in focusing ability, diminished perception of color, and glare from lights. Once cataract has developed, the only means of restoring complete vision is by surgical replacement. There is a small category of patients for whom such surgery is not appropriate (such as patients who have longterm structural eye problems and those with severe retinal problems or blood in the vitreous chamber).

What is the specific goal of surgery?

The surgeon's goal is to enter the eye through a small incision at the margin of the cornea and, working through a widely dilated pupil, to open the transparent capsule of the opacified internal lens, to remove the lens, and to replace it with a new, clear plastic lens. The optical power of the replacement lens needed to restore normal vision is determined beforehand using an ultrasound machine to measure the length of the eye and a keratometer to measure the curvature of the external lens. Although there are three different common surgical methods, the basic procedure is the same except that one method involves removing the natural lens and the entire surrounding capsule. Here, we will describe what is called the extracapsular method.

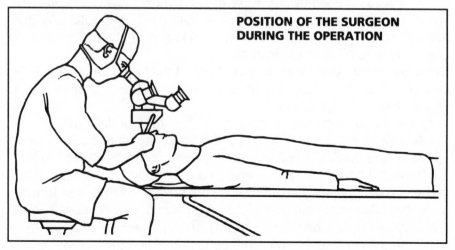

POSITION OF THE SURGEON DURING THE OPERATION

© DIAGRAM

There is a popular misconception outside opthalmic circles that cataract can be treated by means of a laser. Following a successful extracapsular cataract operation, the remaining rear layer of the lens capsule may sometimes become opaque so that vision is impaired. In such a case, a laser is commonly used to cut a hole in the center of the capsule to allow light rays to pass. However, lasers are never used to treat actual cataract.

Exactly what is involved in the surgical operation?

Most cataract surgery is performed using only local anesthesia, but some patients may be offered general anesthesia, in which case they will take no food for at least 12 hours before surgery and will be given a preoperative injection about one hour before surgery to dry up internal fluids and encourage drowsiness.

Preliminary steps. If local anesthetic is used, it is injected through a needle passed through the skin of the lower eyelid under the eyeball, through the eye socket, and into the space behind the eyeball. The procedure may move the eyeball so that for a moment you experience double vision, but the anesthetic administered in this way soon blocks your optic nerve so that any vision you have in the eye fades out. Other injections are given into the muscles around your eye. Your other eye will already have been completely covered with sterile operating towels.

Some surgeons find it helpful to press intermittently on the eye for a few minutes before starting the operation. This "ocular massage" makes the eyeball softer and reduces the risk that some of the vitreous humor (the jellylike substance within the eye) might come out during the operation. Vitreous gel prolapse has been associated with serious complications such as retinal detachment, persistent inflammation, and even loss of the eye. But the management of vitreous loss is now well understood and seldom causes major problems.

Your eyelids are gently but firmly held open by a light wire clip or by fine restraining threads called traction sutures. Some surgeons also administer an injection of the drug acetazolamide to further reduce internal pressure within the eyeball.

Step-by-step surgical procedure. First your pupil must be enlarged (dilated) to allow the surgeon access to the structures inside. This is done with eye drops.

To get to the pupil the surgeon must first cut carefully through the tough transparent outer covering, the cornea, that acts as an external lens over the pupil. The incision is made with a tiny blade and follows the form of a perfect curve, parallel to and just outside the upper edge of the cornea. The surgeon then slides the point of a tiny pair of forceps under the edge of the incision, picks up a little cone of iris near its root, and snips it off with miniature scissors. This procedure—iridectomy—results in a tiny elongated hole in the iris. It has no effect on vision.

THE INCISION

The surgeon cuts into the cornea, following the line of the iris beneath.

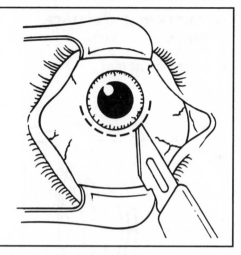

IRIDECTOMY

Slipping tiny forceps under the incision, the surgeon snips off a small cone of iris near its root.

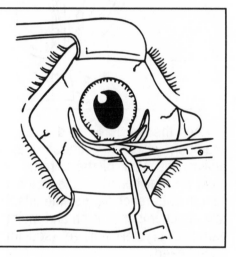

REMOVING THE OLD LENS

After perforating the capsule containing the lens and removing a small piece of it, the surgeon carefully dislocates the lens itself and pulls it out through the cornea.

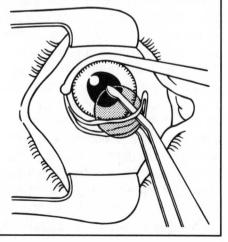

© DIAGRAM

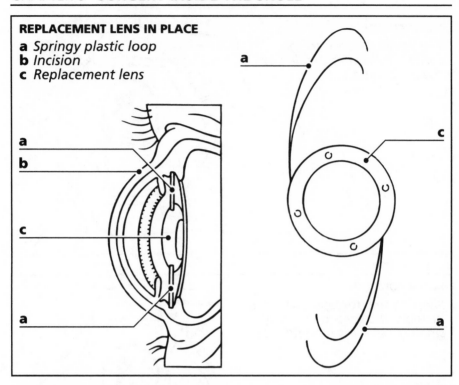

REPLACEMENT LENS IN PLACE
a *Springy plastic loop*
b *Incision*
c *Replacement lens*

When the eye is opened a few drops of water run out of the front chamber, which is obliterated as the iris comes forward to press against the back of the cornea. The space within the front chamber must be maintained or the inside of the cornea may be damaged by instruments reaching into the interior of the eye via the pupil. To maintain the chamber's depth and moistness, most surgeons inject into it a harmless crystal-clear gel (sodium hyaluronate) through a fine blunt-ended needle.

Through the dilated pupil, the lens is now accessible. The surgeon takes a special hypodermic needle and, with a succession of little stabs all around the edge of the pupil, perforates the front of the transparent bag—the capsule—containing the lens (this is sometimes called the "postage stamp method"). The perforations free a large, circular, central portion of the lens capsule, which can then be grasped in fine forceps and pulled carefully out through the cornea. The small piece of lens capsule that has been removed is not replaced, but its absence does not affect vision once the plastic lens has been inserted. A bent needle is now used to hook into the denser nucleus of the lens itself and to draw it out to the front chamber and then out through the cornea. There still remains a considerable quantity of slushy lens material within the now nearly empty lens capsule. Many surgeons remove this material using a miniature double-channeled needle—then, with even more care, using a tool with a minutely roughened edge to rub off whatever lens matter remains on the back of the capsule.

The surgeon then grasps the replacement lens in tiny, angled forceps and skillfully maneuvers it into place, through the cornea and the pupil, and into the opening of the now empty lens capsule. It is then rotated ("dialed") into place so that its hairlike plastic loops settle snugly into the muscle ring (the ciliary body) at the foot of the iris. Rotation also acts to free any part of the iris inadvertently pulled in toward the lens capsule. As a final test, the surgeon may push the lens in a little to make sure that it springs back into position within its capsule naturally.

After cleaning out the front chamber and washing out the sodium hyaluronate, the surgeon closes the incision in the cornea with a zigzag ("bootlace") suture using thread finer than a human hair. The suture is tied, and the knots are pulled into the tissue: it is seldom necessary to remove such sutures afterward.

The surgeon finishes by injecting an antibiotic drug deep behind the lower eyelid. Externally some ointment is applied, and an eye pad and a perforated eye shield are secured in place with adhesive tape.

What is it like immediately after the operation?
Although the operation is conducted mostly under only local anesthesia, it is still customary for a patient to stay at least one night—perhaps even three or four—in the hospital so that specialist and routine checks can be made. Nonetheless, in some circumstances a patient will be encouraged to go home almost immediately, provided that in some way competent medical supervision is guaranteed.

Dressings are usually removed about 24 hours after surgery and a first attempt at vision through the surgically treated eye is then possible. Some cloudiness of the cornea (caused by bending of the cornea during the operation) may partly obstruct vision. But a tremendous improvement in visual clarity and color should certainly be apparent.

What are the longterm effects?
Ideally, the longterm effects are those of complete restoration of vision. But the incision in the cornea takes about five weeks to heal totally, and for a further four weeks or so the actual curvature of the corneal surface may continue to alter, which affects the focus of the eye. New glasses should thus not be prescribed until these changes have settled. The operation may radically alter the basic focus of the eye. Often, distance glasses or contact lenses are not required, but most people will need reading glasses.

Correction of a squint (strabismus)

Why have the operation?

It is important that a squint—strabismus, or the correct alignment of only one eye—in a child should be treated as soon as it is observed. It is best to deal with the condition at a time when the eyes are still developing and early intervention may save the vision in the affected eye. Correction of a longterm squint in an adult is usually of cosmetic importance only—but may be important, especially to people who meet the general public in their work. A squint of sudden onset in an adult commonly causes double vision and may indicate organic disease of the nervous system or of the eye-moving muscles. Such squints require immediate medical attention—but may or may not require surgery. Although operations to correct a squint may overcome double vision in both children and adults, such operations in adults do not restore suppressed vision in the operated eye.

What is the physical cause of the problem?

In a child, a squint is most commonly caused by a failure of the developing nervous system to cope with the effects of overfocusing of the eyes. Alternatively, it may be due to a lack of balance between the muscles that turn the eyes inward and those that turn them out. The result is that when the child tries to focus the eyes on an object, he or she sees double. Such experience quickly causes the brain to suppress vision in the deviating eye, and the sight in that eye may become severely defective.

Such defects should not be confused with the normal lack of focusing seen in a baby's eyes, which is caused by immaturity in the nervous system.

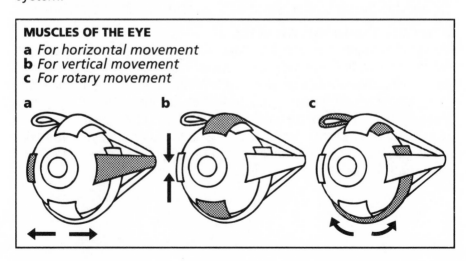

MUSCLES OF THE EYE
a For horizontal movement
b For vertical movement
c For rotary movement

a   b   c

In an adult, not every type of squint can be surgically corrected. A major factor is whether there is already a history of double vision. Only if there is no such history and if both eyes have an almost full range of potential movement is corrective surgery likely to be undertaken.

Preliminary tests can now distinguish those patients for whom surgery is unlikely to be safe.

What is the specific goal of surgery?

The surgeon aims to realign the eyes and restore single binocular vision and a balance in appearance. The operation performed to correct a convergent squint—in which one eye is turned too far inward—is classic for this type of operation, and is the form of surgery described below. When one eye is turned too far outward the result is described as a divergent squint.

Surgery is performed on the muscles that regulate horizontal movement of the eyeball. These two tiny, straplike muscles run from the back of the eye socket, well behind the eyeball, and are fixed to the outer surface of the eyeball (the sclera) about $5/16$ inch from the edge of the cornea on either side. They lie under a thin layer of white tissue—called fascia—that covers the eyeball, and this in turn is covered by the membrane called the conjunctiva.

Exactly what is involved in the surgical operation?

By the time of surgery, prior testing will have determined the amount by which the deviant eye should be turned in order to remain aligned with the other eye.

Preliminary steps. As with all operations involving general anesthesia, you will be given a preoperative injection about an hour before surgery to dry up internal fluids and to encourage drowsiness.

Step-by-step surgical procedure. Once you are anesthetized, most of your head will be wrapped in sterile operating towels, leaving only the eye exposed for surgery. The surgeon starts with the muscle on the inner side, nearer the nose. To reach it, the surgeon turns the eye so that the iris is far to the opposite side, and secures the eye in that position with a fine thread passed through tissues close to the edge of the cornea and clamped to the towels. The surgeon then cuts

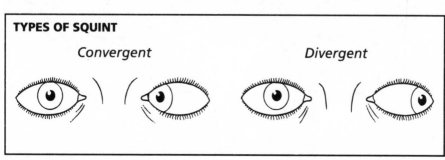

TYPES OF SQUINT

Convergent   *Divergent*

© DIAGRAM

through the conjunctiva and fascia with scissors, and slips a small instrument called a squint hook under the muscle, making sure that the whole width of the muscle is secured. Then, the surgeon very carefully snips through the muscle, as close as possible to its root (**A**). The surgeon secures the snipped end of the muscle and allows it to slide back across the eyeball for the distance assessed in the initial tests (**B**). With fine needles and very thin sutures, the surgeon then sews it back into the surface layers of the white of the eye at that spot. The new attachment is covered with the fascia, and the conjunctiva is closed with a continuous fine stitch. The eye is released from its securing threads.

The eye is then turned to the opposite side (**C**) and once again secured in the same manner. Now the other muscle is exposed, lying slackly on the other side. The next part of the operation is designed to take up this slack by shortening the muscle. First the surgeon puts loose stitches into the muscle at the assessed distance back from its root in the eyeball. The length of muscle between root and stitches is then cut off and removed, and the surgeon uses the stitches to rejoin the muscle—now taut—at the same root (**D**). The fascia and the conjunctiva are then again repaired.

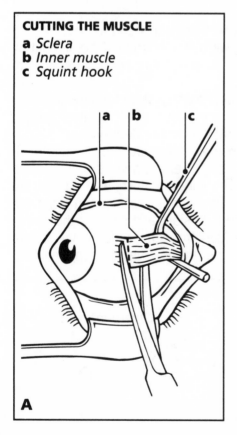

CUTTING THE MUSCLE
a *Sclera*
b *Inner muscle*
c *Squint hook*

A

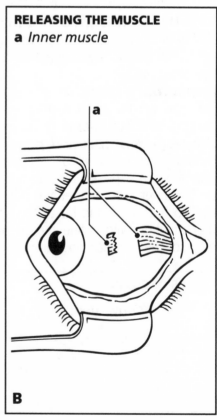

RELEASING THE MUSCLE
a *Inner muscle*

B

What is it like after the operation?

It is likely that you will wake up in your room after the operation wearing an eye pad or at least a shade. Some surgeons choose not to use an eye pad because it slightly increases the risk of infection by raising the temperature of the conjunctiva. But in any case the eye will water a good deal and may be sensitive to light at first. Eye movements may cause a perceptible tugging on the stitches in the muscles, and may be uncomfortable for a period. You may suffer from blurred vision if sticky mucus from the watering eye causes eyelashes to stick together. The white of your eye may turn red through inflammation of the conjunctiva. If it does, it will stay red for some weeks until the cuts in the membrane have fully healed, although in the meantime treatment with eye drops and ointments should relieve the inflammation.

What are the longterm effects?

Ideally, the longterm effects are improved appearance, vision, and morale. A particularly large-angle squint may require operations on both eyes, however. In this case it is usual for a surgeon to perform two separate operations, one on each eye, checking the result of the first before undertaking the second.

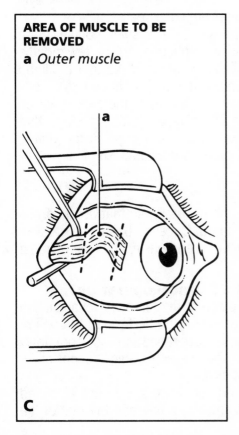

AREA OF MUSCLE TO BE REMOVED

a *Outer muscle*

C

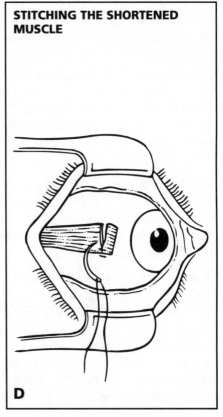

STITCHING THE SHORTENED MUSCLE

D

© DIAGRAM

CHAPTER 6
SURGERY TO THE HEAD

Removal of a basal cell carcinoma

Why have the operation?

The basal cell carcinoma, also known as a rodent ulcer, is the most common tumor that occurs on the skin of the face—and is one of the most common forms of all cancers. Such cancers do not metastasize to other parts of the body as do other cancers, but may spread locally and gradually, destroying tissue. They may penetrate deeply, involving not only the skin but also underlying structures such as the bones of the skull, the eye, or the brain. If such cancers are diagnosed and treated early, a complete and permanent cure is relatively easy. If neglected, they may eventually cause death.

What is the physical cause of the problem?

Basal cell cancers occur mainly on areas of skin exposed to the sun. This is why they are so common on the face—usually around the bridge of the nose, often near the inner corner of the eye, or on a lower eyelid. They are also common on the outer rim of the ear.

A basal cell carcinoma starts as a small, firm, shiny nodule, often with a pearly appearance, which gradually enlarges. After a few months the center of the tumor becomes slightly depressed, so that the lump appears to have a raised rim. In some instances, small red streaks—representing blood vessels—run over the rim from the center, which becomes dimpled and crusted. It is following this crusting stage that surgery to remove the tumor becomes more complex. In the United States, virtually all basal cell carcinomas are treated surgically at or before this stage.

What is the goal of surgery?

The aim of surgery is to remove the tumor totally, so that no abnormal tissue remains and the condition is cured. Because basal cell carcinomas remain so localized, a permanent cure is easier than with almost any other kind of tumor.

Exactly what is involved in the surgical operation?

A biopsy—the slicing off of a small piece of the tumor for examination under the microscope by a pathologist—may be performed to confirm that the tumor is cancerous. The actual operation is most commonly performed under local anesthesia in the surgeon's office, especially if the tumor is on a fairly loose area of skin.

Preliminary steps. The tumor and surrounding skin are cleansed and then sterile towels are placed so that your hair and the rest of the face apart from the tumor site are covered. A local anesthetic is injected, after which you will feel the pressure of the surgeon's manipulation but no pain.

Step-by-step surgical procedure. If the skin around the tumor is fairly loose, it will probably be sufficient for the surgeon to cut out the lump within an ellipse of full-thickness skin and to bring the cut edges together with a few fine stitches. The basal cell layer of the skin is not particularly deep: if there are no signs of attachment to underlying tissues, there is no need to remove more than the skin. But if there is doubt of any kind, the surgeon will remove some of the fat and other tissues beneath the skin.

If the tumor is on skin that does not stretch easily—such as on the side of the nose—it will be necessary for the surgeon, having removed the lump, to undermine the free edges of the skin so that they can be mobilized sufficiently to bring them together for stitching. Undermining like this is done with blunt-pointed scissors that are pushed under each edge and then opened wide to separate the layers of skin tissue. It is important that the edges are aligned accurately against each other in order to produce the thinnest possible (and thus least conspicuous) scar afterward. With luck the scar can be made to coincide with an already existing skin crease.

In the case of a basal cell carcinoma that has been allowed to grow to some size upon an eyelid, the surgeon must (as before) remove some full-thickness healthy skin around the tumor, which, in this case, may mean the loss of a portion of the eyelid. An absence of one-quarter to one-third of an eyelid can be repaired simply by bringing the cut edges together, especially in senior citizens. But if the gap in the eyelid is any larger, plastic surgery involving a flap or a skin graft will be necessary, preferably by an ophthalmic plastic surgeon.

In the rare case of a basal cell cancer being neglected to the stage of penetrating to deeper structures, more complex surgery, under general anesthesia, is required—if surgical removal is possible at all.

What is it like immediately after the operation?
In spite of having a few fine but temporarily conspicuous stitches on your face, you may, if your tumors were large, look better after the operation than you did before. Pain and discomfort are minimal (even when the surgery has involved an eyelid), and there is every reason for you to resume your normal activities on the following day.

What are the longterm effects?
The outlook is excellent. Treated early, a basal cell carcinoma should not recur. Having had one basal cell carcinoma, however, suggests that you are more susceptible than average to this type of tumor; you should be especially careful to avoid overexposure to sunlight.

Surgery to treat otosclerotic deafness

Why have the operation?

Otosclerosis is a condition of the middle ear that causes deafness. It is progressive, and although a hearing aid may provide temporary assistance, a point will come when no measures short of surgery are effective. An untreated ear almost always becomes deaf. Most commonly (in 90 percent of cases), both ears are affected.

Before undergoing surgery, however, there are some risks of which you should be aware:

- There is a slight possibility—calculated at between one chance in 100 and one chance in 50—that the ear operated on may lose its hearing altogether.
- Even more rarely, temporary paralysis of the muscles on the same side of the face may occur.
- Other possible neural side effects are a persistent unpleasant taste in the mouth and the persistent underproduction of saliva.
- Occasionally the operation affects other parts of the ear, resulting in vertigo and loss of balance while standing.

Such conditions are seldom severe, but for people of certain lifestyles—such as athletes or dancers—they can be devastating. Complications like these remain unlikely for most patients.

What is the physical cause of the problem?

Sound vibrations in the air are focused in the outer ear and passed into the middle ear through the tympanum, or eardrum. The vibrations of the eardrum are in turn transmitted across the middle ear to the inner ear by a chain of three tiny bones (the auditory ossicles) that convert the comparatively large and free vibrations of the drum into smaller, more powerful vibrations within the fluid in the canals of the inner ear. The innermost of the three bones, the stapes (Latin for "stirrup"), is named appropriately for it is shaped like a stirrup. Its "footplate" fits in an oval opening in the outer wall of the inner ear. In a healthy person, this footplate is surrounded by an elastic seal that allows it to vibrate freely. In a person with otosclerosis, the bone that surrounds this seal becomes inflamed and gradually converts the seal itself to bone. The footplate thus becomes fixed solid and cannot vibrate; sound is not transmitted, and the result is deafness.

Otosclerosis is thought to be hereditary. In the United States the condition is restricted almost exclusively to the white population, and women are affected twice as often as men. The disease can begin at any age but commonly becomes evident in the patient's 20s or 30s.

If both ears are affected, and tests prove that the inner ear mechanism is fully functional, surgery is generally advised. The more affected ear is usually selected for the first operation.

What is the goal of surgery?

The overall aim of the surgeon is to restore hearing. It is impractical to free the seal around the footplate of the stapes, so surgery is directed at providing a new way for the vibrations of the eardrum to be conveyed to the fluid in the inner ear. The operating area is tiny and lies deep within the ear, so precision microsurgery is used.

Exactly what is involved in the surgical operation?

Before surgery there will be a full ear-nose-and-throat examination and detailed audiometric analysis (to measure how deaf you are in each ear and to confirm otosclerosis).

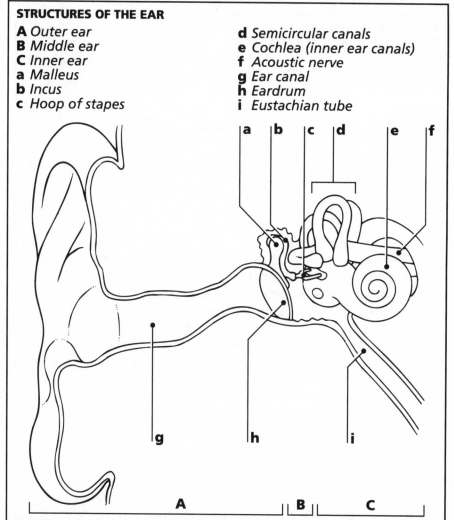

STRUCTURES OF THE EAR

A *Outer ear*
B *Middle ear*
C *Inner ear*
a *Malleus*
b *Incus*
c *Hoop of stapes*
d *Semicircular canals*
e *Cochlea (inner ear canals)*
f *Acoustic nerve*
g *Ear canal*
h *Eardrum*
i *Eustachian tube*

© DIAGRAM

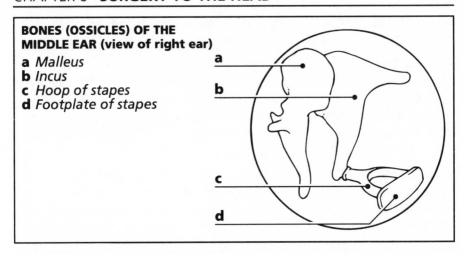

**BONES (OSSICLES) OF THE
MIDDLE EAR (view of right ear)**

a *Malleus*
b *Incus*
c *Hoop of stapes*
d *Footplate of stapes*

a
b
c
d

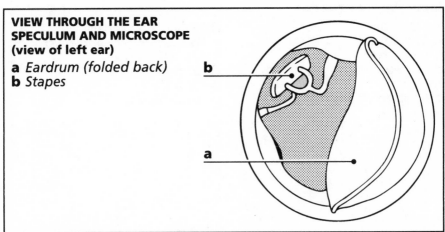

**VIEW THROUGH THE EAR
SPECULUM AND MICROSCOPE
(view of left ear)**

a *Eardrum (folded back)*
b *Stapes*

b
a

Preliminary steps. As with any operation involving general anesthesia, you will be given a preoperative injection about an hour before surgery to dry up internal fluids and to encourage drowsiness.

Step-by-step surgical procedure. Once you are anesthetized, you will be positioned on the operating table so that the operating microscope can be conveniently aligned. To straighten the outer ear canal and bring the eardrum into the view of the microscope, a conical metal or plastic device known as an ear speculum is gently inserted down the outer ear canal.

The surgeon then carefully cuts around most of the edge of the eardrum in order to gain access to the middle ear and the ossicles, and the eardrum is folded back out of the way.

One of several alternative surgical procedures may be performed to remove the hoop of stapes. Most surgeons prefer to separate the "hoop" of the stapes from its "footplate," to cut off the incus at its junction with that bone, and to drill a tiny hole, about 1/24 inch (1mm) in

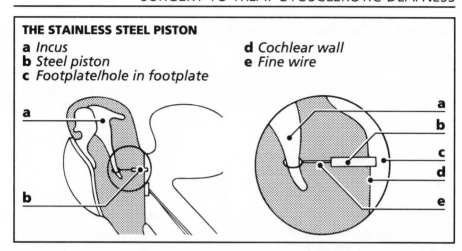

THE STAINLESS STEEL PISTON

a *Incus*
b *Steel piston*
c *Footplate/hole in footplate*

d *Cochlear wall*
e *Fine wire*

diameter, in the center of the disease-thickened footplate. The hole in the footplate can be bored with a miniature rotating twist drill or with a laser. A tiny piston made of stainless steel or polytetrafluoroethylene (a plastic used on nonstick pan surfaces) is inserted into the hole. The piston is then linked by a fine wire that is hooked on to the end of the middle of the three ossicles, the incus, and crimped tightly on with special forceps.

Some surgeons prefer instead to remove the entire footplate of the stirrup or the whole stirrup (stapedectomy), to cover the oval opening with a graft of natural tissue (such as muscle or fascia), and to attach to it a metal or plastic prosthesis joined to the incus.

Once the internal procedure is completed, the surgeon replaces the eardrum and stitches it up.

What is it like immediately after the operation?
After successful surgery, hearing is restored to virtually normal. You may experience a remarkable improvement in the quality of your hearing. There will probably be very little pain: healing around the edge of the eardrum is quick. You should be able to get up as soon as you have slept off the anesthetic. Try to avoid putting pressure on the eardrum for a few days (as, for example, by sneezing forcefully, descending rapidly in high-rise elevators, swimming under water, or taking an airplane flight), although a repaired eardrum is generally secure.

What are the longterm effects?
In most cases the longterm effect is of continued good hearing. In a small proportion of cases, the metal or plastic piston becomes displaced and the hearing is lost suddenly, sometimes for no apparent reason, and sometimes months or even years after the operation. When this happens, a further operation is required to replace the piston or correct the problem.

Washing out nasal sinuses

Why have the operation?

Washing out a nasal sinus under general anesthesia is performed only when other therapeutic measures—which normally succeed in clearing the sinus of the potentially infective mucus that is the problem—have failed. It is also possible for infection to spread from the sinus to the surrounding bone, an advance that may, through progressive contamination, lead to the formation of an abscess in the brain.

What is the physical cause of the problem?

The sinuses are the bony cavities in the parts of the skull that surround the nose. They are lined with mucous membrane. Inflammation of the membrane—sinusitis—affects millions of people every time they catch a cold or flu. In a healthy person, there is ample opening from the sinuses into the nasal passages to allow mucus to drain and escape. Congestion through infection or allergy may block that escape and cause an accumulation of mucus in the sinus—mucus that inevitably contains infective organisms that now find themselves in ideal circumstances for reproduction. In a severe case, the consequent inflammation results in the formation of pus within the sinus, which causes tension and pain and may lead to infection elsewhere.

There are several ways to alleviate sinus congestion:

- decongestants. Drugs such as ephedrine, which is included in many commercial cold "cures," shrink the membrane lining of the nasal passages and are successful in unblocking the passages sufficiently for the mucus to drain. (The shrinkage creates more space for the mucus to escape.)
- steam inhalations. These moisten the mucus and thin it to assist its running out.
- antibiotics. If the infection is bacterial (which it usually isn't), antibiotics can be administered to reduce the bacterial count.
- antral lavage or antral irrigation (as this surgery is called). This is a totally effective last resort.

Even then, the problem may be seated more deeply: the infection of the nasal sinus may have a cause that is quite unsuspected, especially if the sinusitis is of long standing or is recurrent. Washing the sinus may not cure the problem (although it usually does)—but may help to diagnose the real problem.

What is the goal of surgery?

The most common method of antral lavage is to make a temporary artificial opening into the sinus through which it can be washed out, with the hope and intention of draining it through the natural opening. It is a comparatively minor procedure.

THE SINUSES
A *Frontal view of the sinuses*
B *Cross-section of skull showing sinuses*

a *Frontal sinus*
b *Ethmoidal sinus*
c *Sphenoidal sinus*
d *Maxillary sinus*
e *Skull*

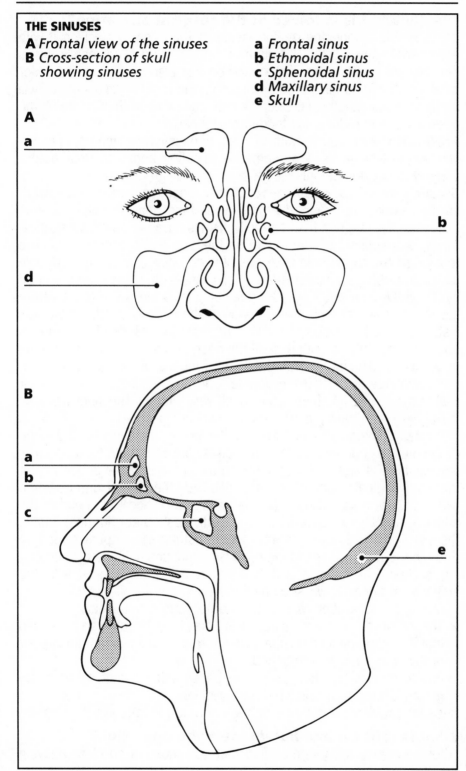

© DIAGRAM

Exactly what is involved in the surgical operation?

It is possible to anesthetize the inside of the nose by packing it with gauze soaked in a strong solution of cocaine, and occasionally this is the only anesthetic used. The operation can also be performed under local anesthetic administered by injection. But most often a surgeon will prefer general anesthesia. Cocaine may still be used then to shrink the nasal lining and reduce any tendency to bleed.

Preliminary steps. As with all operations involving general anesthesia, you will be given a preoperative injection about an hour before surgery to dry up internal fluids and to encourage drowsiness.

Step-by-step surgical procedure. Once you are anesthetized, sterile toweling is wrapped around your face, leaving only the nose exposed. The surgeon then carefully inserts a pair of miniature surgical tongs (a speculum) up the nostril on the side to be operated on. The tension of the tongs holds the nostril wide open. A thin, rigid, double tube comprising a sharp-pointed inner cylinder (the trocar) surrounded by a slightly wider outer cylinder (the cannula) is then used to penetrate the sinus cavity through the side wall of the nose. The site of entry is just under the lower bony shelf that projects inward about half an inch above the nostril. The side wall of the nose at that point is of light bone only; it is not difficult to force the point of the trocar through it. The surgeon continues inserting the double tube until feeling it touch the far wall of the cavity; it is then drawn back very slightly. The inner trocar is then gently withdrawn, leaving the cannula in place.

A syringe is then attached to the outer end of the cannula, and some of the mucous contents of the sinus cavity are drawn out for laboratory examination. (If any of the infective organisms are bacterial, identifying them may indicate appropriate antibiotic drug therapy.) A larger syringe filled with warm salt solution (saline) is then attached to the end of the cannula, and the sinus cavity is repeatedly flushed out. In most cases, the saline injected flows out through the natural sinus opening, and so through the nostril. Irrigation in this way continues until the fluid emerging is clear. The cannula is then carefully withdrawn—the hole in the side wall of the nose will soon heal over.

During this operation, one or two complications may occur:

- The membrane lining the sinus cavity may have become so thickened that it may be difficult for the surgeon to determine when the interior of the cavity has been reached.
- Pus formed within the cavity may be so viscous that it has to be greatly diluted with saline before it will flow.

But such problems merely cause the operation to take slightly longer.

What is it like immediately after the operation?

When you wake up, you may find that your nose is so clear—having

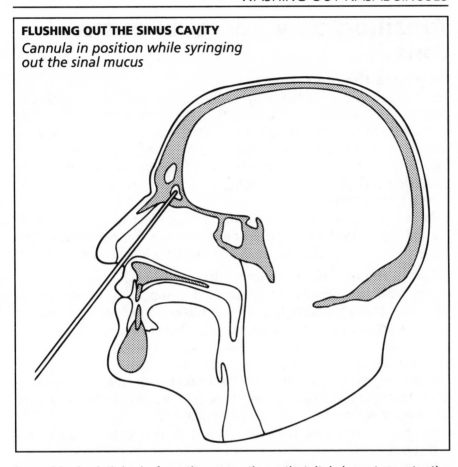

FLUSHING OUT THE SINUS CAVITY
*Cannula in position while syringing
out the sinal mucus*

been blocked tight before the operation—that it brings tears to the eyes to breathe through it. Some surgeons place a pad in the nostril that can be removed after a few hours. There may be considerable pain and neuralgia at the front of the face, much of which may be relieved with painkilling drugs. The severity of such symptoms may determine whether you are encouraged to leave the hospital on the same day or stay in for 24 hours or occasionally longer. If bacterial organisms were discovered within the sinus, you will also be given antibiotics to prevent further infection.

What are the longterm effects?
The longterm effects depend on what caused the sinusitis and how bad it had become. Ideally—and most often—the operation cures the problem. But if the lining of the sinus had been permanently damaged by longterm inflammation, irrigation as described above will relieve the condition only for a matter of hours or days. If the former symptoms then return, further surgery may be needed to create a more permanent drainage channel (in an operation known as radical antrostomy).

© DIAGRAM

Tonsillectomy: removal of the tonsils

Why have the operation?

The tonsils are part of the body's immune system and comprise two pads of glandular tissue on each side of the back of the mouth. While defending the body against infection via the mouth, the tonsils may frequently become inflamed and enlarged in the condition known as tonsillitis. If the inflammatory attacks become frequent and severe, or are prolonged and cause complications, a surgeon may suggest that you have a tonsillectomy.

Nonetheless, the operation is almost always elective—the patient (or the patient's parent or guardian) decides to have it performed—and there are seldom medical reasons that make such surgery essential.

What is the physical cause of the problem?

During childhood the tonsils contain large numbers of lymphocytes—white blood cells that identify and immediately act to neutralize invading infective organisms. When, after puberty, this area of lymphoid tissue shrinks and its protective function wanes, infections may occur. However, because high levels of antibodies to most of the common infective organisms are present in the blood in late childhood, removal of the tonsils at this time is unlikely to affect the body's immune system, and a tonsillectomy may be advised to deal with:

● recurrent attacks of tonsillitis, with high temperature, pain, and distress
● prolonged inflammation (chronic tonsillitis)
● persistent enlargement of the lymph nodes (glands) in the neck, which are closely associated with the tonsils
● recurrent infection of the middle ear (otitis media) linked to tonsillitis
● enlargement of the tonsils that obstructs breathing or swallowing
● an abscess on a tonsil (quinsy)
● recurrent bronchitis or other chest infections linked to tonsillitis

Less commonly, tonsillectomy may be advised to deal with throat infections by streptococcal bacteria, which sometimes lead to serious conditions such as rheumatic fever or nephritis. Much more rarely, the operation may be necessary to treat nutritional deficiencies in a child caused by enlarged and persistently infected tonsils.

What is the goal of surgery?

The surgeon's aim is to remove the focus of infection by removing all tonsillar tissue.

Exactly what is involved in the surgical operation?

Before surgery, you will be given a complete physical checkup. You (or the patient's parent or guardian) will be asked about your previous illnesses and especially whether you have any abnormal bleeding tendency (such as hemophilia). The precise state of your tonsils will be ascertained—active inflammation can lead to complications under the anesthetic and can also increase the chances of severe postoperative hemorrhaging. If the tonsils are actively inflamed, a two- to three-week course of antibiotics is used to control the infection before surgery is performed.

Tonsillectomy is always performed under general anesthesia.

Preliminary steps. You will be given a preoperative injection about an hour before surgery to dry up internal fluids and to encourage drowsiness. This virtually painless injection is particularly important in the case of child patients who may be unduly tense and anxious. (If the thought of the injection itself is stressful, you can ask for an oral preoperative.)

Step-by-step surgical procedure. When you are anesthetized, the surgeon passes a tube through the nose and down the trachea (windpipe). This ensures that you will be able to continue breathing and allows the rest of the back of the throat to be packed with absorbent

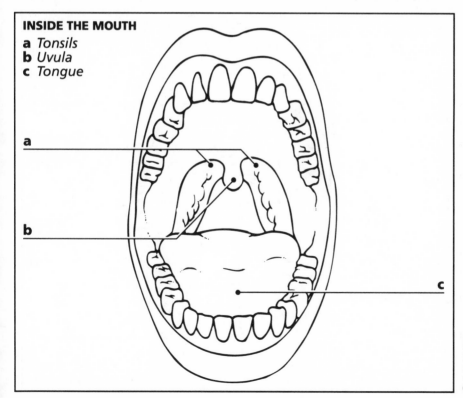

INSIDE THE MOUTH
a *Tonsils*
b *Uvula*
c *Tongue*

© DIAGRAM

material so that blood cannot escape down the back of the throat. To achieve this the mouth is held wide open by means of a "gag," a stainless steel ratchet-and-catch instrument that also acts to keep the tongue out of the way. The surgeon usually wears a lamp on a band around the head so that illumination can be directed where required.

The surgeon begins by grasping the first tonsil in toothed forceps and pulling it toward the front of the mouth so that it is stretched. A careful incision is made through the mucous membrane lining the mouth close to the body of the tonsil, and the tonsil is then stripped from its base by separating layer from layer, with minimal cutting. Bleeding from blood vessels is stopped by securing the vessels in forceps and tying them off with fine catgut (if they are relatively large) or by cauterizing them (if they are small). A suction system may have to be used to clear excess blood. Minor hemorrhage is controlled with pressure from gauze swabs.

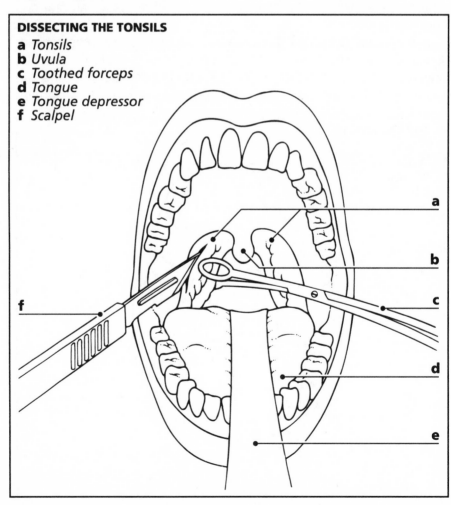

DISSECTING THE TONSILS
a *Tonsils*
b *Uvula*
c *Toothed forceps*
d *Tongue*
e *Tongue depressor*
f *Scalpel*

When the procedure has been repeated on the other tonsil, the surgeon checks that all bleeding has ceased, removes the packing and the gag, and finally takes out the tube from the nose.

What is it like immediately after the operation?

You will wake up with a very sore throat (no matter how careful your surgeon may have been). For a time you will find swallowing liquids unpleasant and swallowing solid food intolerable. You will probably not be permitted (or able) to take anything by mouth for at least four hours after surgery—until the main risk of hemorrhaging has passed—during which time it is likely that you will be kept lying on one side or the other, to prevent choking should bleeding occur. Later, you will be encouraged to use your throat: the more you swallow, the easier it will become. This is the time when you may find yourself wanting to gorge ice cream. You will probably be given a painkilling drug (and possibly a sedative drug) the night following surgery. The next day you can get out of bed, and you will be encouraged to resume a normal diet. You should not need to stay in the hospital for more than a day or two. The soreness of your throat may, however, persist for between 14 and 20 days, especially at mealtimes.

Rarely, severe bleeding occurs several hours after the operation and may necessitate a speedy return to the operating room where—again under general anesthesia—the bleeding blood vessel can be tied off.

What are the longterm effects?

There are virtually no perceivable longterm effects—although the incidence of throat infection is often markedly reduced once the tonsils have been removed.

© DIAGRAM

Tooth extraction

Why have the operation?

Not long ago, tooth extraction was considered an easy solution to almost every kind of dental problem. Today, the emphasis is on conservation of teeth, and many teeth that might once have been routinely taken out are instead treated and saved, maintaining both their practical and cosmetic functions. Teeth are normally extracted when they are

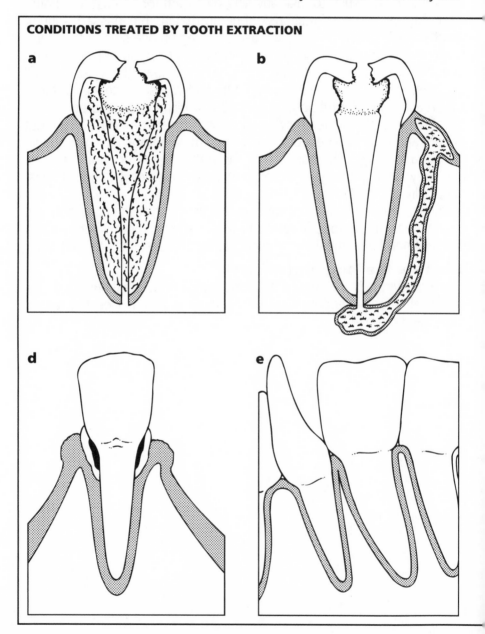

CONDITIONS TREATED BY TOOTH EXTRACTION

a

b

d

e

too damaged or decayed to be saved or because they have grown or are growing incorrectly and cannot be corrected by alternative methods of treatment.

What is the physical cause of the problem?

Severe decay often results from poor dental hygiene (see *Root canal treatment*, p.124), allowing the formation and accumulation of plaque (a sticky coating of saliva, bacteria, and food debris) and calculus (tar-

c

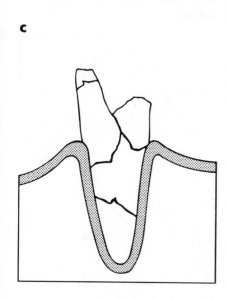

Among the conditions treated by tooth extraction are:
a *Decay (caries) so severe that little remains of root or crown*
b *An abscess of a type or size unsuitable for root canal treatment (see p.124)*
c *A fracture of the tooth so severe that it is impossible to build up or crown*
d *Gum disease so severe that the tooth is loose*
e *Crowding: a tooth impinging upon adjacent teeth and perhaps displacing them, causing pain*
f *Impaction: neighboring teeth growing so close that they prevent the growth and eruption of a tooth (especially a "wisdom tooth")*
g *Malocclusion: overlapping teeth resulting in a defective bite (overbite and underbite)*

protruding upper teeth

g

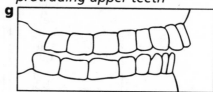

protruding lower teeth

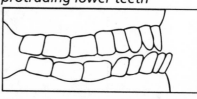

f

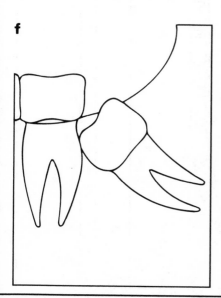

tar: a hard deposit). The bacteria in the plaque convert the sugars in the food into acids, which eat into the tooth's enamel and the underlying dentin. This in turn causes damage to the fine fibers that hold the tooth firmly in its bony socket (the periodontal membrane), initiating gum disease that makes the tooth loose. If the bacteria and other infective organisms reach the soft, living interior (pulp) of the tooth, the blood

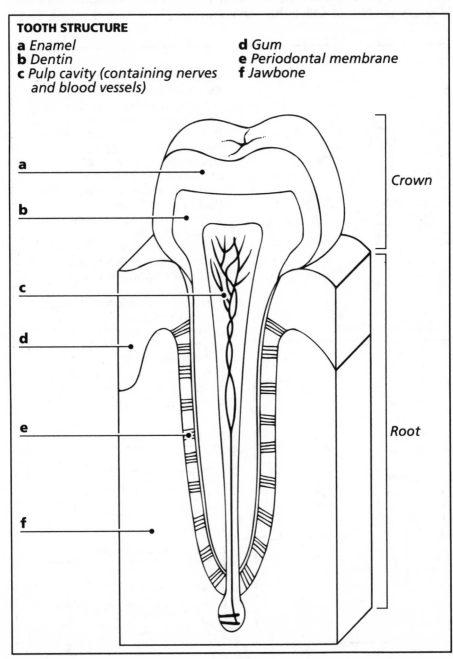

TOOTH STRUCTURE

a *Enamel*
b *Dentin*
c *Pulp cavity (containing nerves and blood vessels)*
d *Gum*
e *Periodontal membrane*
f *Jawbone*

Crown

Root

vessels and nerves that maintain the vitality of the tooth become infected and destroyed. The tooth may then die. Infection may continue to spread down the tooth into the root canals and to the bone of the socket, where it may cause an abscess or even an infection of the bone itself (osteomyelitis).

When decay is not the ultimate cause, the problem is usually one of abnormal growth or is due to some physical trauma.

What is the goal of surgery?

A major aim of surgical extraction is to relieve the pain caused by severe dental problems. In particular, dental extraction relieves the pain caused by an abscess at the roots of a tooth, allowing the abscess to drain and the infection to heal. But there may be additional practical intentions: to allow a neighboring tooth to grow where before it was being impeded, or to improve the patient's ability to bite, for example. Occasionally there are further cosmetic implications.

Exactly what is involved in the surgical operation?

Most dental extractions can be performed with minimal discomfort under local anesthesia, although general anesthesia may be used for patients who are sensitive to local anesthetic in the tissues of the mouth, who are subject to anxiety, or who need the extraction of more than one tooth. It may also be used when treating children. Most single extractions are still performed in a dentist's office, but if many teeth have to be removed (for example, dental clearance), this is usually done in the hospital under a general anesthetic.

Preliminary steps. The local anesthetic administered by the dental surgeon may numb the area surrounding a single tooth, or it may be a "nerve block" and numb one complete side of the jaw. It may be supplemented by an injection of diazepam, which relieves anxiety. If the surgeon intends to use a general anesthetic, you will instead be given a preoperative injection about an hour before surgery to dry up internal fluids and to encourage drowsiness.

Step-by-step surgical procedure. When you are anesthetized, the surgeon uses a pair of dental forceps or a dental elevator to remove the tooth. Dental forceps have jaws that, when moved down the neck of the tooth, cut through the periodontal membrane. The fibers of this membrane must be broken before the tooth can be loosened. The jaws of the instrument also gradually expand the tooth socket, and so free the roots. A dental elevator is a corkscrew-like steel instrument that is pushed down between the roots under the main body of the tooth and rotated in order to force the entire tooth upward and out. It is used to avoid breakage of the tooth at the roots, such as in the extraction of molar or premolar teeth.

Occasionally, after breakage at the roots or when a tooth refuses to budge, for example, a surgical incision is made in the gum at the side of the tooth, a flap of gum is lifted, and a small piece of socket bone is removed. This reveals the roots of the tooth. When the tooth has been extracted, the gum flap is closed with stitches.

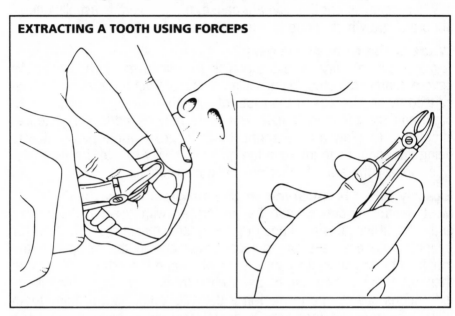

EXTRACTING A TOOTH USING FORCEPS

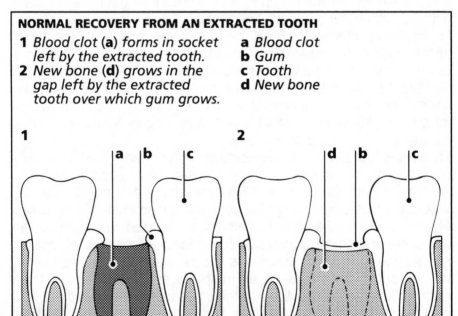

NORMAL RECOVERY FROM AN EXTRACTED TOOTH

1 *Blood clot (**a**) forms in socket left by the extracted tooth.*
2 *New bone (**d**) grows in the gap left by the extracted tooth over which gum grows.*

a *Blood clot*
b *Gum*
c *Tooth*
d *New bone*

1

|a |b |c

2

|d |b |c

What is it like immediately after the operation?

You will be conscious of the gaping hole in your jaw where the tooth used to be—but do not try to dislodge the blood clot in the socket, which should remain there until healing is complete. If bleeding occurs, it can almost always be controlled by biting firmly on a folded piece of gauze or clean cloth for about half an hour. But within a short space of time you should entirely lose the sensation of alteration within your mouth.

As a rule, you should need no special treatment after tooth extraction, unless the condition of your other teeth indicates it. As the anesthetic wears off, your jaw will be sore for a time, but this is seldom severe and may be relieved by painkilling drugs. You should normally be able to go home immediately after surgery, although if you have had a general anesthetic it is inadvisable to drive yourself (usually for the rest of the day). Eating and tooth cleansing should be performed with great care until the gum has healed, however—it is important to avoid excessive rinsing of the mouth. Toothbrushing and flossing can continue as long as you avoid the cavity—usually for about two weeks.

What are the longterm effects?

In the great majority of cases, recovery is swift and uneventful. Rarely, the blood clot fails to form in the socket, or a formed clot may be accidentally dislodged and fail to re-form. The result is a condition known as dry socket, in which infection is inevitable, causing pain, an unpleasant taste in the mouth, and foul breath. Spicules of bone may be exposed within the dry socket. The condition requires dental therapy that involves cleaning the socket and applying a soothing antiseptic paste.

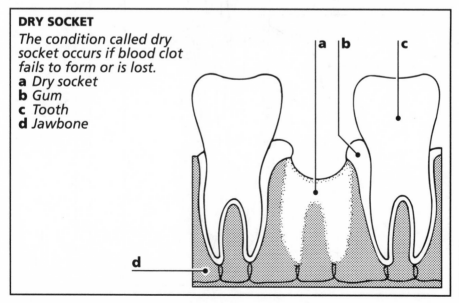

DRY SOCKET
The condition called dry socket occurs if blood clot fails to form or is lost.
a *Dry socket*
b *Gum*
c *Tooth*
d *Jawbone*

© DIAGRAM

Root canal treatment

Why have the operation?

Root canal treatment is a method of preserving a tooth that is dying from disease and infection or is already dead. Fortunately, because of the dense nature of dental enamel and the strength of the underlying dentin, a dead tooth may, if properly modified, retain its full function and last indefinitely.

What is the physical cause of the problem?

Infection of a tooth is often the result of poor dental hygiene.

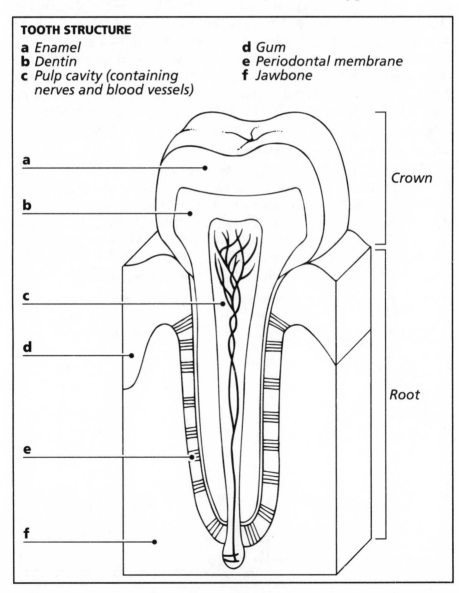

TOOTH STRUCTURE

a *Enamel*
b *Dentin*
c *Pulp cavity (containing nerves and blood vessels)*

d *Gum*
e *Periodontal membrane*
f *Jawbone*

a

b

Crown

c

d

Root

e

f

TOOTH DECAY

1 *Poor dental hygiene results in the formation and accumulation of (**a**) plaque (a sticky coating of saliva, bacteria, and food debris) and (**b**) calculus (tartar: a hard deposit).*

2 *The bacteria in the plaque convert the sugars in the food into acids, which eat into the tooth's enamel.*

3 *Once the enamel has been penetrated, acids eat into the tooth's dentin.*

4 *The resultant decay may eventually permit the bacteria and other infective organisms to reach the soft internal tissue (pulp) of the tooth, infecting, swelling, and constricting the blood vessels and injuring the nerves.*

1   a   b

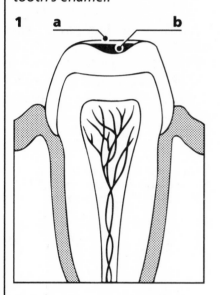

2

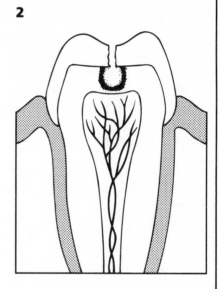

3

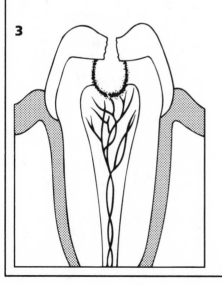

4

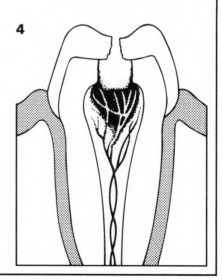

© DIAGRAM

What is the goal of surgery?

The aim of the surgeon is to clear out the pulp and to replace it with a synthetic material that is less susceptible to infection. If the central cavity of the tooth contains nothing that can form a bed for infection, the tooth may stay structurally unchanged permanently.

Exactly what is involved in the surgical operation?

The procedure is usually performed in the surgeon's (or periodontist's) office. First, X-ray photos are taken to show the extent of the pulp cavity that is to be filled.

Preliminary steps. The procedure is usually performed under local anesthesia, administered by injection either to numb an area just around the tooth or to deaden sensation in one side of the jaw (a "nerve block"). It is important that saliva—which contains many potentially infective organisms—is kept away from the tooth under treatment. This is done by means of a rubber "dam," a sheet of thin rubber in which a hole is punched for the tooth to pass through, and which is secured in a small frame.

ROOT CANAL TREATMENT

a *The biting surface (enamel)*
b *Infection*
c *Pulp cavity*
d *Rubber dam*

1 *A hole is drilled in the biting surface and the contents of the pulp cavity are extracted.*

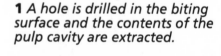
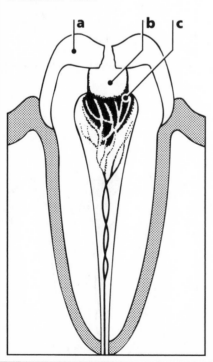
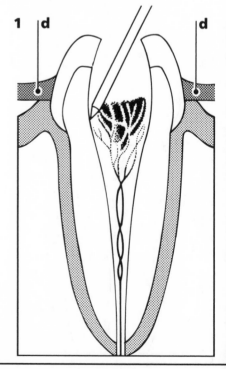

Step-by-step surgical procedure. The dental surgeon gains access to the pulp cavity by drilling a hole through the biting surface at the crown of the tooth. He or she then removes the soft internal material within the cavity. The cavity itself is widened using fine-tipped instruments. To avoid breaking out through the walls of the cavity down at the roots, the surgeon may monitor the progress of the enlargement with repeated X rays. The enlarged cavity is thoroughly washed out and is packed with an antibiotic paste, which is then sealed in with a temporary filling. The tooth is left alone for several days (perhaps up to a week) to ensure that any remaining infective organisms are duly destroyed by the antibiotic.

During this time, careful eating and drinking is permitted. There may be slight residual pain in the jaw as the anesthetic wears off, but if pain is sharp and persistent, you should ask your dental surgeon to deal with it, and not simply endure it until the proposed time for the second part of the operation.

At the appointed time you will be anesthetized once more, and the

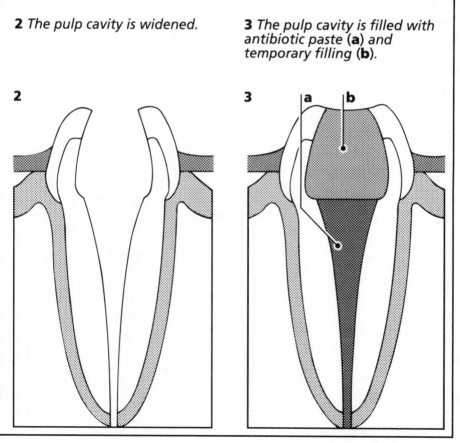

2 *The pulp cavity is widened.*

3 *The pulp cavity is filled with antibiotic paste (**a**) and temporary filling (**b**).*

© DIAGRAM

dam will be replaced in its frame around the tooth under treatment. The dental surgeon removes the temporary filling and the antibiotic packing in the cavity, and, when satisfied that the interior of the tooth is properly sterile, the surgeon inserts into the cavity a permanent root canal filling in the form of a sealant paste or a solid mixture of resin, zinc oxide, and other materials (together known as "points"). Points are tiny, pointed pieces of material that fill up the long pointed cavity in the tooth. The opening in the crown is sealed with a final filling compound, the dam is removed, and you are asked to rinse out your mouth.

What is it like immediately after the operation?

Because all sensory nerves to the tooth have been destroyed, there is no pain other than perhaps a slight residual ache in the jaw as the anesthetic wears off; that should fade rapidly. Nor should there afterward be any undue sensitivity of the tooth to cold or to percussion. The tooth appears normal, and after an hour or so (to let the filling set) you can eat and drink normally.

ROOT CANAL TREATMENT (continued)

4 *The temporary filling and antibiotic paste are removed.*

5 *The cavity is filled with "points"* (**a**) *and a permanent filling* (**b**).

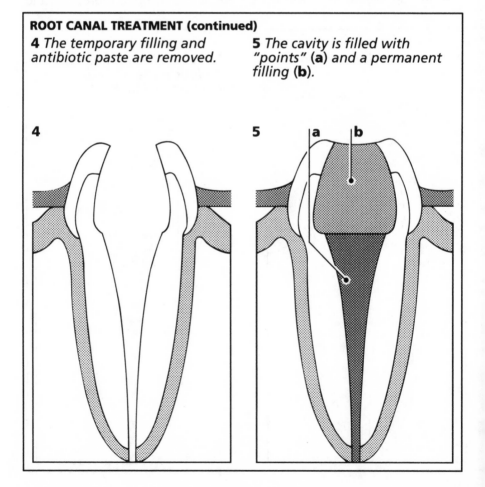

What are the longterm effects?

Assuming that all infection was eradicated, that there has been no damage to the fine fibers (the periodontal membrane) that hold the tooth in place within its bony socket, and that subsequent dental hygiene at home is adequate, the tooth should retain its position and strength indefinitely. Teeth treated by root canal dentistry are dead, however, and may change color over a period of some months to a bluish or grayish tint. There are a variety of cosmetic dental treatments available to deal with this discoloration, including bonding, bleaching, and fitting a crown (see box below).

In the rare cases when surgery is unsuccessful, the tooth may become loose and need to be extracted. There is no pain involved because there are no longer nerves in the tooth, but if a gap among the teeth is to be avoided, a denture or implant will have to be fitted.

Treatment for discolored teeth

Cosmetic methods of dealing with discolored teeth include:
- Bleaching with chemical substances
- Bonding on an acrylic or porcelain veneer
- Fitting an artificial crown

Bonded tooth

The surface of the tooth is roughened using a weak solution of acid. This allows the liquid cement to adhere to the tooth. If the tooth is damaged, this cement can be used to rebuild the shape of the tooth. Then the bonded veneer (made of acrylic or porcelain and preshaped to fit the tooth) is secured over the cement, covering the tooth. The procedure must be renewed every five years or so.

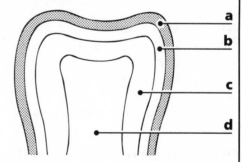

Cross-section through a tooth that has been bonded to hide discoloration
a *Bonded acrylic or porcelain veneer. This should match the color of adjacent teeth as closely as possible.*
b *Enamel*
c *Dentin*
d *Pulp*

Crowned tooth

Fitting a crown involves replacing the tooth's natural crown, using porcelain (for front teeth) or gold for stronger crowns. An impression of the tooth is made so that an artificial crown can be formed. Then the tooth is filed down to a peg shape, over which the new crown is securely cemented.

© DIAGRAM

CHAPTER 7
NECK SURGERY

Radical neck dissection: removal of lymph nodes in the neck

Why have the operation?

The surgical removal of lymph nodes in the neck (radical neck dissection) is performed to stop the spread of cancer. The surgeon has the opportunity to remove nodes that are diagnosed as likely to contain cancerous cells, and to cut out tissue from other nearby organs to which the cancer is presumed to have spread. If cancerous lymph nodes are not removed, the disease usually becomes widespread and inoperable.

What is the physical cause of the problem?

Lymph nodes are junctions in the network of small vessels that make up the lymphatic system. Because that system drains the fluid called lymph from all over the body and is intimately related also to the blood circulation, cancer that involves lymph nodes tends to spread quickly and widely. It is rare that cancer actually begins in the lymph nodes of the neck: it commonly spreads from elsewhere (such as the tongue, tonsils, esophagus, thyroid gland, larynx, breast, or lung).

Although radiotherapy is commonly used to treat cancers elsewhere in the body, radiotherapy powerful enough to destroy all cancer cells in the neck would be damaging to vital structures within the neck. Surgery is therefore the only method that may be successful in these circumstances.

What is the goal of surgery?

Surgery is designed to free the whole area from cancer by gaining access to, and removing, a considerable quantity of tissue. Although the focus of surgery is usually one side of the neck, it is occasionally necessary to operate on both sides, in which case the second side may be dealt with at the same time as the first, or after an interval of a few weeks.

Exactly what is involved in the surgical operation?

The lymphatic system is part of the body's immune system that deals with infection. Therefore, the surgeon will first assess the state of your oral health—if you have any mouth ulcers, for example, they will be treated in advance in order to avoid the risk of infection spreading to the operation site (where, after the operation, you will have less protection than previously).

Preliminary steps. If you are a man, your face, neck, and upper chest will be shaved on the morning of the operation. As with all operations involving general anesthesia, you will be given a preoperative injection about an hour before surgery to dry up internal fluids and to encourage drowsiness.

Step-by-step surgical procedure. Once you have been anesthetized, a tube will be passed down your windpipe (trachea) to ensure that a clear airway is maintained at all times. An antiseptic solution is applied to the whole area of the operation, and sterile towels are fixed in place around the neck with clips or stitches.

The operation begins with an incision through the skin to expose the internal tissues. Any of various incisions may be used, at the discretion of the surgeon, but all allow for a number of large flaps of skin and underlying flat muscle to be folded aside to give free access to the structures beneath. The lower flap is cut low enough to expose the upper surface of the collarbone (clavicle). Also exposed is the most prominent muscle of the neck, which is severed just above the point at which it joins the collarbone and upper border of the breastbone (sternum). From there the surgeon works back until the front edge of one of the large, triangular muscles of the back (the trapezius) is visible. This brings into view the large, external jugular vein, which is then tied off and cut.

7

The back area of the exposed part of the neck can now be completely cleared of lymph nodes. Other neck muscles are exposed and cut through to gain access to underlying tissue planes in which further lymph nodes (and soft tissues) lie. These nodes too are systematically cleared, although the surgeon must at the same time be extremely careful to avoid damage to the several important nerves also located there.

There are six main jugular veins: an external, an internal, and an anterior (front) on each side of the neck. The internal jugular vein and the main artery of the neck—the carotid, which supplies the brain and the

POSSIBLE INCISIONS

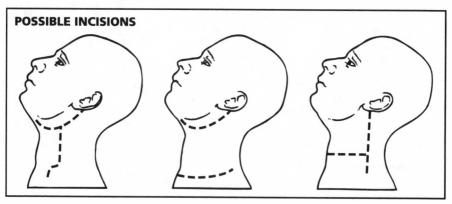

© DIAGRAM

EXTERNAL STRUCTURES OF THE NECK AND CHEST

a *Sternocleidomastoid muscle*
b *Sternohyoid muscle*
c *Trapezius muscle*
d *Sternothyroid muscle*
e *Jawbone (mandible)*
f *Collarbone (clavicle)*
g *Breastbone (sternum)*

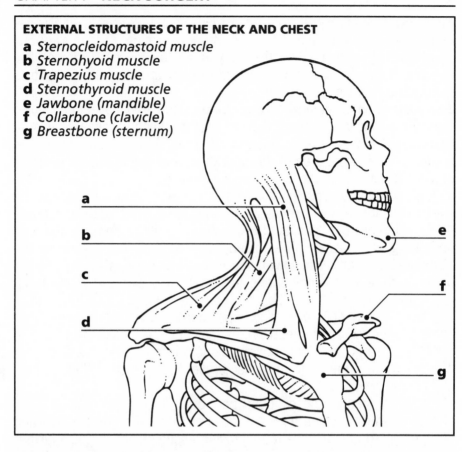

INTERNAL STRUCTURES OF THE NECK

a *Lymph nodes*
b *Jugular vein*
c *Carotid artery*
d *Thyroid gland*
e *Windpipe
   (trachea)*

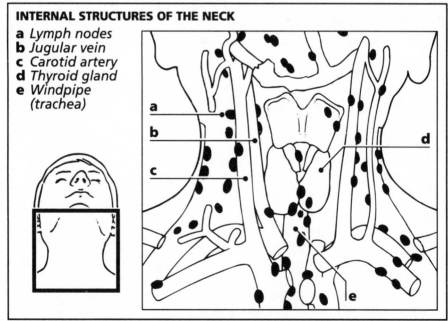

face—are now exposed. The vein is tied off and as much of it removed as is necessary, together with all the lymph nodes and soft tissue surrounding it. Because of the profuse interconnection of other smaller blood vessels, the blood can readily return to the heart even when the full length of vein is removed. If necessary, small veins will later enlarge to carry the increased blood flow. Around the carotid artery is a network of lymph vessels and nodes: these are also carefully removed. Injury to the artery must be avoided.

As the surgeon proceeds upward with the dissection, the salivary gland that lies under the jawbone (mandible) is removed. Any other tissue evidently involved in the cancer process is likewise removed.

The surgeon completes the operation by folding the flaps of skin and muscle together again. Before closing up the skin incisions the surgeon inserts plastic drainage tubes in position; connected to a suction pump, the tubes prevent the accumulation of fluid in the spaces left by tissue removal. Finally,the skin incisions are closed with fine stitches.

What is it like immediately after the operation?
You will wake up lying on your back with your head and shoulders raised to reduce the pressure in the veins of your neck. Drainage tubes will emerge from your neck. Most of the fine nerves that normally carry pain impulses from around the operating site will have been removed, so there will be little actual pain (in spite of having undergone so major an operation). A careful check will be kept for signs of hemorrhaging under the skin and for any indication of obstruction to your airway (to guard against which, the instruments for performing an emergency tracheostomy—the surgical creation of an air outlet at the front of the throat—may be retained close at hand). You should be able to eat normally, unless surgery had to be extended into the mouth, in which case you will be fed by tube for a time.

The danger of fluid accumulation will have passed after four or five days, and the suction drainage tubes can then be removed. The stitches in the skin will be taken out after about a week.

The duration of your stay in the hospital depends on whether cancer is diagnosed elsewhere in the body.

What are the longterm effects?
Healing is usually excellent, and scars are generally inconspicuous. The loss of tissue from the neck will inevitably cause some collapse of the skin, just as the loss of muscle tissue will cause some longterm stiffness and weakness of head movement. If both sides of the neck have been operated on simultaneously, the resultant severe swelling of the face may persist for several weeks. There are six salivary glands, and removal of the small salivary glands under the jawbone will not be missed. At worst, there might be occasional dryness of the mouth.

Laryngectomy: removal of the larynx (voice box)

Why have the operation?

This operation is performed only for the strongest of reasons: to save life when it is threatened by well-established cancer of the vocal cords and associated organs. If the cancer is discovered at an early stage, there is a fair chance that radiotherapy alone may effect a cure. Alternatively, a few surgeons in certain circumstances are willing to try a partial laryngectomy. But not all laryngeal cancers respond well to radiotherapy, and in general most surgeons believe that the only statistically effective treatment is total removal of the larynx.

What is the physical cause of the problem?

The vocal cords are thin, bladelike flaps of tissue slung as a parallel pair across the top of the trachea (the windpipe that ducts air to and from

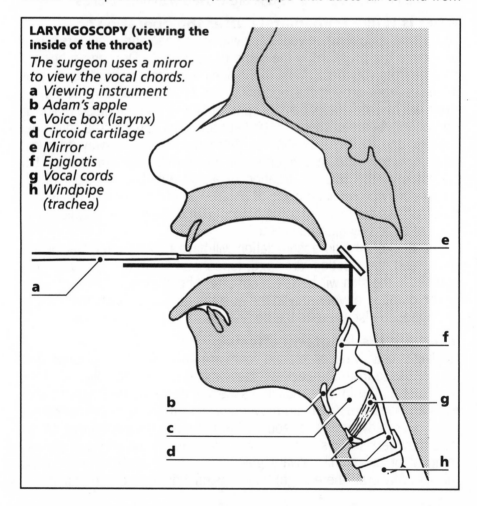

LARYNGOSCOPY (viewing the inside of the throat)

The surgeon uses a mirror to view the vocal chords.
a *Viewing instrument*
b *Adam's apple*
c *Voice box (larynx)*
d *Circoid cartilage*
e *Mirror*
f *Epiglotis*
g *Vocal cords*
h *Windpipe (trachea)*

the lungs). Muscular movement of these flaps to open or close the thin gap between them modifies the flow of air breathed out via the tough, cartilaginous resonance chamber immediately above (the larynx), and so produces the basic sound of the voice and alterations in its pitch. (The vowel and consonantal sounds of speech are imposed upon the voice later within the mouth and nose.) Cancer of the vocal cords thus not only distorts speech tone but also imperils breathing.

Most often, detection of laryngeal cancer occurs only after the tumor has spread from the vocal cords to associated organs and has affected speech tone and breathing. Tests, including the use of a laryngoscope, then confirm the diagnosis.

What is the goal of surgery?

Removal of the larynx means that you will no longer be able to breathe through your mouth or nose or speak normally. The aim of the operation is to remove the cancer and allow continued breathing. It may well be possible for you, over time, to relearn a method of speech.

VIEW OF THE VOCAL CHORDS (as the surgeon sees them in mirror)
The vocal chords open and shut as we speak.

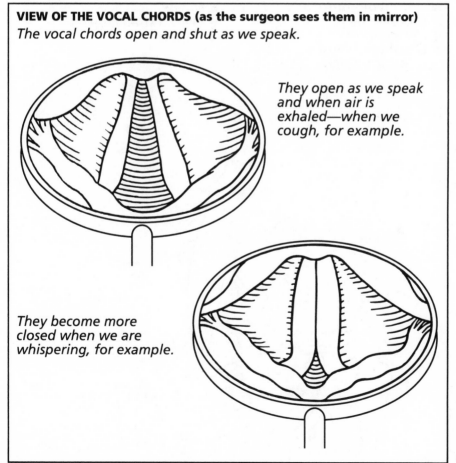

They open as we speak and when air is exhaled—when we cough, for example.

They become more closed when we are whispering, for example.

© DIAGRAM

Exactly what is involved in the surgical operation?

Preliminary steps. As with all operations involving general anesthesia, you will be given a preoperative injection about an hour before surgery to dry up internal fluids and to encourage drowsiness. In surgery of this kind, however, general anesthesia itself is most commonly induced via a tube passed down through the mouth and larynx.

Step-by-step surgical procedure. The surgeon first makes an incision in the front of the neck—usually down the midline but sometimes transversely following one of the skin creases. Either way, the tissues of the neck organs must be exposed from the top of the breastbone (sternum) right up to the hyoid bone at the junction of neck and chin. This incision reveals the long central strap muscles of the neck that extend up the length of the trachea and run up in front of the larynx to the hyoid bone.

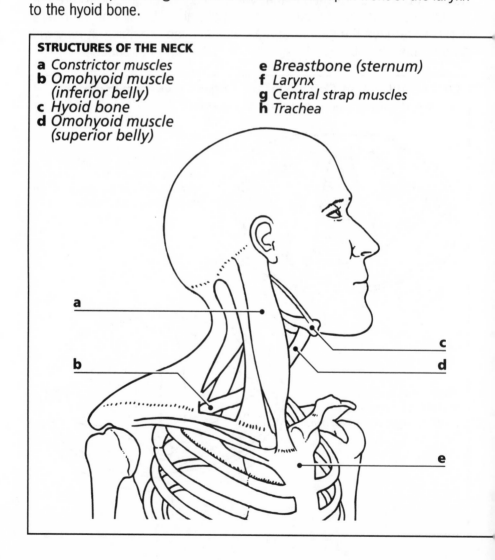

STRUCTURES OF THE NECK

a *Constrictor muscles*
b *Omohyoid muscle (inferior belly)*
c *Hyoid bone*
d *Omohyoid muscle (superior belly)*

e *Breastbone (sternum)*
f *Larynx*
g *Central strap muscles*
h *Trachea*

Depending on how far the cancer has spread, some or all of the muscles surrounding the larynx may have to be removed, together with the body of the hyoid bone. The larynx is now open to view, and can be manipulated first to one side and then the other to expose and detach the constrictor muscles of the throat, which hold the larynx horizontally in place. Immediately behind the larynx lie the throat and the top of the esophagus (the gullet, the passage for food down into the stomach). The surgeon must check carefully to determine whether or not the cancer has also spread to these areas in order to plan supplementary treatment such as radiotherapy and the insertion of a feeding tube through the esophagus and into the stomach.

The larynx is now relatively free and can be pulled forward, and its arteries, veins, and nerves can be tied off tightly with catgut thread. The separation of the (cartilaginous) larynx from the (muscular) esopha-

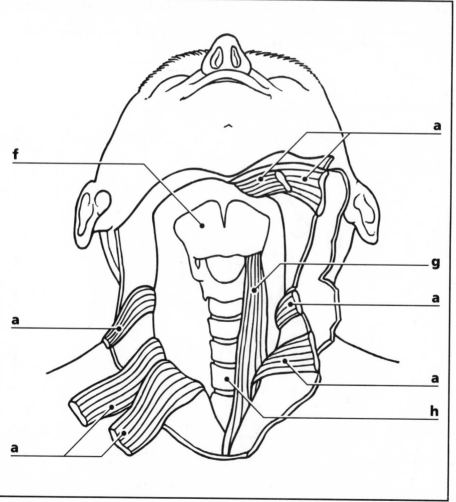

© DIAGRAM

gus behind it must be carried out with extreme care, working from the top downward until all that holds the larynx in place is the trachea (windpipe) beneath it. The trachea itself is then cut partly through at an oblique angle, the incision higher at the back than at the front. At this point the anesthetic tube is removed from the mouth, the cut is completed all around the trachea, and the larynx with the severed top of the trachea is taken away. The anesthetic tube is then replaced, but directly in the top of the remaining trachea from the front so that anesthesia can continue. (Even if there is a delay in replacing the anesthetic tube at this stage, there is no chance that you will wake up.)

Once the larynx has been removed, the remaining muscles may be replaced, and the edges of the skin incision are carefully sewn back together—except at the level of the throat, where the skin is sewn instead around the cut upper end of the trachea, which, thanks to the oblique angle at which it was cut, is now protruding horizontally forward. Once these raw edges in contact with each other heal together,

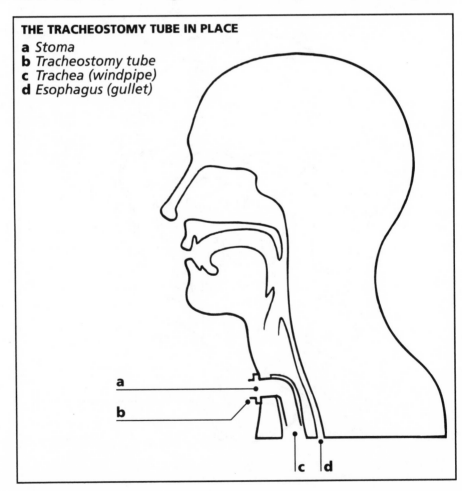

THE TRACHEOSTOMY TUBE IN PLACE

a *Stoma*
b *Tracheostomy tube*
c *Trachea (windpipe)*
d *Esophagus (gullet)*

there will be a permanent opening (stoma) in the neck: a natural yet arti-ficially direct airway to the lungs.

Just before you recover from the anesthetic and are able to breathe on your own, however, the anesthetic tube is removed from the stoma and a small, curved, double-walled tracheostomy tube is put in its place. This ensures that as the tissues heal, the opening in the neck does not become too narrow; when healing is complete, the tube is no longer needed and can be discarded.

What is it like immediately after the operation?
On waking up, you may be surprised at how easy it is to breathe—but your neck may feel cold. The air in your room will most likely be humid-ified because air is passing more directly into your lungs instead of being filtered and moistened through your nose and mouth. Humidifying should help to reduce mucus production, but a nurse will drain the tra-cheostomy tube as a matter of routine from time to time during the first week or two. If the stoma becomes clogged with mucus, the inner tube can be slid out and cleaned separately.

Because of inevitable surgical trauma to the esophagus it will not be safe for you to swallow for about ten days, so at first you will be fed via a thin, soft tube passed through your nose and down into your stom-ach. (This sounds uncomfortable, but you will hardly notice it after the first few hours.)

Depending on the quantity of muscle tissue removed from your neck, you may find it difficult at first to keep your head upright or to move it from side to side. Also, you will be unable to speak; you will be provided with some means of communication (like a buzzer or bell to summon, and a scribble pad for messages).

What are the longterm effects?
If the cancer has been completely removed, there is a fair chance of total recovery of health and fitness, although extra attention to the con-stituents of the air breathed is always necessary (especially where atmospheric water, water vapor, or dust particles are at unusually high levels).

There is even the possibility of speech, achieved in either of two ways. In one—esophageal speech—air is first swallowed then emitted in a sort of controlled burping manner to produce a noise modified by mouth, tongue, and lips into distinguishable words. This takes a lot of practice. The other method is easier, and makes use of an electronic oscillator which emits a buzzing sound: when the oscillator is pressed against the neck, the buzz can be modified by movements of mouth, tongue, and lips so that clear (if somewhat tonelessly robotic) speech is produced.

Thyroidectomy: removal of part of the thyroid gland

Why have the operation?

One symptom of an overactive thyroid gland is swelling of the gland (sometimes to huge proportions) at the front of the neck, in the bulge known as a goiter. Goiter is now far less common than it once was (mostly because of societal dietary changes), and the cases that do occur can generally be successfully treated by drugs and controlled diet or by administration of small amounts of radioactive iodine. Surgery may be performed if:

- goiter is putting pressure on other local structures
- goiter is interfering with respiration or swallowing
- the usual course of antithyroid drugs to treat hyperthyroidism (thyrotoxicosis) has failed to work and radioactive iodine is not appropriate to the patient (as for example during pregnancy)
- a tumor is detected on or in the thyroid gland

What is the physical cause of the problem?

Located at the bottom of the neck, the thyroid gland may be the site of local or general inflammation, or of a tumor (which may be benign or malignant). In all cases the gland changes its shape, mostly by swelling up to form a goiter (which may be a diffuse or a nodular swelling), and greatly increases production of thyroid hormone. This hormone affects the body's metabolism, acting on body cells to regulate their rates of activity. Excessive production of the hormone tends to accelerate a number of body processes and can result in severe illness. Removal of part of the gland (subtotal thyroidectomy) is usually sufficient to effect a cure.

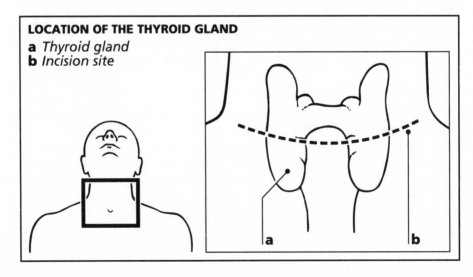

LOCATION OF THE THYROID GLAND
a *Thyroid gland*
b *Incision site*

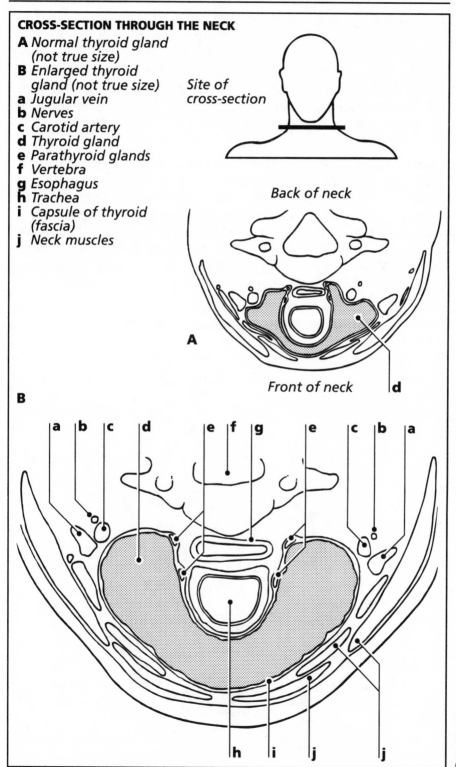

CROSS-SECTION THROUGH THE NECK

A Normal thyroid gland (not true size)
B Enlarged thyroid gland (not true size)
a Jugular vein
b Nerves
c Carotid artery
d Thyroid gland
e Parathyroid glands
f Vertebra
g Esophagus
h Trachea
i Capsule of thyroid (fascia)
j Neck muscles

Site of cross-section

Back of neck

Front of neck

A

B

a b c d e f g e c b a

h i j j

© DIAGRAM

What is the goal of surgery?

The overall intention of surgery is to remove enough of the gland to reduce the hormone output of the thyroid to normal levels. If the gland is suspected of containing a focus of cancer the aim of surgery is to remove all cancerous tissue. If enlargement of the gland is the major problem, and this is affecting local structures (and possibly the wind-pipe nearby), the aim is to relieve these effects, again by removal of part of the gland.

Exactly what is involved in the surgical operation?

Before surgery, an effort will be made to ensure that you are in the best possible overall physical condition. Thyroid overactivity will be reduced as much as it can be by antithyroid medication. In spite of this, sudden increases in the output of thyroid hormone may occur just before—or even during—surgery, and you may be given beta-blocking drugs (which slow the heart rate, reduce anxiety, and also inhibit thyroid activity) such as acebutolol or metoprolol.

THE EXPOSED NECK SHOWING INTERNAL STRUCTURES

a *Carotid artery*　　　**e** *Thyroid cartilage*
b *Jugular system*　　　**f** *Lymph nodes*
c *Trachea*　　　　　　**g** *Collarbone (clavicle)*
d *Salivary gland*　　　**h** *Thyroid gland*

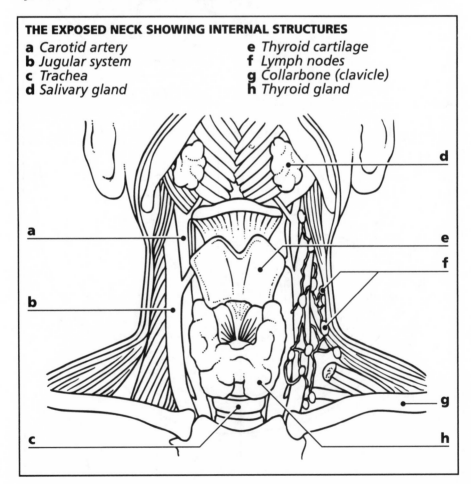

There will also be many tests and scans. These will enable the surgeon to determine whether cancer is part of the problem, and if so how much, and will permit the anesthetist to ensure that your windpipe (trachea) is not distorted. The anesthetist may also check for signs of weakness or paralysis in your vocal cords through encroachment of the swollen gland upon the nerve that activates the cords (this nerve runs closely behind the thyroid gland).

Preliminary steps. As with all operations involving general anesthesia, you will be given a preoperative injection about an hour before surgery to dry up internal fluids and to encourage drowsiness. Because thyroid activity itself may increase anxiety, you may feel more apprehensive about the coming surgery than other patients would feel before another type of surgery. You may be given a drug to put you to sleep before you are taken to the operating room.

Step-by-step surgical procedure. Once you are anesthetized and positioned on the operating table, your neck will be swabbed with antiseptic solution before being surrounded with sterile surgical towels or with a sterile adhesive plastic drape.

The surgeon makes the first incision, horizontally, about 2 inches long and 1½ inches above the notch that marks the top of the breastbone. It usually follows the line of an already existing crease so that after healing it will be imperceptible.

The incision passes through the skin and the underlying flat muscle (the platysma); bleeding points are secured in forceps, and larger blood vessels are tied off or closed by diathermy (electric application of heat). The surgeon then frees the tissues under the upper and lower edges of the incision so that the edges can be pulled apart to expose the thyroid gland. A self-retaining retractor holds the wound open.

POSITION OF THE PATIENT DURING THE OPERATION

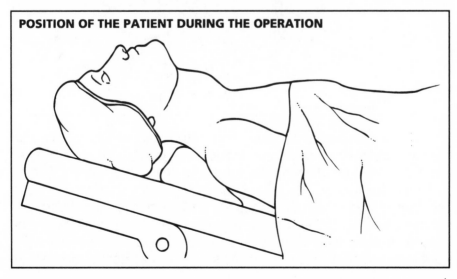

© DIAGRAM

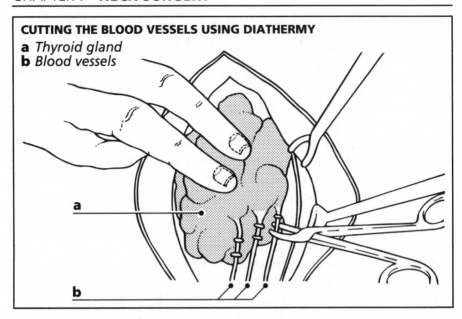

CUTTING THE BLOOD VESSELS USING DIATHERMY
a *Thyroid gland*
b *Blood vessels*

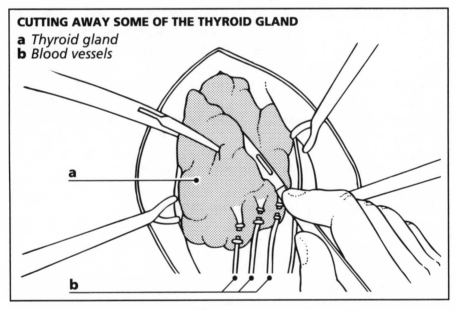

CUTTING AWAY SOME OF THE THYROID GLAND
a *Thyroid gland*
b *Blood vessels*

It is now possible for the surgeon to cut vertically through the thin layer of tissue (the fascia) that covers the gland and, with another retractor, to pull out the straplike muscle on one side of the gland so as to expose the gland's side lobe. If the gland is very swollen, it may be necessary to cut some of the supporting neck muscles in order to gain sufficient access. The exposed lobe is now freed by careful snipping or separation of its securing tissues, so that the lobe can be brought forward to the center of the wound. The surgeon must identify the arteries supplying blood to this side of the gland, tie them off, and sever them. (He or she must at the same time identify the nerves to the muscles that tense the vocal cords, and be sure to avoid damage to them. If these nerves are inadvertently cut, the voice is seriously affected.) The veins that surround the gland lobe are similarly cut away. The whole procedure is now repeated in relation to the lobe on the other side of the gland.

The surgeon then removes most of each lobe of the gland, taking care not to injure or remove the parathyroid glands that lie immediately behind the thyroid gland, within the thyroid tissue. Bleeding points are treated with diathermy. To complete the operation, the deeper tissues are closed with absorbable stitches, drainage tubes are inserted to drain blood that accumulates where the lobe has been removed, the muscle layer is replaced, and (except where the drainage tubes emerge) the skin is closed with clips or stitches.

What is it like immediately after the operation?
When you wake up you will be lying on your back, with your head and shoulders slightly raised and drainage tubes at your neck. There should be little pain, and what there is can be controlled by painkilling drugs. You will be asked to avoid extending your neck for a time.

Possible but relatively rare complications at this time include localized accumulations of blood (hematomas), which may cause pressure on the windpipe, making it difficult to breathe. Occasionally (especially when neck muscles have been severed), kinking of the windpipe occurs. In either of these cases, a tube may be passed down your throat for a few days to ensure respiration; in extreme cases, and as an emergency, a temporary tracheostomy (the creation of an artificial outlet in the trachea through the wall of the neck) may be performed. If the nerves to the larynx (voice box) have been damaged, there may be severe—but ordinarily temporary—hoarseness or loss of voice.

Healing of the wound is usually rapid: the stitches and the drainage tubes are generally removed after a few days, and the patient is allowed to leave the hospital. If necessary, after a large part of the thyroid gland has been removed you may be given instruction on medication (hormone replacement therapy) prior to your leaving.

What are the longterm effects?
The results of this kind of surgery are normally excellent. The scar is seldom apparent. Monitoring of thyroid hormone production may continue for some months after the operation, to check whether too much or too little is being produced. In a few cases parathyroid insufficiency develops some time later. Hormone or mineral replacement therapy successfully treats either case.

© DIAGRAM

Tracheostomy

Why have the operation?

Tracheostomy has been understood since the first century BC. It is an operation to create an opening through the front of the neck and into the windpipe (trachea) in order to allow a patient to breathe. Tracheostomy is done for two main reasons:

1 when there is an obstruction in the larynx and an emergency opening must be made to allow spontaneous breathing and save life

2 when a person is unable to breathe spontaneously and must be artificially ventilated, long term

In combination with a ventilation machine, the procedure allows safe artificial respiration and may also be performed:

• in some cases of laryngeal tumor

• following the accidental swallowing of a large foreign body

What is the physical cause of the problem?

If the body is deprived of oxygen for more than a few minutes, the outcome may be brain damage or even death. A variety of conditions and circumstances can endanger the air supply by causing obstruction. These include:

• congenital (inherited) abnormality of the larynx or trachea

• acute inflammation of sensitive tissues in the throat

• neck or mouth injury involving major tissue deformity and displacement (such as a cut throat)

• inhalation of corrosive material, smoke, or steam

• the presence of a large foreign body that sticks to the larynx

• paralysis of muscles in the mouth, throat, or neck, particularly those that affect swallowing and whose impairment might permit food or drink that is swallowed to go to the lungs instead of to the stomach

• longterm unconsciousness or coma (during which saliva may also find its way to the lungs)

• swelling of the laryngeal lining following radiation therapy for cancer

• removal of the larynx to treat cancer

In most of these cases the tracheostomy is only temporary. A few cases—such as surgical removal of the larynx—demand tracheostomy on a permanent basis.

What is the goal of surgery?

A short tube is passed through the front of your neck and into the windpipe. This acts as mouth and nose for the purpose of breathing air freely and normally in and out of the lungs.

Exactly what is involved in the surgical operation?

Preliminary steps. Preparation depends on whether or not surgery has to be performed as an emergency. If there is time, your air pas-

EMERGENCY INCISION

*In an emergency the surgeon may make a stab incision directly through the crico-thyroid membrane (**a**), part of the larynx that is particularly thin. This gives immediate access to the airway.*

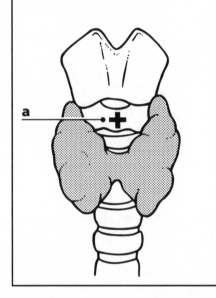

NONEMERGENCY INCISION

*In nonemergency circum-stances the surgeon makes an incision through the skin in the vertical midline at the bottom of the neck, immediately over the trachea (**a**) between the Adam's apple (**b**) and the notch in the top of the breastbone (sternum) (not shown).*

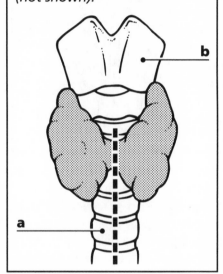

sages will be cleared using methods such as:

- the administration of antibiotic drugs
- medication with expectorants or inhalants
- postural drainage (involves positioning the patient so that secretions can be removed by gravity, aided by slapping or thumping)
- physical therapy (the physical therapist helps with postural drainage and teaches effective breathing)

You may also undergo:

- counseling (which will include supporting you in quitting smoking cigarettes if you smoke)
- lung function tests to find out how effectively the oxygen is getting from the atmosphere to the blood

If your breathing is already labored, a tube may be placed in your mouth and down the trachea to assist respiration. This is an emergency measure necessary to overcome obstruction in the larynx. It may be done at any time. Most commonly, a tube is passed after a general anesthetic has been given for surgery but may suddenly become necessary before there is time to arrange surgery. In an acute emergency a tube

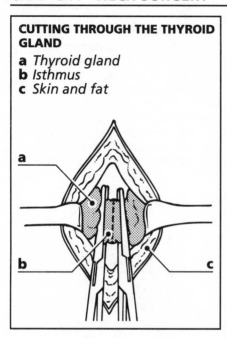

CUTTING THROUGH THE THYROID GLAND

a *Thyroid gland*
b *Isthmus*
c *Skin and fat*

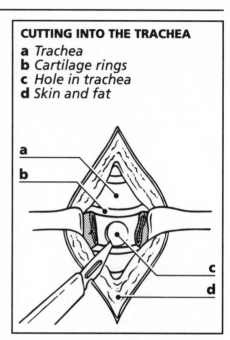

CUTTING INTO THE TRACHEA

a *Trachea*
b *Cartilage rings*
c *Hole in trachea*
d *Skin and fat*

may be passed under local anesthesia or even without an anesthetic. It is often a life-saving procedure.

Step-by-step surgical procedure. You will be positioned lying on your back, your head tilted up and backward, your neck extended with the support of a pillow.

The skin of the neck is opened, the neck muscles are carefully separated, and the central part of the thyroid gland is cut through or pulled upward. This exposes the tough cartilage rings that make up the outer wall of the trachea. The surgeon then cuts into two of these rings and inserts a tracheostomy tube, which effectively closes off all flow of air in the windpipe above that point. Each half of the thyroid gland has its own blood supply and its function is not affected by being cut across the isthmus or pulled higher into the larynx. The neck muscles are replaced, and the skin edges are sewn up around the flange (the flat portion) of the tube where it exits the windpipe. A surgical gauze dressing is applied under the flange of the tube, which is held firmly in place by a tape passed around the neck and tied to each side of the flange of the tracheostomy tube.

If you are unable to breathe spontaneously, the tube will be connected to a mechanical ventilator. The ventilator ensures that blood is at all times fully oxygenated so personal regulation of breathing is not necessary, nor would it be possible. A person on a ventilator will always be lying quietly in bed.

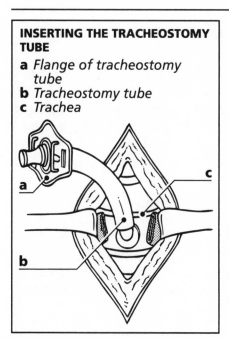

INSERTING THE TRACHEOSTOMY TUBE

a *Flange of tracheostomy tube*
b *Tracheostomy tube*
c *Trachea*

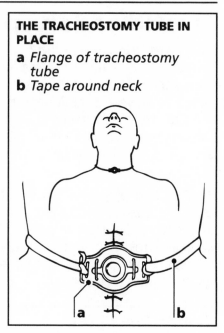

THE TRACHEOSTOMY TUBE IN PLACE

a *Flange of tracheostomy tube*
b *Tape around neck*

What is it like immediately after the operation?

On waking up, you should find that you have been provided with some means of communication—like a bell or buzzer to summon, and a scribble pad for messages. Normal speech will be impossible because air is no longer passing between the vocal cords. The air in your room will most likely be humidified because air is no longer filtered and moistened through your nose and mouth. Humidifying should help to reduce mucus production, but the nursing staff will drain the tracheostomy tube, especially during the first two days.

If your larynx (voice box) is intact and open, you may find it possible to speak by temporarily covering the opening of the tracheostomy tube with one finger so that air once more passes between the vocal cords.

For a time you may be fed intravenously through a drip attached to one hand or wrist. But how you feel, what you are able to do, and how quickly you recover is likely to depend on the condition that required you to have the tracheostomy in the first place.

What are the longterm effects?

If the tracheostomy is temporary, the tube will eventually be removed. The opening in both windpipe and skin will close over and heal very quickly, leaving a minimal scar on the outside. If the tracheostomy tube is permanent, the hole remains open. It does tend to close, but the tube prevents this from happening completely. Sometimes further surgery is needed to widen it.

Carotid endarterectomy

Why have the operation?

Carotid endarterectomy involves the removal of plaque from any of the four carotid arteries that supply blood to the neck and head. It is performed to prevent a stroke and is almost always advised following a series of strokelike attacks in which the effects are merely temporary (transient ischemic attacks) but that suggest a full-scale stroke is imminent. Stroke can result in brain damage, permanent disability, and death.

What is the physical cause of the problem?

Transient ischemic attacks and strokes are caused by a blockage of the blood flow to the brain. In many cases, the blockage results from the extreme narrowing of a major artery due to the accretion of cholesterol and degenerate muscle tissue (together called plaque or atheroma) on the inside wall of the artery—a condition known as atherosclerosis.

RIGHT CAROTID ARTERY

Each of the two common carotid arteries, right and left, *has an internal carotid (**a**) and an external carotid (**b**).*

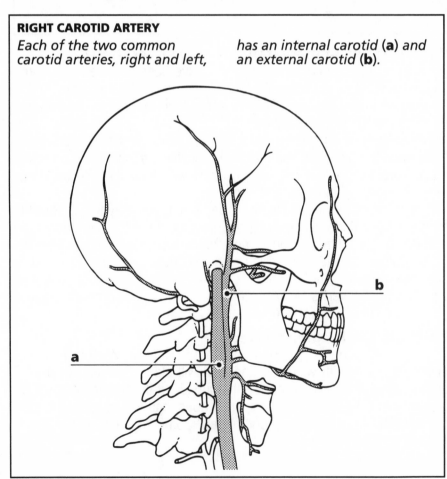

Atherosclerosis may have any or all of four direct effects:

- Blood flow through the artery may be reduced to the point at which the tissues supplied can no longer function.
- Small particles may be dislodged from the plaque and carried in the bloodstream to block smaller artery branches.
- Blood clots may form on top of the plaque, and may then block the major artery completely.
- A diseased and weakened artery may balloon out and burst, causing a dangerous local hemorrhage.

Surgery for carotid atherosclerosis carries risks. Surgical intervention involves some interruption to the blood flow through the artery and may involve actual closure of the artery: paralysis or other stroke effects are possible. Paralysis is usually one-sided and may be of any degree and extent. Other stroke effects include facial paralysis, loss of sensation, double vision, loss of half the field of vision, defects of speech comprehension or articulation or both, and personality changes.

What is the goal of surgery?

Removal of plaque in the carotid artery should restore the supply of blood to the brain. If removal is successful, and if smaller branches of the artery are not affected by plaque as severely as the carotid itself, surgery should relieve all strokelike symptoms and eliminate further ischemic attacks.

Exactly what is involved in the surgical operation?

Before surgery you may undergo a number of investigative procedures. Angiography (or arteriography: the use of X-ray photography following the injection of a contrast medium) should determine the precise state of the interior of your carotid arteries, and may be used also to examine the condition of the interior of other major arteries within your body, particularly of the coronary arteries that supply the heart with blood. In addition, a full medical evaluation is normally made to assess any indi-

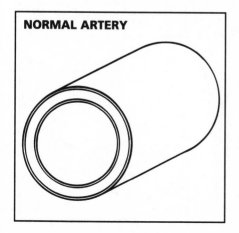

NORMAL ARTERY

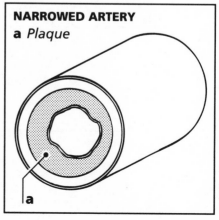

NARROWED ARTERY
a *Plaque*

a

© DIAGRAM

vidual dangers, with specific reference to other types of arterial disease (such as arterial disease resulting from longterm diabetes mellitus).

Preliminary steps. As with all operations involving general anesthesia, you will be given a preoperative injection about an hour before surgery to dry up internal fluids and to encourage drowsiness.

Step-by-step surgical procedure. Once you have been anesthetized, you will be positioned on the operating table with your head turned slightly away from the side of surgery.

The surgeon makes the first incision through the skin down and along the front border of the prominent underlying strap muscle of the neck. The skin edges are then carefully separated to expose the main artery and vein of the neck. Before any further action is taken, the surgeon identifies a number of important nerves in the area to ensure that none is damaged during the rest of the operation.

Cloth tape loops are passed around the artery above and below the point of internal obstruction. The ends of the loops are passed through short lengths of rubber tubing so that loops and tubing together can act as tourniquets. The surgeon now makes a longitudinal incision in the artery between the tape loops and positions a bypass shunt tube to

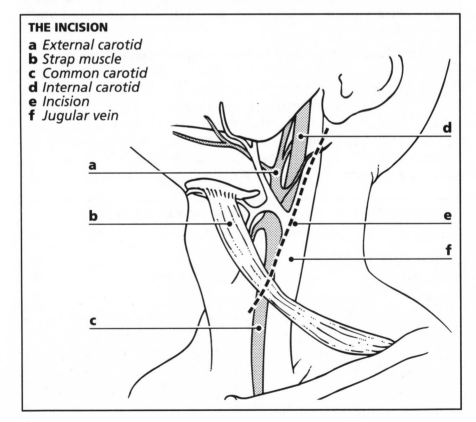

THE INCISION
a *External carotid*
b *Strap muscle*
c *Common carotid*
d *Internal carotid*
e *Incision*
f *Jugular vein*

carry blood from one end of the incision to the other, thus leaving the area with the plaque deposit open for treatment. The tourniquet tapes are tightened around the two ends of the tube so that no blood is lost and the flow is maintained under normal blood pressure.

The surgeon now gently removes the plaque from the artery using a blunt dissecting instrument, then bathes the clean wall in salt solution

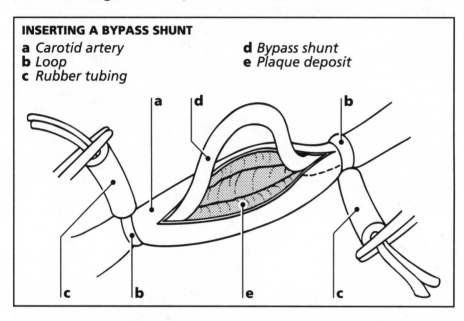

INSERTING A BYPASS SHUNT
a *Carotid artery*
b *Loop*
c *Rubber tubing*
d *Bypass shunt*
e *Plaque deposit*

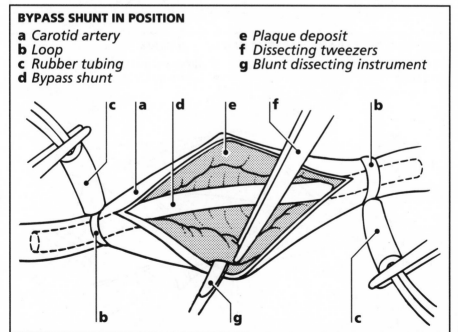

BYPASS SHUNT IN POSITION
a *Carotid artery*
b *Loop*
c *Rubber tubing*
d *Bypass shunt*
e *Plaque deposit*
f *Dissecting tweezers*
g *Blunt dissecting instrument*

© DIAGRAM

that also contains the natural anticoagulant heparin. The incision in the artery is stitched until just enough space is left to allow removal of the bypass shunt tube. The tube is removed and stitching of the artery is completed. After checking to make sure there is no leakage of blood, the surgeon sews up the skin wound.

REMOVING THE PLAQUE DEPOSIT

a *Carotid artery*
b *Loop*
c *Rubber tubing*
d *Bypass shunt*

e *Plaque deposit*
f *Dissecting tweezers*
g *Blunt dissecting instrument*

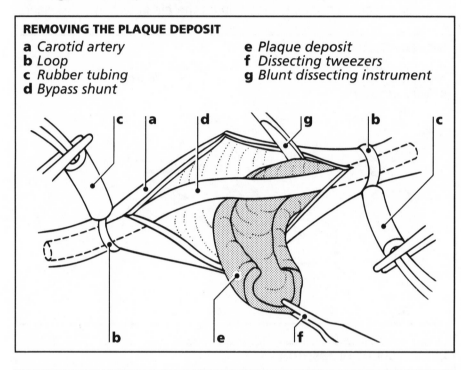

BATHING THE CLEANED ARTERY IN SALT SOLUTION

a *Carotid artery*
b *Loop*
c *Rubber tubing*

d *Bypass shunt*
e *Saline solution*

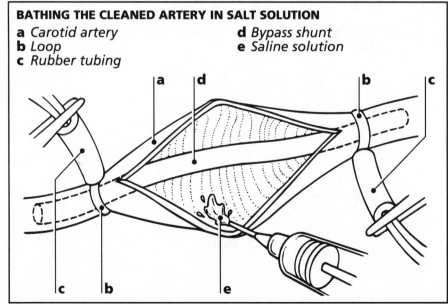

CLOSING THE ARTERY AND REMOVING THE BYPASS SHUNT
a *Carotid artery*
b *Loop*
c *Rubber tubing*
d *Bypass shunt*
e *Clamp*
f *Dissecting tweezers*

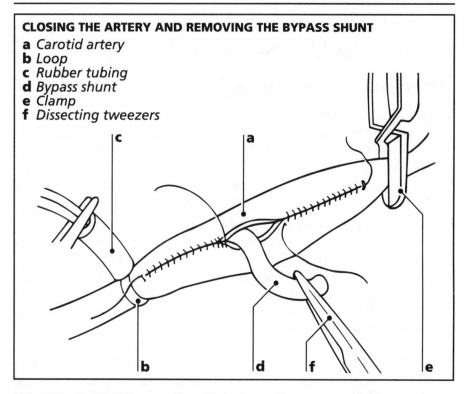

What is it like immediately after the operation?

If all has gone well, you should feel fine when you wake up after the operation—although the greatly increased blood flow in what was previously a seriously narrowed artery may cause a severe headache or lightheadedness at first. This is not a cause for alarm, and should soon pass. If any of the nerves in the neck have been bruised during surgery, you may notice a slight local loss of sensation in the skin and perhaps even a droop of one corner of your mouth; this too should correct itself in time.

What are the longterm effects?

The results of successful surgery for plaque removal are excellent. Remember, however, that atherosclerosis is a general disease that affects most of the arteries of the body. This operation has dealt with only one area of involvement, and affected arteries elsewhere can cause equally dangerous problems. Changing to or maintaining a low-fat, low-cholesterol diet and a no-smoking program is important, especially if diet and lifestyle contributed to the condition.

CHAPTER 8
ARM AND LEG SURGERY

Removal of a bunion

Why have the operation?

A bunion is a painful (and often disabling) prominence at the base of the big toe that causes continual discomfort, especially while walking in shoes. Managing the condition involves wearing pads over or around the bunion, or using special footwear. Bunions do not cure themselves but tend instead to worsen. Surgery is almost always fully effective.

What is the physical cause of the problem?

A bunion is caused by an abnormality in the position of the bones in the foot and big toe. Instead of being in line, meeting flatly end-to-end, the bone along the inside of the foot (the first metatarsal) and the first bone of the big toe (the phalanx hallucis) meet at an angle. Over time, the pressure of footwear causes inflammation of the fluid-filled pad (the bursa) that acts as a shock-absorber at the joint, and the whole joint swells painfully.

The deformity is worsened as the metatarsal bone grows a bony pro-trusion (an exostosis), and the tendons that provide movement in the toe slip from the top and the bottom around to the inside of the metatarsal bone (see box opposite). The tendons may eventually become tight, adding to the pain and disability. If footwear is worn con-tinuously, the skin over the swelling may blister and become subject to

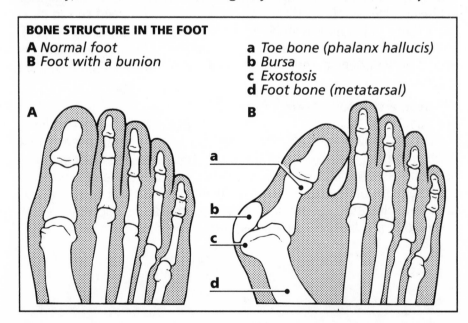

BONE STRUCTURE IN THE FOOT

A *Normal foot*
B *Foot with a bunion*

a *Toe bone (phalanx hallucis)*
b *Bursa*
c *Exostosis*
d *Foot bone (metatarsal)*

A

B

a

b

c

d

calluses or corns. And because the bones of the joint meet at an abnormal angle, they wear irregularly, which may result in osteoarthritis.

A deformed bone joint such as this commonly results from wearing high-heeled shoes that are too tight and too narrow at the toes, forcing the big toe bones to collapse inward. This is why the problem occurs much more in women than in men, and is almost unknown in people who normally go barefoot. Sometimes the condition results from an inherited abnormality in the shape of the metatarsal bone.

Once the toe begins to deviate to the side, there is little that can be done to halt the process. The tendons that bend and straighten the toe soon slip to the inside of the metatarsal bone and, acting like bowstrings, progressively increase the deformity. Later, the tendons shorten (contract) and make matters worse.

What is the goal of surgery?
There are more than a hundred different operations to treat a bunion, all designed to correct the deformity, relieve the symptoms, and restore full, painless function. Ideally, surgery also prevents it from recurring. An effective operation removes the excess bone, straightens the toe, and relieves pressure on the skin and the bursa, allowing normal, slim shoes to be worn comfortably. The most commonly performed procedure is known as the Keller arthroplasty: it is this operation that is described here.

Exactly what is involved in the surgical operation?
Before surgery, the surgeon checks that the skin of each affected foot is healthy and free from infection. You may be required to put aside a

8

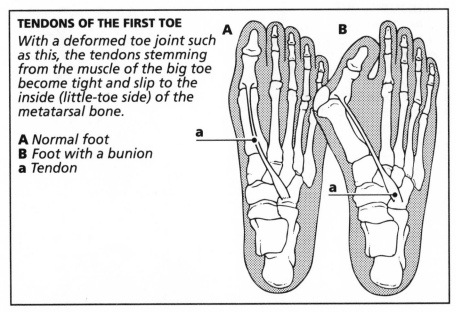

TENDONS OF THE FIRST TOE

With a deformed toe joint such as this, the tendons stemming from the muscle of the big toe become tight and slip to the inside (little-toe side) of the metatarsal bone.

A *Normal foot*
B *Foot with a bunion*
a *Tendon*

© DIAGRAM

short time every day for a week or so for careful washing, drying, and powdering of the foot.

For the operation, the surgeon may use spinal anesthesia, in which case you may retain consciousness throughout although you will be numb from the waist down, or a general anesthetic that will put you to sleep for the duration of the procedure.

Preliminary steps. If your operation is to be performed under general anesthesia, you will be given a preoperative injection about an hour before surgery to dry up internal fluids and to encourage drowsiness.

Step-by-step surgical procedure. Once you are anesthetized, you will be positioned on the operating table lying on your back. A tourniquet will be applied so that the surgeon can operate on your foot with little or no bleeding. The skin of the foot is thoroughly cleaned with swabs held in long forceps and dipped in antiseptic solution. All parts of the leg other than the immediate surgical site are then covered with sterile towels kept in place by clips.

The surgeon's first incision is about 2 inches (5cm) lengthwise along the upper surface of the toe, near the inner edge of the foot. The incision exposes the bone just to the inner side of the tendon that runs along the top of it. The surgeon must be careful not to cause any damage to the tendon or the mobility of the toe will be adversely affected. The tendon is pulled to one side so that the base of the phalanx bone can be completely severed, using an electric rotating saw or a wire two-handed saw. Great care is taken while sawing to prevent damage to the tendon on the underside of the toe. Once the base of the phalanx has

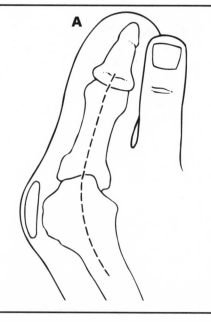

BUNION REMOVAL

A *Possible site of incision*
B *The bony overgrowth (**a**) is trimmed, the bursa (**b**) is removed, and the phalanx (**c**) is cut away.*
C *The joint is then straightened and a new, mobile joint forms in the gap (**d**).*

been removed, the bony protuberance (exostosis) on the side of the metatarsal bone is shaved off with a chisel and mallet so that the end of the bone is considerably narrowed. The surgeon then brings together the ligamentous tissue that overlies the bone on the inner edge of the foot, and stitches it up. He or she sews up the skin and places a firm pad of gauze between the big toe and the second toe to keep them parallel. Finally, the tourniquet is released.

What is it like immediately after the operation?

If your operation was performed under spinal anesthesia, you may suffer a headache after surgery; it should not last long. There should be very little immediate discomfort because the source of the pain has been removed. Function should be virtually normal (including walking), although the big toe is now shorter than before. The foot will be tender at first, but this will soon pass. Balance is unaffected. In the new, straight toe, the tendons soon shorten to take up any slack, restoring the full bending and straightening capacity of the toe necessary for normal walking. You will be encouraged to exercise and resume your usual activities as soon as possible. You should be able to leave the hospital the day after your operation.

What are the longterm effects?

The gap between the metatarsal and phalanx bone is bridged by the formation of a new, mobile joint. The results of the Keller arthroplasty are generally excellent. You should avoid wearing the kind of footwear that might lead to a recurrence of the problem.

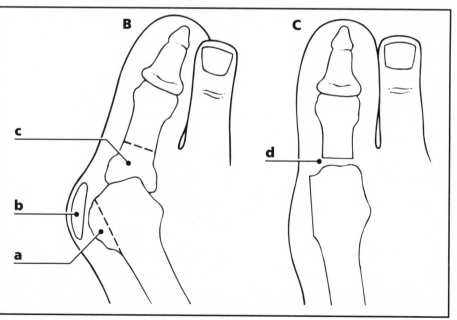

© DIAGRAM

Surgery to treat varicose veins in the leg

Why have the operation?

Varicose veins occur in approximately fifteen percent of all adults but especially in women. They can be treated in a variety of ways including:

- wearing elastic support stockings, taking regular exercise, avoiding standing still for long periods of time, and sitting with the feet raised off the floor
- sclerotherapy—injecting an irritant solution into the varicose vein to cause blockage of the vein so that the blood has to find an alternative (and nonvaricose), deeper channel instead
- surgery—performed for varicose veins that cause pain (and possibly embarrassment) in spite of the above treatment, and when they are in the process of ulcerating through the skin, causing bleeding. The operation itself, which uses a technique known as "stripping," takes roughly one half hour.

What is the physical cause of the problem?

Veins are thin-walled and collapse easily. Blood returning to the heart from the legs has to fight gravity and is barely helped by the force of the heart. The movement of blood in the main leg veins is aided by compression from contracting muscles through which they run and by a

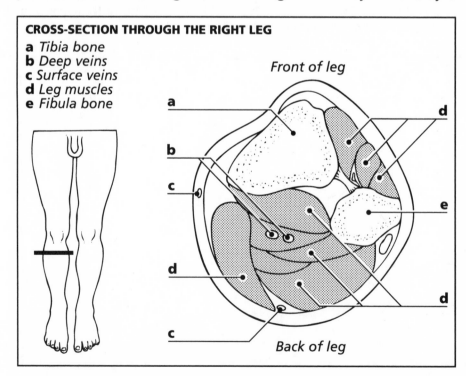

CROSS-SECTION THROUGH THE RIGHT LEG

a *Tibia bone*
b *Deep veins*
c *Surface veins*
d *Leg muscles*
e *Fibula bone*

Front of leg

a
d
b
c
e
d
d
c

Back of leg

series of one-way valves that prevent the backflow of blood. Much of the vein pumping is done by the contraction of the calf muscles during walking.

Veins on the outside surface of the leg have a lower blood pressure than those located within leg muscles and are not aided by the pumping action that these muscles provide. Instead, they must rely more on their one-way valves. Valve damage is a common feature of severe varicose veins, and the blood flow results in outward pressure on the vein walls, causing them to bulge, widen, extend, and twist.

Alternatively, if valve damage occurs in the short connecting vessels (perforating veins) that connect the deeper leg veins and the surface veins, the higher blood pressure in the deeper veins is transmitted to the surface veins and may then cause valve damage in those, too.

Varicosity leads to stagnation of the blood flow and a poor supply of oxygen, glucose, and other nutrients to the surrounding tissues, causing brown-blue discoloration of the skin at the site and a tendency to ulceration after minor knocks and abrasions.

Varicose veins may be caused by:
- obesity
- pregnancy
- prolonged daily standing
- vein constriction from underwear that is too tight
- insufficient exercise

The tendency to develop varicose veins may also be inherited.

COMPARISON BETWEEN A NORMAL VEIN AND A VARICOSE VEIN

*These illustrations show cross-sections of valves in a normal vein (**A**) and a varicose vein (**B**). In a normal vein, blood is prevented from flowing back the way it came when the valve closes. In a varicose vein, however, the weak valves allow blood to flow in both directions.*

A   **B**

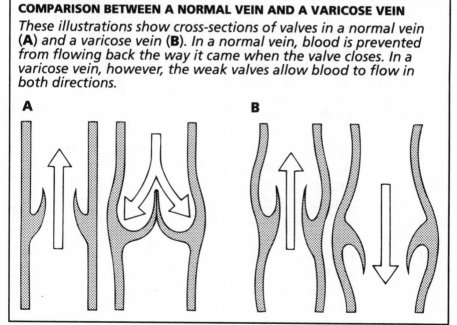

© DIAGRAM

What is the goal of surgery?

The surgeon's aim is to remove (strip out) the main surface veins (the great and small saphenous veins) that have been affected. The blood flow through the leg should then naturally be taken over by healthy deeper veins.

Exactly what is involved in the surgical operation?

Before surgery, the surgeon will make sure any ulceration at the site has healed. This is usually achieved over a period using compression bandaging and elevation of the leg. You may be asked to shower thoroughly, using a hexachlorophene soap. Your groin may be shaved, as may your leg. The veins to be treated will be marked on the leg skin surface with indelible ink.

Preliminary steps. The operation is performed under general anesthesia (which will cause you to sleep through the procedure) or spinal anesthesia (during which you may be conscious but unable to feel anything from the abdomen down). Prior to general anesthesia, you will be given a preoperative injection about an hour before surgery to dry up internal fluids and to encourage drowsiness; you may or may not receive a similar preoperative injection before spinal anesthesia. On the operating table you will be positioned so that the full length of the leg for treatment is available to the surgeon, who will swab the entire leg with antiseptic solution.

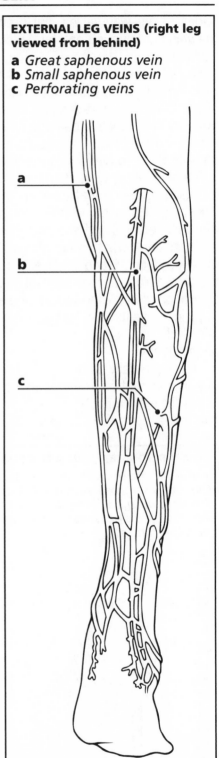

EXTERNAL LEG VEINS (right leg viewed from behind)

a *Great saphenous vein*
b *Small saphenous vein*
c *Perforating veins*

Step-by-step surgical procedure. The main surface vein of the leg, the great saphenous vein, runs from the ankle to the groin along the inner side of the leg. The surgeon makes the first incision high in the groin, about 2 inches long, exposing the upper end of the vein at its junction with the main vein of the groin, the large femoral vein.

The top of the saphenous vein is clamped with two almost adjacent clamps and is severed between the clamps, and the femoral vein end is tied off with a silk ligature; the saphenous vein end remains merely clamped. Four or more large vein branches enter the saphenous vein just below the femoral vein: all these must also be severed and tied off.

The surgeon now turns to the lower end of the vein, at the ankle, and makes a short incision just in front of the bony prominence of the ankle, exposing the saphenous vein there. Again, vein branches that join locally are severed and tied off. A short incision is made in the vein itself. An instrument called a vein stripper is now used. This is a long,

THE INCISIONS (left leg)

*An incision is made first at the thigh, to expose the femoral vein (**a**) and great saphenous vein (**b**). During the operation a second incision is made at the ankle.*

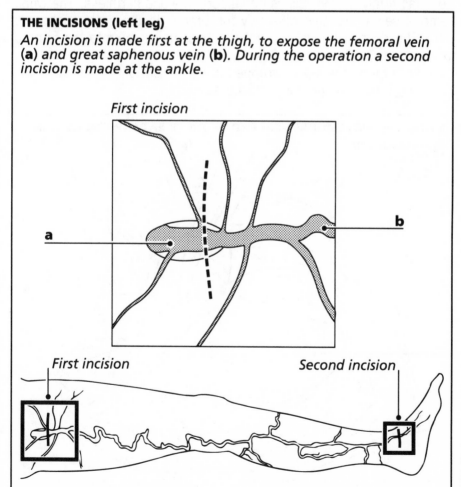

First incision

a

b

First incision

Second incision

© DIAGRAM

flexible cable with a smooth but narrow swelling at one end and a larger, metal, conical knob at the other. The surgeon slips the narrow end into the vein at the ankle and pushes the cable on through and up the vein to the groin, until it strikes the clamp there. Returning to the groin end, the surgeon removes the clamp, takes a firm grasp of the cable that then protrudes, and pulls it slowly but firmly out of the incision. As the conical knob passes through the length of the leg, it brings with it the telescoped thin-walled vein, completely concertinaed, up and out of the wound. Any blood left in the channel now departed by the vein can be compressed out. The corresponding small saphenous vein can be dealt with in like manner, if necessary.

Some surgeons use the vein stripper in the reverse direction, pulling it through from the ankle.

The skin incisions are then closed with a few stitches. The silk ligature remains in place within the tissues until long after the cut end of the vein has firmly healed. Silk is nonabsorbable and harmless. The whole femoral vein is not tied off—only the branch to the great saphenous vein. The deep leg veins are not touched; these run into the femoral vein.

After surgery, the leg is wrapped in elastic cotton gauze and firmly strapped with a compression elastic bandage.

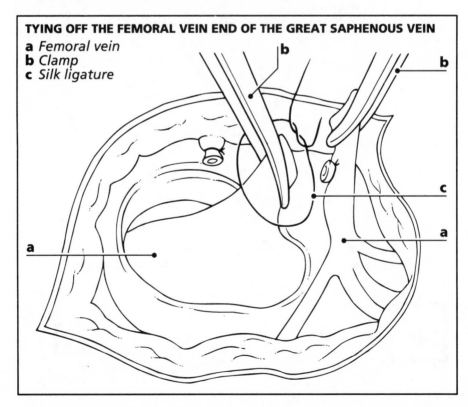

TYING OFF THE FEMORAL VEIN END OF THE GREAT SAPHENOUS VEIN

a *Femoral vein*
b *Clamp*
c *Silk ligature*

What is it like immediately after the operation?

When you recover from the anesthetic you will find that your feet have been elevated 10 to 15 degrees. If you had spinal anesthesia you may suffer from a postoperative headache. You will be encouraged to start walking as soon as you can, but will be instructed to avoid prolonged standing and to keep your legs raised when sitting. There may be some pain through the whole length of the leg, but it should not last long and can in the meantime be treated with painkilling drugs. Your leg will at first appear considerably bruised and discolored. The surgery dressings are replaced after two days with tight elastic stockings that should then be worn all day long for two or three weeks, until the appearance of your leg has returned to normal.

What are the longterm effects?

The results of this operation are usually excellent. If all the varicosities have been removed, the condition may be considered cured. This does not preclude the need for future attention to diet and exercise, however, since obesity and lack of exercise may have been contributing factors causing the varicose veins.

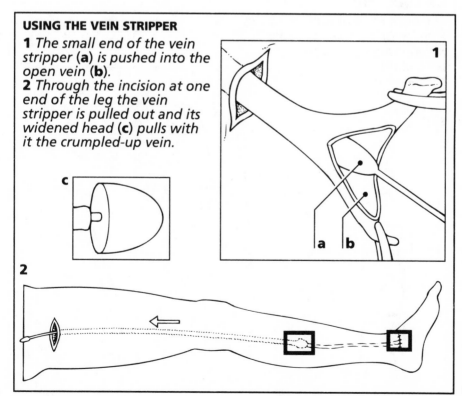

USING THE VEIN STRIPPER

1 *The small end of the vein stripper (**a**) is pushed into the open vein (**b**).*
2 *Through the incision at one end of the leg the vein stripper is pulled out and its widened head (**c**) pulls with it the crumpled-up vein.*

© DIAGRAM

Meniscectomy: surgery for knee cartilage damage

Why have the operation?

A torn and displaced knee cartilage is painful and may cause the knee to lock when the leg is fully extended (preventing the knee from bending) or to buckle and give way suddenly, causing the patient to fall over.

The condition occurs particularly in active individuals (such as athletes) for whom a quick recovery may be essential. A minor tear in the cartilage can take weeks to heal of its own accord, during which time the patient must rest. A major tear or full displacement of the cartilage will not heal by itself and requires surgery.

What is the physical cause of the problem?

The cartilages are attached to (and serve as the connecting material between) the femur (the bone above the knee) and the tibia and fibula (the bones below the knee). If the bones are violently pushed or twisted apart from one another, one of the two crescent-shaped disks of cartilage (the menisci) that support and promote smooth movement at the knee can be stretched until it tears. A sudden blow on the knee from the

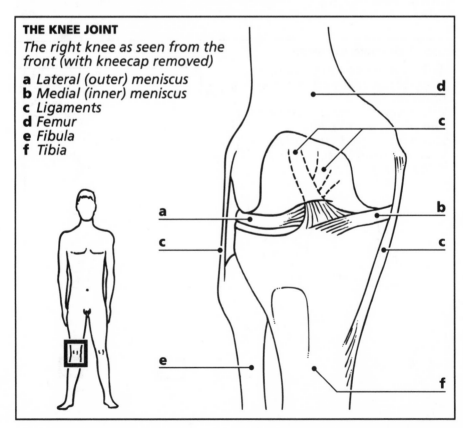

THE KNEE JOINT

The right knee as seen from the front (with kneecap removed)

a *Lateral (outer) meniscus*
b *Medial (inner) meniscus*
c *Ligaments*
d *Femur*
e *Fibula*
f *Tibia*

side can tear the medial meniscus (the cartilage on the inner side of the knee joint) and the medial ligament. An abrupt turn of upper leg can cause a tear if the lower leg is restricted from also turning by an immovably planted foot. The medial meniscus is the one much more commonly torn or detached.

What is the goal of surgery?

The surgeon's aim is to restore full, painless function to the knee. A minor tear may be treated by the removal of fragments of cartilaginous material. A major tear, or the complete detachment of the meniscus, most commonly requires the surgical removal of the meniscus.

Surgery alone will not restore full, painless knee function or cure the

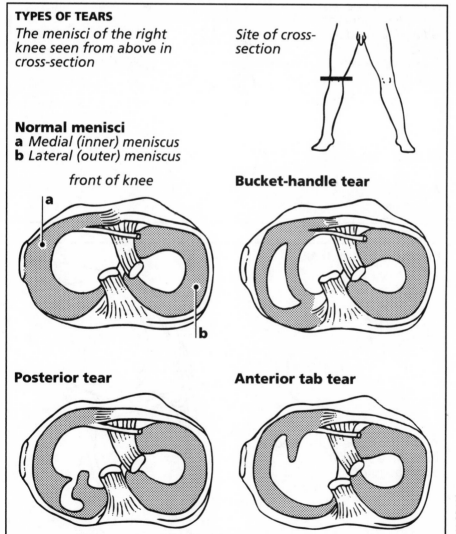

TYPES OF TEARS

The menisci of the right knee seen from above in cross-section

Site of cross-section

Normal menisci
a *Medial (inner) meniscus*
b *Lateral (outer) meniscus*

front of knee

Bucket-handle tear

Posterior tear

Anterior tab tear

© DIAGRAM

propensity of the knee to lock, a tendency that may continue unless the meniscus is completely removed. A period of physical therapy and rehabilitative exercise will also be needed.

Exactly what is involved in the surgical operation?

Before surgery, you will undergo a full clinical examination including arthroscopy: the use of a fine fiberoptic viewing instrument passed

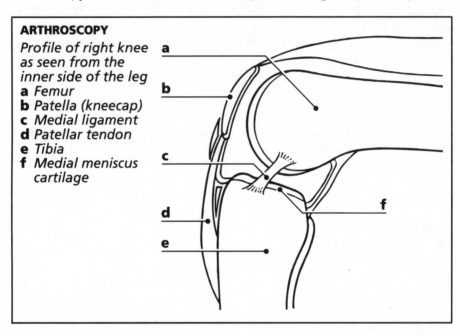

ARTHROSCOPY

Profile of right knee as seen from the inner side of the leg
a *Femur*
b *Patella (kneecap)*
c *Medial ligament*
d *Patellar tendon*
e *Tibia*
f *Medial meniscus cartilage*

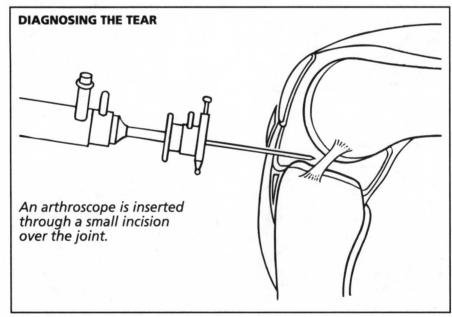

DIAGNOSING THE TEAR

An arthroscope is inserted through a small incision over the joint.

through the skin and into the joint under local anesthesia to view the knee's interior. Arthroscopy permits the site of the tear in the cartilage to be established and an exact diagnosis to be made. Increasingly, surgeons are repairing a damaged meniscus using instruments attached to the arthroscope. Total removal of a meniscus (meniscectomy), however, is more commonly performed by conventional surgical methods, including general anesthesia. This is the procedure described here.

Preliminary steps. Some time before the operation, your knee will be thoroughly washed with antiseptic soap. As with any operation involving general anesthesia, you will be given a preoperative injection about an hour before surgery to dry up internal fluids and to encourage drowsiness.

Step-by-step surgical procedure. Once you are anesthetized, you will be positioned on the operating table lying on your back. The blood supply to the affected leg is reduced by compression, using a flat rubber bandage (an Esmarch bandage) wrapped tightly around the leg all the way up from toes to thigh. A pneumatic tourniquet is then applied at the top of the leg to prevent further blood from entering. No harm results from this procedure, which lasts for only a strictly limited duration and greatly facilitates surgery. With the thigh supported on a sandbag, the knee is again thoroughly cleansed with antiseptic solution and surrounded with sterile towels. Many surgeons choose to operate with one end of the operating table removed and the patient's foot in their lap, the bent knee positioned directly in front of them. The first incision is made at the side of the knee, usually the inner side, about 2 inches down from the border of the kneecap.

Immediately under the skin lies the fibrous capsule that surrounds the bony inner edges of the joint; it is lined by a membranous lubricant

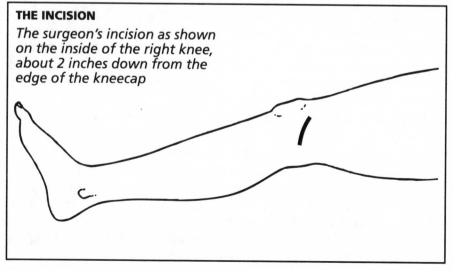

THE INCISION

The surgeon's incision as shown on the inside of the right knee, about 2 inches down from the edge of the kneecap

© DIAGRAM

CUTTING THE TORN MENISCUS
*The right knee as viewed from
above in cross-section*
a *Scalpel*
b *Surgeon's hook*

c *Torn meniscus*
d *Posterior meniscus horn*
e *Ligamentous attachments*
f *Anterior meniscus horn*

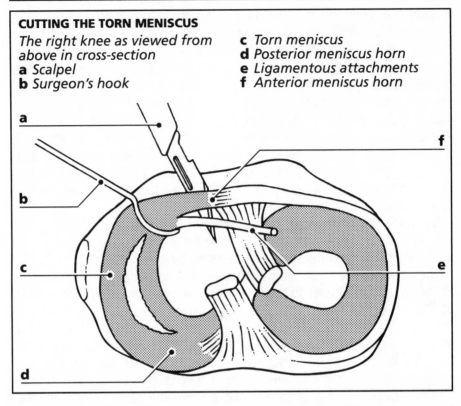

layer, the synovium. The surgeon cuts through both of these layers and inspects the workings of the joint through the narrow gap. Visibility can be increased by bending and extending the knee, by stretching the incision, and by retracting the inner of the two ligaments within the knee joint. It is even possible to examine the back of the kneecap at the same time.

The surgeon slips a hook over the nearer (anterior) horn of the crescent-shaped meniscus and carefully cuts the meniscus free from its retaining ligamentous attachments, using a fine scalpel passed through into the joint. The cartilage can now be grasped more firmly, in toothed forceps. It is put under tension, and the remaining ligamentous attachment to the bone is cut away at the edge.

The ligamentous attachment to the rear (posterior) horn must now be severed. This is the most problematical part of the procedure, for the horn is reached only with great difficulty, and there are other important ligaments in and around the joint that must not be injured. The knee may have to be manipulated with some vigor in order to attain adequate exposure. The surgeon may sever the final horn by holding the scalpel still and drawing the cartilage over its blade with the forceps: this ensures that the incision is made accurately. A selection of scalpels curved at different radiuses is available for this task.

Once the meniscus is free, it can be removed from the wound. The surgeon checks to make sure that no fragments of damaged meniscus remain, and then separately stitches up each of the three covering layers—synovium, capsule, and skin. A firm crepe bandage is applied: some surgeons also apply a plaster cast to act as a temporary splint. Finally, the tourniquet is removed.

What is it like immediately after the operation?

Bed rest, keeping the knee still, is usual for at least the first 36 hours after surgery. There should be little or no pain. After this, mobility is encouraged, although you must be careful how you put weight on the knee. You will be encouraged to exercise in order to maintain muscle tone in the quadriceps muscles of your thighs: the muscles there become weak very quickly if not used, and strong thigh muscles are necessary to help stabilize the knee. In the four or five days of hospitalization following the operation, you will probably receive counseling and instruction on techniques of exercising these muscles. You may also be expected to undergo physical therapy as an outpatient for some weeks after leaving the hospital.

If you have been given a plaster splint, it will be removed after about seven days.

What are the longterm effects?

You should take it easy and not expect to undertake strenuous activity for at least four weeks after surgery. Then, provided you have benefited from the exercises to strengthen your thigh muscles, the longterm prospects are excellent. The absence of a meniscus cartilage seldom causes any further problems.

Athletes should resume previous physical activities gradually under the advice of their surgeons. In many cases it will be possible for them to return eventually to their standard of performance prior to the surgery.

In a very few cases, however, the joint may later become subject to osteoarthritis.

Surgery for hand contracture

Why have the operation?

No one with Dupuytren's contracture will be in any doubt about the answer to this question. The hooklike deformity, in which the ring finger (and often adjacent fingers) are permanently drawn into the palm of the hand, interferes with a variety of activities requiring finger mobility. The condition, which usually occurs on one hand only, is not only disabling but also unsightly and often causes embarrassment.

What is the physical cause of the problem?

No one really knows for certain what causes this strange condition, first described by Baron Guillaume Dupuytren in 1832. Initially it was thought to be due to repeated occupational trauma to the hands in manual workers, but this idea has now been disproved. Dupuytren's contracture affects men twice as often as women and occurs mainly in people of European origin. The condition is rare in young people but becomes

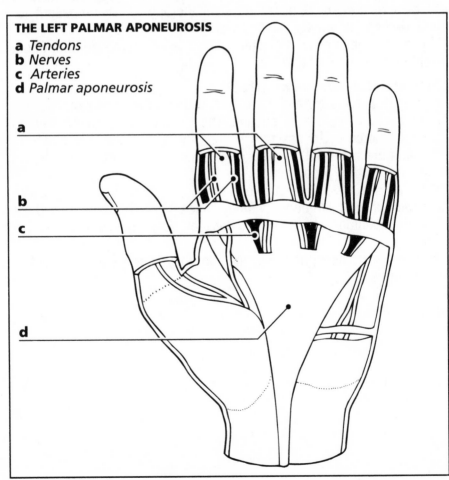

THE LEFT PALMAR APONEUROSIS

a *Tendons*
b *Nerves*
c *Arteries*
d *Palmar aponeurosis*

a

b

c

d

increasingly common with age. When it affects the young it is usually rapidly progressive and very severe.

It seems likely that there is a genetic basis for the problem, but other factors also appear to be important. It is common in people with longterm chest diseases such as tuberculosis. People with epilepsy often have Dupuytren's contracture, as do chronic alcoholics, especially those with cirrhosis of the liver.

Lying just under the palm is a triangular structure of fibrous tissue called the palmar aponeurosis. It covers the tendons of the palm of the hand, holding them in place and preventing them from bending away from the palm when the fingers are bent against resistance. Dupuytren's contracture results from the thickening and shortening of part or all of this aponeurosis. The condition first shows itself as a thick nodule or a short cord on the palm, just below the base of the ring finger. Fibrous tissue (similar to that of the aponeurosis) forms between the aponeurosis and the skin—which then becomes puckered. This fibrous tissue slowly extends and tightens until eventually the ring finger cannot be fully straightened. As the condition progresses it is common for the little finger also to become involved. Dupuytren's contracture is usually confined to these two fingers, but is occasionally more widespread. In severe cases neglected for years, the contraction spreads to involve the capsules of the finger joints, which become permanently immobilized. In such cases, contraction is irreversible and treatment may necessitate amputation of a finger.

What is the goal of surgery?
The aim of surgery is to sever the fibrous attachments between the aponeurosis and other tissues, and so release the contraction. Finger movement should then be permanently restored to normal.

If the problem is confined to a single finger, and the contracted band is well localized, it is sometimes possible to free the finger by simply severing the band under the skin. But if the aponeurosis is more widely affected, and especially if more than one finger is bent, the surgeon may decide to remove the whole of the aponeurosis.

Exactly what is involved in the surgical procedure?
Before the operation, the surgeon may ensure that the skin of your palm is healthy and free from infection: careful and repeated cleansing of the skin with antiseptic solutions may be supervised by the hospital staff.

The operation can be performed under a general anesthetic or a local anesthetic nerve block administered by injection in the armpit. In the latter case you will probably remain conscious throughout the operation, although you may not actually be able to watch the procedure.

© DIAGRAM

Preliminary steps. If you are to have a general anesthetic, you will be given a preoperative injection about an hour before surgery to dry up internal fluids and to encourage drowsiness. You may or may not receive a preoperative injection if you are to have a local anesthetic for this operation.

Step-by-step surgical procedure. Once you have been anesthetized, you will be placed on the operating table lying on your back, with your affected hand and arm stretched out on a separate board. The whole of your hand and forearm is first thoroughly swabbed with an antiseptic solution. All but the palm is then wrapped in sterile operating towels secured with clips; only the palm is left exposed.

The location of the surgeon's initial incision depends on the proposed extent of the surgery, and differs from case to case and from surgeon to surgeon. But incisions are almost always made following the natural

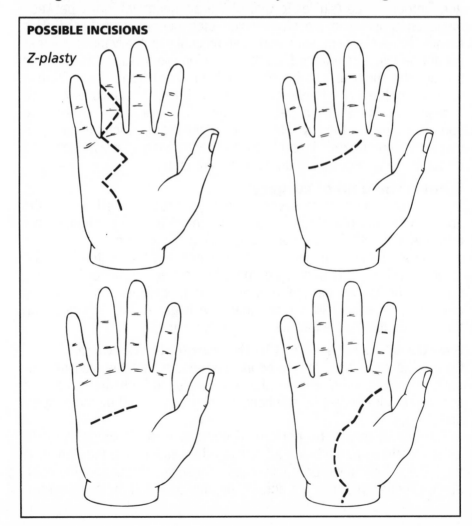

POSSIBLE INCISIONS

Z-plasty

creases of the palm. Many surgeons make zigzag incisions that can be sewn up afterward in such a way as to relieve skin tension (a technique known as Z-plasty).

Once the fibrous sheet that is the palmar aponeurosis has been exposed, the surgeon removes enough of it to allow full straightening of the fingers. The surgeon achieves this by careful dissection, using toothed forceps and a fine-pointed scalpel. A major concern is to avoid damage to the nerves of the fingers and to the arteries of the palm and fingers, all of which lie in close proximity to the aponeurosis. Damage to the blood supply could result in the need to amputate a finger. When the surgeon has removed the fibrous tissues, the skin incision is closed with fine stitches.

Occasionally, the surface skin has contracted so much that it cannot be stretched to cover the increased area of the palm of the now fully opened hand; in such cases a skin graft is required.

What is it like immediately after the operation?
The hand has a complex network of blood vessels and nerves, and is one of the most sensitive areas of the body. Moderate discomfort following hand surgery is inevitable. Severe pain can be controlled with painkilling drugs, although any such treatment should be only briefly necessary. To begin with, your hand will be bandaged with a splint to keep it straight and open, which will make it mostly unusable. From the start there will be a program of physical therapy to retain and increase the overall freedom of movement in the hand imparted by the operation. Inauguration of this program may delay your departure from the hospital for a few days, although if it is more convenient you may instead be required to attend as an outpatient on a daily basis for a time. Maintaining physical therapy will be crucial to the continued mobility of the hand.

What are the longterm effects?
Removal of the entire palmar aponeurosis usually gives an excellent result, in relation to the original severe condition: the cure is generally permanent, although full manual mobility depends on the success of extensive physical therapy. Removing the entire aponeurosis causes little ill effect, although the flexor tendons of the middle fingers may bow forwards.

Physical therapy is needed to prevent the formation of adhesions that might restrict full opening and closing of the hand. The palmar aponeurosis is not essential to normal functioning. Its loss may cause some minor disadvantages, but these are much less disabling than the effects of a severe Dupuytren's contracture.

Surgery for carpal tunnel syndrome

Why have the operation?

Two major nerves pass from the forearm into the hand—the large median nerve and the smaller ulnar nerve. Both cross the front of the wrist, the median nerve centrally and the ulnar nerve to the little finger side, within a passage known as the carpal tunnel. Many tendons passing to the fingers from the forearm muscles also pass across the front of the wrist in the carpal tunnel. To prevent these from bowing forward when the wrist and fingers are bent, there is a strong tendinous strap across the front of the wrist. This is called the transverse carpal ligament, or flexor retinaculum. The median nerve controls sensation and

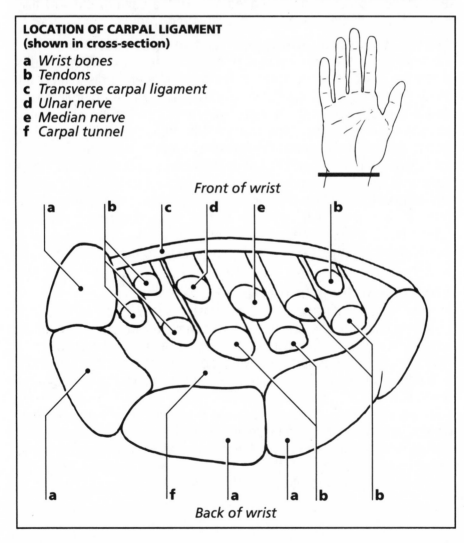

LOCATION OF CARPAL LIGAMENT
(shown in cross-section)

a *Wrist bones*
b *Tendons*
c *Transverse carpal ligament*
d *Ulnar nerve*
e *Median nerve*
f *Carpal tunnel*

Front of wrist

a   b   c   d   e   b

a   f   a   a   b   b

Back of wrist

movement in the fingers. There is little free space under the transverse carpal ligament and, should any swelling occur, the large median nerve can readily be compressed, causing carpal tunnel syndrome. The syndrome can sometimes be effectively treated by keeping the wrist in a splint, especially at night, and by injecting a mixture of local anesthetic and corticosteroid into the area but away from the nerves. A drug that increases the output of urine (a diuretic) and so reduces water retention can also be helpful. These measures are effective in relieving the symptoms in about 40 percent of cases of mild compression. Surgery is necessary if compression of the nerve leads to signs of wasting in the muscles activated by the median nerve. Obvious wasting is a sign of an advanced stage of compression of the nerve. Carpal tunnel syndrome can occur in one or both hands.

What is the physical cause of the problem?
Carpal tunnel syndrome mostly affects women between 40 and 60, but may occur as a result of fluid retention during pregnancy, in the course of rapid weight gain, or as a complication of thyroid underactivity (myxedema). Sometimes the condition is brought on, or made worse, by tight watchbands or rubber gloves. Any movement of the wrist that is repeated many times in a short period is liable to bring on this syndrome, as can repeatedly striking an object with the heel of the hand. Occasionally increased tension under the transverse carpal ligament can be caused by a benign tumor of the sheath of the nerve or of the nerve itself. The syndrome may also occur if dislocation of one of the wrist bones, in the course of an injury, leads to direct pressure on the nerve.

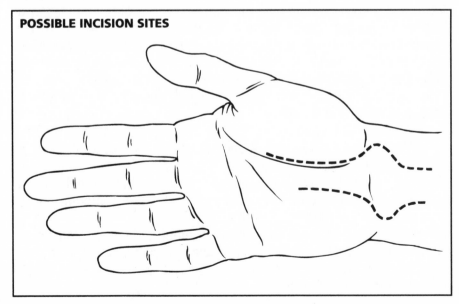

POSSIBLE INCISION SITES

© DIAGRAM

Even a minor degree of swelling under the transverse carpal ligament is sufficient to cause compression of the nerve. This leads to pain, tingling, and numbness in the thumb and the three adjacent fingers, loss of sensation, and wasting of some of the small muscles of the hand. The symptoms are often made worse by grasping with the fingers, especially while the wrist is bent or even when it is extended.

The diagnosis of carpal tunnel syndrome can be confirmed by finding loss of sensation to touch and pinprick in the thumb and adjacent fingers. Various electrical tests of nerve conduction can also show a reduction in the nerve function. Tapping with a finger on the center of the wrist near the palm of the hand can cause tingling in the fingers.

What is the goal of surgery?

Surgery is performed to relieve the pressure on the median nerve so that normal nerve conduction may, once again, occur. In this event, the muscles activated by the nerve may, hopefully, recover their function and normal sensation should be restored to the fingers and thumb.

Exactly what is involved in the surgical procedure?

The surgical procedure involves cutting through the transverse carpal ligament so as to remove the tunnel's roof and relieve the pressure.

Preliminary steps. The operation can be performed on an outpatient basis using local or general anesthesia. If general anesthesia is to be used, you will be given a preoperative injection about an hour before surgery to dry up internal fluids and to encourage drowsiness.

Step-by-step surgical procedure. Once you are anesthetized, the surgeon makes an incision about 2 inches long on the front of the wrist. Different surgeons may place the incision in slightly different places, but a common site is in line with the center of the ring finger at right angles to the crease nearest the palm and extending from this crease for a short distance into the palm. This incision avoids important branches of the median nerve. Alternatively, the incision may be made nearer the base of the thumb on the other side of the nerve.

The incision is held open with retractors, exposing the transverse carpal ligament, and a narrow, flat instrument can be passed into the canal so as to form a guard over the top of the nerve and avoid the danger of the nerve being injured. A fine scalpel, or the blade of a pair of scissors, is now passed under the ligament, which is carefully cut through to relieve the pressure. The surgeon inspects the median nerve to assess the severity of the compression. Severe compression will show as a definite constriction in the nerve.

The skin edges can now be brought together and the incision closed with fine separate stitches or with a single continuous stitch. Many surgeons will leave the stitched wound uncovered; some will apply a plastic spray or a sterile dressing.

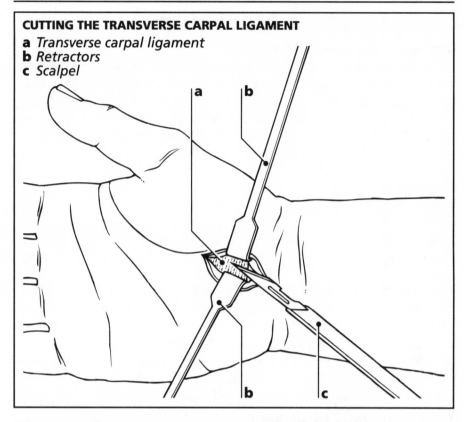

CUTTING THE TRANSVERSE CARPAL LIGAMENT
a *Transverse carpal ligament*
b *Retractors*
c *Scalpel*

What is it like immediately after the operation?

Immediately after the operation your wrist is likely to be somewhat uncomfortable, and there may be some pain, but discomfort should not persist for more than a day or two. You will be encouraged to move your hand and wrist as soon as possible.

If nonabsorbable nylon stitches were used to close the incision, they will be removed once the incision has healed; absorbable stitches are not removed.

What are the longterm effects?

Assuming that adequate decompression of the nerve has been achieved and that permanent damage has not been caused by unduly severe compression, the long-term results should be excellent. The likelihood of recurrence is very small. Persistent symptoms may imply damage from prolonged compression or persistent inflammation of nearby tendon sheaths affecting the nerve.

Bone fracture treatment

Why have the operation?

Some limb fractures can be readily realigned by a physician and then firmly immobilized to allow healing, but complicated fractures may require surgery if the limb is to recover fully in both strength and sensitivity, and some fractures need the surgical application of traction. Surgery thus forms an essential part of fracture therapies.

The most common causes of fractures are:

● automobile crashes
● sporting accidents
● falling from a height
● firearms wounds

Healthy bones require a major force to fracture; bones that are diseased break more easily. Diseases that predispose a bone to fracture include:

Osteoporosis, a condition prevalent among the elderly—and especially among postmenopausal women—in which the bone is weakened and thinned, possibly to such an extent that a mere stumble or trip over the edge of a sidewalk may be sufficient to cause a break.

Secondary cancer in the bones and bone cysts, which can weaken a bone to the point at which it fractures without any trauma at all. Fractures of this type are known as pathological fractures.

What is the goal of surgery?

The initial aim is to realign the ends of bone at the break so that they exactly reconstitute the original bone. This may be done by:

● external manipulation. The bone is pulled from the outer end. Anesthesia may be used.
● open surgery performed under general anesthesia. In complicated fractures, additional surgical techniques will also be required to repair damage to associated tissues surrounding the break.

The second aim of the physician or surgeon is to retain the realignment by immobilizing the limb through the use of:

● plaster casts
● splints
● external fixators, by which the bone fragments are secured to a strong external steel rod by means of steel pins
● traction (the gentle but continuous application of weight). Traction is commonly applied through attachments to a plaster cast, although some methods require additional minor surgery. Immobilization and traction are sustained until healing is complete. Depending on the fracture, this may take from six to twelve weeks, or, in the case of a delayed union, up to two or three years.

Categories of fracture

Fractures are grouped into three important classes according to how much damage has been sustained by the bone and the surrounding structures.

Closed (or simple) fractures

The skin remains intact and adjacent structures—such as arteries and nerves—remain unscathed. Such fractures may involve a relatively complex break in the bone, and may be difficult to manage, but if properly immobilized during healing they will heal well.

Open (or compound) fractures

A broken bone protrudes through the skin or touches a penetrating wound. Infection in the bone may result from contamination from the outside, which could lead to failure of healing and consequent disability.

Complicated fractures

Major surrounding structures are injured in addition to the break. Severe injury to the membrane covering the bone (the periosteum) or to adjacent arteries, veins, or nerves is common in connection with fractures caused by high-velocity force. Such additional injuries may be responsible for delayed union of the break, or even permanent nonunion.

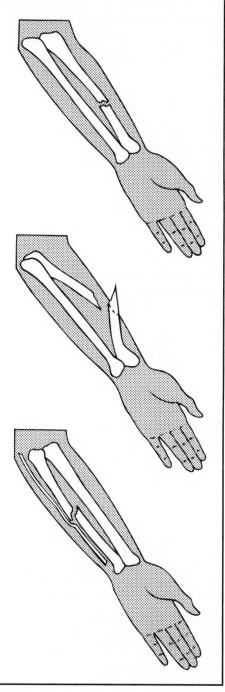

© DIAGRAM

Types of fracture

Fractures may also be categorized according to the way in which the bone has broken.

Type of break

Linear (or simple) fracture
A break with a single fracture line—not to be confused with closed (or simple) fractures

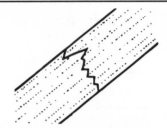

Spiral fracture
A break that spirals around the bone

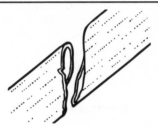

Comminuted fracture
The bone is smashed to pieces. Often there is severe soft-tissue injury.

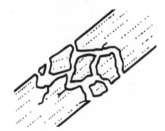

Transverse fracture
A break straight across the width of the bone

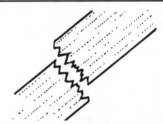

Greenstick fracture
A break on one side of the bone (the convex side) that does not extend to the other side (the concave side). Limited almost entirely to children and adolescents whose bones contain less calcium than adults' bones.

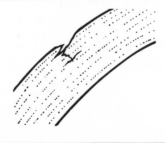

Cause	Outlook for fracture repair
Caused by direct or indirect forces that cause the bone to bend beyond its elastic limit.	*Heals quickly after appropriate immobilization.*
Caused by rotational or torque force, such as may occur during sport (skiing in particular) when the foot is held solidly and the leg is twisted.	*Once a closed spiral fracture is correctly realigned (reduced), healing is generally rapid and uncomplicated.*
Usually caused by a direct blow or a crushing force.	*Closed comminuted fractures can often be realigned by simple external manipulation, and then immobilized for healing. Alignment may occasionally require sustained traction to keep fragments from impacting or overriding each other.*
May be caused by a heavy fall across a narrow ledge.	*Recovery depends on whether the fracture is closed (simple) or open (compound).*
Softness of the bone together with the strength of the surrounding membrane (periosteum) may lead to the kind of break described, causing a bend in the bone (angulation) at the fracture site, but no other displacement.	*The outlook in greenstick fractures is better than in any other type of fracture. Healing is rapid and usually complete in three or four weeks.*

© DIAGRAM

Exactly what is involved in the surgical operation?

The need for surgery depends on the location and nature of the fracture and the amount of surrounding tissue damage. Diagnosis must be as complete and rapid as possible because a patient with a fracture is in pain (unless unconscious) and liable to be in shock. X-ray photographs are taken so that if surgical skills are required, all the background information possible is available. Local anesthesia should relieve pain.

A general anesthetic can be administered once the full extent of the injury is known and a plan of action has been formulated.

1. Surgery to reduce a fracture

Confronted with a complicated open fracture, the surgeon's first decision is how to approach the wound in order to get inside and sort out the bits of bone that have been displaced while making the least disturbance possible. Once the surgeon has gotten inside, disrupted blood vessels may have to be tied off or cauterized, and any dirt or other contaminants cleaned away.

BONE GRAFT TECHNIQUES

A *A graft of spongy bone may be taken from the crest of the pelvis and used to pack the gap.*
B *Small chips of bone taken from a (dead) donor can be used to make up for lost bone if extra support is all that is required. Such chips can be surgically inserted as inlay grafts (**a**), sliding them into carefully prepared slots in the original bone ends, or as onlay grafts (**b**), attaching each end of a chip to a broken bone end with a pin.*
C *(not shown) In extreme cases of nonunion, bone grafts complete with an artery to provide a good blood supply can sometimes be used. This requires microsurgical techniques to connect the blood vessel.*

The wound is then closed and the limb immobilized. Inlay and onlay grafts do not, by themselves, provide sufficient structural strength to allow weight-bearing until at least some natural healing has occurred.

The final operation may involve:

- microsurgical repair of blood vessels and nerves. If required, the surgeon will operate with the aid of microscopic projection, using specially designed and ultrafine instruments and hairlike (but strong) sutures crimped into small, curved needles to bring together the ends of severed arteries and nerves in snug apposition. Incisions are closed afterward in the usual way, and healing is ordinarily excellent.
- bone graft. If examination of the fracture (with confirming X-ray photographs) shows that a quantity of bone has been lost as a result of the breakage—and especially if there is an actual gap between the broken bone ends—the surgeon may decide that a bone graft is essential to avoid greatly delayed healing.
- fixation. If a bone graft is not used, the bone will have to be fixed in place to stabilize it (see illustrations on pp.186–87).

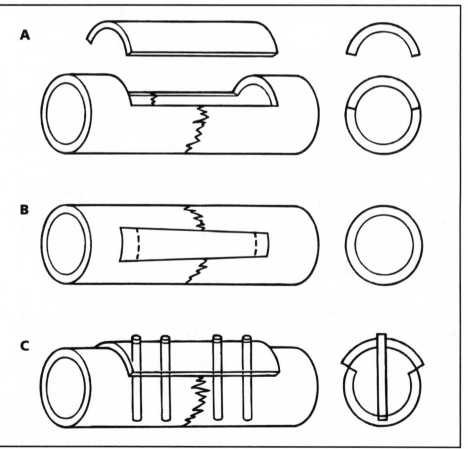

2. Fixation of a fracture

If bone grafting is not necessary, some method of stabilizing a fracture once reduced may be essential for proper healing in addition to the usual immobilization.

Internal fixation (using screws, pins, or plates temporarily or permanently attached to or in the bone). Internal fixation is usually avoided if there is any risk of infection, but it often allows early mobility. (It is the standard method of fixing a fracture of the neck of the femur, for instance.)

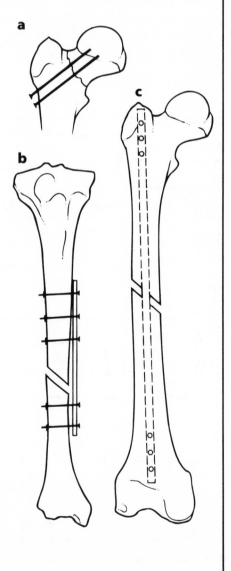

METHODS OF INTERNAL FIXATION

a *Using one or more screws inserted across the break*
b *A steel plate held by screws. To fit a plate, the bone is first drilled, and screws are inserted through the plate and right through to the other side of the bone to hold the plate on.*
c *A metal pin also affixed by screws. A long, fluted pin with holes in it is driven down the shaft of the bone from one end, and screws are passed through the bone and through a hole in the pin.*

   The skin incision is then closed in the usual way. One great advantage of internal fixation is that it is by no means always necessary or desirable to remove it once healing has been completed. A pin driven down the center of a bone is usually left permanently in position and seldom causes trouble. Pins, screws, and plates need to be removed only if they cause problems.

External fixation (using pins through the bone attached to a steel rod outside the limb). External fixation is used primarily to stabilize transverse fractures, and is becoming increasingly common. No other form of immobilization (such as a plaster cast) is required. Some external fixators allow a degree of compression at the fracture site; it has been suggested that this may contribute to more rapid healing. External fixation offers very secure immobilization and allows almost immediate mobility.

METHOD OF EXTERNAL FIXATION

To apply a fixator, the surgeon first selects a device made from noncorrosive steel, makes a long incision to expose the areas of bone where the pins will be inserted, drills the bone, and screws in the threaded pins, passing them through additional small incisions. The pins pass right through the bone. Alignment need not be perfect because the brackets that secure the squared-off top ends of the pins to the external longitudinal steel rod allow for some sideward adjustment. The skin incision is then closed. The length of time such external fixation devices are left in place varies from a few weeks to many months. Once the fracture is healed, all parts of the device are removed.

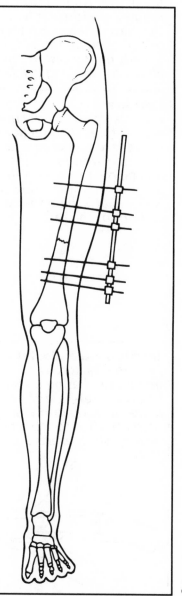

© DIAGRAM

**SIMPLE METHODS OF
IMMOBILIZING A FRACTURE**

Plaster cast
*Most common method of
immobilization, effective in
most cases*
1 *The arm is thoroughly
bandaged.*
2 *Wet plaster is applied over
the bandage. Once hardened,
the plaster is split into two,
roughly semicircular halves, and
the plaster halves are then
rebandaged on the outside.*
3 *Splitting the cast in this way
allows for swelling inside the*
*cast and for limited movement,
as when bending the arm.*

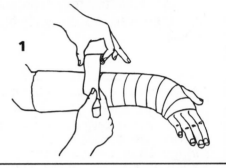

Cast brace
*Cast braces are mainly used for
leg fractures. Two sections of
plaster are prepared and
wrapped around the leg above
and below the knee. While the
plaster is still wet a flexible join
is fitted, attaching the two
sections of the cast.*

Traction via a plaster cast
*First, the fracture is
immobilized using a splint
(shown here)—a stiff support
made of wood or metal. This is
then attached to a traction
device, which exerts a pulling
force.*

*Traction of arm or leg fractures
usually lasts for only a few
weeks. After that there is some
danger that the joint will
stiffen, so a different method
of immobilization is applied.*

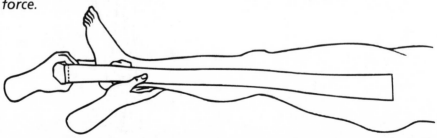

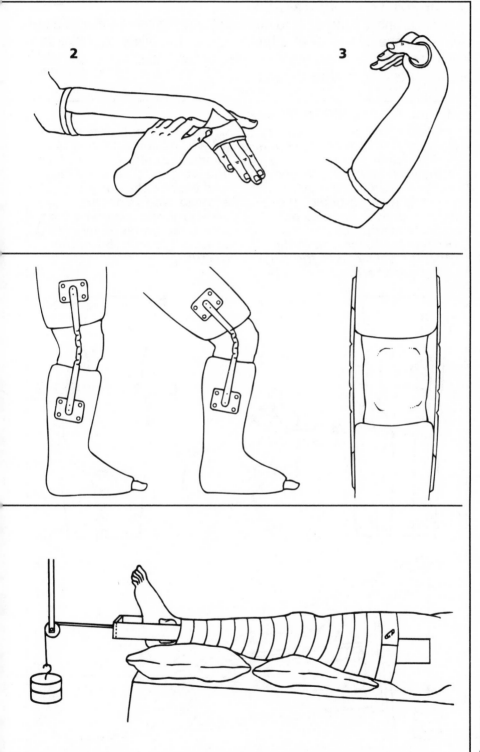

3. Surgery to apply traction

Traction is applied surgically to maintain the realignment either of a broken thighbone (femur) or of a broken spine. The minor operation is in each case ordinarily carried out under general anesthesia, and strict aseptic precautions are essential.

METHOD OF TRACTION TO THE LEG

*Traction is applied to the tibia (shinbone) in order to realign a broken femur (the large bone in the upper leg). The surgeon makes a small incision below the knee on each side of the leg and drills a threaded pin (called a Steinmann pin) through from one side to the other (**a**). Each end of the pin is then tightly secured, by a set-screw, in a strong steel stirrup (**b**) which allows traction to be applied by means of nylon cord and weights (**c**). Some rotation of the pin in the bone is allowed. No stitches are necessary, and traction alone by this method is generally sufficient to immobilize the fracture.*

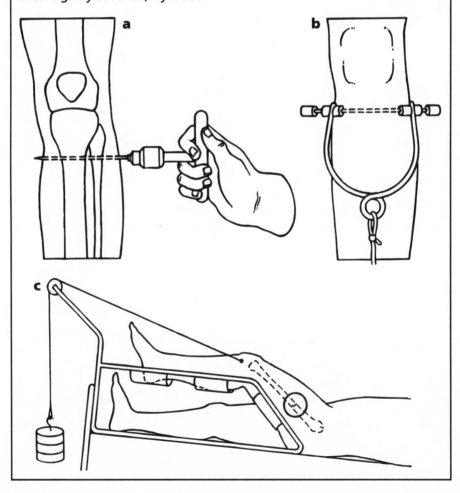

What is it like immediately after the operation?

You will soon discover that life, for a time at least, will be very different from what it was, especially if you are now in traction. With or without traction, there may at first be pain at the fracture site; this should dull to a constant ache that may or may not require painkilling drugs. The

---

METHOD OF TRACTION TO THE SKULL

Traction is applied to the skull in order to align the vertebrae of the spine.
***a** The surgeon makes three incisions in the top of the scalp to expose the bone.*
***b** Holes are then drilled in the skull to accommodate the points of a large pair of tongs (called Gardner-Wells tongs). Alternatively, a cranial halo made of steel can be attached*

to the skull using a ring of threaded pins.
***c** Tongs or halo are fixed to the head of the bed, and traction is applied by means of weights and cords attached to the waist or legs.*

A plaster cast is not usually necessary. Provided the spinal cord has not been injured, good recovery is to be expected.

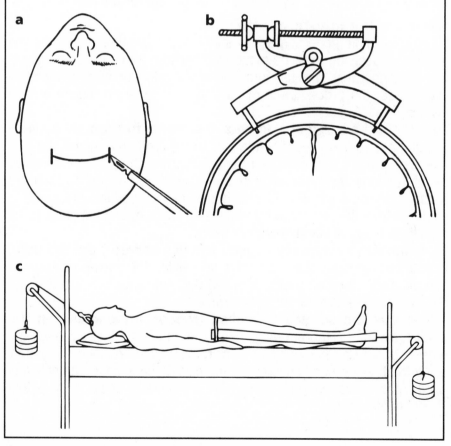

a

b

c

© DIAGRAM

injured limb is now immobilized, but you will nonetheless be expected to exercise it (despite the unaccustomed weight of the plaster cast) in order to maintain the strength and health of the limb muscles, which would begin to waste away without such activity. This is particularly true if the limb is in traction, and although care must be taken to avoid too much exertion, you will at a fairly early stage be put on a regimen of exercises designed to tense, maintain tension, then relax the muscles. Rapid rehabilitation after the fracture has healed is possible only if the muscles have been kept in good form.

How long you will have to stay in the hospital depends on factors such as the bone concerned, the presence of infection, the state of the blood and nerve supply, other injuries, your ability and willingness to exercise the muscles involved, and your age and state of health. Simple, uncomplicated fractures heal in up to six weeks. Most fractures heal within three months. Delayed union occurs when fractures do not heal within three months, and it leads to the formation of a kind of "false joint" of fibrous tissue. In the case of a fracture of the leg it is probable that even after you return home you will be advised to attend physical therapy sessions at the hospital as an outpatient for a time.

What are the longterm effects?

If you have undergone surgery to stabilize the fracture or to maintain traction, a decision must be made whether to remove the surgical elements temporarily inserted into the now healed or healing bone. In every case, the procedure is minor and may not even require a local anesthetic.

To remove the surgical elements of external fixation, the surgeon unbolts the brackets securing the pins to the rod and removes the rod. The healed fracture is checked for solidity, and the pins are screwed out of the bone using a spanner on their squared-off heads. This causes a dull, aching pain that lasts only during this procedure. Antiseptic is applied where the pins penetrated the skin surface, and the small holes are left to heal (no stitches are needed).

To remove the surgically applied traction stirrup from the tibia, the surgeon loosens the set-screws and slides the stirrup off the pin. The pin itself can then easily be pulled out. Antiseptic is applied where the pin ends penetrated the skin surface.

To remove the surgically applied traction attachments in the skull following vertebral realignment, the surgeon either releases the tension of the Gardner-Wells tongs or removes the cranial halo by loosening the brackets and unscrewing the pins. In each case, the only outward signs of traction that remain are a couple of scalp wounds that should heal quickly.

REMOVING A PLASTER CAST

a *Cutting through the plaster cast*

b *Separating the cut plaster cast for removal*

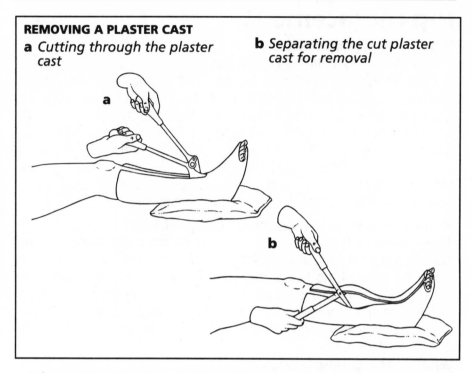

It is usually not necessary to remove internal fixation devices. Metal pins and plates inserted surgically are left permanently in position in most cases and cause very few ill effects. Internal fixators are only removed in the rare cases when they produce or encourage infection.

Recovery of limb fractures is usually excellent, although the duration of healing depends on your age and physical fitness, among other natural factors. Ideally, full mobility of the limb will be regained, although a fracture at a joint may become the site of intermittent rheumatic or arthritic pain.

Hip replacement

Why have the operation?

The hip joint is essential to normal mobility, and is accordingly subject to considerable stress in everyday life. Little wonder then that the joint is prone to arthritis and rheumatism—diseases that are associated with aging and that cause fierce pain and debilitating stiffness. Older people are additionally liable to fall heavily on the hip joint, the resultant fracture often snapping off the rounded head of the femur (the upper leg bone), the ball in the ball-and-socket joint of the hip at the pelvis. In later life fractures heal slowly, and sometimes badly, and hip replacement surgery is in these circumstances the ideal remedy.

What is the physical cause of the problem?

The problem is caused by deformity or deficiency in the bone that makes up the hip joint. In osteoarthritis, the thin layers of cartilage that cover the ends of the bones that form the joint become fissured and flake off, so that bone rubs on bone, causing roughening and inflammation with considerable pain. Osteoporosis, which occurs particularly in postmenopausal women, may weaken the bone and predispose the joint to fracture.

What is the goal of surgery?

The surgeon's aim is to remove the rounded head of the femur and replace it with a metal substitute, cemented firmly into the top end of the remaining femoral shaft and fitting comfortably into a corresponding metal or plastic cup-shaped socket surgically set within the pelvic bones. The result is almost always immediate restoration of normal and painless function of the hip.

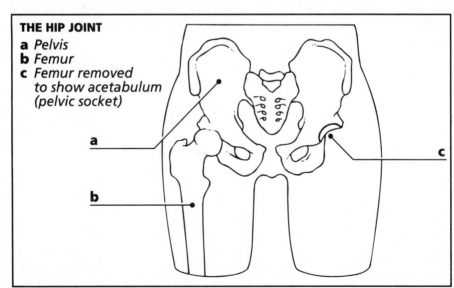

THE HIP JOINT

a *Pelvis*
b *Femur*
c *Femur removed*
   to show acetabulum
   (pelvic socket)

Exactly what is involved in the surgical operation?

The principal risk to the success of this operation is infection of the operation site. To help reduce this risk it is likely that you will be asked to come into the hospital a couple of days before the operation, to be put on a regimen of antibiotic drugs.

Preliminary steps. You will be encouraged to have a bath or shower as the time for surgery approaches. Afterward, the skin over and around the affected hip may be specially cleaned with antiseptic fluid. As with all operations involving general anesthesia, you will be given a preoperative injection about an hour before surgery to dry up internal fluids and to encourage drowsiness.

Step-by-step surgical procedure. Once you have been anesthetized, the surgeon will arrange your body so that the hip is optimally positioned for the line of approach. Operative technique varies from surgeon to surgeon, and the incision may be at the front, side, or back of the hip. Padded wedges wrapped in sterile towels may be used to tilt your body at the appropriate angle. More sterile towels are applied and fixed in place with clips until only the site of the surgeon's incision is left exposed. The site of the incision is again painted with antiseptic fluid.

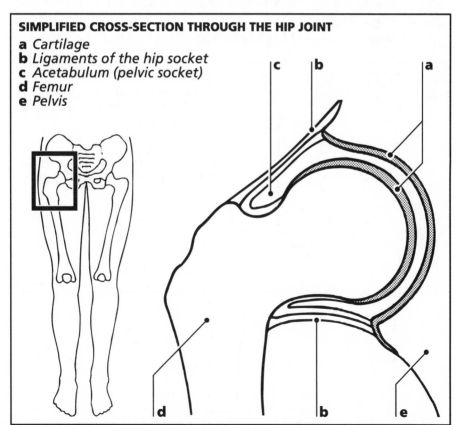

SIMPLIFIED CROSS-SECTION THROUGH THE HIP JOINT

a *Cartilage*
b *Ligaments of the hip socket*
c *Acetabulum (pelvic socket)*
d *Femur*
e *Pelvis*

© DIAGRAM

The surgeon makes an incision and exposes the pelvis and femur, which lie just under the skin. Bleeding points are secured or cauterized. The surgeon now separates the femur from its pelvic socket and removes the head of the femur with an oscillating power saw or a two-handled wire saw (a Gigli saw). The pelvic socket (the acetabulum) is hollowed out further, using an instrument known as a reamer, to clear it of cartilage and soft tissue in order to accommodate the prosthetic cup. The surgeon then drills several keying holes. These are holes drilled into the pelvis and then filled with liquid acrylic cement when the prosthetic cup is fitted in place. The solid cement "pegs" that form in the keying holes when the cement solidifies increase the area for adhesion and greatly strengthen the joint. The center of the top end of the femur is in turn reamed or filed to clear it of loose and spongy bone. The femoral part of the artificial joint is now pushed down the reamed shaft, and its ball is tried in the cup. Several of these femoral parts, of slightly variant sizes, may have to be compared until a satisfactory joint position is found. The one finally selected is cemented into the shaft of the bone, and is held still until the cement has set. The ball is fitted into the cup. Muscles and tendons temporarily moved or cut to keep them out of the way are put back or repaired, and the outer incision is then closed with stitches.

The operation may last from two to four hours or even longer.

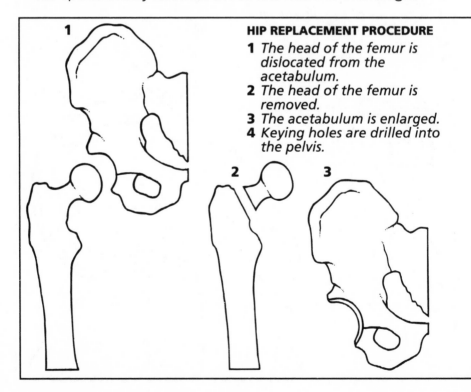

HIP REPLACEMENT PROCEDURE
1 *The head of the femur is dislocated from the acetabulum.*
2 *The head of the femur is removed.*
3 *The acetabulum is enlarged.*
4 *Keying holes are drilled into the pelvis.*

What is it like immediately after the operation?

How you feel after your operation depends on the skill of your anesthetist, on the amount of blood lost, and on the degree of difficulty experienced by the surgeon. Pain control may or may not be necessary. However, the joint remains unstable (liable to displacement) for a time after the operation. Some surgeons therefore arrange for their patients to lie with their feet well apart for a few days. Others are anxious to get their patients mobilized as soon as possible, and you may find yourself out of bed, walking with crutches or a walker learning new techniques to get in and out of the bath, all on the second day, and home within five to ten days. Early mobilization reduces some of the complications common to elderly patients, such as blood clots.

What are the longterm effects?

In general, the results of total hip joint replacement are excellent, and full, painless mobility is restored. Joints currently being inserted are expected to give at least 20 years of good service—the weak point perhaps being the cement by which both shaft and cup are affixed. If either part of the replacement does work itself loose, or if infection occurs, reoperation may be necessary.

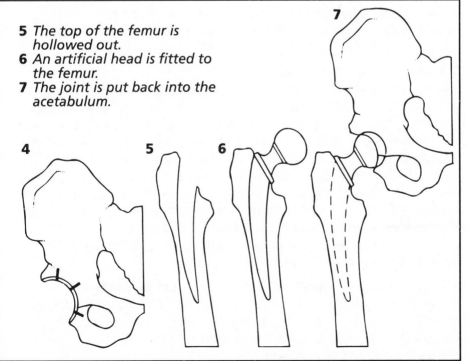

5 *The top of the femur is hollowed out.*
6 *An artificial head is fitted to the femur.*
7 *The joint is put back into the acetabulum.*

© DIAGRAM

Leg amputation

Why have the operation?

Limb amputation is normally performed only as a last resort to treat disease or injury when there is no safe or possible alternative. A limb that is useless is often also a danger to the continued health of the rest of the body.

What is the physical cause of the problem?

Main reasons for having to resort to limb amputation are:

- the death of tissue (gangrene) in the limb, caused by a loss of its blood supply—usually at the end of the limb farthest from the trunk—and resulting from the disease atherosclerosis (hardening of the arteries), prolonged exposure to cold, or as a complication of diabetes mellitus, by which blood clot formation has obstructed at least one major artery
- severe infection, either that is life-threatening by its presence in outer tissues or that is so persistent in the bone tissues (osteomyelitis) as to be uncontrollable with antibiotic drugs
- cancer, especially the type known as sarcoma of bone. Amputation may offer the only reasonable chance of saving the patient's life.
- severe deformity and malfunction. Such a condition may be present at birth (congenital), or due to artery or nerve damage, longterm infection, large bedsores (pressure sores), or extreme swelling through the obstruction of lymph vessels (lymphedema).
- severe injury, in which the tissues, arteries, and nerves in the limb are so damaged that there is no chance of saving the limb

What is the goal of surgery?

The surgeon's aim is to remove all diseased tissue and to fashion the stump so that an artificial limb (prosthesis) can be fitted to it. It is rarely necessary to remove an entire limb, and a length of limb left as a stump will allow the joint at the trunk to bend freely, assisting overall balance and movement. Ideally, the muscles that cross from the trunk to the limb, including their attachment to the bone, are preserved (so that they can continue to flex and extend the hip joint). The longer the stump, the greater the leverage that remains, the better the muscle control, and the more easily an artificial limb can be fitted and used.

A classic limb amputation involves surgery through the thigh: it is this operation that is described here.

Exactly what is involved in the surgical operation?

If infection is present, you will first undergo an intensive course of selected antibiotic drugs. Local infection of the skin at the proposed amputation site may delay the operation until the infection clears up, unless the delay itself is dangerous.

GUILLOTINE AMPUTATION

If the amputation is being performed on an emergency basis, the surgeon may make a simple surgical incision right around the leg and perform what is known as a "guillotine" amputation. In that case, a second operation will be required at a later time in order to produce a usable stump.

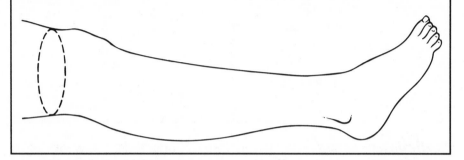

CROSS-SECTION THROUGH THE THIGH

a *Bone (femur)*
b *Muscles (shaded black)*
c *Sciatic nerve*
d *Skin and fat*
e *Femoral artery and vein*

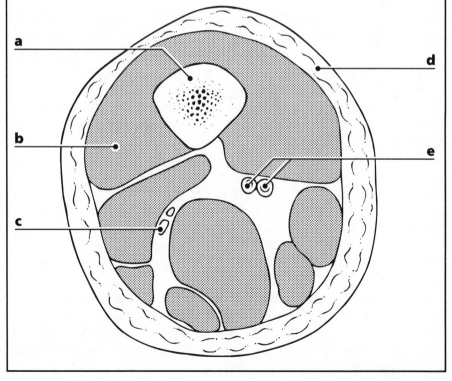

© DIAGRAM

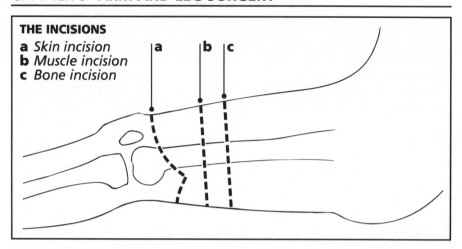

THE INCISIONS
a *Skin incision*
b *Muscle incision*
c *Bone incision*

Preliminary steps. The night before the operation, the whole leg is shaved (or treated with a depilatory) from the groin to below the knee. It is then scrubbed with an antiseptic soap. Amputation at the thigh is usually performed using an anesthetic injected into the cerebrospinal fluid surrounding the spinal cord toward the base of the spine (low spinal anesthesia), but many surgeons prefer to administer a general anesthetic in addition. In that case, you will be given a preoperative injection about an hour before surgery to dry up internal fluids and to encourage drowsiness.

Step-by-step surgical procedure. Once you are anesthetized, you will be positioned on the operating table on your back with the limb to be removed close to the table's edge. The surgeon might apply a tourniquet above the site of amputation: it considerably reduces bleeding but at the expense of making the major arteries less readily identifiable. The leg for amputation is now brought out at the side of the operating table, again thoroughly cleansed with antiseptic solution, and wrapped in sterile towels.

The surgeon creates two specially shaped flaps of skin and underlying soft tissues, the flap at the front larger than the flap at the rear so that when they are stitched together the line of stitching does not lie over the cut end of the bone. The skin and the soft tissues always retract by quite a margin, so the surgeon's incisions must be made at least 6 inches (15cm) below the point at which the bone is to be cut. Muscles below the soft tissues are cut through at a slightly higher level because they retract less.

The surgeon has to be careful in cutting the muscle in order to avoid damage to the main artery and vein in the thigh, the femoral vessels. When these are exposed, they are clamped, securely tied off with catgut, and then severed. New connections between the arteries and veins soon form to restore circulation to the limb.

The surgeon now identifies the main nerve of the leg, the sciatic nerve. It is pulled down as far as possible, crushed in clamps, tied off, and then severed and allowed to shorten again, retracting upward into the leg.

Retraction is particularly important for the nerve because if it were left at the end of the stump it might become the focus of a regenerat-

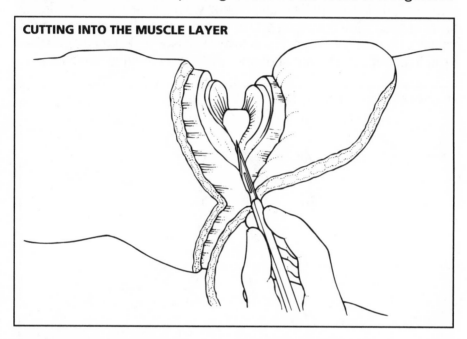

CUTTING INTO THE MUSCLE LAYER

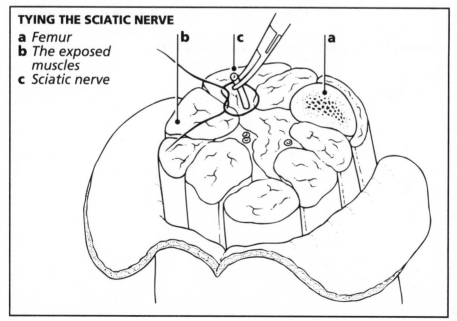

TYING THE SCIATIC NERVE
a Femur
b The exposed muscles
c Sciatic nerve

© DIAGRAM

ing mass of nerve tissue (a neuroma) that would make a prosthesis fitted over it very uncomfortable.

The thigh bone is now exposed, and the membrane surrounding it (the periosteum) is stripped off. The surgeon saws through the bone and rounds off the end with a rough steel rasp. The muscles are closed over the end of the bone and stitched together. Finally the surgeon sews the skin flaps together, and a fluffy wool and firm bandage dressing is applied. Some surgeons also at this time fit a temporary, rigid plaster cast over the dressings, within which is a socket for a "pylon"— a rod that can act as a leg support—which can be fitted almost imme-

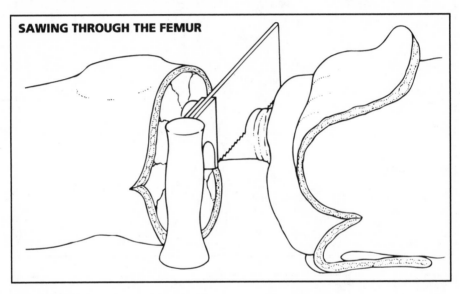

SAWING THROUGH THE FEMUR

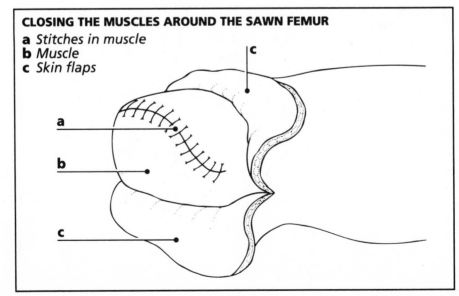

CLOSING THE MUSCLES AROUND THE SAWN FEMUR
a *Stitches in muscle*
b *Muscle*
c *Skin flaps*

CLOSING THE SKIN FLAPS
*The skin flaps are closed in such
a way that the join does not
fall across the muscle sutures.*

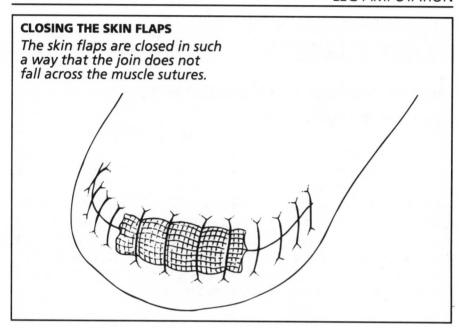

diately. The pylon is also temporary and is intended to help you begin walking as soon as possible.

What is it like immediately after the operation?
The spinal anesthetic may result in a temporary headache. Pain focused around the stump is usually moderate and can be controlled with painkilling drugs. If your stump has been fitted with a pylon, you will be encouraged to start walking (with elbow crutches to support you) within a day or so, and to walk without crutches as soon as possible. Exercise like this accelerates healing, reduces pain, and prevents muscle deformation. At first, firm cotton-elastic bandages are kept tightly in place and are renewed every four hours or so to encourage the stump to shrink down.

What are the longterm effects?
It may take six weeks for the stump to stabilize and for the skin incisions to fully heal, and a permanent prosthesis can be fitted only when the process is complete. You will inevitably suffer from the "phantom limb" phenomenon, by which you seem to feel sensations in the missing leg. The phenomenon usually disappears after a prosthesis has been worn for some time.

There is usually a planned program of training and rehabilitation. The longterm prospects for the mobility of a leg amputee depend much on the patient's age, health, and mental resilience, and on whether the use of the prosthesis causes pain.

CHAPTER 9
HEART SURGERY

Heart valve replacement

Why have the operation?

The operation is most commonly performed when disease in one or more of the four valves within the heart is causing symptoms that threaten life. By this stage it is usual for a patient already to have undergone surgical treatment for defects of the valves: less critical forms of valve disease can be remedied without physical replacement of the valves, and for many patients such therapy is all that is ever required. But in a proportion of cases, the valves finally become so badly damaged as to demand more than the simpler surgical procedures. Valve replacement has a high ratio of success and commonly results in a striking improvement in the condition of the patient.

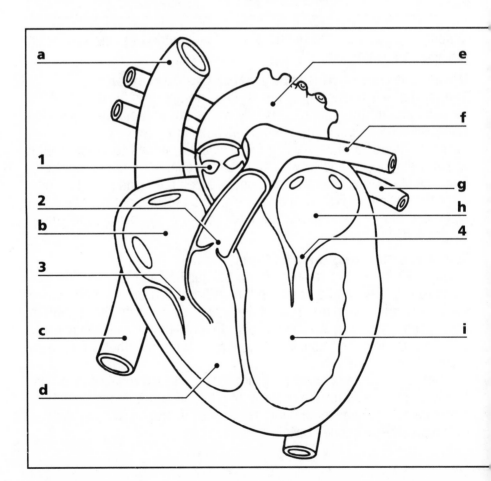

What is the physical cause of the problem?

Correctly functioning heart valves are essential in maintaining the steady, efficient blood circulation that is vital to life. A properly functioning heart valve allows blood to flow in one direction, and closes to prohibit flow in the other direction. The effect of longterm heart disease is for one or more valves either to close so imperfectly as to allow leakage back down past the valve (incompetence), or to narrow so considerably (stenosis) as to seriously inhibit flow at all. Either way, the effect on the heart is to require more effort, and eventually the heart produces signs of an inability to function well at that increased rate of operation (heart failure).

What is the goal of surgery?

The surgeon aims to replace the damaged valve or valves with:
- a mechanical valve made from plastic and metal
- tissue taken from a human or animal donor and fashioned to the correct shape, or
- a complete valve taken from a human or animal donor

THE CHAMBERS AND BLOOD VESSELS OF THE HEART

a Upper (superior) vena cava
b Upper right chamber (right atrium)
c Lower (inferior) vena cava
d Lower right chamber (right ventricle)
e Aorta
f Pulmonary artery (to the lungs)
g Pulmonary vein (from the lungs)
h Upper left chamber (left atrium)
i Lower left chamber (left ventricle)

Heart valves
1 Aortic valve
2 Pulmonary valve
3 Tricuspid valve
4 Mitral valve

CROSS-SECTIONS THROUGH HEART VALVES

The cusps (**a**) are bowl-shaped sections of the valve that open and close with the flow of blood to and from the heart.

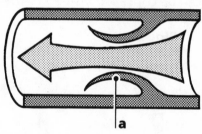

Normal valve, with slim cusps

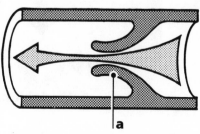

Narrowed valve, with enlarged cusps

9

© DIAGRAM

The choice of replacement valve is the surgeon's, whose decision will take into account various factors such as your age, overall health, tissue type, and the specific nature of the defect in the valve or valves being replaced. Mechanical valves—used successfully in hundreds of thousands of patients to date—tend to require a constant regimen of anticoagulant drug therapy afterward to prevent the formation of blood clots. Tissue from animal donors seldom requires anticoagulant drug therapy, but may be unacceptable to some patients for ethical, religious, or other reasons.

Exactly what is involved in the surgical operation?

Before surgery you will undergo tests to discover the precise condition of your heart valves and the exact reasons behind any symptoms you may be experiencing. The tests may include:

- electrocardiography (ECG or EKG: the monitoring of the electrical impulses involved in the contractions of heart muscle)
- chest X rays
- echocardiography (ultrasonic scanning of the structural composition of the heart)

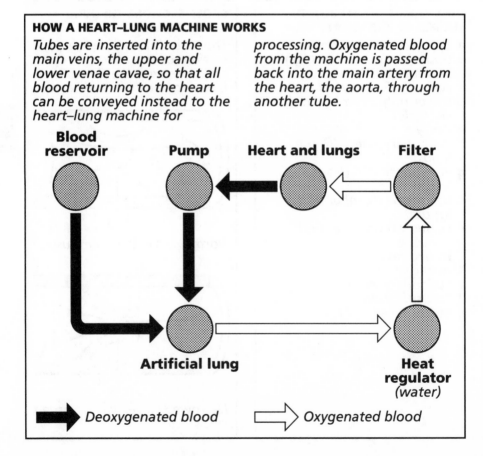

HOW A HEART–LUNG MACHINE WORKS

Tubes are inserted into the main veins, the upper and lower venae cavae, so that all blood returning to the heart can be conveyed instead to the heart–lung machine for processing. Oxygenated blood from the machine is passed back into the main artery from the heart, the aorta, through another tube.

Blood reservoir   **Pump**   **Heart and lungs**   **Filter**

Artificial lung   **Heat regulator** *(water)*

➡ *Deoxygenated blood*   ⇨ *Oxygenated blood*

● cardiac catheterization (to measure the volume and flow of blood through the heart)

The classic operation of this type is replacement of the mitral valve: it is this surgery that is described on the following pages.

Preliminary steps. As with all operations involving general anesthesia, you will be given a preoperative injection about an hour before surgery to dry up internal fluids and to encourage drowsiness.

Step-by-step surgical procedure. The first task for the surgeon is to make sure your circulation is maintained during the operation on your heart—and this means using a heart–lung machine (instead of your heart) to pump the blood around the body. The surgeon makes an incision down the center of the chest, the breastbone (sternum) is carefully sawn through down the middle, and the halves are separated; in this way the heart is exposed.

The heart, once bypassed, is cooled and temporarily stopped, using a cold potassium solution injected through the aorta into the coronary arteries: the low temperature makes it safe for the heart to be stopped for up to four hours. The surgeon then makes an incision in the wall of

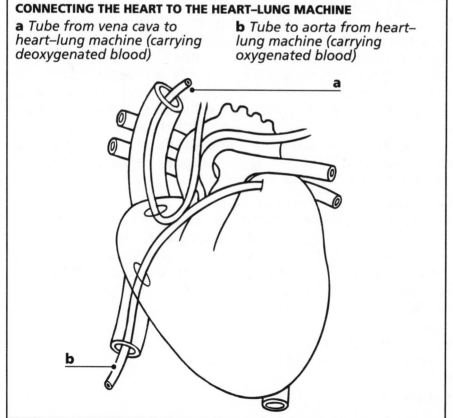

CONNECTING THE HEART TO THE HEART–LUNG MACHINE

a *Tube from vena cava to heart–lung machine (carrying deoxygenated blood)*

b *Tube to aorta from heart–lung machine (carrying oxygenated blood)*

© DIAGRAM

the upper left chamber, and through it can see the diseased and narrowed valve. With a fine scalpel the surgeon now cuts around the valve and removes it, leaving a thin rim of tissue standing out from the blood vessel wall. About 12 to 15 stitches of fine synthetic fiber are sewn through both the rim of tissue and the edge of the replacement valve. When stitches have been inserted all around, the new valve is slid down into place, the ends of the stitches are firmly tied, and surplus suture is cut off.

The outer wall of the heart can then be closed and stitched shut. Blood at normal temperature can now be allowed to flow once more through the heart, which at once starts to beat again. The tubes to the heart—lung machine are disconnected and the small incisions through which the tubes led are repaired. The edges of the breastbone are closed, held together using fine, malleable, stainless steel wire that is threaded through a number of small holes drilled for the purpose. Healing is rapid and the wire need not be removed. Finally, the chest wall is sewn up.

What is it like immediately after the operation?
After the operation you will be in an intensive care unit (ICU) for a day or so. Do not expect the symptoms you were suffering before the operation to have vanished. Breathlessness, for example, may continue for some weeks, and if you were receiving drug treatment to help respiration, that treatment may also have to continue for a time.

All being well, however, you should be able to leave the hospital after a few days. Meanwhile, you will be given antibiotics to avert the possibility of infection and, if your replacement valve is mechanical, the first doses of what will be a lifetime regimen of anticoagulant drug therapy (to avoid blood clots around the valve). You should expect to take only gentle exercise at first but to be able to undertake normal exertion for your age after perhaps four weeks.

What are the longterm effects?
You should take special precautions to avoid infection in the blood circulation—when undergoing dental treatment or other therapies that may expose the bloodstream, for example, ask for antibiotics to be administered first. Follow-up examinations at regular intervals are essential to ensure that the valve is working properly. These may include:
- history-taking
- blood pressure checks
- checks for signs of blood clot formation
- ECG
- angiograms and echocardiograms

EXPOSING THE HEART

a *Incision around the valve*
b *Retractor*

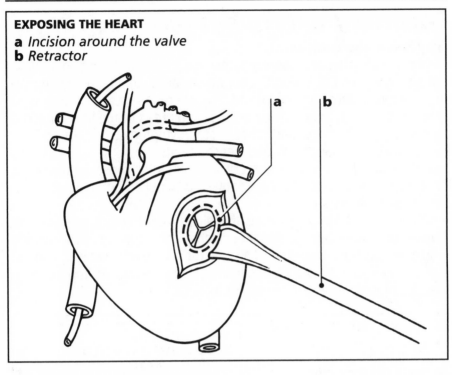

POSITIONING THE REPLACEMENT VALVE

a *Synthetic fiber suture*
b *Prosthetic (artificial) valve*
c *Rim left after diseased
valve is removed*

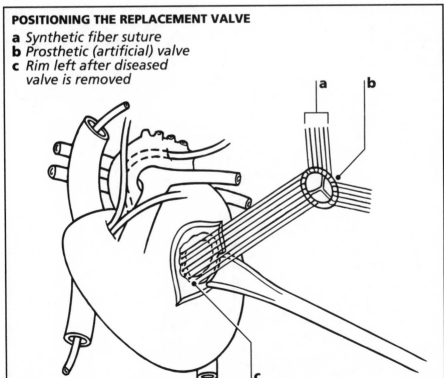

Coronary artery bypass

Why have the operation?

Coronary artery bypass surgery is necessary when the blood vessels that supply nutrient-rich blood to the muscular tissue that makes up the heart become narrowed or blocked. The operation creates a new route by which blood can reach those vessels and areas of the heart that are experiencing deficiency, and so alleviates symptoms of heart disease and reduces the chances of later heart attack.

At the same time, bypass surgery is perhaps the most drastic of the three main methods of treating narrowed or blocked coronary arteries. The other methods are:

- drug therapy both to improve the blood flow through arteries and veins and to discourage the deposition of fatty substances within the arteries, administered according to a regimen that includes a change of lifestyle for the patient—who must lose weight (if appropriate), stop smoking tobacco, and adopt a sensible diet

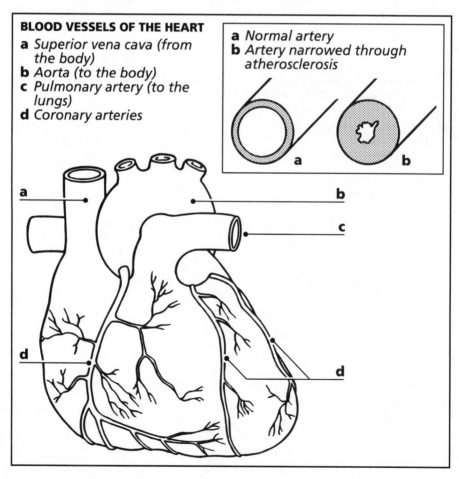

BLOOD VESSELS OF THE HEART
a *Superior vena cava (from the body)*
b *Aorta (to the body)*
c *Pulmonary artery (to the lungs)*
d *Coronary arteries*

a *Normal artery*
b *Artery narrowed through atherosclerosis*

- balloon angioplasty, by which an inflatable probe is propelled down a narrowed artery and inflated until the vessel is sufficiently wide

What is the physical cause of the problem?

The heart is a pump: its force is provided by its muscular walls. Those walls rely on a constant supply of glucose—and of oxygen-rich blood through the arteries that run around its surface. A restriction in this supply causes first the "warning sign" of angina pectoris—severe heart pain—and may then go on to cause heart disease accompanied by heart attack.

The main reason for restriction of the blood supply is that deposits of fats have built up within the arteries—a condition called atherosclerosis—narrowing the blood vessels and causing them to lose flexibility.

A decision as to the most appropriate form of treatment is made only after full discussion with your physician—and with a full appreciation of the implications. The decision takes into account:

- your previous cardiac history, as documented (and, if necessary, as investigated and researched)
- your present symptoms and degree of disability
- the result of coronary angiography, an X-ray technique used to establish
    - the number of arteries, or branches, involved
    - the exact site/sites of blockage
    - the state of the arteries beyond the site/sites of blockage

What is the goal of surgery?

The surgeon's goal is to reposition a length of vascular tissue from within your own body (generally a piece of vein from the thigh or lower leg, or of artery from the chest wall) in such a way as to create a new channel from a major blood vessel at the top of the heart down to wherever on the heart's surface the blood flow is deficient.

The bypass operation involves major surgery and considerable input of the hospital's most modern and expensive machinery. During the operation the heart is stopped for a period of one to two hours through the use of a solution of potassium and a clamp over the main outlet of the heart (the aorta), for which time the blood circulation is maintained via a heart–lung machine (see p.206) that is connected to the heart through tubes tied in to the main veins and the largest artery. In this way oxygen is added in continued normal fashion to the blood and carbon dioxide is removed as a waste gas. The heart is also cooled and kept at a temperature below 59°F (15°C): this allows it to be safely stopped for longer than would otherwise be possible.

Advanced age is, in itself, no bar to the operation. What matters is the improvement in the quality of life afterward.

Exactly what is involved in the surgical operation?

Preliminary steps. As with all operations involving general anesthesia, you will be given a preoperative injection about an hour before surgery to dry up internal fluids and to encourage drowsiness.

Step-by-step surgical procedure. Soon after administration of the general anesthetic, the length of vein or artery that is to form the bypass graft is taken from the thigh, leg, or chest wall through several short incisions which are closed and stitched immediately afterward. At the same time, another surgeon makes an incision down the center of the patient's chest, divides the breastbone, separates the two halves of the ribcage, and opens the membranous sac that encloses the heart (the pericardium): the heart is then exposed. The heart–lung machine can now be attached, and the heart stopped and cooled.

One end of the graft is first attached to the affected coronary artery at a site below the obstruction, within the area affected by deficient blood supply. If there is to be more than one graft involving more than one artery, the surgeon works on each coronary artery in turn, making a slit in the artery wall, enlarging this to a narrow oval opening, and carefully sewing on the end of the graft vessel which has been precut at an angle. In sewing, the surgeon uses very fine synthetic suture material.

Once the lower end of each graft is secure, the clamp is removed from the aorta and the heart is allowed to start beating again. Simultaneously, the upper end of each bypass graft is implanted into

THE OPERATION SITE
a *Blocked coronary artery*
b *Fine suture used to stitch graft to oval cut in coronary artery*
c *Cut edge of oval incision in coronary artery*
d *Vein graft*

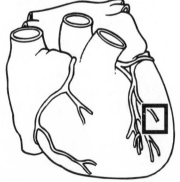
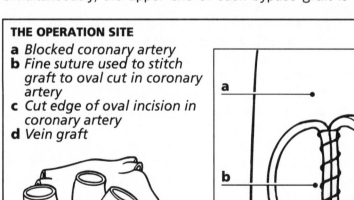
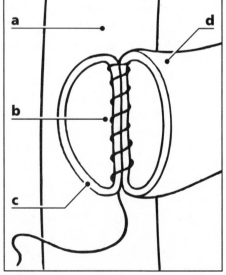

the aorta so that blood at high pressure will flow through. When the bypass is established, a satisfactory flow can be monitored by means of a flowmeter. The heart–lung machine is then redundant and can be disconnected: all the tube entry sites are stitched up with care. That done, the two halves of the breastbone are wired together, and the skin above closed with stitches or clips.

What is it like immediately after the operation?

For the first two or more days after surgery you will be in a cardiac intensive care unit (ICU) under close surveillance by staff and machine. Provided the operation was successful, you should not experience any heart pain. Careful watch will be kept for heart irregularities, which, if they occur—for they are common—may be controlled by drug therapy or (if necessary) electrical cardioversion—restoration of a normal heart-beat by giving an electrical shock to the front of the chest. Pain will likely be limited to the site of the incision. You may expect to leave the hospital between a week and two weeks after surgery but this depends on whether there have been any complications, such as bleeding or infection, and on your general condition and state of heart muscle before surgery.

What are the longterm effects?

In the continued absence of complications, you should after about six weeks be able to live a completely normal life, without any restriction. You will even be encouraged to participate in physically active sport.

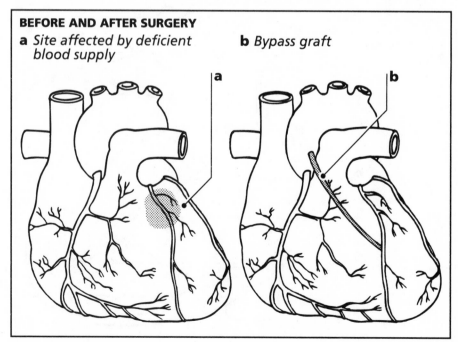

BEFORE AND AFTER SURGERY
a *Site affected by deficient blood supply*
b *Bypass graft*

© DIAGRAM

Pacemaker implantation

Why have the operation?

Narrowing of some of the branches of the coronary arteries from disease may cause certain parts of the heart muscle to be deprived of sufficient blood supply. One of the effects of this is to interfere with the functioning of the natural pacemaker of the heart or with the conducting tissue that controls the spread of contraction throughout the heart muscle. So the heartbeat may fail to respond to the demands of the moment—to speed up during exercise, or to slow down afterward. At worst, the heartbeat may slow down to a dangerously low rate. Such a condition strongly suggests the replacement of the natural pacemaker with an artificial one, by means of surgical implantation.

What is the physical cause of the problem?

The heart's natural pacemaker consists of a group of specialized cells known as the sinoatrial node located within the wall of the upper right chamber of the heart. It is connected to the main muscle mass of the heart by a bundle of specially sensitive muscular cells, which channel the electrical impulses of the sinoatrial node down to the lower chambers of the heart. Both the sinoatrial node and the impulse-transmitting

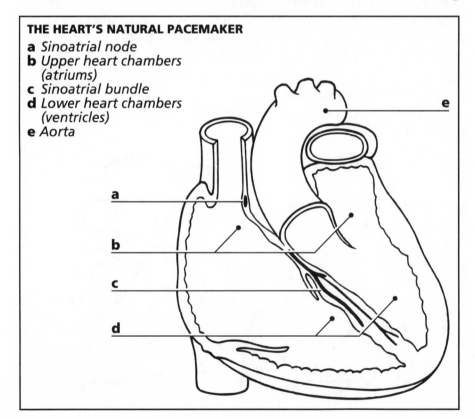

THE HEART'S NATURAL PACEMAKER
a *Sinoatrial node*
b *Upper heart chambers*
(atriums)
c *Sinoatrial bundle*
d *Lower heart chambers*
(ventricles)
e *Aorta*

bundle are vulnerable to damage through various types of heart disease, particularly coronary artery disease. Damage causes control of the heart rate to be affected or lost, and the heart is then unable to respond to changing demand.

What is the goal of surgery?

The surgeon's aim is to replace the damaged natural pacemaker with a transistorized electronic oscillator or pulse-generator, a device that can be implanted within the body, not far from the heart itself, and actually connected to the heart by means of an insulated wire. The bare tip of this wire (the electrode) lies either in the heart or on its surface.

Exactly what is involved in the surgical operation?

Before surgery, you will undergo tests to discover the most suitable location for the pacemaking device with its battery. The decision depends mainly on the condition of the veins of the neck, one of which would normally be used as a means of access to the heart. If the vein condition is appropriate, the pacemaker may be located just under the collarbone. If the condition is not appropriate, the device is implanted in the upper abdomen instead. On this decision may also rest the decision whether to use a local or a general anesthetic: a local anesthetic may be all that is required to insert a pacemaker in the chest, whereas the connecting of the device in the abdomen with its electrode in the heart wall is surgically more complicated.

The two types of artificial pacemaker

Modern pacemakers are flat devices about the size of a cigarette lighter.

"Demand" pacemakers

You will probably be fitted with one of the more modern programmable "demand" pacemakers, which can be set to assist your heart whenever it needs help—cutting in when your heart has difficulty but otherwise monitoring your heart's beating without actively doing anything to help. Some models of this type of pacemaker provide impulses whose frequency, strength, and duration can be altered by radio signals from a manual control dial, making it possible to increase the rate at a time of exertion or reduce the rate once exertion has ceased.

"Fixed-rate" pacemakers

None of the above features is available from an older, nonprogrammable "fixed-rate" pacemaker, now largely superseded by the programmable ones. Fixed-rate pacemakers provide a steady and continuous series of impulses to the heart, and may occasionally cause a problem by in effect competing with the heart's own rhythm.

© DIAGRAM

Preliminary steps. If a general anesthetic is to be administered, you will be given a preoperative injection about an hour before surgery to dry up internal fluids and to encourage drowsiness.

Step-by-step surgical procedure.

If the pacemaker is to be located in the chest, a local anesthetic is administered just beneath the collarbone. The surgeon first uses a scalpel to make a short horizontal cut in the skin. Through this cut, the surgeon then separates the top layers of the skin surface from the deeper layers with blunt-pointed scissors, so creating a "pocket" in which the pacemaker and battery can sit. Next, the surgeon exposes a vein in your neck. The insulated wire leading from the pacemaking device is then passed through a tunnel under the skin to the vein, into it, and through it into the lower right chamber of the heart. There, the bare end of the wire is lodged in one of the many internal crevices.

PACEMAKER IN THE CHEST
a *Vein*
b *Vena cava*
c *Pacemaker*
d *Lead (insulated wire)*
e *Lower right chamber of the heart*
f *Electrode (bare tip of wire)*

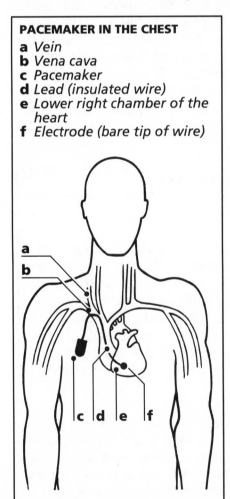

PACEMAKER IN THE ABDOMEN
a *Outer wall of lower right chamber of the heart*
b *Electrode (bare tip of wire)*
c *Lead (insulated wire)*
d *Pacemaker*

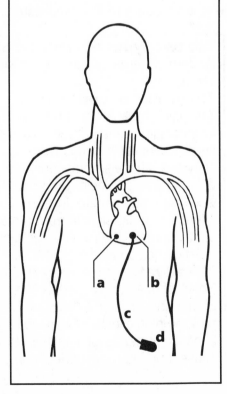

Exact positioning is monitored on-screen by an X-ray intensifier. The small incisions in the neck and chest are closed with a few stitches .

If the pacemaker is to be located in the abdomen, the procedure by which a pocket is created in the skin to carry the device is very much the same. The insulated wire is then led up from it under the skin, and the bare electrode surgically screwed into the outer wall of the lower right chamber of the heart. Incisions are finally sealed with stitches.

What is it like immediately after the operation?

The shallow dome of the pacemaker beneath the skin should be the only outward sign of your operation, and one that need be no inconvenience even in the bath or in bed. Complications of any kind are rare, and center on the possibility of infection. Consequently, you will be given antibiotics for three or four days after the operation. During that time you will be encouraged not to exert yourself, in order to maintain as steady a heart rhythm as possible and establish a standard pacing rate. You will probably be allowed to go home after the antibiotic treatment, and for the next two to three weeks you should also avoid strenuous exertion. At the end of that period you will probably have your first checkup on the pacemaker as an outpatient, at which the pacing rate will be reviewed.

What are the longterm effects?

You should be able to return to work and ordinary activities after a few weeks. Outpatient checkups will be arranged most likely at three-month intervals. You should avoid undue strenuous activity, although moderate exercise is recommended. Sex, too, should be gentle not strenuous.

You should avoid strong electric fields such as:
- power transformers
- high-power radio or radar-transmitting antennas
- short-wave diathermy machines, used by some physical therapists
- airport security screens

These devices are electromagnetic and could cause the pacemaker to change its rate of firing and make the heart beat at an inappropriate rate.

As for changing the battery of the pacemaker: batteries usually last for more than two years each—some last for more than seven—and there is ample warning when the battery needs replacing. Batteries do not suddenly fail—instead, a gradual slowing of the response is experienced, making the user aware of the pacemaker's reduced ability to maintain a high heart rate needed for exertion. Replacing a battery requires a very minor operation performed under a local anesthetic.

Heart–lung transplant

Why have the operation?

A heart–lung transplant is a major operation offered only to those people for whom any other form of treatment for disease of the heart, the lungs, or both simply will not suffice—people who, without such surgery, are likely to die within a short period of time.

What is the physical cause of the problem?

Oxygen in the air is breathed in at the mouth or nose, travels down the bronchi into the lungs, is channeled into smaller bronchioles, and finally reaches the tiny pulmonary air sacs (alveoli), which are surrounded by blood vessels with extremely thin walls through which gases such as oxygen can pass in and carbon dioxide can pass out. Lung disease may cause the walls of the alveoli to collapse, break down, or become thickened. The blood flow is slowed, making it harder for the heart to maintain its special circulation of blood through the lungs. As scarring (fibrosis) of the lungs increases, the circulation becomes even more disrupted, and the right side of the heart (the side that deals exclusively with the lungs) enlarges in an effort to maintain blood pressure. Eventually the heart can increase no further and begins to fail, and the blood circulation through the lungs rapidly becomes worse. By this stage, the amount of oxygen transmitted in blood from the lungs via the heart to the rest of the body has been substantially reduced.

Heart–lung transplants are indicated in cases of chronic lung damage or disease, such as emphysema, conditions causing lung fibrosis, and severe pulmonary inflammation. Even when the heart is not diseased, a heart–lung transplant offers better chances of success than a lung transplant alone.

What is the goal of surgery?

The aim is to replace the damaged heart together with the poorly functioning lungs, as a single unit, in one operation, with a healthy heart and healthy lungs from a recently deceased donor. The donor heart and lungs must also be maintained until the patient is ready for the transplant and, once removed from the donor, are kept chilled by a special cold solution run through the organs' arteries to maintain their condition. The heartbeat of the donor heart is temporarily stopped by the cold temperature, which also helps to preserve it.

Exactly what is involved in the surgical operation?

Preliminary steps. As with any operation involving general anesthesia, you will be given a preoperative injection about an hour before surgery to dry up internal fluids and to encourage drowsiness.

Heart and lung connections

The heart is connected to the lungs by two major arteries and two pairs of veins; it is also connected to the general circulation around the body by a major artery and two large veins. All these connections between heart and blood vessels have to be carefully reimposed when the heart alone is transplanted—whereas in a heart–lung transplant the blood-vessel connections are already present. The new lungs additionally have to be connected to the trachea (windpipe).

For the purposes of simplification we have shown only the air channels (from the trachea) on the left of this diagram and the complex arrangement of veins and arteries on the right. In reality, both lungs contain air channels, veins, and arteries.

a *Trachea*
b *Bronchi*
c *Bronchioles*
d *Right lung*
e *Alveoli*
f *Superior vena cava*
g *Pulmonary artery*
h *Upper right heart chamber*

i *Lower right heart chamber*
j *Inferior vena cava*
k *Left lung*
l *Aorta*
m *Pulmonary arterioles*
n *Upper left heart chamber*
o *Lower left heart chamber*

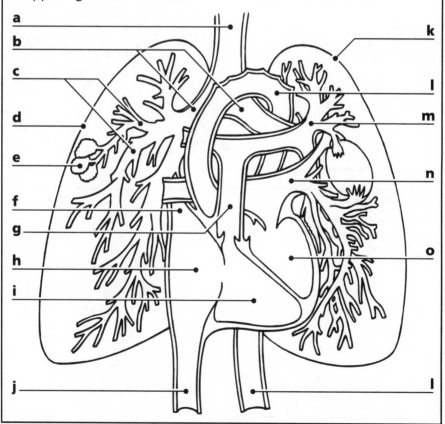

© DIAGRAM

Step-by-step surgical procedure. Once you are anesthetized, the circulation and oxygenation of your bloodstream are maintained using a heart–lung machine. (For an explanation of how a heart–lung machine works, see p.206.) The surgeon makes an incision down the center of the chest, the breastbone (sternum) is carefully sawn through down the middle, and the halves are separated and kept apart with retractors, exposing the heart. Tubes are then firmly attached with stitches into the main veins (the upper and lower venae cavae) so that all blood returning to the heart is instead conveyed to the heart–lung machine for oxygenation. Oxygenated blood is pumped back from the machine through another tube attached to the main artery from the heart (the aorta), and so is passed around the body.

To remove the diseased heart and lungs, the surgeon cuts and removes an area of heart wall. This allows the large veins situated there to be removed together, rather than separately. The same area is cut

DONOR ORGANS

Donor organs are shown here shaded; parts retained by the host are shown white.
a *Trachea*
b *Aorta*
c *Superior vena cava*
d *Inferior vena cava*

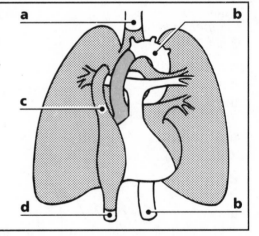

CONNECTION POINTS

Heart and lungs showing connection points after transplant

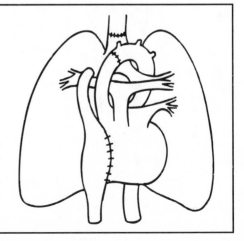

on the donor heart so that only one circular area of stitching is necessary to complete the vein reconnection. The aorta is severed just above the point at which it leaves the heart, and the trachea is cut through just over half an inch (1.5cm) above the point at which it branches to each lung. The diseased heart and lungs can now be removed and the donor organs substituted.

The surgeon now stitches the lower cut end of the trachea to the open upper end of the donor trachea. The free end of the aorta is then stitched firmly to the cut end of the donor aorta. When all the connections have been made and checked over, the new heart can be allowed to return to normal body temperature—which will restart the heartbeat. The tubes to the heart–lung machine are disconnected. The surgeon repairs the incisions by which the tubes were affixed to the blood vessels, brings the breastbone together, and sews up the chest wall.

What is it like immediately after the operation?
You will wake up under close surveillance in an intensive care unit (ICU), linked to various machines that monitor your overall condition, and particularly your heartbeat. Pain—focused mainly at the chest incision—can be dealt with using painkilling drugs that the medical staff will administer. After a few days, the ability to breathe freely, and the accompanying relief at no longer always being breathless, should give you an overriding feeling of renewed vitality.

You will probably remain in the ICU for a few days, until the immediate danger of tissue rejection is past. To lessen this possibility, you will be given immunosuppressive drugs (which you will keep taking for the rest of your life).

What are the longterm effects?
Your new heart does not have the nerve connections that normally control the heartbeat under differing conditions of exertion so will not respond quickly to the demands of exercise. The resting heart rate is also much faster than that of a normal heart: it will probably be about 100–120 beats a minute. But the heart rate is still largely controlled by hormones (such as epinephrine) and by other factors not lost by the transplant, and few transplant patients find they are limited in their activities.

You have an 80 percent likelihood of total recovery. The lifelong immunosuppressive drug treatment makes you susceptible to infection so you must avoid contact with people known to have an infection of any kind.

In rare cases, the joint between the trachea and the donor lung gradually narrows through scarring, or a condition known as obliterative bronchiolitis affects the smaller air tubes in the new lungs. Surgical methods are used to treat either condition.

CHAPTER 10
CHEST SURGERY

Pneumonectomy: lung removal

Why have the operation?

The removal of a lung (pneumonectomy) may be performed:

● in an effort to save life by preventing the spread of lung cancer (bronchial carcinoma)

● if the lung is severely damaged by bronchiectasis (deformity of the tissues of the lung's smaller air channels as a result of repeated infection, blockage by a foreign body, or congenital defect), retains little useful function, and presents a threat to health by remaining

In the case of lung cancer, there are in fact more reasons not to have the operation than to have it. More than half of the people in whom lung cancer is diagnosed show signs of having cancer elsewhere in the body. Most surgeons take this as grounds for not operating, for in such cases the preferred treatment is radiotherapy, chemotherapy, or both.

What is the physical cause of the problem?

Pneumonectomy has become a relatively common operation since the mid-1940s due almost entirely to the sharp increase in the incidence of lung cancer (for which cigarette smoking must be held virtually exclusively to blame). Until 1986 the most common form of cancer in American women was breast cancer; it has now been surpassed in prevalence by cancer of the lung.

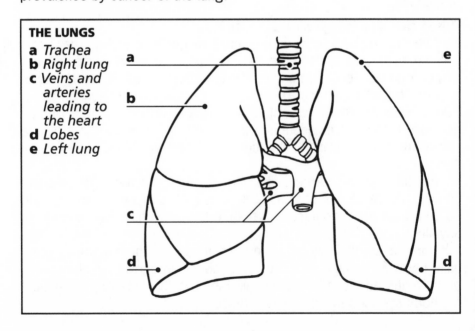

THE LUNGS

a *Trachea*
b *Right lung*
c *Veins and arteries leading to the heart*
d *Lobes*
e *Left lung*

Many lung cancers grow rapidly and, if left untreated, may double in volume in as short a time as three months.

Local spread may:

- cause irritation and cough
- erode the walls of blood vessels
- cause hemorrhage with the coughing up of frothy blood
- affect the nerves of the chest wall or the bones surrounding the chest cavity, causing pain
- obstruct the air tubes, leading to severe breathlessness
- affect the nerves of the larynx (voice box), causing hoarseness and loss of vocal tone

Remote spread (metastasis) can affect any part of the body and may cause similarly severe effects, but quite often it can also lead to extensive metabolic upset due to the production of hormones by primary and secondary tumors.

What is the goal of surgery?

Surgery is designed to provide the patient with the best chance of curing the cancer—or, if this is not possible, at least to extend and improve the quality of life.

If a tumor appears to be well localized in one lobe of the lung, removal of the lobe (lobectomy) is the most usual form of surgery performed. If the main air channel (the bronchus) is involved, however, or if the cancer is more widespread within the lung, the entire lung is removed.

Exactly what is involved in the surgical operation?

If there is time before the operation, you will be encouraged to get your respiratory system in the best possible shape through

- physical therapy
- training in special breathing techniques
- postural drainage (lying in specific positions on a sloping bed in order to drain fluids from different areas of the lung)
- expectorant medication
- antibiotic drugs (in some cases)

Smoking is not permitted. You may be asked to undergo lung function tests.

Preliminary steps. The night before the operation, your chest and armpits may be shaved and scrubbed with an antiseptic solution. As with all operations involving general anesthesia, you will be given a preoperative injection about an hour before surgery to dry up internal fluids and to encourage drowsiness.

Step-by-step surgical procedure. Once you are anesthetized, a tube will be gently maneuvered down your throat into the trachea (windpipe) to supply oxygen and anesthetic gases. Spontaneous breathing

10

© DIAGRAM

will be impossible for you when your chest is opened up, so a ventilator is necessary. You will probably also be positioned on the operating table lying on the side opposite that of the lung to be removed.

The surgeon's first incision is from below the nipple right around the side of the body to below the lower tip of the triangular shoulder blade (an incision technically described as the posterolateral thoracotomy incision). Beneath the skin, the underlying muscles are then carefully separated, exposing the membrane-covered ribs. The membrane over the fifth rib is sliced open so that the surgeon can cut through the rib with bone-cutters and remove it. Alternatively, the muscle between the ribs is cut through. Either way, the lung is exposed, and to increase its visibility a strong self-retaining retractor is used to keep the edges of the incision widely separated.

The surgeon frees any adhesions between the lung and the chest wall and compresses the lung to reveal its root (the central area on the inner surface at which the main bronchus and blood vessels enter it). The large veins and arteries running from the lung to the heart are tied off and severed. The main air tube (the bronchus) of the lung is clamped

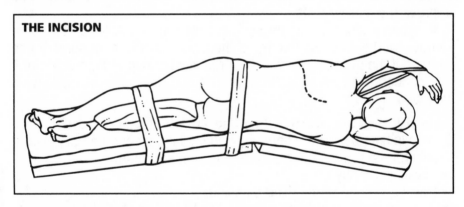

THE INCISION

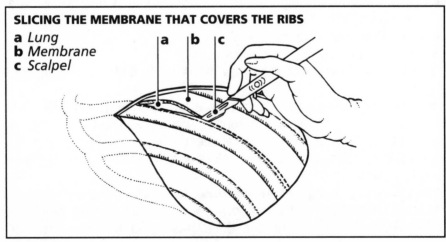

SLICING THE MEMBRANE THAT COVERS THE RIBS

a *Lung*
b *Membrane*
c *Scalpel*

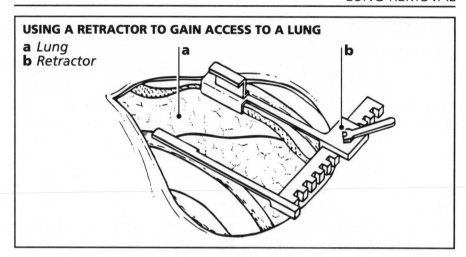

USING A RETRACTOR TO GAIN ACCESS TO A LUNG
a *Lung*
b *Retractor*

a

b

and cut. The lung is now free and is removed, and the cut end of the bronchus is closed with metal staples. The cavity left by the removal of the lung is then filled with sterile salt solution (saline). The surgeon then checks the stapled bronchus for air leakage and, if satisfied, closes up the chest in layers—probably leaving a couple of tubes in the incision for drainage.

What is it like immediately after the operation?
You will wake up under close surveillance in an intensive care unit (ICU), linked to various machines that monitor your overall condition. You may find that your breathing is being assisted by a ventilation machine (respirator) connected to your nose or mouth. There may also be pain, focused mainly on the chest wall, although this may be lessened by a long-acting anesthetic block, injected around the nerves between the ribs during surgery. Any further pain can usually be dealt with using painkilling drugs administered by the medical staff. But above all, you will feel breathless.

The respirator is usually required for less than 24 hours and the drainage tubes are generally removed a day after surgery. But you will probably remain in the ICU for several days, until your general condition has improved.

The stitches in the incision are extracted after about ten days, at which time most patients are allowed to go home. The staples in the bronchus remain: they are biologically inert and do no harm.

What are the longterm effects?
If all the tumor has been removed with the lung and has not spread to other parts of the body, the cancer is cured. In the meantime normal activities must be resumed gradually, allowing time for adaptation of the body to reduced lung capacity. Many pneumonectomy patients are able to go back to work after about 60 days.

Drainage of a lung abscess

Why have the operation?

An abscess in a lung is a serious condition: it causes fever, chest pain, night sweats, clubbing of the fingers, and a racking cough (often with large amounts of foul-smelling sputum). Untreated, an abscess may lead to the accumulation of pus between the membranes that surround the lungs (the pleurae) or to blood poisoning (septicemia), both of which are potentially life threatening. One lung abscess can additionally cause further abscesses elsewhere in the body, such as the brain if infective material is spread within the bloodstream, or the throat or mouth if spread via the air passages. Without effective treatment, an abscess may persist for months or years; antibiotics are of little use, and surgical drainage may be the only remedy.

What is the physical cause of the problem?

A lung abscess is an area of lung tissue that has been broken down, surrounded by an area of infection and inflammation. It takes the form of a rounded capsule in or on the lung; the inner cavity will contain fluid, which shows up on X-ray photographs.

The most common cause of a lung abscess is the accidental inhalation of foreign material (such as a peanut or part of a tooth) that jams in the lung tissue and causes it to become inflamed. Such inhalation occurs in people who are deeply unconscious or who have lost the laryngeal closure reflex (the gag reflex) through epilepsy, stroke, or severe head injury. Lung abscesses may also be caused by the inhalation of harmful organisms—such as the tubercle bacillus (the organism

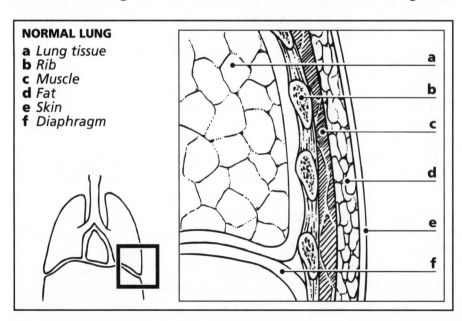

NORMAL LUNG

a *Lung tissue*
b *Rib*
c *Muscle*
d *Fat*
e *Skin*
f *Diaphragm*

Mycobacterium tuberculosis that causes tuberculosis)—or other air-borne septic material.

What is the goal of surgery?

The specific aim of surgery varies depending upon the exact location of the abscess.

- An abscess deep in the lung is treated by conservative surgery rather than by attempting to remove the affected part of the lung. Surgery is performed only when other methods of therapy have failed or are rejected as inappropriate.
- In many cases, a lung abscess can be successfully treated by antibiotic drug therapy in combination with postural drainage and physical therapy. Postural drainage involves positioning the patient so that secretions can be removed by gravity, aided sometimes by slapping or thumping of the patient's back.
- Foreign bodies that cause an abscess in a lung can sometimes be removed without surgery through the use of an instrument called a bronchoscope (a flexible tube introduced into the lung via the mouth), through which the contents of the abscess can be sucked out.
- Surgery is performed when an abscess has formed within the outer tissues of the lung—out of the reach of a bronchoscope—and finally breaks out of the lung altogether, causing pus to collect in the pleural cavity between the lung and the chest wall. This condition is called empyema and is described below. Here the aim of surgery is to provide free drainage of an abscess lying just under the chest wall, thus causing the abscess capsule to collapse, in turn promoting healthy healing.

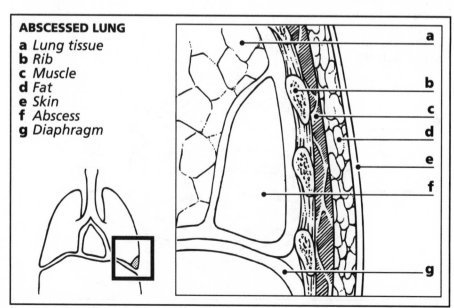

ABSCESSED LUNG

a *Lung tissue*
b *Rib*
c *Muscle*
d *Fat*
e *Skin*
f *Abscess*
g *Diaphragm*

© DIAGRAM

Exactly what is involved in the surgical operation?

Before surgery, the exact location of the abscess is determined by X rays and other imaging methods. Samples of pus are taken by suction through a needle, and are cultured to establish the infective organism involved and thus the most suitable antibiotic. Any anemia that has resulted from the presence of the abscess is also treated.

The operation is usually performed under general anesthesia, although in some cases a local anesthetic that includes a block on the nerves between the ribs may be used instead.

Preliminary steps. If you are to have a general anesthetic, you will be given a preoperative injection about an hour before surgery to dry up internal fluids and to encourage drowsiness.

Step-by-step surgical procedure. Once you have been anesthetized, you will be positioned on the operating table so that you lie on your healthy side, with the arm on the affected side raised above your head. Abscesses with thick pus, granulation tissue, and some surrounding fibrosis necessitate removal of part of a rib (described here). Thin pus in the pleural space can often be removed by aspiration alone, but all abscesses require removing at least part of a rib.

If the abscess lies up against the back of the ribcage, a short section of a rib will need to be removed in order to drain the abscess effectively. The surgeon's incision may be vertical over or horizontal along the line of the specified rib.

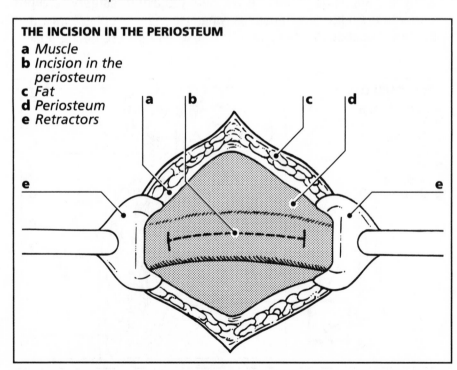

THE INCISION IN THE PERIOSTEUM
a *Muscle*
b *Incision in the periosteum*
c *Fat*
d *Periosteum*
e *Retractors*

Once the incision is made, the underlying muscles are exposed and are carefully separated over the rib in the direction of their fibers. The surgeon retracts the muscle layers until the rib is revealed in its covering membrane (periosteum). He or she then cuts the periosteum and detaches it from the rib, but does not remove it: it is important to preserve the periosteum because a new section of rib can grow from it later.

Using bone shears, the surgeon cuts a 1–1.5 inch (2–4cm) section from the exposed bone. Any sharp edges left on the rib are rounded off with a strong pair of forceps known as a rongeur, and bleeding from the rib ends is stopped with a material called bone wax.

A short incision is now made in the inner layer of the periosteum,

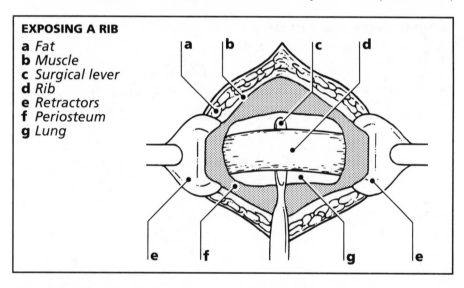

EXPOSING A RIB

a *Fat*
b *Muscle*
c *Surgical lever*
d *Rib*
e *Retractors*
f *Periosteum*
g *Lung*

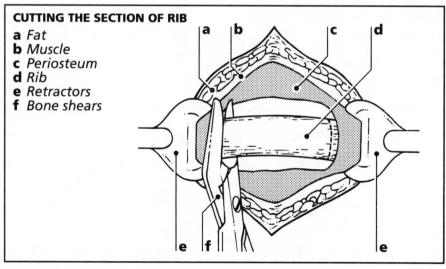

CUTTING THE SECTION OF RIB

a *Fat*
b *Muscle*
c *Periosteum*
d *Rib*
e *Retractors*
f *Bone shears*

© DIAGRAM

through and into the abscess capsule. A suction tube is pushed in to empty the abscess cavity. With a gloved finger, the surgeon feels inside the abscess capsule in order to break down any internal compartments that might limit full drainage. To ensure adequate drainage, the ends of one or more soft rubber tubes are now inserted into the cavity and secured there with absorbable stitches—this prevents the tubes from being sucked into the chest by the action of breathing.

The drainage tubes are left in position as the surgeon folds back the muscle layers and closes the initial incision. The drains remain in position and the soft tissue closes around them—incision stitches are not usually necessary. When the last drain is finally removed, the opening will already be much smaller and will close spontaneously.

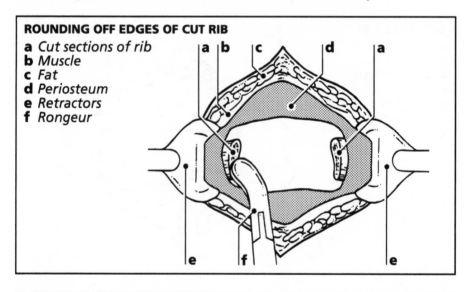

ROUNDING OFF EDGES OF CUT RIB
a *Cut sections of rib*
b *Muscle*
c *Fat*
d *Periosteum*
e *Retractors*
f *Rongeur*

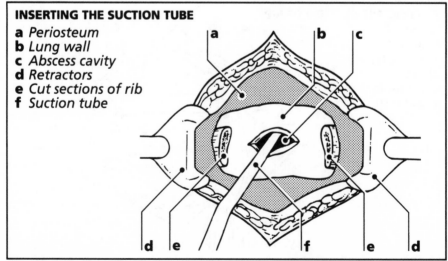

INSERTING THE SUCTION TUBE
a *Periosteum*
b *Lung wall*
c *Abscess cavity*
d *Retractors*
e *Cut sections of rib*
f *Suction tube*

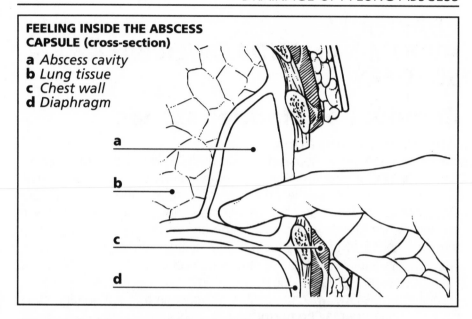

FEELING INSIDE THE ABSCESS CAPSULE (cross-section)

a *Abscess cavity*
b *Lung tissue*
c *Chest wall*
d *Diaphragm*

What is it like immediately after the operation?

You will wake up to find the drainage tubes causing some discomfort as you breathe, although there should be little pain. You will be given advice on breathing, and instructed on how to perform special exercises to stretch the chest wall. Probably after three or four days the abscess cavity will be washed out with sterile salt (saline) solution. How long the drainage tubes remain in place will depend on how quickly the abscess capsule closes down. This can take from a few days to several weeks. Surgeons are reluctant to remove the tubes until there is X-ray evidence that the only thing holding the capsule open is the drainage tube ends. Sometimes smaller drainage tubes are substituted as the capsule closes. But eventually the last tube will be removed, after which the small opening left will quickly close over and heal. You will leave the hospital when the drainage tubes have been removed.

You will be advised to avoid sitting twisted to one side—a position that many patients unconsciously adopt to favor the side of the body on which the abscess was located. Such persistent twisting of the spine can in due time lead to permanent deformity (scoliosis), a recognized complication of empyema.

What are the longterm effects?

Successful drainage and closure of a lung abscess should be followed by complete recovery. Inevitably, there will be some adhesions between the membrane that surrounds the lung and the chest wall, but these should cause no trouble, especially if you have followed the regimen of breathing exercises prescribed. The section of removed rib will grow back within weeks or months.

© DIAGRAM

CHAPTER 11
ABDOMINAL AND LOWER BACK SURGERY

Removal of bladder stones

Why have the operation?

Bladder stones cause spasms of pain in the lower abdomen, intermittent stoppages during urination, and occasionally the passage of small particles of "gravel" in the urine. In men—who suffer from bladder stones about 20 times as often as women—they also cause difficulty in urination while standing and pain in the end of the penis. Other symptoms are those of urinary infection and include burning pain on urination, a slow and weak stream, and, occasionally, blood in the urine. When stones are present, these symptoms do not respond to antimicrobial drug therapy, which is usually effective in treating urinary infections, and surgery may be performed.

What is the physical cause of the problem?

Bladder stones form in urine that has stagnated or become concentrated. They still occur frequently in the tropics (where the heat that causes loss of other body fluids may serve to concentrate the urine) and in men with some obstruction to the outflow of urine (which then tends to stagnate in the bladder). In the latter group the usual cause is enlargement of the prostate gland, which obstructs the bladder outlet (the urethra). Persistent infection of the bladder (cystitis) is a common result, and infection itself produces changes in the urine that promote stone formation.

Other causes of bladder stones include:

- diverticula: small pouches within the bladder wall in which urine can be retained and then stagnates
- foreign bodies within the bladder around which stones can gradually form. Some people push things, such as bobby pins, into the bladder—either deliberately or accidentally—by way of the urethra. This is more commonly achieved by women, who have a much shorter urethra than men. The motive may be to relieve irritation or to overcome a narrowing, but it is sometimes inscrutable.
- blood clots or congealed droplets of pus—located on the lining of the bladder or free in the urine—which can form the nuclei of bladder stones
- cancers, polyps, and other forms of abnormal growth on the lining of the bladder
- longterm catheterization, which commonly leads to incrustations of stones on the catheter and stones in the bladder

- prolonged immobilization of paraplegic patients, which can lead to urine stagnation
- In the tropics, additional causes include dietary factors and parasitic worm infestation. Some diets result in an increased excretion of substances in the urine that can form stones. A particular schistosome parasite commonly infests the bladder in certain tropical areas.

Often only a single stone is present, although the stone may grow to an astonishing size. Some weigh more than five pounds (two kilograms). In the United States, the major constituent of bladder stones is calcium oxalate, a substance occurring naturally in urine and ultimately deriving from dietary intake of such everyday foods as green, leafy vegetables and coffee. It is probably the very normality of these dietary elements that gives bladder stones a tendency to recur: a patient whose stone is surgically removed has a 60 percent chance of developing another stone within the following seven years.

What is the goal of surgery?
The surgeon aims to remove the stone or stones from the bladder, thus eliminating symptoms and permitting any urinary infection to be treated. There are several methods available, some of which require no surgical incision at all. The method chosen depends mainly upon the size of the stone or stones.

Exactly what is involved in the surgical operation?
Before surgery, the inside of your bladder will be examined by the surgeon through a cystoscope: a thin, tubular instrument inserted carefully and gently up the urethra (see p.42 for more information about cystoscopes). This allows the surgeon to make a positive diagnosis and to detect the presence of any other bladder disease.

Preliminary steps. Surgery is performed under general anesthesia or spinal anesthesia (by which sensation is numbed from the waist down following the injection of anesthetic into the cerebrospinal fluid within the spinal column). If you are to have a general anesthetic, you will be given a preoperative injection about an hour before surgery to dry up internal fluids and to encourage drowsiness. A preoperative injection may or may not be administered before spinal anesthesia.

Step-by-step surgical procedure. There are several procedures for removing bladder stones.

- Small stones can be simply flushed out of the bladder by squirting water through the urethra and letting it run out of a tube passed through the same.
- The cystoscope can be used in conjunction with a laser to crush or break up stones in the bladder, and the resultant "gravel" can then be flushed out as above.
- Stones up to 2 inches (5cm) in diameter can be crushed within the

11

© DIAGRAM

bladder by means of an instrument called a lithotrite, also passed through the urethra. Fragments are then flushed out.

- Larger stones may be fragmented from outside the body using a machine called a lithotripter, which produces high-frequency ultrasound shock waves. For this method—known technically as extracorporeal shock-wave lithotripsy (ESWL)—X rays are used to locate the stone. Then, high-power sound waves are focused on the stone and shatter it. The fine gravel is then suitable for passing out in the urine over the following few weeks.

- Stones associated with enlargement of the prostate gland in men are commonly removed by open surgery involving removal of the prostate gland itself. In this case, the surgeon makes a short vertical or horizontal midline incision immediately above the pubic bone. The underlying muscles are carefully separated, and the bladder is exposed. A small incision is made in the bladder, through which the stone is removed with forceps. The lining of the bladder where it sits upon the prostate gland is then cut, so that the entire prostate gland can be shelled out of its capsule by the surgeon's finger and removed. The incision in the bladder is then carefully closed with absorbable stitches, the muscle layers are returned to their place, and the outer incision is also closed.

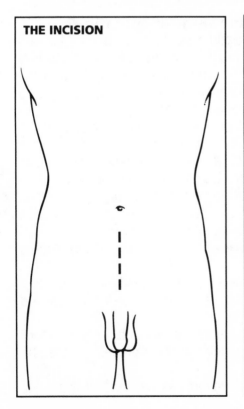

THE INCISION

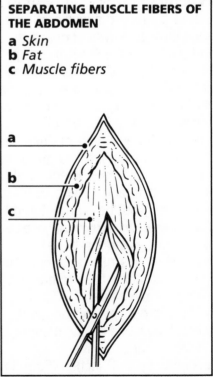

SEPARATING MUSCLE FIBERS OF THE ABDOMEN
a *Skin*
b *Fat*
c *Muscle fibers*

What is it like immediately after the operation?

If the operation was performed under spinal anesthesia, you may suffer a headache for a time afterward. After lithotripsy there may be some bruising of the skin at the point of entry of the shock wave and at its point of exit on the opposite side of the body, and there may be some blood in the urine for a day or so. If you have had the prostate gland removed, you may wake up with a catheter still in place in the urethra to temporarily facilitate urination and, if necessary, bladder irrigation to wash out blood clots.

Instruments inserted up the urethra cause soreness and (in men) penile discomfort that will last for a couple of days.

Most patients are encouraged to get out of bed the day after surgery and may leave the hospital almost immediately, although full normal activity should not be resumed for six or seven days. Patients who have had the prostate gland removed will have to wait a little longer to leave the hospital (five to ten days) and may take some weeks more to fully recover (see *Prostatectomy*, p.378).

What are the longterm effects?

Unless bladder stones recur, the longterm effects are excellent and permanent.

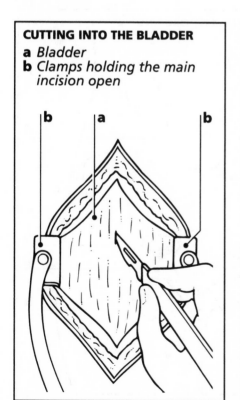

CUTTING INTO THE BLADDER
a *Bladder*
b *Clamps holding the main incision open*

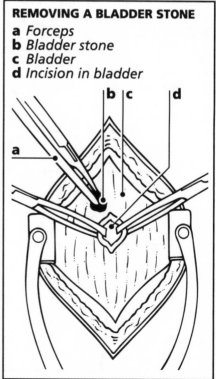

REMOVING A BLADDER STONE
a *Forceps*
b *Bladder stone*
c *Bladder*
d *Incision in bladder*

© DIAGRAM

Removal of a bladder tumor

Why have the operation?

As with surgical treatment for cancer elsewhere in the body, the opera-tion to remove a bladder tumor can be lifesaving. Caught in the early stages, bladder cancer can be cured; in more advanced cases, surgery—in combination with radiation therapy and perhaps other methods of anticancer therapy—offers the best chance, although the outlook is inevitably not as favorable.

What is the physical cause of the problem?

Bladder cancer begins in the membrane that lines the inside of the organ. Changes in the structure of that lining occur gradually and insid-iously, giving few outward symptoms. Yet about half of the bladder can-cer patients who undergo surgery are treated when only the bladder lin-ing has been affected. Because such a tumor can be destroyed fairly easily by direct local surgery, these patients have an excellent chance of complete cure. But if the cancer remains undetected, it may spread from the lining deep into the muscular wall of the bladder. Surgery may then involve partial or total removal of the bladder itself, followed by intensive radiation therapy. In severe cases, the cancer may spread

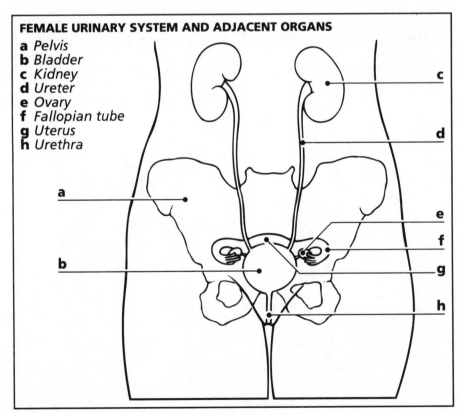

FEMALE URINARY SYSTEM AND ADJACENT ORGANS

a *Pelvis*
b *Bladder*
c *Kidney*
d *Ureter*
e *Ovary*
f *Fallopian tube*
g *Uterus*
h *Urethra*

elsewhere in the abdomen or, at worst, throughout the body, requiring several surgical operations and the full modern anticancer treatment program of radiation therapy and chemotherapy.

Bladder cancer affects three times as many men as it does women. This is partly due—in perhaps about 30 percent of affected men—to occupational hazards in the form of chemicals in the rubber, petroleum, leather, and dyeing industries. But several other causes have been identified, notably alpha- and beta-naphthylamine, substances that are excreted into the urine of heavy cigarette smokers. Persistent smoking is believed to be the cause of bladder cancer in some 50 percent of cases in men and around 30 percent of cases in women.

What is the goal of surgery?

The aim of surgery is to eliminate all areas of cancer. But before surgery is considered, tests will be done to confirm the diagnosis and to establish the stage the cancer has reached. The extent of surgery required depends on how far the tumor has advanced. Examination of the inside of the bladder by means of a cystoscope, under local anesthesia, should indicate the site of the tumor and its probable extent. A cystoscope is a very thin viewing instrument, with several attachments, that is inserted up the urethra (see p.42 for more on cystoscopes).

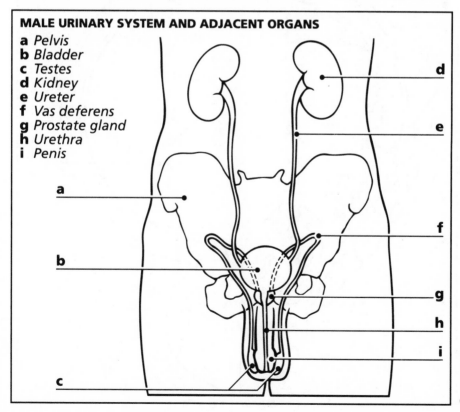

MALE URINARY SYSTEM AND ADJACENT ORGANS
a Pelvis
b Bladder
c Testes
d Kidney
e Ureter
f Vas deferens
g Prostate gland
h Urethra
i Penis

© DIAGRAM

Exactly what is involved in the surgical operation?

Preliminary steps. If a tumor is suspected or actually seen under cystoscopy, you will at once be scheduled for biopsy (cutting out a specimen of the tissue growth) or removal of the tissue mass, performed under general anesthesia. Preliminary studies also include checks into whether there are any signs of secondary spread of the cancer to other parts of the body. As with any operation involving general anesthesia, you will be given a preoperative injection about an hour before surgery to dry up internal fluids and to encourage drowsiness.

BLADDER TUMOR

Cross-section through a male bladder showing the development of a bladder tumor

a *Ureter*
b *Opening of ureters into bladder*
c *Prostate gland*
d *Urethra*

1 *Tumor in bladder lining*
2 *Tumor in muscular bladder wall*
3 *Tumor breaking into fat surrounding the bladder*
4 *Tumor infecting adjacent organ (prostate gland)*

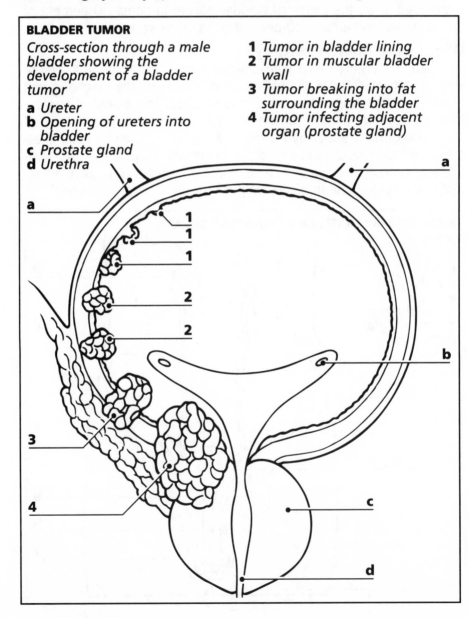

Step-by-step surgical procedure. Once you have been anesthetized, you will be placed on the operating table lying on your back with your feet up in stirrups, your knees bent and wide apart (the lithotomy position). A catheter will then be inserted up the urethra (the urine outlet) and into the bladder to permit the access of sterile water to wash out the bladder and to obtain sample cells of the tumor for laboratory examination under a microscope (exfoliative cytology).

The surgeon then inserts a gloved finger into the rectum while pressing with the other hand on the relaxed wall of the abdomen, to feel for lumps in and around the bladder. If a lump is present, the surgeon continues the manual examination to establish whether the lump is fixed to any adjacent structure.

Finally, the entire inner surface of the bladder is inspected through a cystoscope. Through this instrument, biopsies (tissue samples) of the tumor and any other suspicious areas may be taken for analysis in a laboratory.

The operation from this point differs according to the nature and spread of the tumor. A tumor that is restricted to the bladder lining may be destroyed through the cystoscope using an attachment known as a resectoscope, a small wire loop that can be heated. If the tumor has invaded the bladder wall or spread even further, the surgeon may decide to perform partial or total (radical) removal of the bladder (cystectomy)—a major abdominal procedure. But before undertaking such an operation, many surgeons give a course of radiation therapy, with or without simultaneous chemotherapy. Radiation therapy is commonly administered also at the time of surgery itself.

For both partial and radical cystectomy, the surgeon makes an incision on the midline between navel and pubis or transversely across the lower abdomen. The layers of underlying muscle are carefully separated and held with retractors, and the abdominal wall is penetrated to reveal the bladder and other pelvic organs. Diversion of the urine flow between the ureters and the urethra, bypassing the bladder and providing a means of urine storage, is the next task for the surgeon. In a partial cystectomy, the need for such a urinary diversion will be only temporary; in a radical cystectomy it will be permanent. There are several methods. The ureters, which carry urine from the kidneys to the bladder, may be permanently implanted in the rectum. There is plenty of room in the rectum to accommodate additional volume, and some of the water will be reabsorbed (this is the main function of the colon). The anal sphincters provide a remarkably tight seal. Alternatively, a short length of the ileum (the lower small intestine) can be isolated to form a substitute bladder into which the ureters can be implanted; the outlet from this ileal conduit, as it is called, is made through the front wall of the abdomen, to which a collecting bag is later attached.

REMOVING THE BLADDER
a *Kidneys*
b *Small intestine*
c *Ileal conduit*
d *Ureters*
e *Large intestine*
f *Cutting points*
g *Bladder*

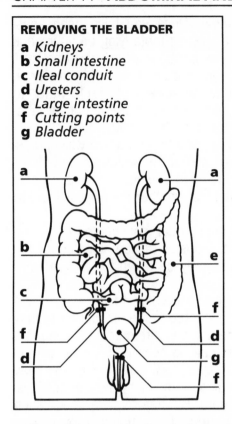

FORMING THE ILEAL CONDUIT FROM THE SMALL INTESTINE
a *Ileal conduit*

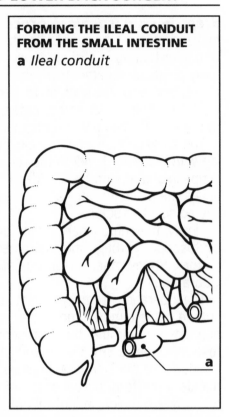

Once the urine is diverted, the bladder is available for surgery. In a partial cystectomy, the area of the bladder wall involved in the cancer is removed, and the free edges are brought together with stitches. In men, radical cystectomy involves total removal of the bladder together with the prostate gland and seminal vesicles and the surrounding fat, lymph nodes, and other tissues. In women, the uterus (womb), Fallopian tubes, ovaries, and lymph nodes must be removed in addition to the bladder—and the operation thus closely resembles the total hysterectomy operation (see p.314). Radical cystectomy involves the removal of other organs besides the bladder because the cancer is sufficiently advanced and is likely to have affected them also.

When the surgeon has partly or totally removed the bladder (and any other organs), he or she checks for residual bleeding and, if satisfied that there is none, closes the abdominal wall and outer muscle layers with stitches, before stitching up the external incision.

What is it like immediately after the operation?
Your postoperative condition will depend on the level of surgery you have undergone. Minimal surgery, performed through the urethra (transurethral surgery), in men might cause some brief residual discomfort in the penis, but in all patients should have little general effect,

MAKING AN OUTLET FROM THE ILEAL CONDUIT

Ureters are attached to the ileal conduit and this in turn is attached to abdominal skin to form an outlet. A collecting bag is attached to the skin.

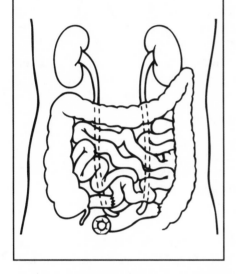

ATTACHING THE COLLECTING BAG

Cross-section through the abdomen showing ileal conduit and collecting bag
a *Collecting bag*
b *Skin of the abdomen*
c *Outlet*
d *Opening of collecting bag secured with adhesive to opening in skin of abdomen*
e *Ileal conduit*

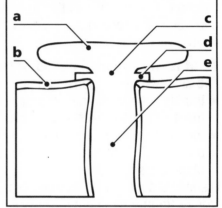

and you should be up and walking almost at once. After abdominal surgery, especially radical, you should expect a period of being confined to bed, with some monitoring of body processes. (There may also be a drainage tube in the wound at first.) You will feel weak, but will be encouraged to move around as soon as you can. It may be possible to leave the hospital about seven to ten days after surgery, but you will have to recuperate at home for several weeks thereafter. Following the surgical creation of an ileal conduit, you will require counseling in the positioning and changing of the urine-collecting bag. The bag lies flat against the skin and is secured with adhesive around the opening, which is below the navel and to one side.

What are the longterm effects?
Bladder cancer commonly recurs: careful medical follow-up is vital. In cases of cancer caught early and dealt with by transurethral surgery, the results are normally excellent. More advanced cases have a less favorable outlook, although modern medicine is improving the prospects for such cases all the time.

© DIAGRAM

Nephrectomy: removal of a kidney

Why have the operation?

The main reason for undergoing nephrectomy is that through disease or injury one of the body's two kidneys is not working properly or not working at all. One kidney can normally take on the full function of both, but if the other is malfunctioning, various unpleasant symptoms may—if untreated—eventually cause considerable discomfort. But the very fact that one kidney can genuinely take on the full function of both also means that it is possible for a healthy kidney of suitable tissue type to be taken from a voluntary donor without the donor's losing any kidney function. And this is another reason (for far fewer people) to undergo nephrectomy: to donate a kidney to someone else—generally a close relative—who needs one.

What is the physical cause of the problem?

The kidneys are responsible for:

• the filtration of the blood in circulation
• the subsequent excretion of liquid wastes (as urine)
• the control of the body fluids' acid-alkali balance
• the secretion of special hormones that regulate blood contents and blood pressure

Disease—such as inflammation of the millions of filtering units of the kidney (glomerulonephritis), diabetic nephropathy, tuberculosis, a kidney stone, or a tumor—or injury cause many different symptoms relating to the specific functions affected most. Kidney failure may occur suddenly (acute renal failure) or gradually over months or years (chronic renal failure); either may result in a life-threatening condition known as end-stage renal failure.

What is the goal of surgery?

The surgeon's aim is to remove the defective kidney and so cure any symptoms its condition may have been causing. Normally, this means at the same time allowing the remaining kidney to take over the full original function of both. If both kidneys are removed, the surgeon will ensure that an easy means of regular access to the blood circulation is made available for the purpose of dialysis (blood filtration via a machine external to the body, or less commonly via a membrane elsewhere inside the body). Most often a short tube ("shunt") connecting an artery and a vein, and with an external access junction, is inserted within the outer tissues of a limb. Similar access is also provided if a kidney is to be transplanted into the patient. It is highly unusual for a transplant to be made immediately after kidney removal: there is generally a gap in time—to reduce overall shock and stress to the body—during which dialysis is regularly performed.

Although nephrectomy is a major surgical operation, the risks are small and mortality from surgery alone is negligible. Survival rates for nephrectomy performed to treat kidney cancer depend on how far the cancer has advanced at the time of initial surgery: if therapy begins at an early stage, the chances of longterm survival are greatly increased.

THE LOCATION OF THE KIDNEYS

a *Adrenal glands*
b *Right kidney*
c *Vein*
d *Ureter*
e *Pelvis*
f *Left kidney*
g *Artery*
h *Bladder*

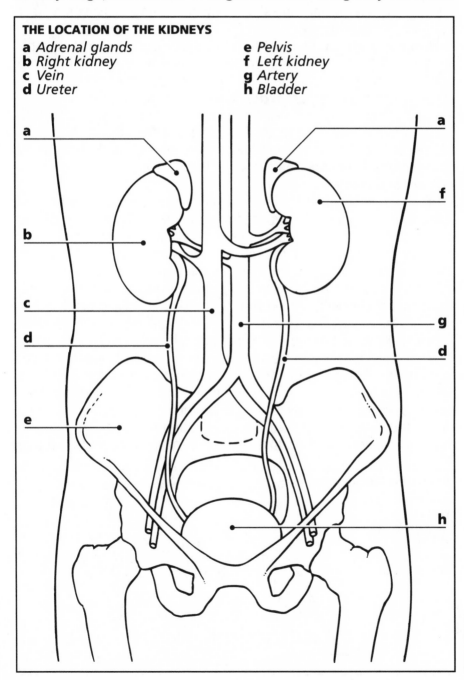

© DIAGRAM

Exactly what is involved in the surgical operation?

To remove a kidney, a surgeon's approach can be either from the front, through an incision in the abdominal wall, or from behind, through one in the lower back. Because each kidney lies close against the back wall of the abdomen—and because it avoids potential complications with masses of interposing intestines—most surgeons use the rear approach, as described below.

Preliminary steps. As with all operations involving general anesthesia, you will be given a preoperative injection about an hour before surgery to dry up internal fluids and to encourage drowsiness.

Step-by-step surgical procedure. Once you are anesthetized, you will be positioned on the operating surface, lying on your side, with the defective kidney uppermost. The surface is then angled sharply in the middle, so that upper and lower parts of your body both slope downward, and the upper part is stretched out, so bringing the kidney area well into reach.

The surgeon then makes a long, curved incision along the lower edge of the ribs, from your spine around toward the front. Beneath the skin is a layer of fat; when this too is cut through, the top muscle layer is exposed. In all there are three muscle layers, and when the third has also been cut through, the kidney is revealed, lying in a bed of fat.

First the surgeon ties two strong ligatures made of catgut (or material of similar strength) around the large artery supplying blood for filtration to the kidney. The artery between the ligatures is then severed. The same action is taken on the vein leading from the kidney and passing filtered blood back into the bloodstream. It is important to tie off the artery before the vein or the pressure of blood in the kidney would rise steeply, with the risk of severe bleeding during and after the operation. Various other blood vessels leading to the kidney may also now be tied off, but the surgeon must take care not to interrupt the blood supply to and from the adrenal gland that sits like a small conical hat on top of

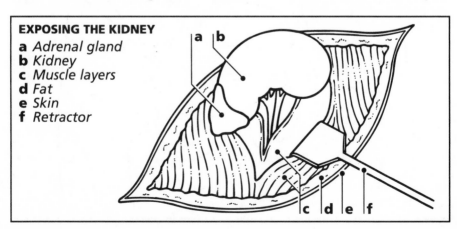

EXPOSING THE KIDNEY
a *Adrenal gland*
b *Kidney*
c *Muscle layers*
d *Fat*
e *Skin*
f *Retractor*

the kidney and that may not immediately be identifiable as a separate organ because of the mass of fatty tissue all around. Finally, ligatures are tied around the ureter—the tube that passes urine from kidney to bladder—and that too is severed between them. The kidney is now free, and can be lifted out of the body.

If cancer is the reason for the nephrectomy, all ligatures are usually tied in place before any severing of blood vessels is performed. This is to minimize the risk of jarring loose any cancerous cells into the bloodstream. A further precaution taken by most surgeons is the removal of the fatty tissue around the kidney, together with all the lymph nodes (glands) in the area, especially those close to the large blood vessels running up the center of the back wall of the abdomen between the kidneys.

The wound is closed, layer by layer, usually with catgut sutures, and the skin is sealed with stitches or metal clamps.

What is it like immediately after the operation?

You will wake up lying on one side, with the side from which the kidney has been removed uppermost. There may well be a rubber or plastic drainage tube leading from the incision (or less commonly, from a separate incision) to a small container somewhere below, inserted just to avert infection and, if present, left in place for between 24 and 48 hours. If infection does occur, you will be put on a regimen of antibiotics and the drainage tube will be left in for longer. You will feel weak, but you may already feel healthier. If necessary, the medical staff can administer drugs to combat pain or high temperature. To begin with, your diet will probably remain the same high-carbohydrate, low-protein diet designed to help kidney function that you will have been consuming prior to the operation. You will be encouraged to be active within fairly restricted limits, and should certainly expect to be on your feet within a few days. You can expect to return to work within a month—longer if your work involves heavy labor. Abdominal exercise could be resumed by about six weeks after surgery.

If both kidneys have been removed, you will have to become accustomed to regular dialysis (usually two to three times per week). It is relatively painless and eventually may seem no more than a boring but necessary routine.

What are the longterm effects?

When using one kidney after the other has been removed, kidney function generally returns to normal in about six months' time. By then your quality of life should be much improved, and almost all everyday activities will be open to you.

Regular tests on kidney function may be carried out at intervals—especially if the reason for the nephrectomy was kidney cancer.

© DIAGRAM

Kidney transplant

Why have the operation?

Kidney transplantation reestablishes the function of organs that are not working. Successful in at least 85 percent of cases—and repeatable in the case of failure, provided that a second suitable donor can be located—the operation allows a patient to lead an independent existence instead of being reliant on regular kidney dialysis. It also allows a liberating return to a normal diet. Regular dialysis is a short-term solution to kidney failure: the blood is artificially filtered through a machine or by diverting the bloodstream through another permeable membrane in the body itself. But the ideal treatment for total kidney failure is kidney transplantation.

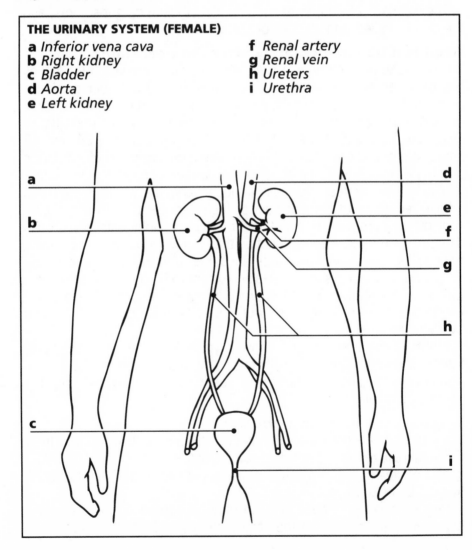

THE URINARY SYSTEM (FEMALE)

a *Inferior vena cava*
b *Right kidney*
c *Bladder*
d *Aorta*
e *Left kidney*

f *Renal artery*
g *Renal vein*
h *Ureters*
i *Urethra*

There are, however, certain disadvantages to the operation: the medication essential to prevent rejection of the transplanted kidney (immune suppression medication) makes you more prone to infection and may cause some redistribution of body fat—your face and body may become permanently rounder. You may also suffer anxiety at the continuing possibility of tissue graft rejection.

What is the physical cause of the problem?

The two kidneys' function is to filter all the blood in the body, purifying it by ridding it of the soluble waste products and excess water that can then be eliminated in the form of urine. Total kidney failure, which may be gradual or sudden in onset, results in the accumulation of these waste products in the blood, and these can poison you unless removed. The causes of kidney failure include:

- infection and inflammation of any part of the kidney structure
- nephrosclerosis: the replacement of ordinary kidney tissues with scar tissue following disease
- damage to kidney tissue through disease or injury
- polycystic kidneys: an inherited condition in which the tissues of the kidneys are gradually destroyed by cysts
- failure of normal kidney development from before birth

What is the goal of surgery?

The aim of surgery is to supply you with a single, fully functioning kidney. One kidney provides more than enough filtration and regulating capacity for all purposes and is grafted into its own position while the existing (nonfunctioning) kidneys remain in place. Your own kidneys are removed only if they cause persistent infection or high blood pressure; they will not interfere with the transplant procedure or functioning of the new organ. As soon as the transplanted kidney is connected to your blood vessels, it will begin purifying your blood of waste products.

Exactly what is involved in the surgical operation?

Your operation relies on the availability of a donor, either a living donor (usually a close relative) or one who has recently died. Accurate tissue typing reduces the risk of rejection, but there are many more different tissue types than there are blood groups and a good match can be difficult to find. Tissue from close relatives offers the best chance—around a 90 percent success rate, which can be improved to 98 percent by giving three transfusions of blood from the prospective donor prior to the operation. Without a willing close relative you may have to wait for some time before a suitable kidney becomes available. And when it does become available it may be at short notice: be prepared to have your operation at any time.

Preliminary steps. As with all operations involving general anesthesia, you will be given a preoperative injection about an hour before surgery to dry up internal fluids and to encourage drowsiness.

Step-by-step surgical procedure. Once you are anesthetized on the operating table, the area of skin over the implant site is thoroughly cleansed and surrounded by sterile surgical towels and drapes. Unless you are a child, this area will be the right lower corner of the abdomen. Here the new kidney can lie in the hollow of the pelvis and can be connected to the large iliac artery and vein that branch out to the legs from the main arterial trunk. The new kidney will also be connected to the nearby bladder. In children, the new kidney is sited almost centrally, and the kidney vessels are joined to the body's main artery (the aorta) and main vein (inferior vena cava).

The surgeon makes a curved and fairly long incision in the lower right

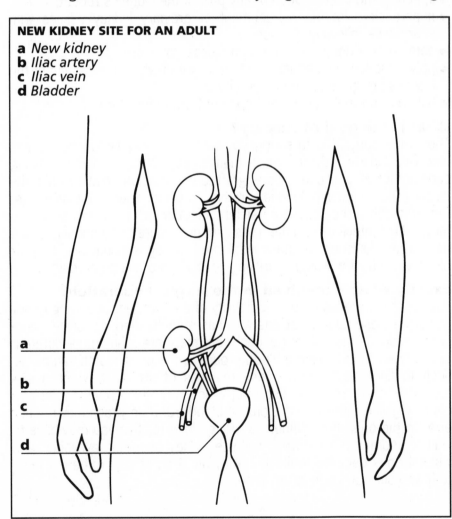

NEW KIDNEY SITE FOR AN ADULT
a *New kidney*
b *Iliac artery*
c *Iliac vein*
d *Bladder*

abdomen (or, in a child, in the midline of the lower abdomen), separates the underlying layers of muscle, and penetrates the membranous abdominal wall. The iliac artery and vein are lifted free and clamped. One of the main branches of the iliac artery is connected by a series of fine stitches end-to-end with the artery supplying the donor kidney. The donor kidney vein is connected similarly to the side of the iliac vein. When all is secure, the vein clamps are gently released, and then the artery clamps. As the artery clamps are removed, the kidney balloons out a little and becomes a healthier pink color. Small spurts of urine almost at once begin to emerge from the (so far unconnected) ureter (urine outlet) of the donor kidney. The end of the ureter is then pushed through a blunt incision in the side of the bladder, and stitched there.

The surgeon then closes up the abdominal wall and the muscle layers with catgut stitches, and closes the skin with nonabsorbable stitches.

NEW KIDNEY SITE FOR A CHILD

a *Main artery (aorta)*
b *Main vein (inferior vena cava)*
c *New kidney*
d *Bladder*

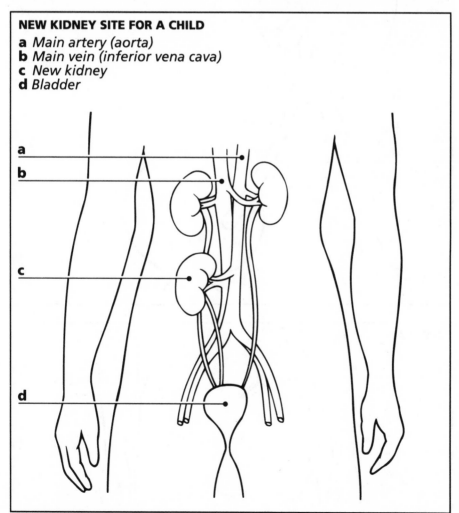

© DIAGRAM

THE GRAFTED KIDNEY
a *New kidney*
b *Iliac artery*
c *Iliac vein*
d *Ureter*
e *Main artery (aorta)*
f *Main vein (inferior vena cava)*
g *Bladder*

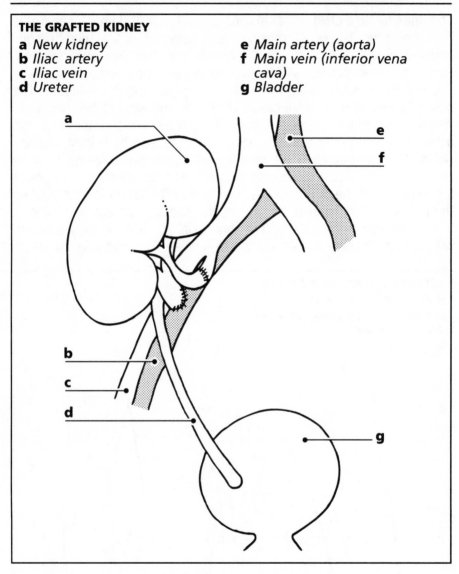

THE SCAR

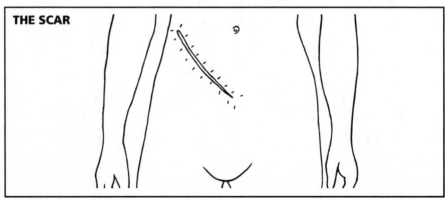

What is it like immediately after the operation?

When you wake up, your main feeling will be one of increasing well-being. In spite of some pain and stiffness in the abdomen, you are likely to feel better than you have for a long time, as the residual waste products are cleared from your body.

You will have to take medication at regular times, without fail, in order to avoid the possibility of tissue rejection. The immunosuppressant drug cyclosporin has revolutionized transplant surgery, especially kidney transplants: it does not affect the entire immune system, only those processes most involved in tissue rejection. Cyclosporin and other immunosuppressant drugs are administered immediately after the operation—sometimes even during the operation—and must be continued indefinitely. For a time you may be confined to an enclosed, purified atmosphere to avoid the possibility of airborne infection.

If all is well, you will be encouraged to get out of bed within a day or so. Urination should be no problem.

The duration of your stay in the hospital depends on the performance of the new kidney and on whether there are any signs of infection or rejection.

What are the longterm effects?

For many people the operation brings longterm good health. But the risks of tissue rejection do not disappear even if the kidney has been well accepted in the early stages. This is why immunosuppressant drugs must be given over a long term, although it is seldom necessary to maintain the high dosages required at first. A small proportion of transplanted kidneys are nonetheless rejected. If this happens, the kidney becomes inflamed and will usually have to be removed. Then the patient is put back on regular dialysis until the operation can be repeated and a new donor kidney can be transplanted.

The scar from the incision becomes less noticeable after some time.

Gastrectomy: removal of part or all of the stomach

Why have the operation?

Removal of the entire stomach is an operation that is performed comparatively rarely, generally in an attempt to save a life threatened by cancer of the stomach. Ulcers—areas of tissue erosion—in the stomach or duodenum (the next sector of the alimentary canal after the stomach) also once used to render the operation a necessity, but advances in the pharmaceutical treatment of ulcerative conditions in those organs have greatly reduced the need for treatment by surgical means, and even partial gastrectomy—removal of a section of the stomach—is now less commonly performed. Nonetheless, partial gastrectomy is still indicated in certain specific conditions:

- when intensive drug and dietary treatment of stomach or duodenal ulcers has failed to halt or heal tissue erosion
- when stomach or duodenal ulcers bleed continuously and copiously, to the extent that blood loss may present a further danger, or
- when the erosion is so extensive that there is a danger that the stomach or duodenal wall may be eroded entirely through (perforated), causing an escape of potentially infective digesting matter and highly acidic juices into the abdominal cavity

Ulcers remain the main reason for partial gastrectomy, although localized tumors near the pylorus (the outlet from stomach into duodenum) may also provide good cause.

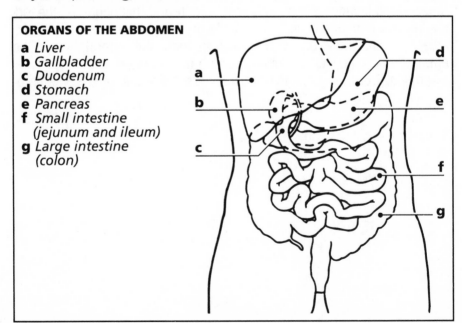

ORGANS OF THE ABDOMEN

a *Liver*
b *Gallbladder*
c *Duodenum*
d *Stomach*
e *Pancreas*
f *Small intestine (jejunum and ileum)*
g *Large intestine (colon)*

What is the physical cause of the problem?

The world incidence of stomach cancer is increasing rapidly, probably influenced in some way by dietary factors. If the cancer is detected early enough, there is a good chance that gastrectomy will prove a complete remedy—but in most cases the cancer has spread elsewhere in the body by the time of the initial diagnosis, and treatment has to include therapies additional to surgery, such as radiotherapy and chemotherapy.

Ulcers in the stomach and duodenum are caused primarily by the acidic effects of the stomach's own digestive juices on the lining of the organ, although they may be related additionally or instead to infection with the bacterium *Campylobacter pylori*. An initial rawness in the lining becomes an area of actual erosion in the tissues that may then bleed and become progressively deeper. Very rarely, a gastric or peptic ulcer may turn malignant.

What is the goal of surgery?

By gastrectomy, the surgeon aims to remove the part of the lining of the stomach on which the ulcer or tumor is situated. To do this, a complete section of the stomach wall has to be removed or, if essential, the entire stomach. The surgeon will make sure, however, that digestion can still take place by joining parts of the alimentary canal on each side of the removed portion; the alimentary canal will thus be shorter, but still functional.

Exactly what is involved in the surgical operation?

Tests and scans should already have pinpointed the problem—the exact position and nature of the tumor or ulcer—before the operation begins. There is no standard gastrectomy procedure, and the way in which the operation is performed is to some extent dictated by those details concerning the tumor or ulcer evident from the tests and scans.

Preliminary steps. As with all operations involving general anesthesia, you will be given a preoperative injection about an hour before surgery to dry up internal fluids and to encourage drowsiness.

Step-by-step surgical procedure. Once you are anesthetized, a soft, pliable tube is passed through your nose into your stomach to suck out any stomach contents. The surgeon then makes an incision, slightly to the left of the midline, running vertically down from below the ribs to just above the navel. The layer of fat beneath the skin, and then the muscle beneath the fat, and finally the fibrous sheath that surrounds and protects the abdominal cavity are all carefully cut through and pulled to one side to expose the abdominal organs inside. Before any incision is made into stomach or intestine, however, large clamps with rubber blades are positioned on both sides of the area for surgery to ensure that any residual contents cannot spill out.

The area of stomach or duodenum wall on which the ulcer or tumor is situated is then cut away. Depending on how much is removed, what remains of the stomach may be reattached to the duodenum or to part of the small intestine farther down. Sometimes, for example, the free end of the duodenum is tightly closed with stitches, and the remaining part of the stomach is united at the incision with a short length of the jejunum (see illustration **C** below).

When all is secure, the clamps are removed and the various layers of tissue over the abdominal cavity are sewn up.

What is it like immediately after the operation?

When you wake up, you will find that the tube through your nose to your stomach is still in position. This is to allow digestive secretions to be sucked out at regular intervals. When the digestive processes have restarted it will be safe for you to take small quantities of fluids by mouth and, if there is no pain or other untoward symptom, it should be possible to remove the tube soon thereafter. It normally takes four or five days to resume even a light diet of semisolids.

Gastrectomy, total or partial, is a major operation that requires a longer than average period of hospitalization and close postoperative care. The normal digestive processes are necessarily disrupted by the operation, and the period of hospitalization may be lengthy to allow treatment for a number of possible and—if they do occur—rather unpleasant side effects. About 20 percent of total gastrectomy patients

OPERATION OPTIONS

A Total gastrectomy
*Following removal of the entire stomach (**a**), the duodenum (**b**) is isolated and a section of the jejunum (**c**) is brought up and attached to the esophagus.*

B Partial gastrectomy
*Following removal of part of the stomach (**a**), the duodenum (**b**) may be reattached to the stomach at the incision.*

C Partial gastrectomy
*Alternatively, the duodenum (**b**) may be isolated and a section of the jejunum (**c**) brought up and attached at the incision.*

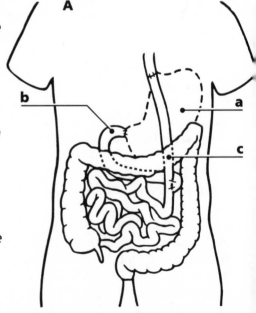

and around 10 percent of partial gastrectomy patients experience relatively severe side effects that may include:

- bloating: discomfort and a sense of fullness, caused mainly by the reduced size of the stomach; it may be more comfortable for you to eat little and often, rather than at set mealtimes
- dumping syndrome: a low blood sugar level caused by raised production of insulin triggered by the unaccustomed speed at which digesting material proceeds through the shorter stomach and on down the intestine; symptoms include nausea, dizziness, sweating, and faintness
- bile gastritis, caused by bile (gall) coming back into the stomach from farther down the intestine; symptoms include pain and vomiting
- the formation of, and pain from, a new ulcer at the pylorus
- diarrhea

Some or all of these effects may require drug treatment and an appropriate dietary regimen. It is possible that a second surgical operation may be necessary if symptoms do not subside.

What are the longterm effects?
Ideally, longterm effects are no more than a necessity to be careful with diet—probably to take vitamin and mineral supplements as directed by the surgeon to compensate for reduced absorptive capability.

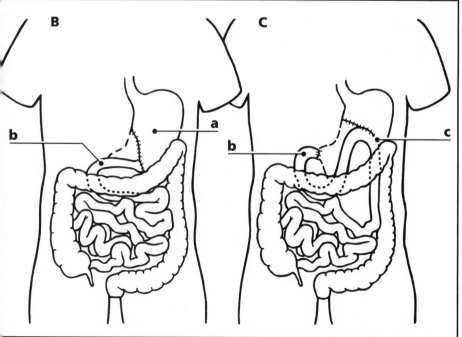

© DIAGRAM

Appendectomy: removal of the appendix

Why have the operation?
The operation is usually necessary on an emergency basis, either to relieve the symptoms of an inflamed appendix (appendicitis), which are painful in themselves, or—even more important—to prevent the inflamed appendix from bursting and releasing its infective material into the abdominal cavity, so precipitating a yet more dangerous medical condition (peritonitis) and necessitating further complex and difficult surgery.

STRUCTURES OF THE ABDOMEN

The appendix is usually about 3¹/₂ inches long and ¹/₂ inch around and hangs behind or below the cecum, the pouch that begins the large intestine. Less commonly, it is longer or shorter, and although stemming from the same place may be tucked up within the folds of the small intestine or even stuck to the back of the cecum itself; in rare cases, the appendix hangs right down into the pelvic region. An inflamed appendix in these circumstances may cause extra surgical difficulty either because it has become attached to other internal structures and will have to be separated, or because the inflammation or infection has spread to nearby organs, which will also have to be surgically disinfected after the appendix is removed.

a *Stomach*
b *Liver*
c *Small intestine*
d *Cecum*
e *Appendix*
f *Large intestine*

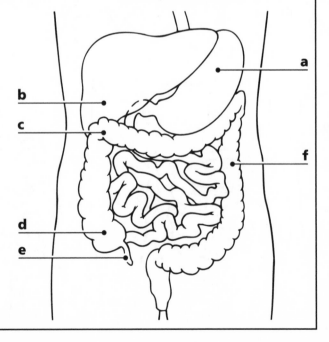

What is the physical cause of the problem?

The appendix is a short, wormlike structure that hangs from the rounded pouch (the cecum) that begins the large intestine, just after its junction with the longer small intestine, in the lower right corner of the abdomen. It has no known function, although in other mammals it assists in the digestion of certain vegetable carbohydrates that in humans are indigestible. The appendix contains lymphoid tissue which elsewhere provides a degree of protection against infection.

No single cause of appendicitis is known. The most common symptoms of appendicitis—nausea and vomiting, constipation, a slightly raised temperature, and a pain that begins dully around or beneath the navel but becomes sharper as it localizes in the lower right side of the abdomen, which then is tender to the touch—are not always all present, and final diagnosis may even require investigative surgery through the abdominal wall (see section on laparotomy, p.41). In cases where diagnosis is tentative, and particularly in small children and senior citizens, it may be best to delay surgery and maintain a close watch on how and whether further, more genuine, signs of inflammation become evident, although this means that if surgery is eventually deemed necessary it may be as a matter of urgency.

What is the goal of surgery?

The surgeon's goal is to remove the inflamed appendix, and so relieve the symptoms, before the condition worsens. If there are signs that peritonitis has already occurred, the surgeon will also have to clear the infective material from the abdominal cavity, disinfect the area, and try to ensure that no further complications occur.

Exactly what is involved in the surgical operation?

Preliminary steps. This operation is usually done under general anesthesia but a spinal anesthetic may be used. As with all operations involving general anesthesia, you will be given a preoperative injection about an hour before surgery to dry up internal fluids and to encourage drowsiness.

If peritonitis is indicated, you will also be given antibiotic drugs and a saline infusion drip may be attached to one arm. The anesthetist will then induce general anesthesia.

Step-by-step surgical procedure. The surgeon starts by swabbing the skin of your abdomen with an antiseptic solution. Sterile towels are then fixed in place with clips so that only the lower right area of the abdomen remains exposed. The surgeon now makes the initial incision through the skin—an approximately 4-inch-long cut roughly parallel to, and 2 or 3 inches above, the fold of the groin. The cut is made through the skin and underlying fat. Any bleeding points are picked up in forceps and sealed with an electric current.

Once the incision is made, an assistant using metal retractors pulls aside the skin edges and their underlying layer of fat, to reveal the flat, fibrous tendon sheet of the external abdominal muscle beneath. This is split in the direction of the fibers. Below are two further layers of flat muscle in which the fibers run in different directions—but it is unnecessary to cut them because they too can readily be split and held apart by retractors.

Under the flat muscles is the smooth membranous layer of the peritoneum, the lining of the abdominal cavity. This too is cut open and is held open with forceps. It is then possible to see the intestines. The cecum should be immediately under the opening. It is carefully turned until the appendix is found and can be inspected. The whole cecum—with the appendix still attached—is then brought out through the wound, for at this point the surgeon's main concern is to avoid bursting a swollen and inflamed appendix and releasing a jet of infective material into the abdominal cavity.

Along one side of the appendix is a short membrane containing blood vessels. The vessels are firmly tied off with catgut ligatures before the appendix itself is tied off and cut away. Most surgeons now bury the stump of the appendix within the cecum by putting a "purse-string" stitch around its base, pulling it tight so as to close up the wall of the cecum, and pushing the stump inside with the end of a pair of forceps

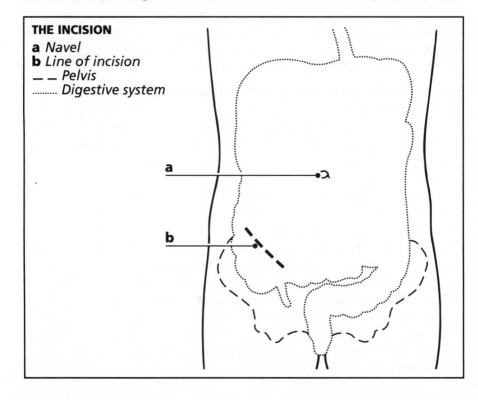

THE INCISION
a *Navel*
b *Line of incision*
− − *Pelvis*
········· *Digestive system*

EXPOSING THE PERITONEUM
a *External abdominal muscle*
b *Retractors*
c *Fat*
d *Flat muscle*
e *Peritoneum*

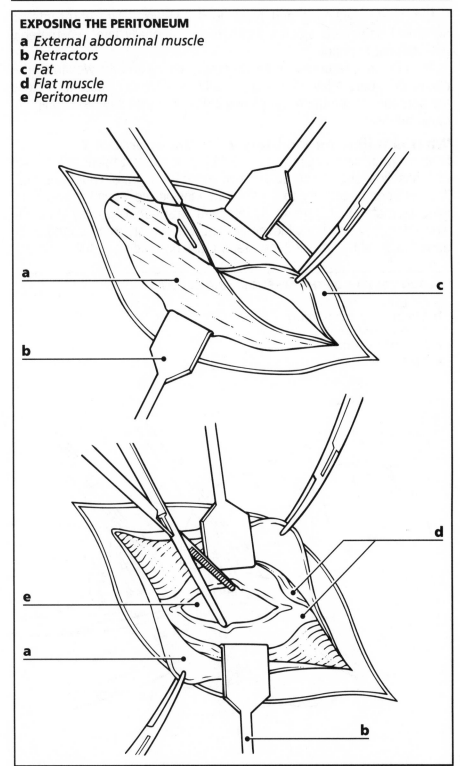

© DIAGRAM

before finally tightening and tying up the suture. This represents an additional safeguard against leakage of potentially infective material from the cut appendix.

The cecum is returned to the abdominal cavity and the wound is now closed in separate layers, using continuous stitches of catgut to close the peritoneum and the muscles and individual nylon stitches or clips to close the skin.

What is it like immediately after the operation?

In an uncomplicated case you should be able to start taking a light diet of semisolids, such as cereals, within about 24 hours of your operation. If it has been necessary to leave a drain inside the wound to clear any infective material, it is generally removed after about two days (and the wound heals soon after). Movement and walking are encouraged at an early stage, although climbing stairs must be taken carefully, and any

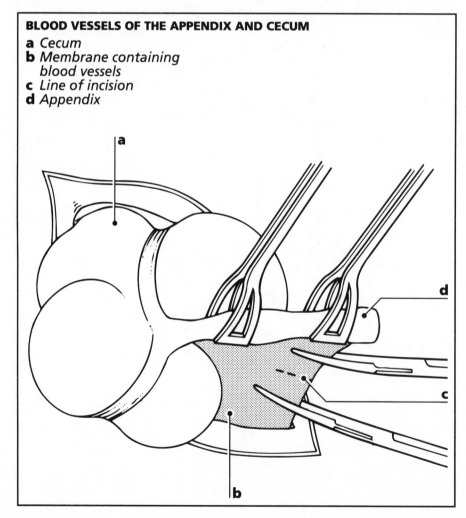

BLOOD VESSELS OF THE APPENDIX AND CECUM

a *Cecum*
b *Membrane containing blood vessels*
c *Line of incision*
d *Appendix*

effort that might cause strain on abdominal muscles—such as lifting with the arms—must be avoided for a time. You should be able to leave the hospital after two or three days. The scar may seem vivid for a while but will fade.

What are the longterm effects?

External stitches are usually removed after about a week or a little more, and you should be able to resume virtually all your former activities in around three weeks, or sooner if you lead a relatively sedentary life. If there are complications, however—if infection persists either within the abdominal cavity or at the site of surgical incision, causing local pain, inflammation, and possibly high temperature—recovery may take much longer and involve a prolonged regimen of antibiotic drug therapy.

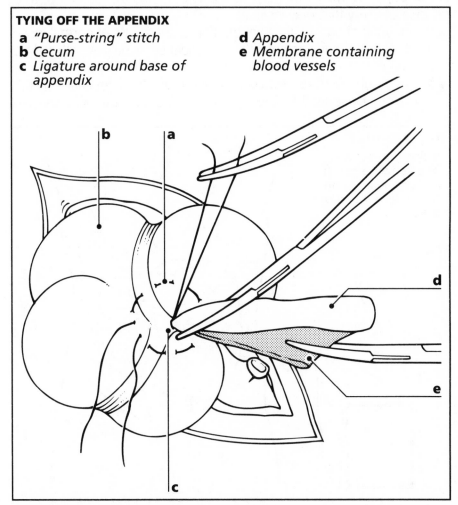

TYING OFF THE APPENDIX

a *"Purse-string" stitch*
b *Cecum*
c *Ligature around base of appendix*

d *Appendix*
e *Membrane containing blood vessels*

© DIAGRAM

Colostomy

Why have the operation?

The colostomy operation creates an outlet in the abdominal wall through which the large intestine (the colon) is brought out to act as an artificial anus. The outlet may be permanent, replacing the rest of the colon, the rectum, and the true anus when those organs are subject to malignant disease or severe injury. Or it may be temporary, allowing lesser disease or injury in those areas time to heal before being brought back into use. A colostomy is required when the normal movement of the intestinal contents is impossible. It is one of the most common of all abdominal procedures, and afterwards it is quite usual to live a normal, active life.

What is the physical cause of the problem?

A temporary colostomy may form part of a larger operation to treat disease or injury that may include:

- the clearing of an intestinal obstruction or the failure of normal movement of intestinal contents that, unchecked, would result in total blockage of the small intestine
- the repair of a perforation (a hole right through the intestinal wall) that would otherwise lead to leakage of intestinal contents into the peri-

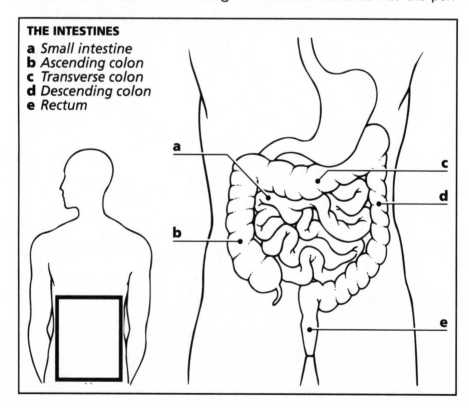

THE INTESTINES

a *Small intestine*
b *Ascending colon*
c *Transverse colon*
d *Descending colon*
e *Rectum*

toneal cavity (the sterile space in the abdomen). This results in infection of the peritoneum (the complex membrane covering the abdominal organs and abdominal wall) in the condition known as peritonitis—another medical emergency.

A permanent colostomy is used to treat cancerous conditions or severe injuries that result in:

- removal of the lower part of the colon together with the top part of the rectum, when remaining parts of the intestine cannot be rejoined
- removal of the rectum and anus
- obstruction of the colon, when the patient is likely to remain too ill or too weak to undergo surgery more radical than colostomy (e.g., total removal of the colon)

In these cases, too, the colostomy may form part of a more extensive surgical operation.

What is the goal of surgery?

The aim of a colostomy is to restore the outflow of feces (stools) from a location in the intestine above one that is healing or has been removed. The operation described here is loop colostomy.

Exactly what is involved in the surgical operation?

Preliminary steps. If the operation is performed as a medical emergency there may be little time for any of the normal preliminaries, except for:

- transfusion of blood or other fluids to prevent shock
- X-ray examination to try to determine the site of any obstruction—although an obstructed colon is generally distended, which may give an indication of where the problem lies and where the surgeon should consider making the first incision
- an emergency barium enema (the introduction of a radiopaque barium solution through the anus and into the rectum and colon). This is a quick way of identifying the site of obstruction. Radiopaque substances are opaque to radiation, and the barium therefore shows up readily on X rays. The "shape" of the barium on the X ray indicates the shape of the interior of the bowel and in this way highlights any bowel defects such as narrowing or "filling" caused by tumors.
- endoscopy (viewing through a fiberoptic instrument introduced through the anus) if required. In this case antibiotics will probably be administered, and a tube will most likely be passed down the windpipe (trachea) so that your airway can be sealed off to prevent harm coming to you should you vomit under anesthesia.

If the operation is not being done on an emergency basis you will be given a preoperative injection about an hour before surgery to dry up internal fluids and to encourage drowsiness. The operation itself is performed under general anesthesia.

© DIAGRAM

Step-by-step surgical procedure. The surgeon makes the first incision in the upper right quadrant of the abdomen. It is usually vertical (although it may instead be transverse) but is always 3–4 inches (8–10cm) long. The underlying muscles are carefully separated, or cut through, and the membranous wall of the abdominal cavity (the peritoneum) is then also penetrated. This exposes the part of the colon that runs straight across the width of the body (the transverse colon). In the case of obstruction, this is often ballooned out under great tension, and it may be necessary to deflate the distended colon with a wide needle. In any event, the connective tissue (the omentum) from which the colon is suspended within the peritoneal cavity is cut through along a short length so that a loop of colon can be gently pulled out of the incision.

A strong, sterile glass rod is passed behind the colon to keep it out of the wound; the rod is kept in place by means of short lengths of rub-

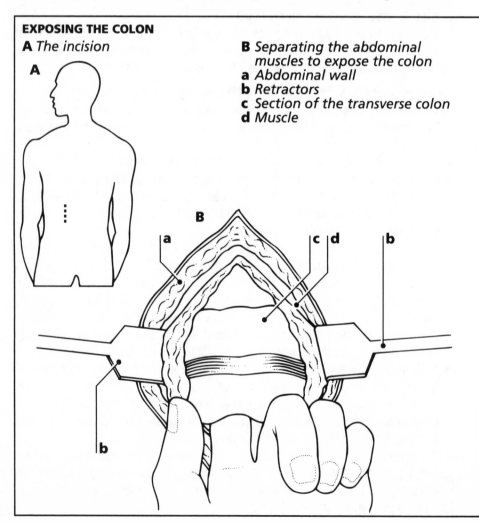

EXPOSING THE COLON

A *The incision*

B *Separating the abdominal muscles to expose the colon*
a *Abdominal wall*
b *Retractors*
c *Section of the transverse colon*
d *Muscle*

ber tubing attached at each end. The under surface of the colon is then stitched to the outer edges of the peritoneal membrane, and both edges of the incision are closed up against the colon, so that only the small loop of protruding intestine remains exposed.

Some surgeons prefer to leave the colon loop as it is for a few days until the edges have sealed and healed. In that case, intestinal contents can be drained from the loop via a catheter passed in through a small incision surrounded by a purse-string suture. Other surgeons prefer to open the loop to make the colostomy at the initial time of surgery. To do so, an opening is made with surgical scissors at the outside extreme of the loop, and the free edges are then carefully stitched to the free skin edges on either side, while at the same time any leaking intestinal contents are rapidly vacuumed away to avoid contaminating the wound.

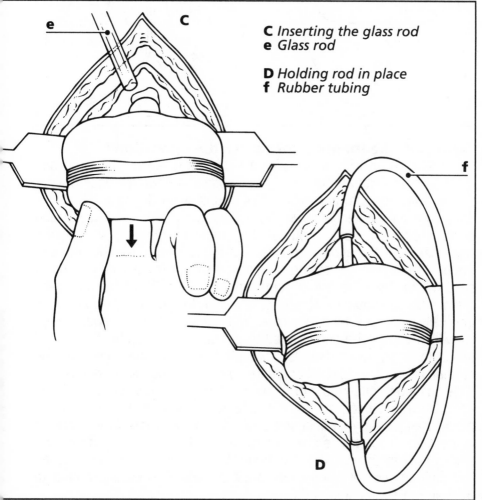

C *Inserting the glass rod*
e *Glass rod*

D *Holding rod in place*
f *Rubber tubing*

© DIAGRAM

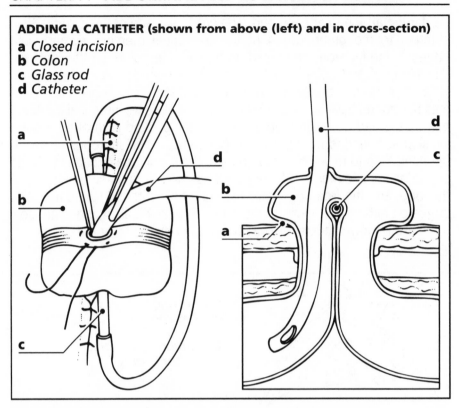

ADDING A CATHETER (shown from above (left) and in cross-section)
a *Closed incision*
b *Colon*
c *Glass rod*
d *Catheter*

What is it like immediately after the operation?

You will wake up with an intravenous drip attached to one hand and most probably with a tube through the nose and down the back of your throat. The drip is to administer fluid nourishment during the first few days. The tube extends down the esophagus into your stomach and ensures constant suction out of the stomach contents, so that the intestines have a chance to recover. For the first few days you will need frequent changes of dressing around the site of the wound and great care will be taken to avoid contamination. Once the tube has been removed, you should be able to take a soft, low-residue diet, and then gradually increase intake to normal. Within a short time afterward—during which you will be encouraged to get up and move about—you will begin to pass feces (stools) through the colostomy opening (the stoma). Normally, intestinal contents do not become fully firm until they have passed through most of the colon; those that pass out of a stoma are generally of a soft, muddy consistency. They pass into a lightweight plastic bag fixed by an adhesive seal around the stoma. While you are in the hospital you will be given instructions in the care of the stoma and shown how to change the colostomy bag. Feces are usually passed into the bag once or twice a day, but it is seldom necessary to change the bag more than once a day.

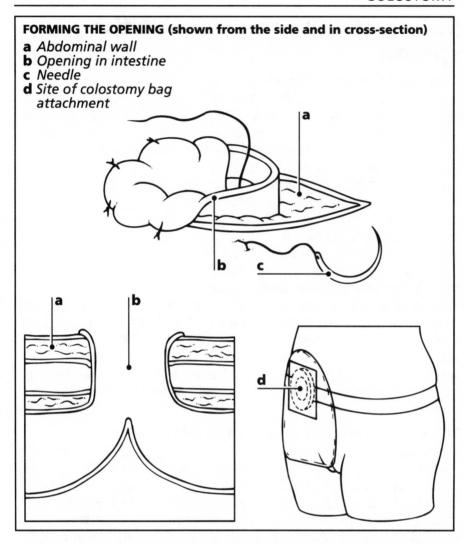

FORMING THE OPENING (shown from the side and in cross-section)
a *Abdominal wall*
b *Opening in intestine*
c *Needle*
d *Site of colostomy bag attachment*

The duration of your stay in the hospital depends on your overall condition, on what other surgical procedures (if any) you underwent at the time of your colostomy, and whether further procedures are required.

After you leave the hospital, you may receive follow-up visits from the stoma care attendant to ensure that all is proceeding well.

What are the longterm effects?

With a permanent colostomy there are usually no complications at all. Digestion and excretion again become part of the background routine of everyday life. Very occasionally, the stoma may narrow and cause problems through partial blockage. Even more rarely, part of the inner surface of the colon may begin to protrude (prolapse) through the stoma. Both of these defects can be quickly and permanently remedied through minor surgery.

Splenectomy: removal of the spleen

Why have the operation?

The most common reason for removal of the spleen is to control severe bleeding from the organ following serious injury to the upper abdomen or to the lower ribs, and the operation is generally performed as an emergency. In such cases removal of the spleen (splenectomy) is life-saving. The spleen may also be removed to treat:

- blood diseases such as anemia, leukemia, and thalassemia
- an enlarged spleen caused by lymphoma
- venal blood congestion
- white blood cell deficiency
- Gaucher's disease, in which the spleen becomes enlarged from deposits of the abnormal substance glucosylceramide

The effect of splenectomy varies. It may:

- result in a striking and permanent improvement where it was per-formed to treat certain blood diseases in which the spleen is respon-sible for the undue destruction of red blood cells (hemolytic anemia)
- lead to a longterm remission of symptoms
- provide the basis for determining the best course of treatment to pursue thereafter (as with the lymphoid cancer known as Hodgkin's disease)

What is the physical cause of the problem?

The spleen's main purpose is to pick out and destroy red blood cells that are no longer effective. It therefore has a comparatively large blood supply at high pressure through its own five-branched artery direct from the main artery of the body, the aorta. Bleeding from a rup-tured spleen is difficult to halt other than by tying off its artery—which inevitably causes death of the organ, necessitating its removal. In an adult, spleen removal ordinarily causes no harm at all: its function can be taken over by the liver and parts of the lymphatic system. In a young child, however, removal may be followed by severe and uncontrollable infection, which may progress to potentially fatal blood poisoning.

Described here is the procedure for a nonemergency splenectomy. In an emergency situation, rapid transfusions may be administered to maintain the body's overall blood volume during the operation. Large quantities of blood may be lost into the abdominal cavity before the artery can be successfully secured and tied off.

What is the goal of surgery?

Surgery is designed to remove the spleen with minimal upset to the patient. In the case of Hodgkin's disease, splenectomy is merely part of

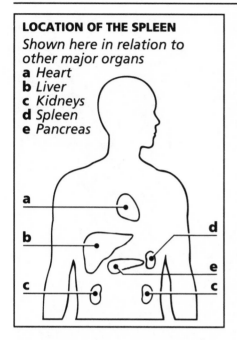

LOCATION OF THE SPLEEN
Shown here in relation to other major organs
a *Heart*
b *Liver*
c *Kidneys*
d *Spleen*
e *Pancreas*

a
b
c
d
e
c

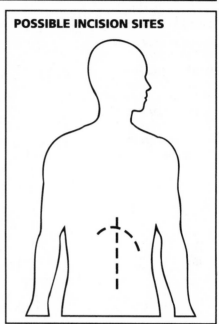

POSSIBLE INCISION SITES

the process of "staging": gauging how far the disease has progressed and obtaining essential information on how treatment should continue.

Exactly what is involved in the surgical operation?

Preliminary treatment will depend on why you are having your spleen removed. For example:

- If you are seriously anemic, you may need a prior blood transfusion.
- If your condition involves the breakdown of excessive numbers of red blood cells (hemolytic anemia), transfusion would be dangerous.
- If shortage of blood platelets is causing a tendency to bleed beneath the skin (purpura), you may be given a transfusion of platelets.
- With a deficiency of white blood cells (part of the immune system), you might be given antibiotic drugs to reduce the risk of infection.

Preliminary steps. As with all operations involving general anesthesia, you will be given a preoperative injection about an hour before surgery to dry up internal fluids and to encourage drowsiness. Once you have been anesthetized, you will be positioned on the operating table lying on your back; the table may be tilted down at the foot to make the spleen more accessible to the surgeon. Emergency supplies of blood and oxygen will be available.

Step-by-step surgical procedure. After making the incision, the surgeon separates the layers of muscle that lie beneath the skin and exposes the abdominal organs. The large transverse colon is held out of the way using large, warm, moist gauze packs. The stomach is held in a sizable clamp and pushed to the right side. Movement of the stomach tightens a thin, broad ligament that connects the stomach to the

EXPOSING THE ABDOMINAL ORGANS
a Retractors
b Stomach
c Skin, muscle, and fat layers
d Spleen
e Ligament connecting the spleen to the stomach

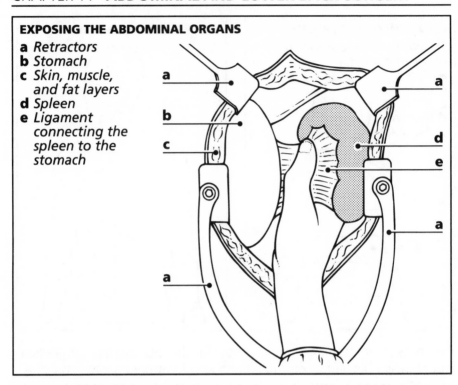

spleen. A hole is made in this ligament and is gradually enlarged; some small blood vessels within the ligament have to be cut and tied off. But the hole is eventually large enough to allow access to the twisting splenic artery immediately behind the ligament. The surgeon passes blunt forceps behind the artery and ties it firmly using one or two strong bands of silk. As blood continues to drain from the spleen via the splenic vein, the organ shrinks because no further blood is reaching it.

The surgeon now cuts through the remainder of the ligament connecting the spleen to the stomach and then forces the spleen toward the right side, thus tightening another ligament that connects the spleen with the left kidney. This too is severed. The surgeon now brings the spleen (still attached to the tied-off splenic artery and the untied splenic vein) out of the wound. In adult patients, clamps and firm ties are applied to artery and vein, and they are severed between ties. In child patients, a healthy fragment of the spleen may be left and reimplanted: such fragments sometimes regenerate to form a new spleen, and it is far preferable for a child not to be left without a spleen if possible.

The cut end of a tied-off artery soon heals, leaving a blind-ended tube. There is no harm in this. The edges of cut ligaments soon heal over as well. The wound is closed in layers—abdominal wall, muscles, skin; each layer is stitched separately.

LOCATING THE SPLENIC ARTERY
a *Stomach*
b *Splenic artery*
c *Ligament*
d *Spleen*

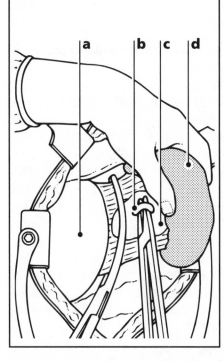

SEVERING THE SPLEEN
The ligament connecting the spleen to the stomach is cut through completely.
a *Stomach*
b *Splenic artery*
c *Ligament*
d *Spleen*

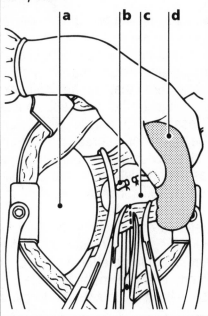

What is it like immediately after the operation?

How you feel after the operation depends largely upon why it was performed and on your condition before surgery. But recovery from the operation should be rapid, and complications are rare. There may be some pain at the site of the incision, but that can be deadened, if necessary, with painkilling drugs administered by the medical staff. You will probably be encouraged to get out of bed within 24 hours, and it is likely that you will be able to leave the hospital in about a week. All being well, you should be able to return to normal activity two or three weeks after leaving the hospital.

What are the longterm effects?

Absence of the spleen slightly increases the risk of infection. Some surgeons advise a daily dose of penicillin for an indefinite period after surgery, and you should avoid contact with people known to suffer from an infection. Children, especially, should be vaccinated against infection by pneumococcal bacteria (which cause pneumonia) and should receive additional doses of antibiotic drugs with longterm potency.

Liver transplant

Why have the operation?

Transplantation provides the only chance of survival for a person whose liver has been destroyed by disease or injury. The liver is vital to life because it is responsible for:

- storing body fuels and vitamins
- synthesizing blood-clotting factors
- managing the products of normal red blood cell breakdown and their conversion to the valuable substance bile
- regulating the quantity of bile produced
- changing poisonous nitrogenous body waste products to the less toxic urea that can be safely excreted in the urine
- changing other toxic substances found naturally in the body to safer, less toxic forms. Detoxified poisons are then excreted.

The operation represents a comparatively recent development. The first successful transplant was performed in 1967, but the operation has been widely accepted only since around 1983. The liver is technically more difficult to transplant than the kidney and, although (in adults) the success rate is not as high, results are steadily improving. Safer methods of preventing tissue rejection by the immune system, better solutions for the preservation of the donor organ, new surgical procedures, and more effective selection of suitable recipients—specific conditions in some (notably certain types of cancer) render them unsuitable—have all contributed to this record of increased success.

What is the physical cause of the problem?

In adults, the most common cause of liver failure is excessive alcohol consumption leading to cirrhosis (a condition in which the clusters of healthy active cells within the liver become separated by increasingly disruptive bands of fibrous scar tissue). The liver has great powers of recovery and rejuvenation and even people who consume large amounts of alcohol (resulting in liver failure) can quickly recover once they have stopped drinking alcohol. Not all liver failure is due to alcohol poisoning. Other conditions that may be responsible include:

- longterm hepatitis B (and other forms of hepatitis)
- poisoning with acetaminophen or similar drugs
- longterm obstruction to the passage of bile or of blood through the liver
- Wilson's disease (an inherited condition in which copper accumulates in the liver)
- hemochromatosis (similar to Wilson's disease but involving iron)
- cancer
- (in children) congenital biliary atresia, an inherited condition in which the bile system of the liver fails to develop

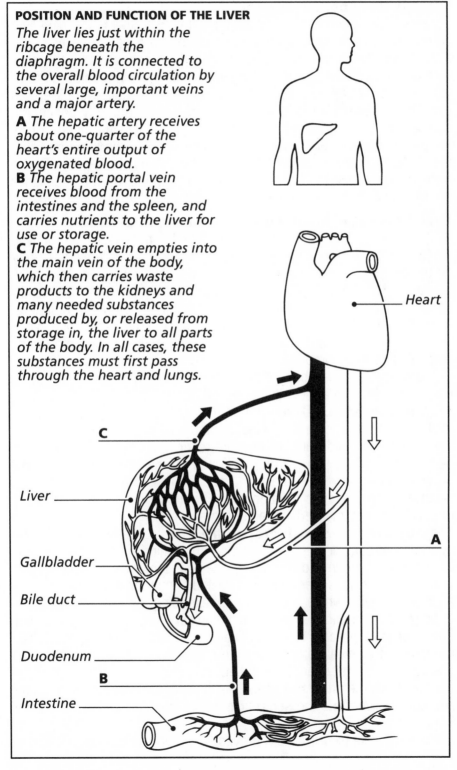

POSITION AND FUNCTION OF THE LIVER

The liver lies just within the ribcage beneath the diaphragm. It is connected to the overall blood circulation by several large, important veins and a major artery.

A *The hepatic artery receives about one-quarter of the heart's entire output of oxygenated blood.*
B *The hepatic portal vein receives blood from the intestines and the spleen, and carries nutrients to the liver for use or storage.*
C *The hepatic vein empties into the main vein of the body, which then carries waste products to the kidneys and many needed substances produced by, or released from storage in, the liver to all parts of the body. In all cases, these substances must first pass through the heart and lungs.*

Heart

C

Liver

Gallbladder

Bile duct

A

Duodenum

B

Intestine

What is the goal of surgery?

Surgery is designed to provide the patient with a new, functioning liver so that the body may return to a state of comparative normality.

The liver donor may be someone recently deceased through accident or, since the beginning of the 1990s, may be a living close relative who donates a segment of his or her own liver. Because the liver has excellent regenerative faculties, a part of a liver (properly connected during transplantation) can increase in size to meet the needs of its recipient's body. In all forms of transplant surgery it is important that the donated organ should be accepted by the patient's body. Tissue from a close relative is less likely to be rejected by the recipient's immune system than is tissue from an unrelated donor.

Exactly what is involved in the surgical operation?

In acute liver failure, an immediate transplant is necessary for survival. When time is less critical, the timing of the operation depends largely on the availability of a donor liver. Washed through with a special solution cooled to 39°F (4°C), a donor liver can be preserved for up to about five hours without risking a loss of vitality. The donor organ may also have to be transported between hospitals. This is another excellent reason for partial donation by a living close relative—both donor and patient can be prepared for the operation together.

The operation described below is the more conventional transplant, using the liver from a recently deceased donor.

Preliminary steps. Depending on the urgency of the operation, you may be given a preoperative injection about an hour before surgery to dry up internal fluids and to encourage drowsiness. Once you have been anesthetized, you will be positioned on the operating table lying on your back, with your chest and abdomen having been thoroughly cleansed with antiseptic solution and with sterile towels covering parts of your body not involved in the surgery.

Step-by-step surgical procedure. The surgeon performs the operation through a long, vertical incision running from just below the breastbone (sternum) to the navel. The layers of muscle beneath the skin are carefully separated to reveal the membranous wall of the abdominal cavity, which is cut through, exposing the internal organs.

So great is the blood flow through the veins that they cannot be shut down even temporarily while the liver is substituted, so bypass tubes are inserted to divert blood from the major veins to veins in the arm. The veins and artery can then be tied off and severed. After detaching the liver from the underside of the diaphragm, the surgeon then gently lifts out the liver (and the semi-enclosed gallbladder) and removes the liver.

Once the diseased liver is removed, the blood vessels of the donor organ are connected to the recipient and the bypass tubes are removed. But the new liver must be connected also with the intestinal tract. The connection can be made in any of several ways. Sometimes a loop of the small intestine is brought up near to the liver so that the bile duct can be implanted into it.

The surgeon closes up the incisions in layers—membrane, muscles, skin; each layer is sewn up separately.

During this operation there is a strong tendency to hemorrhage and measures must be taken to control the bleeding. In former decades, air sometimes got into the large veins and was passed directly to the brain where it caused serious, occasionally fatal, damage; this potential problem has since been virtually eliminated.

What is it like immediately after the operation?
You will wake up under close surveillance in an intensive care unit (ICU), linked to various machines that monitor your overall condition. There may be pain, focused mainly on the incision in your upper abdomen, but this can be dealt with using painkilling drugs administered by the medical staff. In general you are likely to feel much better than you have felt for a long time, and certainly more alert. It may be several days before you leave the ICU, and—if all seems to be going well and there is no sign of tissue rejection—you will be encouraged to get out of bed in about a week.

More than half the people who receive liver transplants survive for five years and longer, and the results are steadily improving. Rejection is the major danger. You will be given drugs (such as cyclosporin) that suppress the immune system's normal processes, although this in turn will increase your susceptibility to infection. About 20 percent of patients suffer graft rejection, liver artery thrombosis, infection, or other complications, and require another graft. In these cases the survival rate is around 70 percent. About 8 percent of grafts fail to function.

What are the longterm effects?
After a few weeks you will be able to return to an almost normal, active life. Unless your graft was donated by a twin brother or sister, however, you will probably have to continue taking immunosuppressive drugs for the rest of your life. These drugs damage the protective function of the immune system so your susceptibility to infection is much greater and infections are likely to be more severe. You should therefore avoid contact with people known to suffer infection of any kind.

Vagotomy: reduction of stomach acid

Why have the operation?

A peptic ulcer is a raw area in the mucous membrane that lines the gastrointestinal tract. Such ulcers are caused by stomach acids, which normally facilitate digestion but which in excessive amounts begin to digest the tissues of their containing organs, causing pain, loss of appetite, weight loss, and vomiting.

Vagotomy involves cutting some of the branches of the major nerves (the vagus nerves) that transmit the impulses that cause the stomach to secrete peptic acid. Some surgeons maintain that the availability of certain drugs makes the operation unnecessary, whereas others insist that vagotomy is a useful operation, especially in cases that do not respond to medical management.

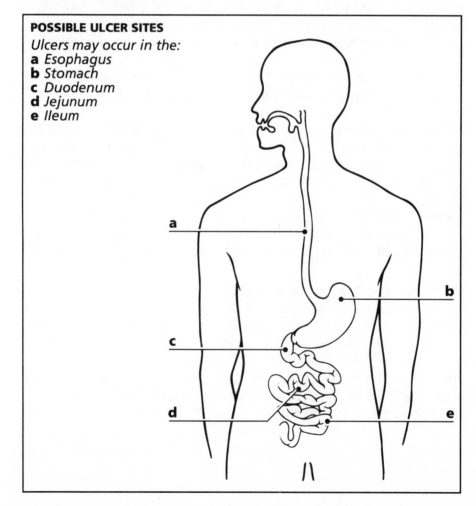

POSSIBLE ULCER SITES

Ulcers may occur in the:
a *Esophagus*
b *Stomach*
c *Duodenum*
d *Jejunum*
e *Ileum*

The drugs used to treat ulcers include:

- histamine-2 blockers—which block the impulse-receiving "terminals" at the nerve ends
- antibiotics—which destroy the bacterium *Helicobacter pylori* present in 90 percent of cases
- mucosal protectors—drugs (such as sucralfate) that can provide a protective coating over the eroded area, allowing it to heal underneath

Where symptoms persist or worsen, surgery is performed to reduce the amount of stomach acid being produced, thereby allowing the ulcer to heal.

Left untreated, peptic ulceration may eventually lead to bleeding from the ulcer; narrowing of the outlet of the stomach into the duodenum; or perforation of the stomach or duodenum, allowing the digesting contents to surround the pancreas or—worse—to leak into the peritoneal cavity and cause peritonitis. Each of these is a medical emergency.

What is the physical cause of the problem?

Factors that contribute to the occurrence of a peptic ulcer include:

- heredity: a family history of peptic ulcers
- excessive intake of irritants such as alcohol or aspirin
- the presence in the stomach of the bacterium *Helicobacter pylori*
- insufficient quantity of protective stomach mucus
- severe physical stress—such as a head injury, burns, severe infection, or major surgery

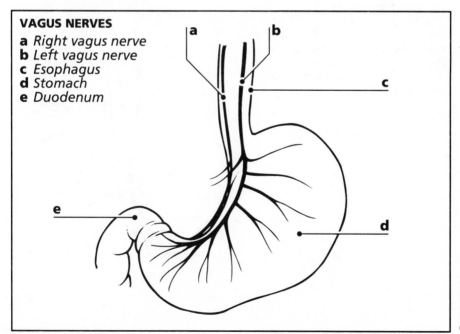

VAGUS NERVES
a *Right vagus nerve*
b *Left vagus nerve*
c *Esophagus*
d *Stomach*
e *Duodenum*

© DIAGRAM

What is the goal of surgery?

There are two vagus nerves: the left vagus nerve lies to the front of the stomach; the right vagus nerve lies behind. The surgeon's aim is to sever and permanently destroy some or all of the branches of the nerves so that acid secretion is greatly reduced. Vagotomy may be "truncal," "selective," or "highly selective" (see illustrations below).

The vagus nerves are responsible not only for the secretion of stomach acid but also for stomach movements that help it to empty when its contents have been digested. For this reason truncal vagotomy—and, less often, selective vagotomy—is nearly always immediately accompanied by a further surgical procedure to ease the passage of digesting contents. This additional surgery might involve widening the exit from stomach to duodenum (pyloroplasty), or connecting the stomach directly with a further part of the small intestine (gastrojejunostomy). Such additional surgery is not required with highly selective vagotomy, the operation described here.

TYPES OF VAGOTOMY

A Truncal
The major nerves are cut near the stomach.

B Selective
Some lesser branches from the nerves are severed.

**C Highly selective
(or superselective)**
The main trunk of each nerve and the lower branches to the stomach remain intact but the very small branches to the upper and middle part of the stomach are cut.

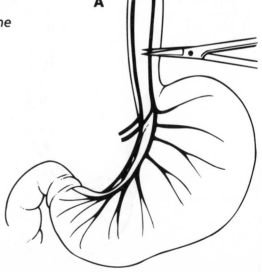

A

Exactly what is involved in the surgical operation?
Prior testing and scans will have allowed the surgeon to determine whether the vagotomy is to be truncal, selective, or highly selective.

Preliminary steps. As with all operations involving general anesthesia, you will be given a preoperative injection about an hour before surgery to dry up internal fluids and to encourage drowsiness.

Step-by-step surgical procedure. Once you are anesthetized, the surgeon makes the first incision, in the midline from the angle of the ribs vertically down to just above the navel. He or she carefully separates the layers of underlying muscles and penetrates the abdominal wall. Such a long initial incision allows adequate exposure of the stomach, enabling the surgeon to inspect the upper abdomen for signs of infection and to examine the outside wall of the stomach and intestine for indications of imminent perforation. The next task is to identify the vagus nerves; this is not always easy.

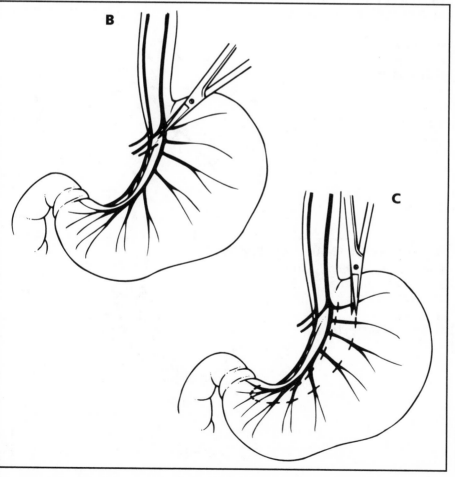

Some surgeons prefer to start at the lower end of the esophagus (just above the stomach), where the vagus nerves are readily visible, and to put them under tension with small hooks so that they can then be traced downward along the inner curve of the stomach. Other surgeons work upward from the underside of the stomach. Either way, the many small nerve branches to the stomach—each accompanied by a small artery and vein—are picked up in artery forceps and severed. The procedure is performed at the front and back of the curve of the stomach. The surgeon must ensure that every single nerve branch in the area is cut: the results depend on the efficiency with which this is done. It has been suggested that just one missed nerve fiber can nullify the effects of this operation.

When all nerve branches are severed, the surgeon closes the abdominal wall and the layers of muscles using absorbable stitches, and closes up the skin with clips or stitches.

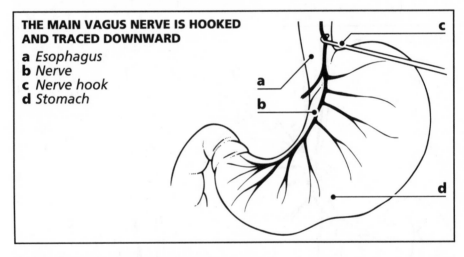

THE MAIN VAGUS NERVE IS HOOKED AND TRACED DOWNWARD

a *Esophagus*
b *Nerve*
c *Nerve hook*
d *Stomach*

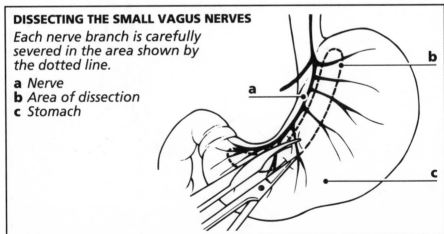

DISSECTING THE SMALL VAGUS NERVES

Each nerve branch is carefully severed in the area shown by the dotted line.

a *Nerve*
b *Area of dissection*
c *Stomach*

THE NASOGASTRIC TUBE
a *Nasal passage*
b *Nasogastric tube*
c *Esophagus (leading to the stomach)*
d *Trachea (windpipe)*

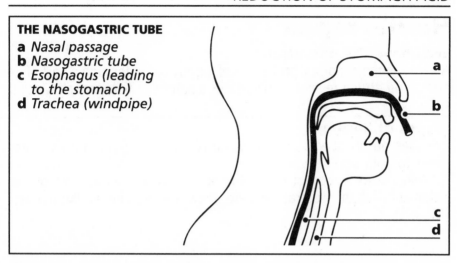

What is it like immediately after the operation?

You will wake up to find a nasogastric tube through your nose and down the back of your throat. The tube extends down the esophagus into the stomach and is intended to apply suction to remove the (fluid) stomach contents until the stomach is capable of emptying itself. It will be removed after four or five days.

An intravenous drip will be attached to supply the body with fluid nourishment, and should be present for between 36 and 48 hours. Neither tube nor drip should cause more than mild discomfort: it should be possible to forget they are there for most of the time. While either of them is there, though, you will be confined to bed. When the tube is removed, you may at first find it difficult to swallow solid food because the lower end of the esophagus may go into spasm. If this occurs, you will be given small, soft meals at regular intervals during the day.

Diarrhea may also be an initial problem.

You will be encouraged to take careful exercise once you are able to leave the bed, and should be able to leave the hospital in ten to fourteen days after surgery.

What are the longterm effects?

In most cases the outlook is excellent—some surgeons claim a 90 percent rate of complete cure. A highly selective vagotomy has very few potential complications. But truncal vagotomy may be followed by the unpleasant side effect known as "dumping syndrome," in which the digesting contents of the stomach are passed prematurely to further sections of the intestines, causing sweating, flushing, weakness, and abdominal discomfort after eating. Dumping syndrome usually fades away of its own accord, although it may take a few months to do so. One way to avoid it is to take small meals without extra fluid.

Hernia repair

Why have the operation?

A hernia is the abnormal protrusion of a body organ through a part of its containing structure via a weakness or a natural orifice through which it

---

Types of hernia

Hernias are of specific types, some restricted to men, others common to both sexes.

With the exception of the hiatus hernia—which shows part of the stomach—all the illustrations here show the intestine as the herniating organ.

Abdominal wall hernia
Also called an epigastric or ventral hernia; both sexes, affecting 1 person in 100 nationwide; technically, however, this group also includes inguinal hernias and umbilical hernias (see below)

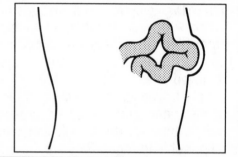

Indirect inguinal hernia
Men only; a loop of intestine passes down the canal from where a testis descends in early childhood into the scrotum; if neglected, this type of hernia tends to increase progressively in size (a "sliding hernia") causing the scrotum to expand grossly

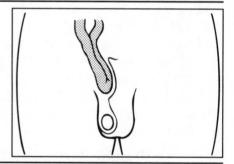

Direct inguinal hernia
Both sexes; the intestinal loop forms a swelling in the inner part of the fold of the groin

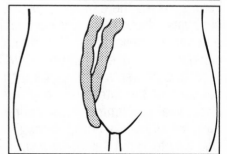

does not ordinarily pass. Hernias cause pain and reduce general mobility; they never cure themselves, even though some can be cured (at least temporarily) by external manual manipulation. Depending on the nature of the protruding organ and the solidity of the structure through which it is protruding, a hernia may cause complications that are medi-

Femoral hernia
Both sexes; an intestinal loop passes down the canal containing the major blood vessels (a) to and from the leg, between abdomen and thigh, causing a bulge in the groin and another at the top of the inner thigh

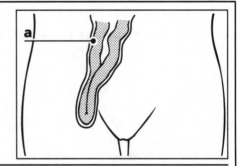

Umbilical hernia
Both sexes; an intestinal loop protrudes through a weakness in the abdominal wall at the navel (a) (but remains beneath the skin)

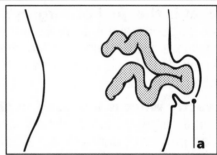

Hiatus hernia
Both sexes; a loop of the stomach (a) when particularly full protrudes upward through the small opening in the diaphragm (b) through which the esophagus (c) passes, thus leaving the abdominal cavity (d) and entering the chest (e)

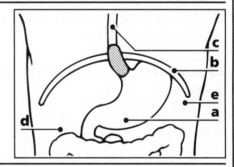

Other hernias
Far less common, but occur either in relation to intestinal loops penetrating a weakness in the abdominal wall (a) where surgery has been performed (an incisional hernia) or in connection with other organs or tissues (such as brain matter) that protrude invasively out of their normal medium

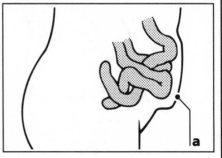

© DIAGRAM

cally dangerous. One major danger of a hernia is that the material within the protruding loop may cease flowing through the intestine (occlusion). More serious still, if the loop itself becomes twisted outside its containing structure, or compressed at the point where it breaks through that structure (a strangulated hernia), the blood supply to the loop will also cease and the entire hernia may undergo tissue death (necrosis). This requires immediate emergency surgery to avoid gangrene.

What is the physical cause of the problem?
A common type of hernia involves a length of intestine that somehow loops through an area of the abdominal wall which for some reason—strain through excessive coughing or over-strenuous exercising, perhaps—has become weakened locally. Abdominal hernias, which represent all the common hernias, mostly arise as a result of such strain on the abdominal wall. Even straining while defecating may cause a hernia, especially in an elderly person.

What is the goal of surgery?
The surgeon's aim is to replace the protruding part, and to repair the weakness in the containing structure so that further herniation is prevented. The classic operation for this type of surgery is the repair of an indirect inguinal hernia, and that is what is described below.

Exactly what is involved in the surgical operation?
Before surgery, you will already have undergone tests for any lung or heart problems; urinalysis will also have checked your kidney function. If the hernia is causing actual obstruction to the flow of material through the intestine, a tube will be passed down your mouth or nose into the intestine so that its contents can be vacuum-extracted. In that case,

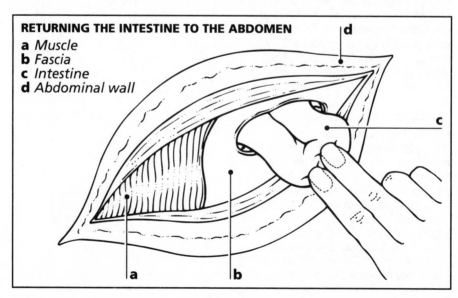

RETURNING THE INTESTINE TO THE ABDOMEN

a *Muscle*
b *Fascia*
c *Intestine*
d *Abdominal wall*

too, you will probably also already be receiving fluids by intravenous infusion and be on a course of antibiotic drugs.

Preliminary steps. Surgery for a hernia is most commonly performed under general, local, or epidural anesthesia. In the case of general anesthesia, you will be given a preoperative injection about an hour before surgery to dry up internal fluids and to encourage drowsiness. Once you are anesthetized, you will be positioned on the operating surface lying on your back.

Step-by-step surgical procedure. To reduce an indirect inguinal hernia, the surgeon makes an incision nearly an inch above—and in the line of—the crease in your groin. The incision is deep enough to cut through the skin and through the underlying fatty tissue. Two or three veins will also be severed and must be tied off. Beneath this tissue is a layer of muscle tendon, which is also cut through to reveal the thick spermatic cord that passes from there down into the scrotum. The outer fibers of the cord must additionally be cut in order to free the saclike structure that surrounds the protruding loop of intestine. The bowel loop is pulled free and is replaced in the abdominal cavity. The neck of the sac is then tightly tied off. When this has been done, the sac is cut off and removed. The surgeon must now reinforce the abdominal wall at the weak point in order to prevent the hernia from recurring. There are a number of options for this purpose, from simple stitching to using a sterile mesh to cover a square area. Finally, the cut muscle is repaired by stitching with catgut, and the skin edges are brought and held together with nonabsorbable stitches, clips, or adhesive strips.

What is it like immediately after the operation?
You are likely to wake up to feel some local soreness at the operation site. Nonetheless, continued medical attention is rarely necessary after a hernia operation, so you will be mobilized fairly quickly and you may even be able to go home the same day, although a stay in the hospital of two or three days is alternatively not uncommon. Coughing, laughing, and particularly walking may be uncomfortable for a few days more. All muscular strain on the abdominal wall should be avoided for at least a week, and lifting heavy objects and other forms of strenuous activity are inadvisable for a minimum of three months.

What are the longterm effects?
Successful surgery results in a complete cure. With many forms of hernia, however—and some more than others, notably with inguinal hernias—there remains a risk of recurrence, generally brought on by inadvertent overexertion.

© DIAGRAM

Hemorrhoidectomy: removal of hemorrhoids

Why have the operation?

Hemorrhoids, or piles, are varicose veins that occur inside, on, or just outside the anus. They can be treated in a number of ways such as by:

- a change of diet
- soothing creams or suppositories
- injection of an irritating (sclerosing) solution that causes the blood in the piles to clot solid and the piles subsequently to shrink
- subjecting them to extreme cold (cryotherapy)
- "banding," a rapid form of surgical treatment that causes them to wither away

All these treatments can be performed on an outpatient basis within a surgeon's office. Full-scale surgery to remove piles (hemorrhoidectomy) is required only when the hemorrhoids are large, have become visible outside the anus, and are causing constant pain and itching. By this time they may also be bleeding and/or discharging mucus.

What is the physical cause of the problem?

Under the mucous membrane that lines the anal canal is a network (plexus) of small veins that extends for 1–1.5 inch to just above the point at which the anal canal joins the rectum. The veins in their membrane form a kind of soft, compressible pad that acts as a seal between the rectum and the anal outlet. If those veins widen, bulge, and twist (become varicose), they may quickly turn painful and obstruct the passage of feces (stools). The bulge may extend from inside the anal canal (internal hemorrhoid) out to the anal outlet (external hemorrhoid) and beyond (prolapsed hemorrhoid).

In most cases the specific cause of hemorrhoids remains unknown. They sometimes result from persistent straining during defecation, especially in people whose diet may be deficient in fiber (piles are almost unknown in societies where the normal diet contains a high proportion of fiber), or who suffer from repeated constipation. Many experts believe that hemorrhoids may be caused by continual high pressure of blood in the veins (the anal veins are at the foot of a venal system with no valves extending through the liver right up to the heart). This high pressure may be the cause of hemorrhoids during pregnancy and in some cases of intestinal cancer or cirrhosis of the liver. Contrary to popular folklore, piles are not caused by sitting on cold, hard surfaces, by prolonged standing, or by sedentary occupations.

What is the goal of surgery?

The surgeon's intention is to restore normal structure and sensation to

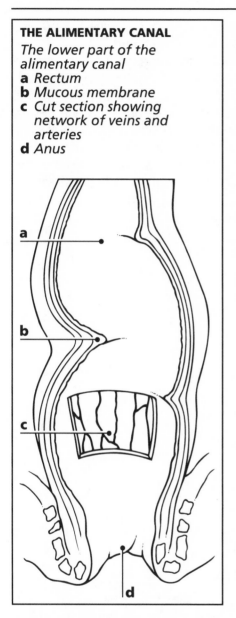

THE ALIMENTARY CANAL

The lower part of the alimentary canal
a Rectum
b Mucous membrane
c Cut section showing network of veins and arteries
d Anus

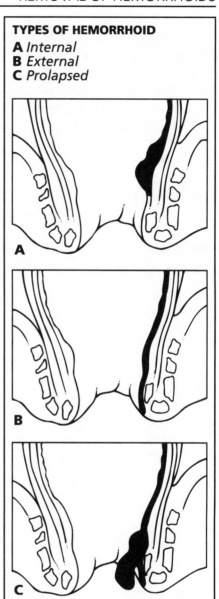

TYPES OF HEMORRHOID
A *Internal*
B *External*
C *Prolapsed*

the anal canal by removing the varicose veins together with the mucous membrane overlying them.

Exactly what is involved in the surgical operation?

Before the operation begins you will have undergone several tests for other conditions. If you are a woman, you will have had an examination to check for pregnancy or tumor. If you are a man, you will have had a rectal examination to check the state of your prostate gland. In all cases, you will probably have undergone an examination of the rectum and lower colon by endoscopy (sigmoidoscopy) and by barium enema

© DIAGRAM

(a solution of barium introduced into the rectum to define the precise internal shape of the rectum on X-ray screen or image).

Preliminary steps. Several hours before surgery—perhaps on the previous evening—you will be given an enema (an internal rectal wash). If the operation is to be performed under general anesthesia, you will be given a preoperative injection about an hour before surgery to dry up internal fluids and to encourage drowsiness. A similar injection may or may not be administered if the operation is performed with spinal anesthesia (lumbar puncture, epidural anesthesia, or sacral block), in which only part of your body will be numbed to sensation and you will otherwise remain conscious. Once in the operating room you will be positioned according to the requirements of the surgeon: either in the "litho-

---

REMOVING A HEMORRHOID

If more than one hemorrhoid is present, this procedure is repeated for each.

A *Pushing gauze swab into anus*
B *Hemorrhoid appearing as gauze swab is pulled out*
C *Grasping hemorrhoid in clamp*

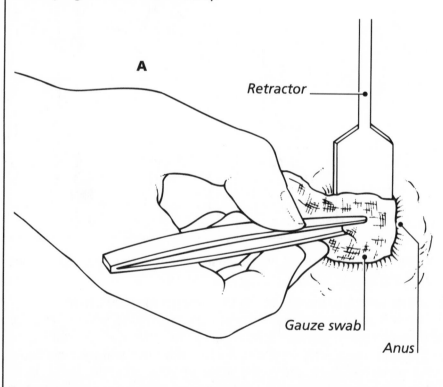

tomy position," lying on your back with your knees and feet held apart in stirrups, or in the prone "jacknife position", face down.

Step-by-step surgical procedure. The procedure starts with an inspection and cleansing of the anal canal, facilitated by the use of a retractor to open the anus and dilate the canal. A gauze swab on forceps is then pushed into the rectum and pulled slowly out, causing the pile(s) to come down and to exit through the anus with the swab. As the piles appear, each is grasped in a hemorrhoid clamp that is left temporarily attached. The surgeon picks up each clamp in turn, pulls on it to tighten the vein, and cuts off the outer layer (the mucous membrane covering the vein). The vein is then clamped and cut off.

Forceps are then applied at the base of the hemorrhoid, squeezed

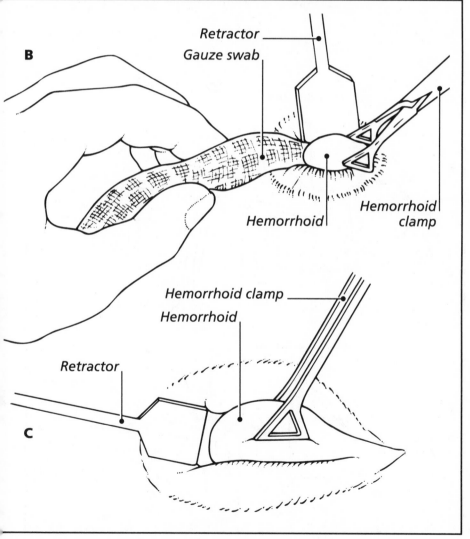

© DIAGRAM

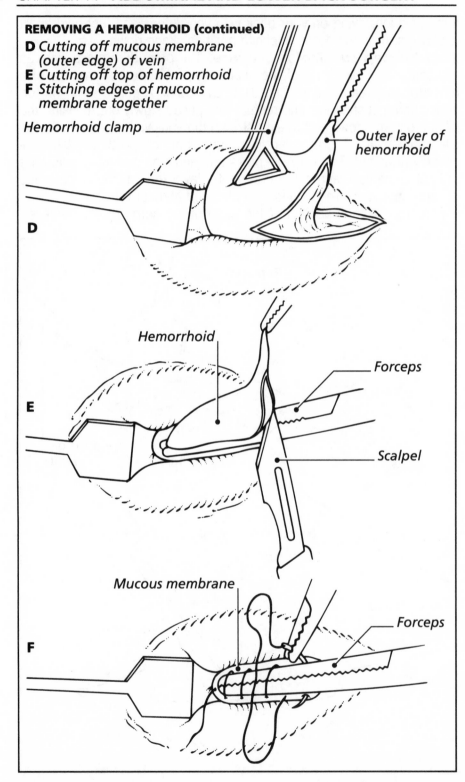

REMOVING A HEMORRHOID (continued)
D *Cutting off mucous membrane (outer edge) of vein*
E *Cutting off top of hemorrhoid*
F *Stitching edges of mucous membrane together*

Hemorrhoid clamp

Outer layer of hemorrhoid

D

Hemorrhoid

Forceps

E

Scalpel

Mucous membrane

Forceps

F

tight, and the entire upper surface of the hemorrhoid is cut off along the top of the forceps. With the forceps still in position, the surgeon then stitches over the mucous membrane edges, removes the forceps, and pulls the stitches tight, bringing the mucous membrane edges together. The skin edges are usually left unstitched in order to allow drainage and prevent the accumulation of fluids in the tissues (edema). This procedure is repeated with each of the other clamps.

Finally, a sterile protective dressing is applied (generally one impregnated with petrolatum).

What is it like immediately after the operation?

If you have had surgery under spinal anesthesia, you may be one of the 20 percent of patients to get a headache afterward. For that and for any serious discomfort in the anal region, ask for painkilling drugs from the medical staff. Over the first two or three days you will be on a restricted diet; on the third day you will probably be given a mineral-oil laxative to help you with the first defecation (bowel movement) after the operation. You will be encouraged to defecate: the first defecation will be extremely painful, but it is better to reestablish regular habits as early as possible than to risk constipation and hard feces (stools). Some pain and discomfort is to be expected on defecation for a time, but healing should occur within three to six weeks. In the meantime, painkilling drugs and frequent warm baths will help. There should be no problem with walking, sitting, and exercising.

What are the longterm effects?

There is a tendency, after the operation, for the anus to close off, and if it does it must be regularly widened (dilated) by the passage of a gloved finger or a smooth metal dilator. This can be performed in your surgeon's office. Once the anus ceases to close down—which sometimes takes many weeks—the dilation can be discontinued. Other longterm effects of surgery are uncommon. Attention to diet, however, may prevent or lessen the chance of recurrence.

© DIAGRAM

Cholecystectomy: removal of the gallbladder

Why have the operation?

Removal of the gallbladder (cholecystectomy) is necessary if that organ is causing persistent and significantly severe symptoms through disease, such as:

- recurrent attacks of acute pain in the upper right abdomen and right shoulder
- sweating and vomiting
- jaundice (yellowing of the skin), especially at night or following a heavy meal

The presence of gallstones in the gallbladder or in one of the bile ducts (as diagnosed through X rays) is not, in itself, justification for the operation: fewer than 10 percent of people with gallstones develop any symptoms at all.

What is the physical cause of the problem?

Gallstones form by crystallization from the concentrated bile in the gallbladder, usually when the bile contains excess cholesterol—about three-quarters of all gallstones are made up mainly of cholesterol. The remainder are formed from bile pigment and other materials, and usually compact into stones as a result of gallbladder infection. Gallbladders often simultaneously contain a sludge of small crystals of calcium carbonates, phosphates, cholesterol, and other substances, all of which together seldom present any problem.

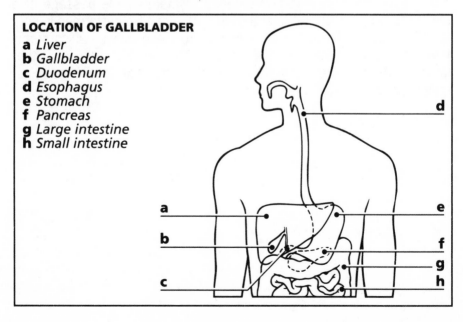

LOCATION OF GALLBLADDER

a *Liver*
b *Gallbladder*
c *Duodenum*
d *Esophagus*
e *Stomach*
f *Pancreas*
g *Large intestine*
h *Small intestine*

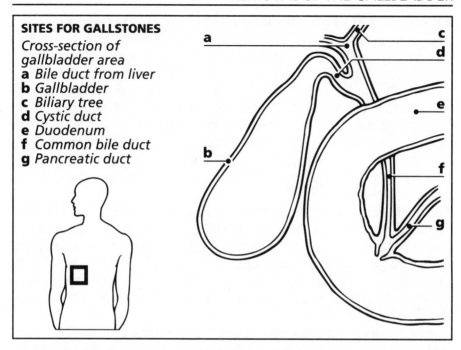

SITES FOR GALLSTONES

*Cross-section of
gallbladder area*
a *Bile duct from liver*
b *Gallbladder*
c *Biliary tree*
d *Cystic duct*
e *Duodenum*
f *Common bile duct*
g *Pancreatic duct*

Many people of middle age and older have gallstones without being aware of it. It is only when the gallstones make their presence felt—either by obstructing the outlet from the gallbladder or by leading to persistent inflammation (chronic cholecystitis)—that they become troublesome. Stones that migrate into the duct leading from the gallbladder to the common bile duct may give rise to biliary colic, a painful condition in which the muscles in the duct's walls repeatedly contract in an attempt to force the stone through. Stones that obstruct the duct completely cause persistent pain, tenderness, and fever, and the gallbladder gradually becomes distended by the continual secretion of mucus. If it then becomes infected, the gallbladder fills with pus.

What is the goal of surgery?
There are several methods of dealing with gallstones. Lithotripsy, in which external shock waves are used to bombard and shatter the stones, is sometimes used but is less successful with gallstones than it is with kidney and uretic stones. Another approach involves injecting into the gallbladder a strong solution that dissolves the cholesterol from which the stones are made.

When symptoms from gallstones are severe, removal of the gallbladder is the best approach. The conventional operation involves major abdominal surgery. The more commonly performed laparoscopic surgery—the procedure described here—is designed to remove the gallbladder as easily and safely as possible and with the smallest possible incision.

© DIAGRAM

Exactly what is involved in the surgical operation?

The most commonly performed procedure for gallbladder removal is laparoscopy, which uses instruments originally designed for gynecological surgery within the abdominal cavity. Laparoscopy is performed by remote control through a fine, fiberoptic viewing and illuminating tube (endoscope) passed in through a tiny opening in the abdominal wall. The endoscope has one or more additional ports through which other instruments can be passed. The great advantages of this method are that the abdomen is not opened in the conventional way of surgery and it involves only tiny incisions. It is laparoscopic cholecystectomy that is described below.

Preliminary steps. Your surgeon will ensure that you are free from chest infection and is likely to investigate the state of your intestinal tract by means of X rays after you have swallowed a (radiopaque) barium meal. The surgeon will probably examine the lower part of your colon and your rectum by direct visual inspection through a sigmoidoscope—a straight, metal viewing tube passed into the lower bowel through the anus.

As with all operations involving general anesthesia, you will be given a preoperative injection about an hour before surgery to dry up internal fluids and to encourage drowsiness.

Step-by-step surgical procedure. Once you are anesthetized, you will be positioned on the operating table, and the skin of your abdomen will be thoroughly cleansed with antiseptic solution. Sterile towels will be fixed in place with clips so that only three small areas—the navel, the upper right quadrant, and the midline just below the breastbone—remain exposed.

The surgeon starts by passing a wide needle through the navel so that carbon dioxide gas can be gently pumped in to inflate the abdomen a little and to get the intestines out of the way. An opening is then made in the navel large enough to push through a tube two-fifths of an inch (1cm) across: this is called a port and is used as an access route for the operating laparoscope. Another port incision of the same size is made in the midline just below the breastbone, and two smaller ports—each half the size of the first two—are inserted in the upper right area, just under the ribs. The central port carries the surgeon's dissecting forceps, scissors, and clip applicator. The two small ports are used for retracting instruments held by the surgeon's assistant.

The procedure is performed under direct vision, often using a video camera attached to the laparoscope and a closed-circuit TV monitor. In this way the surgeon and the assistant can both see exactly what is going on and can cooperate fully.

First, any adhesions around the gallbladder are freed, as are the gallbladder duct and the artery to the gallbladder. The duct and artery are then tightly clipped in two places and severed between the clips. The surgeon then frees the gallbladder from the underside of the liver, and all bleeding points are sealed with electrocautery or a laser. When the gallbladder is completely free, the laparoscope is transferred to the upper port, and forceps are passed through the navel port to grasp the gallbladder. The gallbladder may then be carefully pulled out through the navel port into direct vision. As soon as part of it is outside, the surgeon carefully opens it up; its contents are then evacuated so that it is reduced in size and can more easily be slipped through the port.

The surgeon now removes the ports and, if necessary, repairs the openings in the skin with one or two stitches.

What is it like immediately after the operation?
When you wake up, you may be surprised at how well you feel and how little pain there is. You should also be pleased with the cosmetic appearance of the tiny incisions involved. The chances are that you will be up and about within 24 hours of the operation, and should be able to return to work in about a week.

What are the longterm effects?
This operation does not deprive your digestive system of a regular supply of bile from the liver, but the bile is no longer synchronized with intake of fat. Apart from some possible intolerance to a high-fat diet (which should, in any case, be avoided by all of us), the longterm results are excellent.

Surgery for prolapsed intervertebral disk

Why have the operation?

A herniated (or prolapsed) intervertebral disk causes sharp and persistent back pain. Pressure of the disk upon the sciatic nerve may also lead to permanent weakness and loss of sensation in the leg and foot. It may even become difficult to raise the leg when it is held in a straight position. Surgery is performed to eliminate these conditions.

What is the physical cause of the problem?

The spine is a column of short cylindrical bones one on top of another, with shock-absorbing, disk-like cushions of tissue lying flat between them. Each disk is tough and fibrous toward the outer edge (the "fibrous ring" or annulus fibrosus) and is soft and pulpy toward the center (the "pulpy core" or nucleus pulposus). Degeneration of the fibrous outer ring of a disk may allow some of its pulpy core to be squeezed by

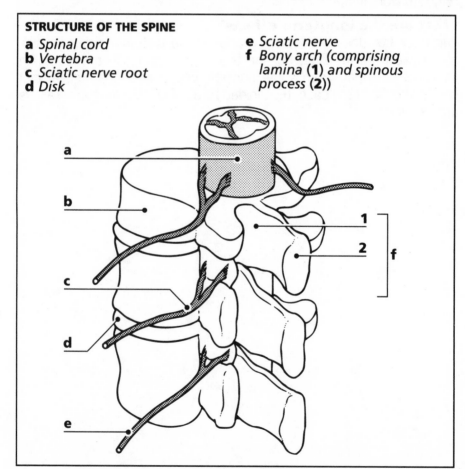

STRUCTURE OF THE SPINE

a *Spinal cord*
b *Vertebra*
c *Sciatic nerve root*
d *Disk*

e *Sciatic nerve*
f *Bony arch (comprising lamina (**1**) and spinous process (**2**))*

the weight of the bones in the column above so that it protrudes (it herniates or prolapses) backwards into the spinal canal in the column. Here it may press on the nerve roots emerging from the spinal cord or on the cord itself.

The sciatic nerve is composed of several such nerve roots that leave the spine to run from buttocks through hips and thighs down to the toes. Pressure from a herniated disk on the sciatic nerve affects the sensitivity and activity of much of the lower half of the body.

Less commonly, pressure is applied by a herniating disk on the bundle of nerve tissue (the "horse's tail" or cauda equina) that runs directly down the rear of the spine within the cylindrical vertebral bones. This can cause severe back pain, urinary retention, and weakness in one or both legs below the level of the knee.

Symptoms of a herniated disk often appear following a triggering factor, such as twisting the back while lifting a heavy weight. The condition is most common in middle-aged men.

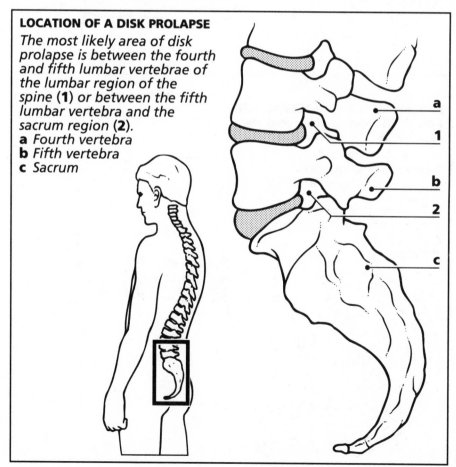

LOCATION OF A DISK PROLAPSE

The most likely area of disk prolapse is between the fourth and fifth lumbar vertebrae of the lumbar region of the spine (1) or between the fifth lumbar vertebra and the sacrum region (2).
a *Fourth vertebra*
b *Fifth vertebra*
c *Sacrum*

© DIAGRAM

NORMAL INTERVERTEBRAL DISK (shown in cross-section from the top (left) and from the side)

a *Hard outer layer (annulus fibrosus)*
b *Soft center (nucleus pulposus)*
c *Vertebra*
d *Nerve root*

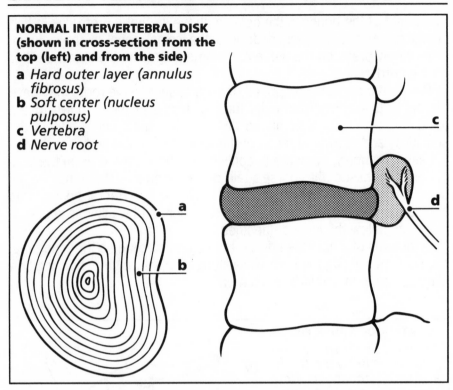

PROLAPSED INTERVERTEBRAL DISK (shown in cross-section from the top (left) and from the side)

Disk with herniated (prolapsed) pulpy core
a *Hard outer layer (annulus fibrosus)*
b *Soft center (nucleus pulposus)*
c *Vertebra*
d *Nerve root*

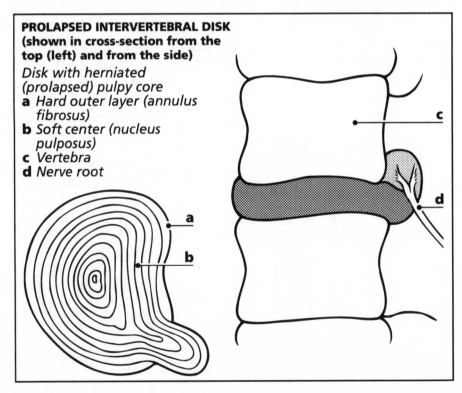

What is the goal of surgery?

The surgeon aims to relieve all pressure on nerves and nerve roots by removing the pulpy material that is protruding from the disk. The operation is called spinal canal decompression and involves a procedure known as laminectomy.

Exactly what is involved in the surgical operation?

Before surgery, X-ray and clinical examinations determine the precise location of the affected disk. The location is often apparent on an X-ray photograph because loss of the pulpy core at the center of the problem disk makes the space between the adjacent vertebrae visibly narrower than spaces between other vertebrae.

Preliminary steps. As with all operations involving general anesthesia, you will be given a preoperative injection about an hour before surgery to dry up internal fluids and to encourage drowsiness.

Step-by-step surgical procedure. Once you have been anesthetized, you will be positioned on the operating table lying face down. The table will be angled so that your spine is bent forward (flexed).

The surgeon makes the first incision in the midline of the back, at the appropriate level. The incision is deepened until the rear-pointing spiky projections (spinous processes) on the back of the vertebrae and the arches between them (the laminae) are exposed. The bulky muscles attached to the spiky projections are temporarily separated from the bone. Using bone-cutting forceps, the surgeon then removes part or all of the spinous processes of two adjacent vertebrae and enough of the arch on the side of the disk protrusion to expose the tough membrane (the dura mater) that surrounds the spinal cord. Very gently, the cord in its membrane is pushed to the opposite side of the enclosing vertebra so that the affected pulpy core of the disk can be seen.

The surgeon removes all protruding material, although to do so it may be necessary to cut through the tough ligament that runs longitudinally down the back of the vertebral column. In rare cases it may also

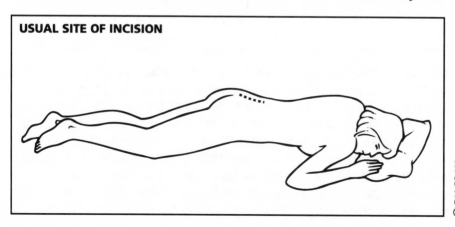

USUAL SITE OF INCISION

© DIAGRAM

LAMINECTOMY

*This shows the removal of part or all of the bony arch (**1**), including the laminae (**a**) and spinous processes (**b**) at the rear of one or more of the vertebrae (**c**) so as to expose* *the spinal cord (**d**) in its protective membrane (**e**). In this way the surgeon can reveal the pulpy core (**f**) of the disk (**g**) that is causing the problem.*

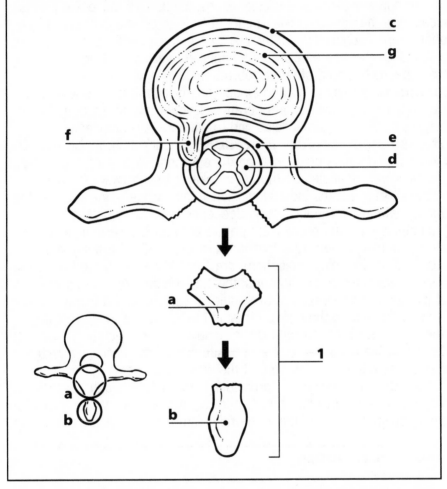

be necessary to remove laminae from several adjacent vertebrae, making the spine potentially unstable as a support for the body's weight. Spinal fusion may be required to ensure that the spine is once again adequately sturdy. Spinal fusion involves total removal of the disk or disks between two or more vertebrae and the roughening of the now adjacent bone surfaces so that the vertebrae heal together. To help promote fusion, reinforcing strips of bone taken from the fibula or elsewhere may be inlaid into grooves cut for them. Sometimes metal rods are used for reinforcing instead of bone strips.

The surgeon returns the muscles to their normal location at the rear of the spine and closes the wound in layers, using absorbable stitches for the muscles and (usually) nonabsorbable stitches for the skin.

What is it like immediately after the operation?

You will wake up to find yourself lying absolutely flat in bed on your stomach—a position that you will have to maintain for at least a couple of days. During that time you may or may not be fed intravenously. You will be able to change position only for the purposes of avoiding bed-sores (pressure sores) and physical therapy (physiotherapy) to tone up the leg muscles. There will be slight pain and stiffness in the muscles of the back until the operative trauma to them has lessened. After between three and six days, you will probably be encouraged to get up, and by that time much of the muscle ache will have subsided. Recovery of full mobility and sensation (and, in severe cases, of bladder control) depend on how much and for how long neurological symptoms—such as pain, muscle weakness, muscle wasting, sensory loss, and loss of bladder control arising from pressure on the nerve roots or cord—were present before surgery and on whether any damage was sustained to the nerves or to the spinal cord during the operation.

All being well, you should be able to leave the hospital within five to seven days and resume all normal activities (such as daily work) after four to six weeks of recuperation at home.

What are the longterm effects?

You will be advised to sleep on a firm mattress and to avoid frequent bending at the waist, lifting of heavy weights, and sitting in one position for long periods (such as in a bus or car).

The degenerative process that led to the herniation of one disk might later affect other, adjacent disks.

© DIAGRAM

Surgery for aortic aneurysm

Why have the operation?

An aortic aneurysm—in which the side wall of the body's largest arterial blood vessel, the aorta, balloons out under pressure and threatens to burst—is a dangerous condition. If it is not dealt with quickly a rupture of the aorta may follow, involving a massive hemorrhage that may be fatal. Surgery is also performed in an attempt to prevent further complications such as:

- the formation of blood clots (thrombosis) that may then be carried (as emboli) to block smaller arteries
- complete blockage of the aorta by a large blood clot
- the abnormal connection under pressure of the aorta with the adjacent main vein (thus reducing or even halting blood flow further down the aorta)
- severe infection at the site of the aneurysm

What is the physical cause of the problem?

Subject to the greatest blood pressure of all blood vessels, the aorta is usually thick walled and strong, but like all arteries it may be weakened by the gradual deposit within it of fatty substances (atherosclerosis), which narrows the channel. This condition may in turn lead to the internal splitting (a dissecting aneurysm) of the aorta's wall.

The most common site for an aortic aneurysm is just above the junction with the iliac arteries, in the lower abdomen.

What is the goal of surgery?

The surgeon's intention is to replace the section of the aorta that has become weakened and ballooned out with a synthetic (plastic-weave) graft.

Exactly what is involved in the surgical operation?

Before surgery, you will undergo a number of routine tests, including a blood count (monitoring the levels of different constituents in your blood), a chest X ray, an electrocardiogram (ECG: a measure of the electrical activity of the heart), and most likely an ultrasound examination of the aorta; all are painless. If the tests suggest that atherosclerosis is also seriously affecting the coronary arteries, the surgeon may propose an initial operation to perform coronary bypass surgery (see p.210) in order to avoid the possibility of a heart attack.

Several units of blood are cross-matched and set aside for transfusion. You will be given a wide-spectrum antibiotic to prevent infection.

Preliminary steps. You will be given a preoperative injection about an hour before surgery to dry up internal fluids and to encourage drowsiness. Once you have been anesthetized, you will be positioned on the operating table lying on your back, your legs most probably held

THE BODY'S ARTERIES

The aorta is the principal artery in the body. It arises directly from the left side of the heart, arches over the heart, and runs down alongside the spine until it divides into two main branches. These branches are the iliac arteries—one for each leg.

a *Carotid artery*
b *Aorta*
c *Subclavian artery*
d *Pulmonary artery*
e *Hepatic artery*
f *Messentric artery*
g *Renal artery*
h *Iliac artery*
Some organs served by the arteries
1 *Heart*
2 *Liver*
3 *Kidney*

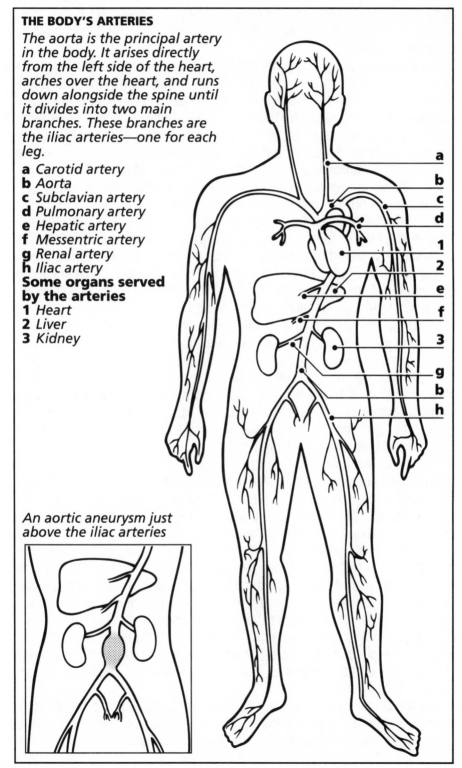

An aortic aneurysm just above the iliac arteries

© DIAGRAM

fairly tightly within inflatable leggings to prevent deep-vein thrombosis (blood clot formation) during the short time that the blood flow is reduced or halted.

Step-by-step surgical procedure. The surgeon makes a long incision, down the midline of the abdomen, usually from well above the navel down almost to the pubis. The contents of the abdomen are examined for other disease, then the small intestine—which covers the aorta—has to be kept out of the way. The surgeon either loops the intestine up in a plastic bag outside the abdomen or packs it out of the way inside the abdominal cavity with large, moist, sterile, gauze packs. Care is taken during the operation to avoid any damage to the important branches off the aorta to the kidneys and intestines.

When the full area of the aneurysm is exposed and examined, a plastic-weave graft of appropriate size and shape is selected. (If the aneurysm involves the fork of the aorta a bifurcated graft is required). The graft is soaked in blood, which soon clots to seal the openings in the weave. At the same time, the surgeon administers an intravenous injection of the natural anticoagulant heparin.

Next, clamps are applied to the aorta, above and below the site of the aneurysm. Blood flow below the upper clamp is completely stopped, so the surgeon must proceed quickly. As soon as the prosthesis is in place and securely stitched, the clamps are removed so that blood can flow. If the aneurysm is just above the fork, as it usually is, clamps have to be applied to both of the iliac arteries below. The surgeon cuts right through the front wall of the aneurysm, from top to bottom, and all blood clot is cleared out.

The upper and lower ends of this incision are then extended sideways so that the aneurysm can be opened widely. The surgeon first stitches the upper end of the graft in place. The graft is clamped and, just for one heartbeat, the clamp on the aorta is released to test for leaks in the stitching line. If all is well, the surgeon goes on to stitch the lower end of the graft within the aorta—or, if the aneurysm is extensive enough, to the two iliac arteries, ensuring that all the original branches of the aorta and of the iliac arteries remain open. All the clamps are released gradually—over about five minutes—to prevent a dangerous drop in blood pressure. Again the surgeon checks for leakage. Finally, the surgeon folds the limp sac of the aneurysm around the graft, and stitches it in place as additional strengthening (and to prevent the graft coming into contact with the intestines, to which it might otherwise adhere).

The small intestine is returned to its normal location, and the abdominal wall is stitched closed in layers: the surgeon uses catgut to seal the inner layers and nonabsorbable stitches or clips for the skin.

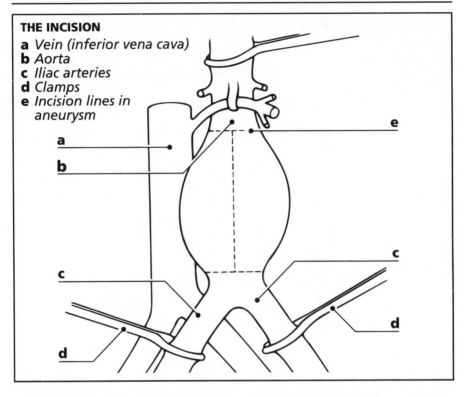

THE INCISION

a Vein (inferior vena cava)
b Aorta
c Iliac arteries
d Clamps
e Incision lines in aneurysm

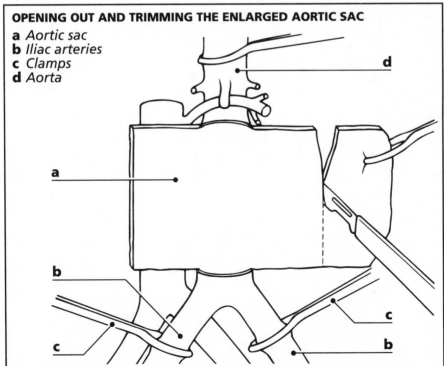

OPENING OUT AND TRIMMING THE ENLARGED AORTIC SAC

a Aortic sac
b Iliac arteries
c Clamps
d Aorta

© DIAGRAM

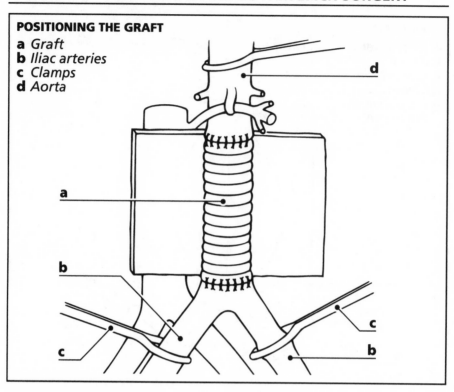

POSITIONING THE GRAFT
a *Graft*
b *Iliac arteries*
c *Clamps*
d *Aorta*

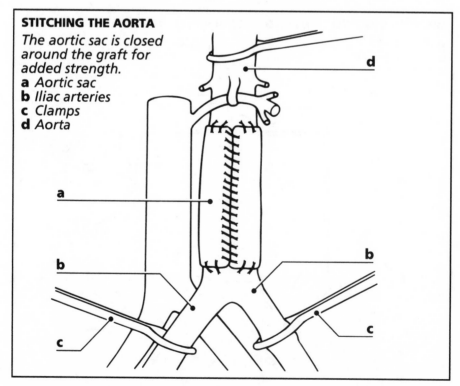

STITCHING THE AORTA
The aortic sac is closed around the graft for added strength.
a *Aortic sac*
b *Iliac arteries*
c *Clamps*
d *Aorta*

What is it like immediately after the operation?

You will probably feel tired and wan for a week or two. Most of your discomfort and pain will come from the long incision. For the first few days you will probably be confined to bed. It is important to follow your surgeon's instructions implicitly on the subject of exercise, and especially in relation to leg movements. The surgeon will advise you to avoid exercise that might raise your blood pressure (which in turn might put pressure on the aorta and cause leakage through the stitches). A normal, light diet is recommended. In most cases patients can be discharged from the hospital within a week.

Complications are relatively uncommon but do occur. They include leakage from the graft stitch lines, blockage of leg arteries by blood clots from the graft (or, rarely, at the graft), and distention of the small intestine following its repositioning (which may require the passage of a tube through the nose down into the intestine to release trapped gas). Sexual function may be permanently affected in men.

What are the longterm effects?

The longterm effects depend on the condition of the rest of the arterial blood circulatory system. But even in cases where atherosclerosis is severe, the prospects are by no means dismal. The mortality rate following surgery for aortic aneurysm is around 5 percent or less; the five-year survival rate is above 70 percent even among patients over age 70. Most deaths that do occur are due to associated atherosclerosis that affects the arteries supplying the heart or brain.

© DIAGRAM

CHAPTER 12
THE REPRODUCTIVE SYSTEM

Dilatation and curettage

Why have the operation?

Dilatation and curettage (D & C) is primarily an investigative procedure intended to help diagnose specific problems in the uterus. As such, it is used in a considerable range of patients' conditions. By itself, however, it can be used as a form of treatment—particularly in the removal of abnormal tissue from the uterus—with the result that D & C is one of the most frequently performed gynecological operations.

What is the physical cause of the problem?

The usual reason for having a D & C is bleeding from the uterus, ordinarily apparent as vaginal hemorrhage. Principal causes include:

- abnormally heavy menstrual bleeding (menorrhagia)
- the presence of polyps (which may be removed by the procedure) on the lining of the uterus
- uterine infection

Other symptoms that need investigation also include:

- bleeding after sexual intercourse
- postmenopausal bleeding
- some forms of infertility
- various uterine disorders

D & C is additionally used as a method of terminating a pregnancy at an early stage, and is commonly employed to remove the retained products of a pregnancy in which the fetus has died (known technically as an incomplete abortion).

What is the goal of surgery?

The surgeon's aim is to dilate first the vagina and then the cervix (neck) of the uterus in order to gain access for the insertion into the uterus of the curette, a spoonlike instrument that is used to gently scrape away a proportion of the endometrium, the lining of the uterus. Removal of the endometrium—even in entirety—causes no harm (for it naturally regrows during the following menstrual cycle) and may, in certain circumstances, by itself constitute the remedy for the patient's condition. Generally, however, the endometrium removed is then analyzed under a microscope in a laboratory with regard to possible further medical treatment, if necessary, following assessment.

Exactly what is involved in the surgical operation?

The operation is almost always performed under general anesthesia although it is a comparatively minor procedure. So little preoperative preparation is required that a D & C is sometimes done on an outpatient basis. In these circumstances you will have been warned not to eat or drink after midnight on the night previous to surgery.

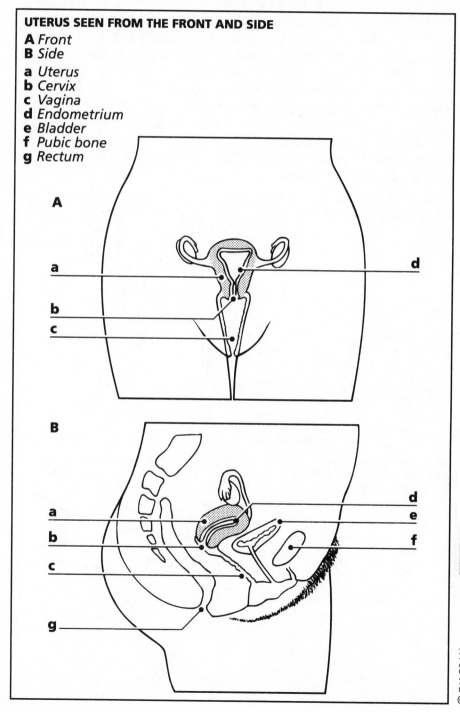

UTERUS SEEN FROM THE FRONT AND SIDE

A *Front*
B *Side*

a *Uterus*
b *Cervix*
c *Vagina*
d *Endometrium*
e *Bladder*
f *Pubic bone*
g *Rectum*

A

B

© DIAGRAM

Preliminary steps. As with all operations performed under general anesthesia, you will be given a preoperative injection about an hour before surgery to dry up internal fluids and to encourage drowsiness. Once you are anesthetized, you will be positioned lying on your back, your feet lifted up and outward in canvas slings attached to metal pillars. This is the lithotomy position, and it allows the surgeon easy access to vagina and uterus. The external genitalia are then swabbed with a mild antiseptic solution, and sterile towels and drapes are wrapped around until only the vulva is exposed.

Step-by-step surgical procedure. The surgeon now carries out a vaginal examination with a gloved hand, simultaneously feeling the uterus by pressing carefully on the front wall of the abdomen. This "bimanual examination" establishes the size, shape, and exact position of the uterus for the surgeon.

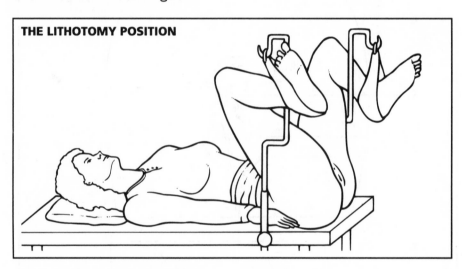

THE LITHOTOMY POSITION

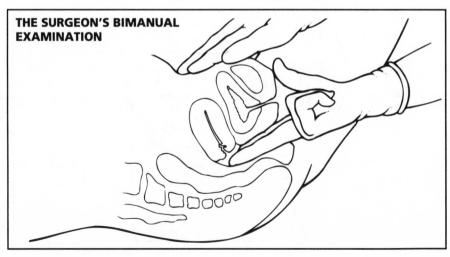

THE SURGEON'S BIMANUAL EXAMINATION

A vaginal speculum is now inserted. This is a metal or plastic instrument designed to expand the vagina and allow access to the cervix of the uterus. There are various types of speculum, the two most common being the "duckbill" speculum (which is inserted closed, and then opened to expand by turning a screw thread) and the alternative type, which acts principally by virtue of its own weight, widening and pulling down the back wall of the vagina. Either way, the vagina is extremely flexible, extends readily, and is not harmed at all by the instrument.

Once the cervix is exposed, its front lip is grasped in the pull of a long, sharp-pointed pair of forceps called a vulsellum, and pulled slightly down into the vagina, causing the mouth of the uterus to open a little. The surgeon then passes a fine, blunt-tipped probe called a uterine sound into the uterus to measure its internal length. This is done with great care, in order to avoid the possibility of perforating the wall

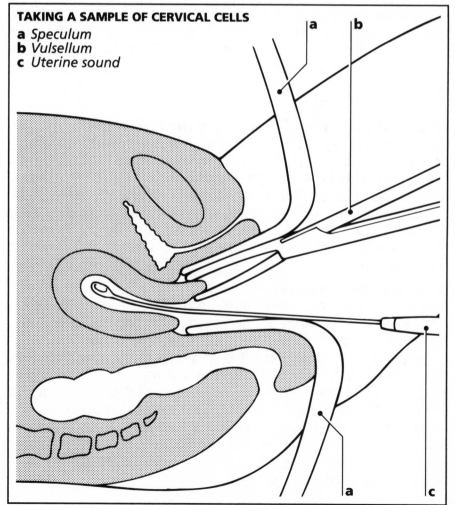

TAKING A SAMPLE OF CERVICAL CELLS
a *Speculum*
b *Vulsellum*
c *Uterine sound*

© DIAGRAM

of the uterus. With the end of the probe, a small sample of the cells on the surface of the cervical canal is taken for laboratory analysis; it is bottled in a saline-and-formalin solution, and labeled.

The next stage is the widening (dilatation) of the inner mouth of the cervix (the internal os) as it opens into the uterus. The surgeon does this using a graded series of smooth, round-tipped metal rods (dilators), commencing with the narrowest and progressing slowly upward through the sizes. If a dilator is tightly gripped at the os, it is left in place for a short interval to allow the os to expand in its own time around it. Force is never used, for that might tear or otherwise injure the cervix.

Once the cervix has been sufficiently dilated, the curette can be inserted. The curette most commonly used is spoon shaped but has sharp edges, and is employed in a systematic manner all around the interior of the uterus to scrape away the endometrium. Less often, the surgeon may use a low-suction vacuum curette, which sucks out tissue through a fine tube. This procedure is not always suitable for older patients because the endometrium is usually much thinner and less free to come away. In either event, the scrapings are also placed in a container and sent away to the pathology laboratory for analysis.

The instruments are then withdrawn.

What is it like immediately after the operation?

You should wake up feeling absolutely normal. Some patients experience cramping but this is not a major problem. There is usually no reason for you not to be able to go straight home after a couple of hours' rest—provided you are not driving yourself—pending the results of the laboratory analysis. You may, however, be kept in the hospital for a day or so if you lost a lot of blood prior to the operation. The only restriction on your activity meanwhile is that sexual intercourse is best avoided for a week or two.

What are the longterm effects?

Removal of the lining of the uterus has no ill effects and is often beneficial, especially if the lining has thickened unduly and is causing heavy menstrual periods. The lining grows again each menstrual cycle.

Investigation of material from the lining may reveal other conditions that require further medical treatment. These are in no way caused by the D & C itself. Nonetheless—and very rarely—dilatation of the internal os can lead to permanent slackness in the walls of the cervix (cervical incompetence) which may, if pregnancy follows, cause spontaneous miscarriage. Cervical incompetence can, however, be readily controlled by means of an encircling stitch, inserted after confirmation of pregnancy and removed before delivery.

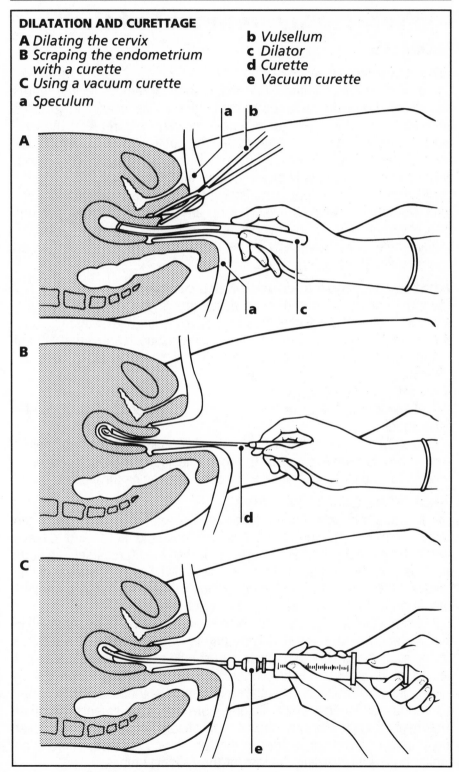

DILATATION AND CURETTAGE
A *Dilating the cervix*
B *Scraping the endometrium with a curette*
C *Using a vacuum curette*
a *Speculum*
b *Vulsellum*
c *Dilator*
d *Curette*
e *Vacuum curette*

Hysterectomy: removal of the uterus

Why have the operation?

There are several conditions that make surgical removal of the uterus necessary, some more urgently than others. Diseases and growths account for most of these conditions—and require careful diagnosis—but in some women the natural cycle of menstruation may also cause unusual degrees of menstrual flow or of associated pain every month which can be relieved only by removal of the uterus itself.

Hysterectomy is no longer routinely performed as a method of sterilizing women who wish to avoid having any or more children. For one thing, hysterectomy is not reversible.

Nonetheless, hysterectomy is one of the most frequently performed operations in the Western world.

What is the physical cause of the problem?

The most common forms of extra tissue growth in the uterus are:

- fibroids (benign but sometimes obstructively large growths)
- endometriosis (the growth of uterine-lining tissue in areas that are not appropriate, such as the uterine wall, the Fallopian tubes, and the cervix
- cancer (a malignant tumor)

Any of these might require hysterectomy. Hysterectomy may also be performed:

- as a treatment for excessive menstrual bleeding or menstrual pain
- on a woman whose uterus has become internally displaced or is liable to turn inside out and slip through the vagina (prolapse)

What is the goal of surgery?

The aim to some extent depends on the reason for the surgery. When cancer is not the problem, the aim is to remove the uterus and to leave surrounding organs (and even perhaps part of the uterus itself) as complete as possible. If cancer is the cause, however, the removal of the Fallopian tubes and the ovaries in addition to the uterus may be necessary in order to prevent the spread of the tumor.

It is important for you to know exactly what is going to be removed in the operation before you undergo surgery. Are you to have a total or partial hysterectomy? In particular, you should ascertain whether or not you will be able to keep your ovaries. Ovaries are not just for producing eggs: they also produce essential sex hormones, the loss of which may be serious and necessitate lifelong hormone supplements or other treatment. If you have any choice, you should request that whatever might be saved of your ovaries is duly preserved in place. There is no similar concern regarding the loss of the Fallopian tubes.

Exactly what is involved in the surgical operation?

The operation may be performed through the vagina, but more commonly—and more easily—the uterus is removed through a conventional incision in the front wall of the abdomen. The abdominal approach is always used if organs other than the uterus are additionally to be removed. This is the operation described here.

PARTS OF THE FEMALE REPRODUCTIVE SYSTEM

A *Front view*
B *Side view*
a *Fallopian tube*
b *Ovary*
c *Uterus (shaded)*

d *Endometrium (uterine lining)*
e *Cervix (neck of the uterus)*
f *Os (mouth of the uterus)*
g *Vagina*

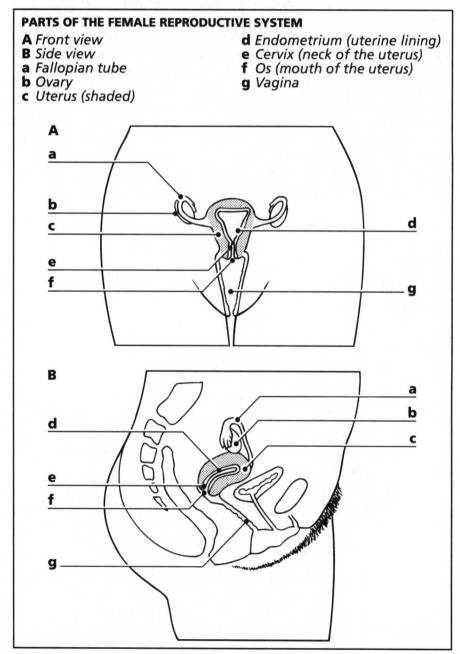

© DIAGRAM

Preliminary steps. As with all operations involving general anesthesia, you will be given a preoperative injection about an hour before surgery to dry up internal fluids and to encourage drowsiness.

Step-by-step surgical procedure. Once you are anesthetized, the surgeon makes an incision in the abdomen: either "vertically" along the length of the body from navel to pubis but slightly to one side of the middle, or "horizontally" across the body at the top of the pubic hair. The vertical incision makes the operation easier for the surgeon; the horizontal incision leaves a less conspicuous scar; both heal equally well and neither is more or less painful than the other. The muscle fibers in this region also run vertically, and may be split or pulled to one side with retractors. There are two layers of muscle sheath—in front of and behind the muscle—both of which must be severed. The uterus is now visible behind the bladder.

A strong stitch or a pair of retractors grips the uppermost part of the uterus and is held under tension by an assistant, so that the weight of the uterus is taken off the body. On either side of the uterus, connecting it to the side wall of the pelvic cavity, is a sheetlike structure called

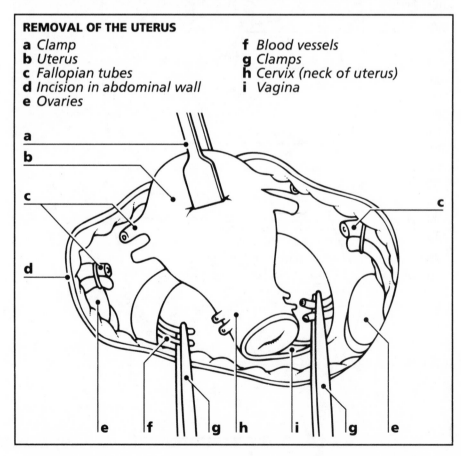

REMOVAL OF THE UTERUS

a *Clamp*
b *Uterus*
c *Fallopian tubes*
d *Incision in abdominal wall*
e *Ovaries*
f *Blood vessels*
g *Clamps*
h *Cervix (neck of uterus)*
i *Vagina*

the broad ligament, which also encloses a Fallopian tube and an ovary, and a ligament called the round ligament, which supports the uterus. The front leaf of the broad ligament on both sides is cut with scissors to expose the Fallopian tubes, while the uterus is carefully separated from the bladder and its assorted blood and urinary vessels. The Fallopian tubes are then tied off and severed—unless the ovaries are also to be removed, in which case there is no need to sever them for they will be removed together with uterus and tubes. The round ligaments on both sides are cut. Finally, the arteries and veins connected to the uterus are identified, tied off, and severed at the base of the broad ligament.

The uterus can now be pulled upward, mostly free but attached still to the vagina. Upward pulling stretches the vagina and brings it into view so that it becomes easy to sever it from the uterus at the junction with the cervix. The uterus is now free, and is removed. The top end of the vagina is closed tightly with stitches, and the ligaments that previously supported the uterus are then stitched to it so that the vagina remains supported within the pelvic cavity. Layer by layer the abdominal incision is now closed. A drainage tube may be left inserted at the site.

What is it like after the operation?

You may wake up to find a drainage tube leading from the site of the incision to a holding container, and a blood or saline infusion may be running. There may also be some vaginal discharge of blood and other fluids that may cause some discomfort. You will feel sore and weak, but serious pain can be avoided by asking the medical staff for painkilling drugs prescribed specially. The body area will remain tender for two to three weeks. How long you stay in the hospital depends on your age, your overall health, and whether any complications (such as infection) arise—although complications are not common. Most patients leave the hospital about a week after the operation. You will be encouraged to take reasonable, but not strenuous, exercise once the drainage tube has been removed.

What are the longterm effects?

You should have completely recovered within about four to six weeks, by which time sexual intercourse can safely be resumed. The vagina is extremely elastic and, although now slightly shorter, will recover normally. There will be no more menstrual periods or the monthly symptoms that went with them. If the ovaries have been removed also, you will undergo tests to see what and how many hormone supplements are most suitable to be taken on a regular basis.

© DIAGRAM

Induced abortion

Why have the operation?

The operation of induced abortion is performed in various circumstances: when continuation of the pregnancy involves danger to the life of the woman or threatens her physical or mental health; if the baby is likely to be seriously handicapped; and when the pregnancy is unwanted. In the last two circumstances, abortion may be allowed only up to a certain stage of the pregnancy, and may not be allowed at all, depending on local laws.

The availability of controlled, medical abortion has greatly reduced the incidence of criminal abortion, with its attendant risks to the woman. Most induced abortions are performed early in the pregnancy, within three months of the last menstrual period.

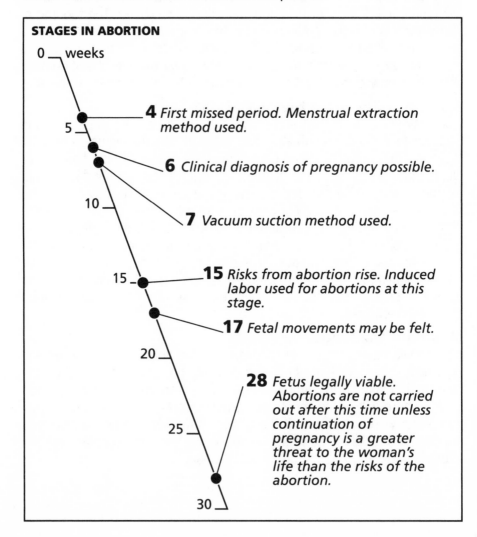

STAGES IN ABORTION

0 __ weeks

4 *First missed period. Menstrual extraction method used.*

5

6 *Clinical diagnosis of pregnancy possible.*

10

7 *Vacuum suction method used.*

15

15 *Risks from abortion rise. Induced labor used for abortions at this stage.*

17 *Fetal movements may be felt.*

20

28 *Fetus legally viable. Abortions are not carried out after this time unless continuation of pregnancy is a greater threat to the woman's life than the risks of the abortion.*

25

30

What is the physical cause of the problem?

Abortion is a procedure undertaken to terminate pregnancy. As elective surgery, it is generally the decision of the woman involved, up to about 21 weeks into the pregnancy. The decision to abort is usually made for personal reasons, although health risks can also be determining factors, especially later in pregnancy.

What is the goal of surgery?

The surgeon's intention is to terminate the pregnancy by removing the fetus from the uterus. How this is done depends largely on the stage of the pregnancy you have reached by the time of surgery.

Exactly what is involved in the surgical operation?

If you are still at a very early stage of pregnancy—within two weeks of a missed menstrual period and before pregnancy has actually been confirmed—you will probably undergo an operation known commonly as menstrual extraction, which requires only local anesthesia. For pregnancy from about six to twelve weeks' duration, the vacuum suction method is used, requiring either local or general anesthesia. If local anesthesia is being used, before going to the operating room you will be asked to urinate to empty your bladder. Surgery at all stages later than this is performed under general anesthesia—in which case you will be given a preoperative injection about an hour before surgery to dry up internal fluids and to encourage drowsiness.

Preliminary steps. Once you have been anesthetized, you will be positioned lying on your back, your feet lifted up and outward in canvas slings attached to metal pillars. This is the lithotomy position, and it

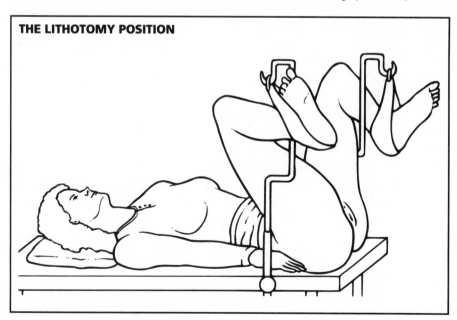

THE LITHOTOMY POSITION

© DIAGRAM

In pregnancy of up to six weeks' duration

For menstrual extraction, the surgeon first inserts a vaginal speculum—a metal or plastic instrument designed to expand the vagina and allow access to the cervix of the uterus. Once the cervix is exposed, its front lip is grasped in the pull of a long, sharp-pointed pair of forceps called a vulsellum and pulled slightly down into the vagina, causing the mouth of the uterus to open a little. The surgeon then injects local anesthetic into the cervix at three equally distanced positions, and waits a couple of minutes for the drug to take effect. A flexible plastic tube about one-quarter of an inch in diameter is then passed through the cervical canal into the uterus itself. A tube of this size is thin enough not to require measures to widen (dilate) the cervical canal. The tube has a blunt, rounded end and a hole on one side near the tip. A vacuum device or a large syringe is now attached to the outer end of the tube, and suction is generated down it as the tube is pushed gently in and out and rotated, so that the hole comes into contact with the entire surface of the uterus. All embryonic tissue is sucked out. The whole procedure takes about five minutes. The instruments are then withdrawn.

In pregnancy of up to three months' duration

The procedure for vacuum suction is initially identical to that for menstrual extraction. The procedural difference arises—as does the need for general anesthesia—because a larger quantity of material has to be removed from the uterus and the cervical canal therefore has to be dilated to allow its passage. Cervical dilation is a gradual process in which the surgeon inserts into the canal one after another a series of smooth, round-tipped metal rods, commencing with the narrowest and progressing slowly upward through the sizes. Ultimately, the cervix is wide enough to insert into the uterus a tube of appropriate diameter, made of plastic and attached to a vacuum device by noncollapsible tubing. The tube is moved in and out of the uterus and rotated, so that suction is effected over the entire surface of the uterus. All material on the wall of the uterus is sucked away. Simultaneously, the hormonal drug oxytocin is injected into a vein and causes the uterus to contract. The instruments are then withdrawn.

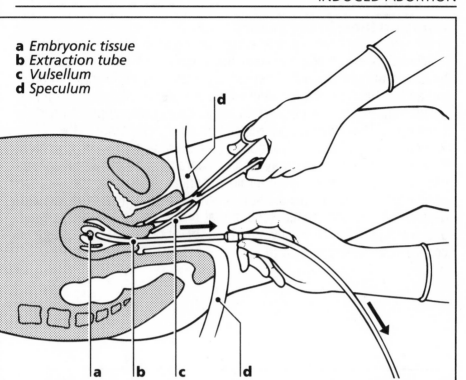

a *Embryonic tissue*
b *Extraction tube*
c *Vulsellum*
d *Speculum*

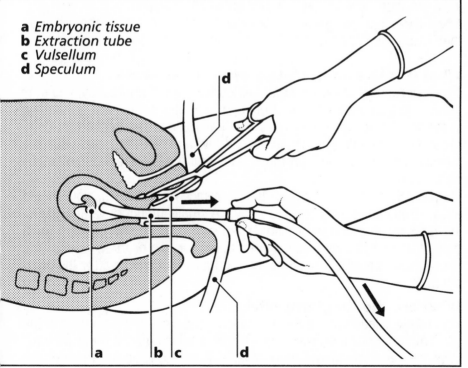

a *Embryonic tissue*
b *Extraction tube*
c *Vulsellum*
d *Speculum*

© DIAGRAM

Abortion later in pregnancy
Most commonly, prostaglandin drugs are injected intravenously or are instilled into the space between the membranes that surround the fetus and the uterine wall. Alternatively, they may be injected through the abdominal wall into the fluid within the uterus or may be administered in the form of a pessary (a vaginal suppository) placed high in the vagina. They have the effect of causing natural labor within 12 to 24 hours, with strong contractions of the uterus expelling its contents. Pain during this process may be considerable, and the simultaneous use of painkilling drugs is generally essential. Afterward, the surgeon ordinarily administers an anesthetic and with the help of a vacuum device ensures with gentle suction that there are no embryonic products retained. An alternative method of abortion at this stage is cesarean section (see p.328).

allows the surgeon easy access to vagina and uterus. The external genitalia are then swabbed with a mild antiseptic solution.

Step-by-step surgical procedure. The procedure the surgeon then follows is dependent on the stage of the pregnancy reached.

What is it like immediately after the operation?
If the operation was performed at an early stage of pregnancy, you may be able to go home virtually at once; if at a later stage, you will remain in the hospital for one or two days so that you can be checked for complications. Possible complications are few and rare, however. But any suspicion of infection will prompt the inauguration of a regimen of antibiotic drugs.

Physical recovery from abortion is rapid. Nonetheless, you should avoid strenuous activity for a few days. A small amount of vaginal bleeding is likely, and you may also experience mild uterine cramps for a time. It is best to avoid sexual intercourse for two or three weeks. You should have a normal menstrual period four to six weeks after the operation.

What are the longterm effects?
Very rarely, dilation of the cervix can lead to permanent slackness in the walls of the cervix (cervical incompetence), which may, if pregnancy follows, cause spontaneous miscarriage. If the condition is recognized,

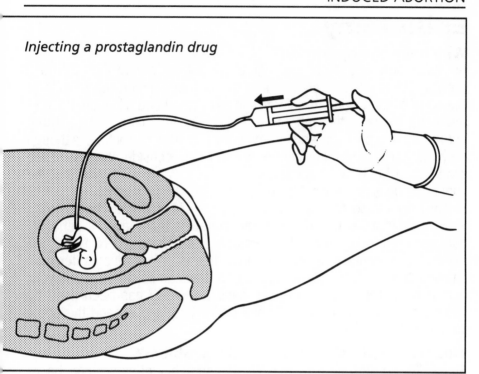

Injecting a prostaglandin drug

miscarriage can be prevented by the insertion, early in the pregnancy, of a simple, nonabsorbable, encircling stitch around the cervix. This is easily removed just before labor is due. Another possible—and rare—complication is infertility through blockage of the Fallopian tubes. In some cases this is believed to be caused by infection spreading from embryonic material accidentally retained in the uterus.

Episiotomy

Why have the operation?

An episiotomy is a minor procedure carried out during the birth of a baby. A cut is deliberately made in the skin and underlying muscle at the edge of the vagina to enlarge the birth canal and allow the head of the baby to pass through more easily. Obstetricians and obstetric nurses do not perform episiotomies as a matter of routine, although they are performed quite commonly and may considerably assist the progress of the birth. It is not until you are about to give birth that the final decision is made whether or not to have the procedure.

You may refuse to have an episiotomy. Many women hold strong views on the subject, and will readily accept a tear—even a seriously damaging tear—as a natural consequence of delivering a baby, but will resent (as unnatural interference) a cut that is in fact much safer than an uncontrolled tear. If you choose not to have an episiotomy, ask your doctor or midwife about perineal massage, which has been used by some women during pregnancy and delivery to help expand the opening naturally.

What is the physical cause of the problem?

Surgically, episiotomy is a minor procedure but at times can be of major importance: when tearing of the vaginal skin may be extensive and involve other organs, for example, or when the way the baby is coming out (the presentation) requires more than the usual clearance.

An uncontrolled tear may take place in the vaginal wall, stretched to breaking point by the baby's head, and yet the external skin may appear intact. The appearance of blood at the opening may suggest that this is happening. If the skin of the perineum (between the vaginal outlet and the anus) begins to split, the matter is even more urgent. Tearing of the anal sphincter (the muscular ring around the anus) should be avoided at all costs, for this may lead to persistent trouble with defecation later, and possibly to fecal incontinence. A ragged, irregular tear is more difficult to repair satisfactorily than a clean surgical cut.

A major tear of this kind is more likely:
- if the baby's presentation is with its face to the front (rather than the more usual back-of-the-head to the front)
- if there is scarring of the vaginal outlet from previous tears
- if there has been previous surgery to repair a tear or a prolapse (external protrusion) of the vagina or uterus

If the baby is coming out in the breech position (bottom first), an episiotomy reduces the risks to the baby. Without an episiotomy, the baby's legs have little room to spare in the birth canal. The arms may also be extended on each side of the head, which has little enough room and is thus placed in real danger of being crushed.

If some form of emergency occurs during childbirth, episiotomy may be a means of rescue. There may, for example, be some difficulty in presentation, so that forceps are required to assist the baby's exit. An inexplicable delay during labor may leave the baby's head continually pressing down on the mother's perineum, and may finally cause the baby to show signs of perinatal distress. The appearance of a loop of umbilical cord may suggest possibly dangerous complications. In all of these cases, an episiotomy may allow a speedy and safe delivery and avert considerable difficulties.

What is the goal of surgery?

The aim of the procedure is to enlarge the outlet of the birth canal so that the baby can more easily pass through without danger to itself or further damage to you. This is achieved by making a harmless controlled cut involving minimal bleeding that can be efficiently repaired soon after the baby is born.

THE PERINEUM DURING DELIVERY

The underlying muscles of the pelvic region shown as the baby's head emerges
a *Baby's head emerging through the vagina*

b *Pubic bones*
c *Perineum*
d *Anus*
e *Muscles of the pelvic region*

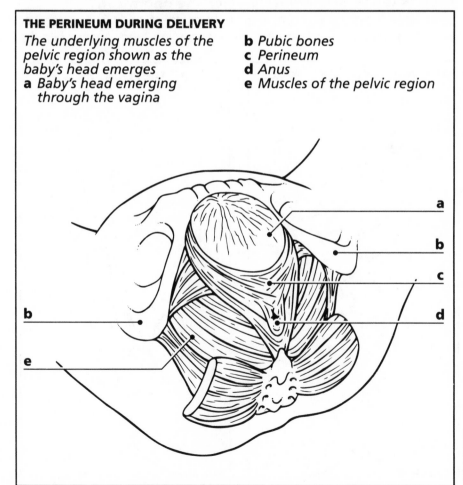

© DIAGRAM

Exactly what is involved in the surgical operation?

Preliminary steps. During childbirth, the stretched tissues of the perineum are often relatively insensitive—nonetheless, a local anesthetic can be quickly injected into the tissue to be cut. Frequently an epidural anesthetic (or a pudendal nerve block) will already have been administered to relieve pain during the birth and will leave the area numb.

A general anesthetic is occasionally administered where special problems are anticipated.

Step-by-step surgical procedure. During a contraction, when the baby's head is stretching and distending the mother's perineum, the obstetrician uses blunt-pointed scissors with straight blades to make the episiotomy cut. The cut is usually 1 inch (3–4cm) long and, unless shorter than this, is always directed to one side so as to avoid the anal sphincter. It should cause no pain whatever at this time.

What is it like immediately after the operation?

Soon after the baby is born, the obstetrician or midwife (or another physician) will put your feet into stirrups to keep them apart while the

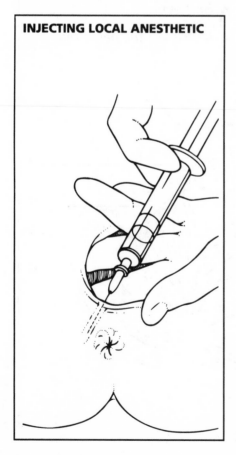

INJECTING LOCAL ANESTHETIC

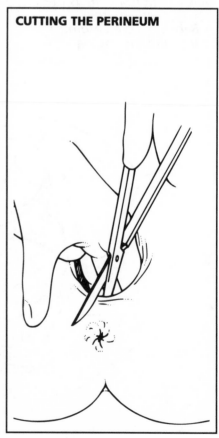

CUTTING THE PERINEUM

episiotomy is stitched up with great care to avoid leaving any spaces in which blood may collect and infection gain a foothold. If you find this painful, the obstetrician or midwife may again inject local anesthetic. He or she will also inspect the birth canal for internal tears that may require repair. Vaginal tears are usually closed with a continuous stitch of fine catgut. Separate stitches are used for the deeper tissues of the perineum, and a continuous buried stitch for the skin. None of these has to be removed, and all will soon soften and be absorbed.

You can walk as soon as you feel able.

What are the longterm effects?

In most cases healing is straightforward and rapid, although episiotomies (or vaginal tears) repaired with nylon or other relatively prickly tension stitches may remain painful for well over two weeks. Occasionally, painkilling drugs may be prescribed to help; icepacks may give some relief.

Because of the good blood supply to the area, episiotomies heal well. Most women experience no appreciable longterm effects, even with repeated episiotomies.

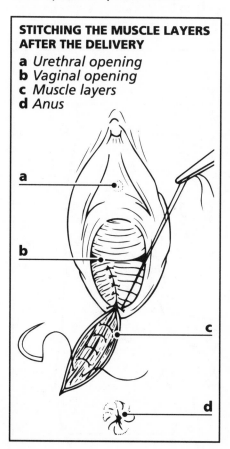

STITCHING THE MUSCLE LAYERS AFTER THE DELIVERY
a *Urethral opening*
b *Vaginal opening*
c *Muscle layers*
d *Anus*

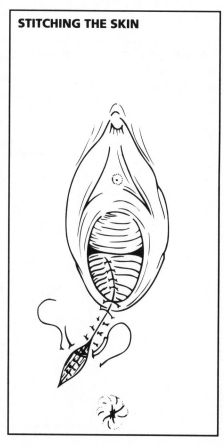

STITCHING THE SKIN

© DIAGRAM

Childbirth by cesarean section

Why have the operation?

At one time, cesarean section—the delivery of a baby through a surgical opening made in the front wall of the abdomen and through the wall of the uterus—was performed only in emergency situations. As surgical and anesthetic techniques have improved, this operation has become a common method of giving birth in the United States. In some areas as many as 25 percent of all births are effected in this way. The operation is often performed where:

- the danger to the mother or baby would be greater by vaginal delivery
- things go unexpectedly wrong during a vaginal childbirth

What is the physical cause of the problem?

Cesarean section may be performed if there is a problem concerning the overall physical condition of the mother and the baby at the end of the pregnancy, such as:

- obstruction or severe distortion in the mother's birth canal (such as caused by a pelvic tumor or by fibroids in the cervix or vagina)
- severe, pregnancy-induced high blood pressure in the mother

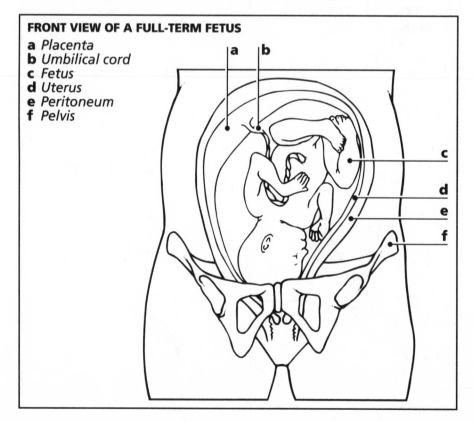

FRONT VIEW OF A FULL-TERM FETUS

a *Placenta*
b *Umbilical cord*
c *Fetus*
d *Uterus*
e *Peritoneum*
f *Pelvis*

- a history of previous problems for the mother during childbirth
- maternal diabetes, and a consequently large fetus
- severe hemolytic disease in the fetus. (Hemolytic disease causes a massive breakdown of red blood corpuscles resulting in the release of hemoglobin.)
- severe prematurity of the fetus

Problems occurring during labor that might necessitate cesarean section include:

- the presence of the placenta across the uterine outlet (*placenta previa*)
- abnormal activity or inertia of the uterus
- abnormal presentation of the fetus (anything but head or buttocks first, including the umbilical cord)
- breech position (buttocks first) plus other adverse factors
- fetal distress during labor
- premature separation of the afterbirth, causing hemorrhaging
- obstructed labor, with a dead fetus (now very rare)

Major complications such as those listed above occur in only a tiny proportion of cases, and the decision to perform the operation is usually made on the balance of advantages for mother and child.

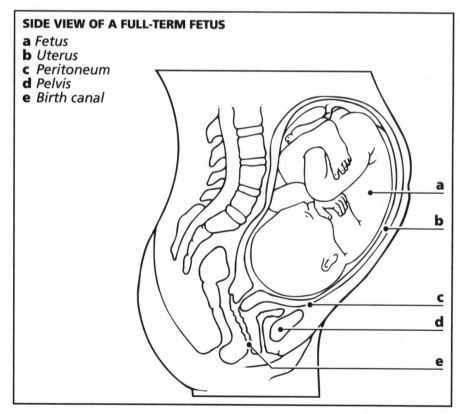

SIDE VIEW OF A FULL-TERM FETUS

a *Fetus*
b *Uterus*
c *Peritoneum*
d *Pelvis*
e *Birth canal*

© DIAGRAM

What is the goal of surgery?

The aim is to produce a live, healthy child with minimum risk to both mother and child.

Exactly what is involved in the surgical operation?

Cesarean section is most commonly performed under general anesthesia. A decision to operate at short notice may make it necessary to pass a tube through the mother's nose (or mouth) to the stomach in order to evacuate the stomach contents: if the stomach is not emptied, there is a serious danger that the mother may inhale vomit produced under anesthesia.

Preliminary steps. A preoperative injection is normally administered about an hour before surgery to dry up internal fluids and to encourage drowsiness and is limited to drugs that do not depress respiration in the fetus. Moreover, in order to minimize the duration of all drug therapy, the anesthetic is itself not administered until everything is ready to start the operation. The bladder is emptied with a catheter, and a saline drip-feed attached to your hand or arm. The surgeon checks that cross-matched blood is available for transfusion, in case there is a need for it.

Anesthesia is then induced, most commonly with a short injection into a vein, followed by a second injection of a muscle relaxant. A breathing tube is at the same time passed into the trachea (windpipe). Alternatively, the entire abdominal area may be rendered numb by an epidural block, an injection of local anesthetic into the epidural space surrounding the spinal cord toward the base of the spine.

Step-by-step surgical procedure. The surgeon makes an incision through the skin and the muscles of the abdominal wall either vertically or transversely below the navel, exposing the peritoneum—the membrane enclosing the abdominal organs—which is cut through transversely. The incision is held open with retractors. Beneath the peritoneum is the bladder, which the surgeon maneuvers gently from its

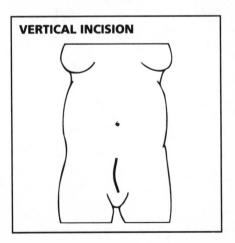

VERTICAL INCISION

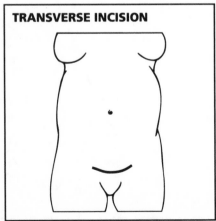

TRANSVERSE INCISION

position on top of the lower part of the uterus. The uterus itself is now fully in view.

The surgeon then very carefully makes a short, transverse cut in the lower part of the uterus, gradually deepening it until the membranes that line the uterus and contain the fetal sac show through. The surgeon inserts two index fingers in the incision and, solely by finger traction, extends the incision sideways to a width of about four inches (10cm), exposing the outer surface of the membranes. The membranes themselves are at this point ruptured with surgical scissors. The surgeon

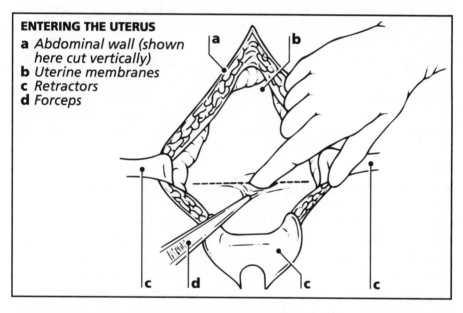

ENTERING THE UTERUS

a *Abdominal wall (shown here cut vertically)*
b *Uterine membranes*
c *Retractors*
d *Forceps*

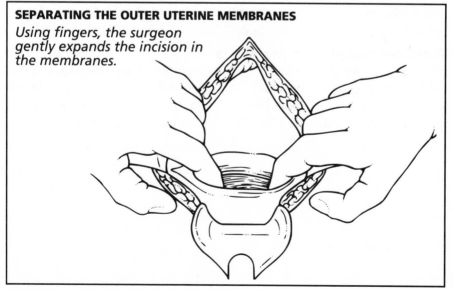

SEPARATING THE OUTER UTERINE MEMBRANES

Using fingers, the surgeon gently expands the incision in the membranes.

© DIAGRAM

immediately slips one hand inside the uterus to locate and identify the baby's head, which is grasped with obstetric forceps and eased through the incision. Once the baby's head is safely delivered, the surgeon administers an injection to the mother of the natural hormone oxytocin (or perhaps the alkaloid vasoconstrictor drug ergometrine maleate), which causes the uterus to contract firmly and prevents excessive bleeding. The baby's shoulders are eased out carefully to avoid enlarging the incision; and the baby is finally brought entirely out, remaining attached only by the umbilical cord.

Immediately following delivery, the baby is held upside down while mucus in the mouth and throat is gently sucked out with a soft vacuum tube. The umbilical cord is clamped, tied, and may be cut. Soon afterward, the afterbirth (the placenta and other maternal tissues) naturally separates from where it has been attached to the mother's uterine wall lining and is brought out through the incision. The birth is now over, and the surgeon stitches closed the incisions in the uterus and its membranes using two layers of catgut or other absorbable material, swabs away any blood or other material from the uterus, and closes the incisions in the muscle walls and skin with further sutures.

What is it like immediately after the operation?
A cesarean section is a major abdominal operation and you will be treated accordingly. You will have a good deal of discomfort in the lower abdomen for which you may need painkillers. You will be encouraged to move your legs frequently and to get up from the bed as soon as you can. There is no reason why you should not breastfeed after a cesarean section—any drugs you may have had are unlikely to affect your baby through your milk.

Complications are extremely rare, and you should be able to go home about a week after the operation.

What are the longterm effects?
After a cesarean section there is always some risk that the wound scar will rupture in subsequent labor. This does not, however, imply that all subsequent deliveries should be by cesarean section: often a woman who has had this operation can, afterwards, deliver babies vaginally.

USING OBSTETRIC FORCEPS

*Obstetric forceps are used to grasp the baby's head within the uterus (**1**) before easing it gently out through the abdominal wall (**2**) and (**3**).*

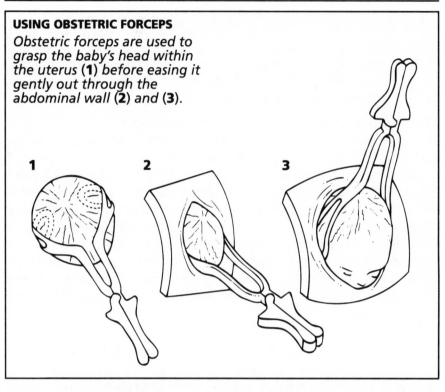

CLOSING THE INCISIONS
a *Incision in peritoneum*
b *Incision in uterus*
c *Abdominal wall*
d *Retractor*

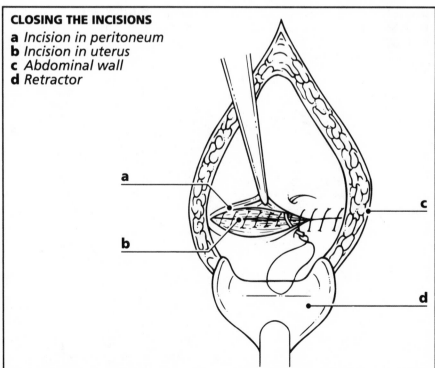

© DIAGRAM

Surgery for ectopic pregnancy

Why have the operation?

Ectopic pregnancy is an extremely painful condition often accompanied by severe—potentially life-threatening—hemorrhaging. The operation is frequently performed as an emergency procedure in order to save life.

What is the physical cause of the problem?

After conception, the fertilized ovum (egg) normally travels down the final length of the Fallopian tube and out into the uterus, where it implants itself in the uterine wall lining. In an ectopic pregnancy the fertilized ovum does not move into the uterus and instead embeds itself in either the Fallopian tube (the most common location) or, much more rarely, in an ovary or in the abdominal cavity. There it continues to grow and develop like a normal embryo, but encroaches ever further into the tissue in which it is lodged. Sooner or later it encounters a blood vessel and causes hemorrhaging. If an artery is damaged, bleeding is severe and continuous and is normally internal (although some vaginal bleeding may also occur).

The passage of a fertilized ovum may be delayed as a result of:
• previous inflammation of the tube lining (salpingitis), often as a

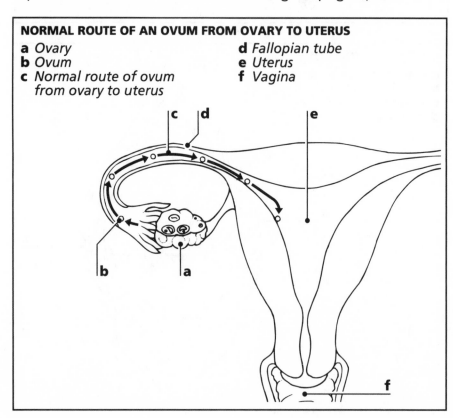

NORMAL ROUTE OF AN OVUM FROM OVARY TO UTERUS

a *Ovary*
b *Ovum*
c *Normal route of ovum from ovary to uterus*
d *Fallopian tube*
e *Uterus*
f *Vagina*

byproduct of pelvic infection, which may destroy the fine hairs (cilia) that ordinarily waft the ovum along the tube or may cause adhesions in the tube and so partly block it. (Adhesions of this type may not obstruct the passage of sperm but may hold up the much larger ovum.)

- blind cavities (diverticula) in the Fallopian tube
- abnormal length of the Fallopian tube
- scar tissue from previous surgery on the Fallopian tube (such as anoperation to reverse tubal sterilization)

It is difficult to distinguish a normal pregnancy from an ectopic one because the hormonal changes that take place—and the enlargement of the uterus during the first few weeks of pregnancy—are often the same. Hemorrhaging (either internal or external) is generally the first sign that something is wrong; the blood may stem from a damaged artery or from a ruptured Fallopian tube, either of which may cause dangerous loss of blood volume in the circulation (shock), severe pain, fainting, and collapse. Blood may also accumulate inside the abdominal cavity instead of finding an escape through the vagina. It is rare for an ectopic pregnancy to advance beyond about eight weeks without serious hemorrhage.

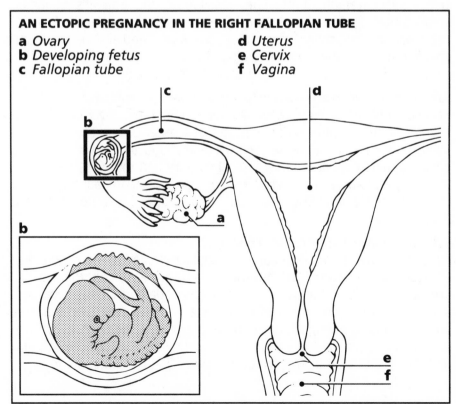

AN ECTOPIC PREGNANCY IN THE RIGHT FALLOPIAN TUBE
a *Ovary*   **d** *Uterus*
b *Developing fetus*   **e** *Cervix*
c *Fallopian tube*   **f** *Vagina*

© DIAGRAM

What is the goal of surgery?

Surgery is usually the only option and is often necessary to save the life of the pregnant woman, especially if there is severe bleeding. The aim is to terminate the pregnancy by removing the embryo. In such a case there is no question of trying to preserve the life of the embryo.

Exactly what is involved in the surgical operation?

Swift diagnosis is essential. If there is evidence of significant hemorrhage, the first priority must be a blood transfusion—this reduces shock but will increase blood pressure, leading to further hemorrhaging even as it reduces shock. There must be no delay in operating. A general anesthetic is administered and the patient brought at once to the operating table.

Step-by-step surgical procedure. The surgeon's first incision is made vertically in the abdominal wall below the navel and near the midline; it exposes the pelvic organs. In most cases the ectopic pregnancy is in a Fallopian tube that has ruptured; ectopic pregnancy in other organs is slightly more complex to deal with. The surgeon will remove the embryonic tissue and either repair or remove the tube (see box opposite). The abdominal wall is then surgically closed.

In cases where bleeding into the abdominal cavity has accumulated in the pelvic region, it may be possible—if the patient's condition remains stable—to drain out the blood through the upper part of the back wall of the vagina using a special wide needle. Afterward, the opening made by the surgeon is closed with a single stitch.

Antibiotics are administered to prevent infection.

What is it like immediately after the operation?

How you feel after the operation will depend upon the severity of the situation just before surgery. If you have lost a great deal of blood you will naturally feel weak and fragile, and will take longer to recover. Your condition will also depend on how radical surgery had to be in treating the ectopic pregnancy—you may have lost part or all of an organ. You should normally be able to leave the hospital after two to three weeks, if not sooner.

What are the longterm effects?

If a Fallopian tube has been partly or wholly removed, there is bound to be a reduction in overall fertility—but there is no reason not to have children in the future, if the other tube remains undamaged. It is even possible for normal conception to take place in a Fallopian tube that has been conserved during a prior ectopic pregnancy, although the risk of a second ectopic pregnancy in the tube is higher than was the risk of a first. Further tests may resolve exactly what that risk amounts to.

DEALING WITH ECTOPIC PREGNANCY

There are three methods of dealing with ectopic pregnancy in a Fallopian tube.
A *If the tube is ruptured, the damaged section is removed after tying it off on both sides of the rupture. The tube is now nonoperational and is held in place by small ligaments.*
B *It may be possible to conserve a tube that is not ruptured by* gently squeezing the embryonic tissue out of the outer end of the tube.
C *Sometimes, where the tube remains intact, a fine, longitudinal incision is made by the surgeon in the tube, and all embryonic tissue is removed. The tiny incision can then be repaired with delicate stitches.*

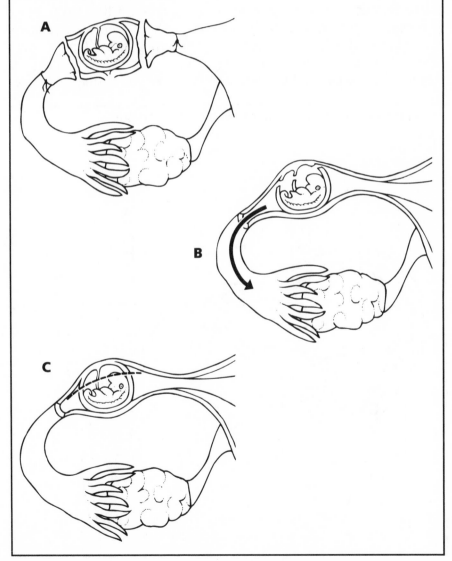

© DIAGRAM

Female sterilization

Why have the operation?

The most common reason for undergoing sterilization is as a method of contraception: to avoid having any or more children and to be able to continue sexual intercourse without risking that consequence. Medical reasons for sterilization include the likelihood of severe disorders in a child as a result of the genetic makeup of one or both parents or the likelihood that pregnancy would endanger the woman's health.

Whatever your reasons, you should be clear about them before considering sterilization. The chances of the operation's being a failure are minimal—1 in 2,000 woman years (for example, if 2,000 operations are performed in a year, on average one will fail). If that failure does take place, there is a slightly increased risk of ectopic pregnancy (implantation of a fertilized ovum (egg) occurring inside the Fallopian tube before it can reach the uterus, causing potentially dangerous symptoms). In addition, the operation may make you permanently ster-

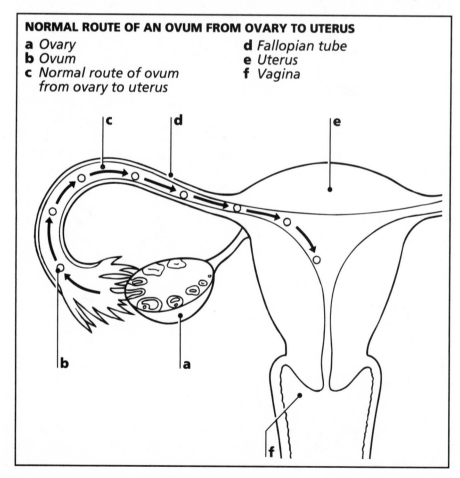

NORMAL ROUTE OF AN OVUM FROM OVARY TO UTERUS
a *Ovary*
b *Ovum*
c *Normal route of ovum from ovary to uterus*
d *Fallopian tube*
e *Uterus*
f *Vagina*

ile, never able to have any or more children, for although in many cases such surgery can be reversed, there is at least a one in four chance that it cannot. Moreover, after a reversal there is again a slightly increased risk of ectopic pregnancy.

What is the physical cause of the problem?
Conception occurs when a sperm ejaculated inside the vagina travels by its own locomotion up the uterine wall, into a Fallopian tube, and there penetrates and fertilizes an ovum released by an ovary. Sterilization simply blocks this process: the ovum is not fertilized and does not travel back down into the uterus and implant itself in the uterine wall there. Instead, ovum and sperm are kept apart.

What is the goal of surgery?
The surgeon aims to ensure that sperm and ovum never meet, either by surgically severing the passages in the body where such encounters occur (the usual method), or by inserting strong plugs to block those passages from both directions.

Exactly what is involved in the surgical operation?
There are several different methods of sterilization. It is now rare for a surgeon to make a full-scale incision in the abdominal wall to reveal all the internal organs. Instead, the most common modern approach is laparoscopy—the use of one or two thin, hollow tubes inserted very carefully through the abdominal wall; the incision is so fine as afterward to leave virtually no mark at all, and not even to require stitches.

Preliminary steps. Laparoscopic sterilization can be performed as an office procedure, but many gynecological surgeons prefer to admit the patient to a hospital 24 hours beforehand. Occasionally, surgery is performed under local anesthesia; most commonly it is undertaken using a general anesthetic—in which case you will be given a preoperative injection about an hour before surgery to dry up internal fluids and to encourage drowsiness. Once you are anesthetized, you will be positioned lying on your back, probably with your legs drawn up (in the lithotomy position, see p.319) in case there is need for access to the uterus also via the vagina.

Step-by-step surgical procedure. For a laparoscopic sterilization, the surgeon first very carefully passes a short, hollow tube through the wall of the abdomen just below the navel; through it a quantity of carbon dioxide gas is pumped, just sufficient to move any inconveniently sited intestines out of the way. A slightly wider double tube is then also forced gently through the abdominal wall, this time on one side, and is pushed deeper with a slow, screwing motion. Its sharp-pointed, inner stylus (the trocar) is then removed, leaving room for a fine viewing instrument (the laparoscope itself) to be introduced down the outer tube (the cannula). Generally, yet another small incision is

© DIAGRAM

made in the abdominal wall, on the opposite side, through which a second cannula is inserted, by means of which various instruments can also be introduced to the abdominal cavity and viewed and guided directly by the surgeon through the laparoscope.

In this way, any of several instruments can be positioned on or by the Fallopian tubes and observed as they perform whatever is the chosen surgical method. The tubes may be burned through with a fine, electrically heated wire (diathermy); they may be clamped tightly shut with plastic clips; a short length of each tube may be cut out and each section tied off; or plastic bands can be used to constrict small loops in each tube. This last method is the least traumatizing to the tubes, and also offers the best chance of reversal afterward—but it is probably also the least reliable.

When both tubes have been treated, the laparoscope, instruments, and cannulas are withdrawn. No stitches are necessary and scarring is minimal.

Some women are sterilized soon after childbirth, while the uterus is still enlarged and the Fallopian tubes are still higher in the body than usual. In this event, you may undergo a form of minor surgery known as a minilaparotomy, rather than a laparoscopic sterilization. A small incision is made below the navel, through which the Fallopian tubes are accessed, tied off with double ligatures, and severed between the ties. In a few cases, access to the Fallopian tubes is made through the vagi-

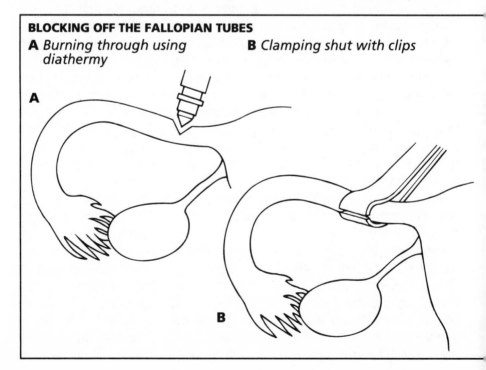

BLOCKING OFF THE FALLOPIAN TUBES

A *Burning through using diathermy*

B *Clamping shut with clips*

A

B

nal wall instead of through the abdominal wall. These methods may require a small amount of stitching to complete the operation. An approach through the vagina, using an instrument passed from there through the uterus and into the Fallopian tubes, may alternatively be used for simply putting a flexible block within each tube.

What is it like immediately after the operation?
Following general anesthesia, you will wake up probably feeling only sleepy but otherwise quite normal except a little tender in the abdomen.

You will be kept in the hospital for another 24 hours just for surveillance. Rarely, and following surgery under the less common local anesthetic, you will be allowed to go home the same day. Sexual intercourse may be resumed as soon as you feel able, although if the vaginal approach has been used surgically, you may not feel able for at least a week.

What are the longterm effects?
The major effect is that other contraceptive methods are no longer necessary. There are no physical longterm effects of this method of sterilization as long as no complications of the operation arise. These include perforation of the bowel by a hot loop diathermy and damage to a blood vessel causing hemorrhage. Accidental injury to a loop of a bowel may lead to a late perforation and peritonitis. Such complications are, however, rare.

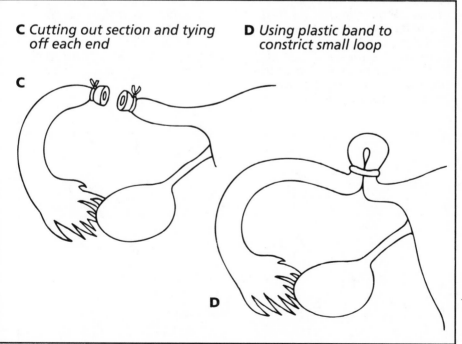

C *Cutting out section and tying off each end*

D *Using plastic band to constrict small loop*

C

D

Removal of fibroids in the uterus

Why have the operation?

Fibroids (fibromyomata) are benign tumors that grow in or from the muscular wall of the uterus. They are common—about one woman in five aged over age 30 has them—but generally cause no symptoms and no problems, even though they may be present in some numbers. Sometimes, however, one or more may grow to a size or in a location that does present a problem. For example, they might:

● impinge on the urinary organs

● put pressure on the final length of the intestinal system

● interfere with reproductive processes

● degenerate or become infected, leading to fever and pain

Surgery is the only way of getting rid of fibroids and may involve a hysterectomy (complete removal of the uterus) or a myomectomy (removal of the fibroids alone). Hysterectomy remains the most common method of treating the condition—but hysterectomy naturally causes total and permanent sterility and women of childbearing age may prefer myomectomy.

TYPES OF FIBROIDS

*Any part of the uterus (**a**) may become subject to fibroids, including the cervix (**b**).*
***A** The most common type grows within the uterine wall, inside its own capsule, enclosed in the muscle tissue (or between the muscle tissue and the inner or outer lining of the uterus) and causing it to bulge, thus potentially putting*

pressure on adjacent organs and disrupting the normal menstrual process.
***B** A less common type grows from a nucleus in the uterine wall out on a stalk into the uterus. Such fibroids may become distended and twisted, causing pain, vomiting, and shock.*

A

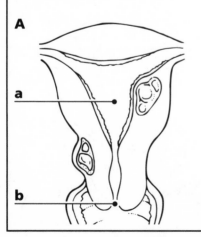

B

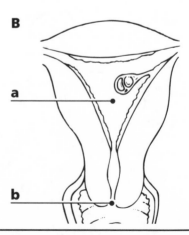

What is the physical cause of the problem?

Fibroids, as their name suggests, are tumors that are composed mainly of fibrous muscular material. Their growth is thought to be linked with the presence of estrogen, sex hormones on and within the muscular wall of the uterus. Oral contraceptives and pregnancy can both cause fibroids already present to enlarge; after menopause, fibroids tend to shrink. The majority are small, but some grow to the size of a pumpkin and can weigh as much as 44 pounds.

Surgery may be performed if there is excessive menstrual bleeding or any other form of disruption to the reproductive cycle, or if there is evidence of the involvement of the urinary system or colon or rectum. Fibroids that are particularly large in young women should be removed surgically, even if they are not currently causing symptoms, because further growth—perhaps with complications—is likely.

What is the goal of surgery?

Surgery is designed to remove the fibroids without interfering with the strength or function of the uterus. Statistically, the removal of one or two fibroids presents the same surgical risk as a hysterectomy (one of the most commonly performed surgical operations, and one of the safest); the removal of multiple fibroids, however, is more complex and slightly more risky.

Exactly what is involved in the surgical operation?

The surgeon may ask you to undergo an ultrasound scan to try to locate the fibroids before surgery. The surgeon will also determine whether you are anemic (and prescribe suitable medication if so) and whether you have any urinary infection (which will be treated if present).

Preliminary steps. The night before the operation you will probably have a cleansing enema (a medicated solution introduced through the anus into the rectum); you may also be given an antiseptic vaginal douche.

The operation is commonly performed under general anesthesia, although some surgeons prefer to administer spinal or epidural anesthesia (the injection of anesthetic into the cerebrospinal fluid that surrounds the spinal cord in the lower back). If you are to have a general anesthetic, you will be given a preoperative injection about an hour before surgery to dry up internal fluids and to encourage drowsiness. If you have a spinal or epidural anesthetic, you may or may not be conscious during the entire operation, but you will be numb from the waist down.

Once you are anesthetized, your pubic hair will be shaved and the whole area of the vulva and perineum (between vagina and anus) will be swabbed with antiseptic solution. Sterile towels and drapes will be secured around the operating site.

Step-by-step surgical procedure. It is likely that dilatation and curettage will first be performed (see p.308) to check for irregularities in the inner surface of the uterus that might indicate the presence of fibroids just under the lining.

You will then be repositioned at an angle, with your head lower than your pelvis, so that the intestines in the abdomen move up toward the diaphragm and thus out of the way of the surgeon.

The initial incision may be either a horizontal line just above the pubis (the "bikini" incision) or a vertical incision in the midline. Either way, the surgeon carefully separates the muscle layers that underlie the skin and makes an opening in the membranous abdominal wall (peritoneum) beneath. Bleeding points are clamped and tied, or sealed by electrocoagulation. Retractors hold the incision open as the surgeon examines the lower abdominal cavity. If the uterus is greatly enlarged by fibroids, it is brought gently forward out of the incision and temporarily retained there.

Most fibroids visibly glisten under the exposed outer surface of the uterus. A careful incision is made over each to reveal it in its own capsule; it is then grasped in toothed forceps and shelled out of its muscular bed. To free it completely, curved surgical scissors are often necessary. Every opening in the uterine wall is finally secured with two layers of catgut stitches.

EXPOSING AND REMOVING THE TUMOR
a *Fallopian tubes*
b *Ovaries*
c *Uterus*
d *Incision over tumor*
e *Surgical scissors*
f *Tumor*

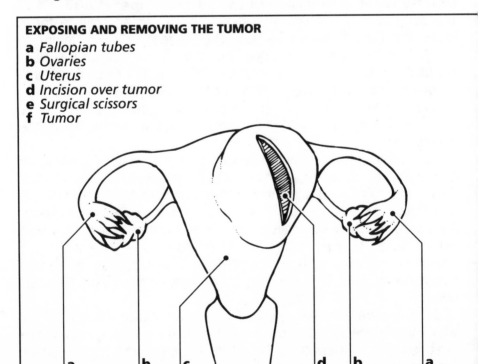

a   b   c   d   b   a

The surgeon checks the whole area to ensure that there are no more bleeding points (and that all swabs have been removed). The peritoneum and muscle layers above are separately closed with absorbable stitches, and the skin is closed with clips or nonabsorbable stitches.

What is it like immediately after the operation?

If you were operated on under spinal or epidural anesthesia, you may wake up with a headache. If fibroids had been causing intestinal problems you may be receiving fluids through an intravenous drip attached to the arm or hand. A tube may be in place through the nose and down into the stomach to remove stomach contents. Pain and bleeding are likely, although pain is likely to be relieved by drugs.

You will be encouraged to get out of bed as soon as possible, and certainly within 24 hours of the operation.

What are the longterm effects?

Recovery from the operation should mean an end to the symptoms you had been suffering. The removal of fibroids does not affect fertility, but if there are recurrences there is an increased risk of miscarriage. Smaller fibroids will not have been removed, so you should have your uterus checked from time to time in case they grow. Fibroids cause the uterus to enlarge, and often they become nodular. They can be detected by manual examination.

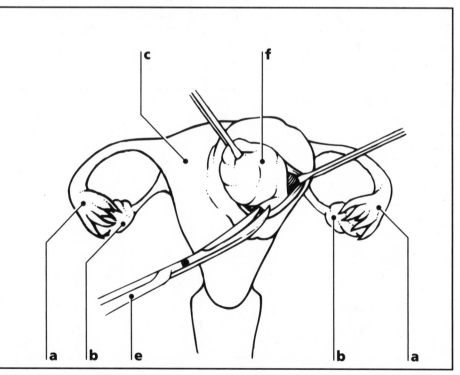

© DIAGRAM

Surgery for cervical precancer

Why have the operation?

The operation is performed when a cervical smear test (a Pap smear) has shown the presence of precancer of the neck (cervix) of the uterus. Precancer is the condition in which surface cells of the cervix have undergone early cancerous changes but have not penetrated the membrane that separates them from the deeper parts of the cervix. This membrane is called the basement membrane and it offers a partial barrier to the deeper spread of the disease into the tissues of the uterus. Changes confined to the surface cells are in the layer known as the epithelium; this condition is called cervical intraepithelial neoplasia (CIN).

If cancer cells have penetrated the basement membrane, the condition of cervical cancer is established and the treatment will probably involve removal of the uterus (see *Hysterectomy*, p.314) or radiation therapy, or both. If they have not, the chances of a cure by surgery are very high.

A positive Pap smear result may mean no more than that the cells scraped off for examination are mildly abnormal. These cells may return to normal without intervention. On the other hand, a positive Pap smear may mean that the cells are moderately or even severely abnormal. Any positive result should be followed by further investigation to determine the severity of the abnormality. With severely abnormal cells, there is serious danger that the cells may break through the basement membrane and establish cancer of the cervix. For this reason it is essential that an operation is performed.

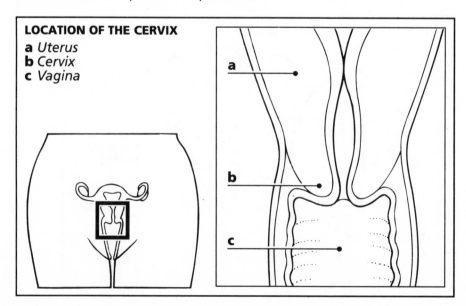

LOCATION OF THE CERVIX

a *Uterus*
b *Cervix*
c *Vagina*

What is the physical cause of the problem?

The exact reasons for the malignant changes that occur in cervical cells remain unclear. Cervical cancer is more common in women infected with some strains of the genital wart virus, but it is not known for certain that these viruses actually cause the cancer. Genital warts are transmitted sexually, and the greater the number of sexual partners the greater the likelihood of wart virus infection.

Cervical cancer is also more common in women who smoke than in those who do not.

What is the goal of surgery?

The goal of surgery is to eliminate all abnormal cells. Assuming that the diagnosis has been made at a reasonably early stage and has progressed no further than CIN, the surgery has a high success rate.

Exactly what is involved in the surgical procedure?

One of several methods may be used to destroy all abnormal cells:
- high-frequency (short-wave) electric diathermy
- electrically heated wire loops or diathermy loops
- lower-temperature electrodes
- cryotherapy (freezing) with very low-temperature applicators
- laser destruction

Preliminary steps. Prior to surgery a Pap smear test will have been done and suspicious cells found. This will invariably be followed by a direct microscopic examination of the cervix—a procedure known as colposcopy. This involves lying on your back on an examination couch with your thighs separated and your feet supported in stirrups (the lithotomy postion). A smooth metal speculum is used to keep the vagina open, as for the Pap smear test, and a binocular microscope is brought to within a few inches of the vaginal orifice. This enables the specialist to carry out a detailed optical examination of the state of the cervix—a procedure that takes about five minutes. Photographs of the cervix may be taken through the microscope for record purposes. Further surface scrapings will probably be taken, and it is likely that a small piece of solid tissue—a biopsy—will also be taken for pathological examination. You may feel a slight pain while this is being done.

Step-by-step surgical procedure. Either general or local anesthesia may be used with any of the surgical procedures. If general anesthesia is used, you will be given a preoperative injection about an hour before surgery to dry up internal fluids and to encourage drowsiness. The laser method is commonly done after a small injection of local anesthetic directly into the cervix and is entirely painless. An advantage of the diathermy loop is that it allows a reasonable-sized sample of tissue to be obtained for pathological examination. Freezing can be done without any anesthetic.

© DIAGRAM

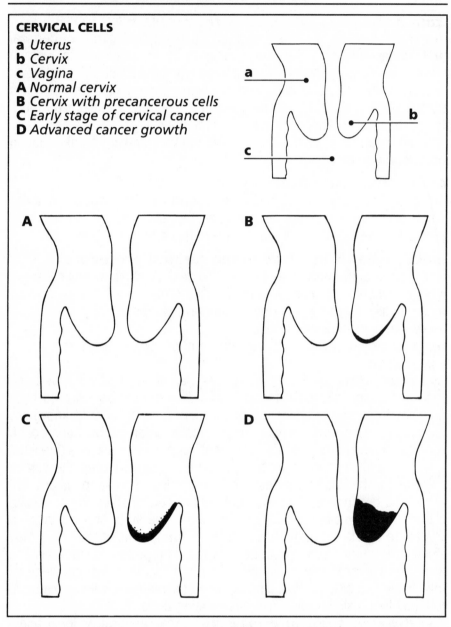

CERVICAL CELLS
a *Uterus*
b *Cervix*
c *Vagina*
A *Normal cervix*
B *Cervix with precancerous cells*
C *Early stage of cervical cancer*
D *Advanced cancer growth*

If the specialist is uncertain that such methods can be relied on to destroy all abnormal cells, he or she may decide that a cone biopsy is required. This will also be necessary if the specialist is unable to see the whole of the cervical area by colposcopy. The procedure requires general anesthesia and involves removing a cone-shaped or cylindrical section of the center of the cervix, using a scalpel or a laser. If a scalpel is used, the area will be stitched or diathermy or freezing will be used to close the wound and stop the bleeding.

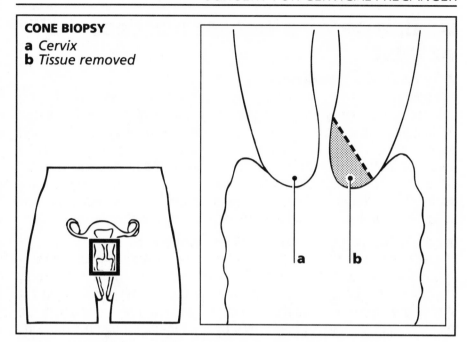

CONE BIOPSY
a *Cervix*
b *Tissue removed*

What is it like immediately after the operation?

In most cases you will be unaware of any symptoms, beyond a dull ache in the lower abdomen. After a cone biopsy, which may involve a hospital stay, there is usually more discomfort, and this will be increased if the vagina must be packed with gauze to control bleeding. Healing usually takes about two weeks after diathermy/laser treatment and up to about five weeks after a cone biopsy.

What are the longterm effects?

If you have had a cone biopsy, the outlet of the womb may tighten up considerably and you may possibly suffer quite severe cramping pains with your periods for a time. This can be treated. There is also a risk that the cervix may not be able to remain sufficiently tightly closed during a later pregnancy. This is called cervical incompetence and it may lead to miscarriage. Cervical incompetence can, however, be controlled by the use of a "purse-string" stitch inserted around the cervix at the 14th week of pregnancy and removed at the 38th week.

If the procedure has successfully removed or destroyed all abnormal cells, complete recovery is the result. For two years following surgery, however, you should have twice-yearly Pap smears, then annual Pap smears, as a matter of course.

Drainage of a breast abscess or cyst

Why have the operation?

A breast abscess is a collection of pus within the tissues that form the milk-producing mammary gland or in the tissues that underlie it. Caused by infection, it is seldom dangerous, although it may be extremely painful. An abscess while forming may cause a high fever (and associated symptoms); milk from the breast may be infectious to a baby. Once an abscess has fully formed, antibiotic drugs cease to have any useful effect, the patient experiences a severe and continuous general upset, and the only remedy is to release the pus surgically.

What is the physical cause of the problem?

Breast abscesses occur almost exclusively in women who are nursing (breastfeeding) a baby. Some form of infection—most commonly staphylococcal bacteria—finds its way through small abrasions in the skin of the nipple and infects the internal tissues; the tissues become inflamed and, as part of the body's own attempt to defend itself, pus accumulates.

In the early stages it is often possible to clear the infection with antibiotics before the abscess has a chance to form fully. But even at this stage milk from the affected breast should not be given to the baby because of the risk of infection: an abscess can communicate with the milk ducts and the milk ducts would then contain the organisms that caused the abscess. An abscess near the nipple may cause the nipple to become inverted and therefore useless to the baby. If the abscess comes to maturity, nursing must be terminated (at least until after the birth of a subsequent child). Nursing from the breast without an abscess can be painful and carries the risk of local contamination from the surface of the skin. Local heat to the affected breast, a good bra for support, and relief from pain through analgesic drugs are all helpful until surgery can relieve the condition.

Abscesses may be single or multiple and occur

- most commonly in women during the second week after the delivery of their first child
- more often in blonds than brunets
- more often in mothers who have had their babies in a hospital than in those who have had them at home
- in the second breast of about one in every five mothers who have an abscess in one breast

What is the goal of surgery?

Surgery is designed to ensure that all collections of pus within the breast are fully discharged, to prevent fibrous tissue from forming, and to promote complete healing in affected areas. A longterm abscess may have developed a tough outer capsule and may have to be removed completely.

CROSS-SECTION THROUGH A BREAST WITH ABSCESSES

a *Abscess*
b *Alveoli*
c *Nipple*
d *Milk duct*
e *Chest muscle (pectoral muscle)*
f *Rib*
g *Chest wall*

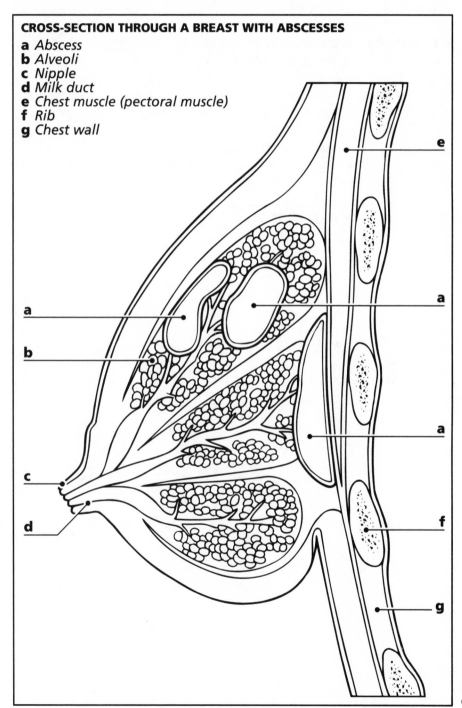

© DIAGRAM

Exactly what is involved in the surgical operation?

The precise location of the abscess or abscesses must be determined before surgery. Local heat or infrared radiation is applied to the breast until each abscess reveals itself as a fluid-filled mass under an area of red, glazed, and swollen skin.

Preliminary steps. As with all operations involving general anesthesia, you will be given a preoperative injection about an hour before surgery to dry up internal fluids and to encourage drowsiness.

Step-by-step surgical procedure. Once you are anesthetized, you will be positioned on the operating table lying on your back, with the side with the affected breast near the edge of the table. The skin over the whole of your chest is cleansed by swabbing gently with an antiseptic solution. Sterile drapes and towels are used to cover all parts except the operation site.

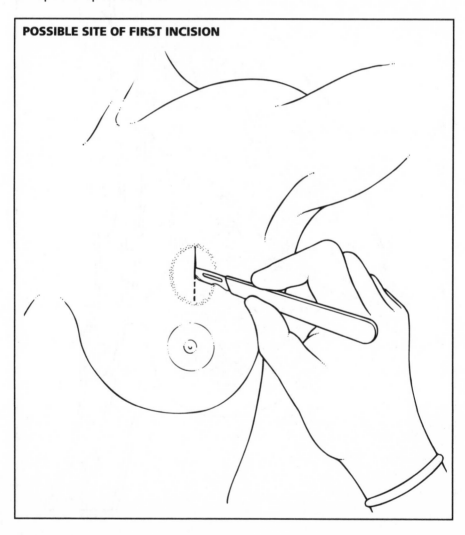

POSSIBLE SITE OF FIRST INCISION

Where the surgeon makes the incision depends upon the position of the abscess.

Abscesses near the nipple may be opened by incisions that curve around the edge of the areola, and are thus nearly invisible afterward. If the nipple has become inverted, it may be carefully undercut and pushed out, so that the appearance is restored to normal.

An abscess behind the breast tissue is drained through an incision made in the crease under the breast.

A visible abscess not near the nipple is opened by an incision over the most prominent part of the abscess.

Longterm (chronic) abscesses may be more complex both in the initial incision and in the amount of dissection required to free the abscess from the breast tissue. Some of them resemble breast tumors. If there is any doubt over whether the surgeon is dealing with an abscess or a

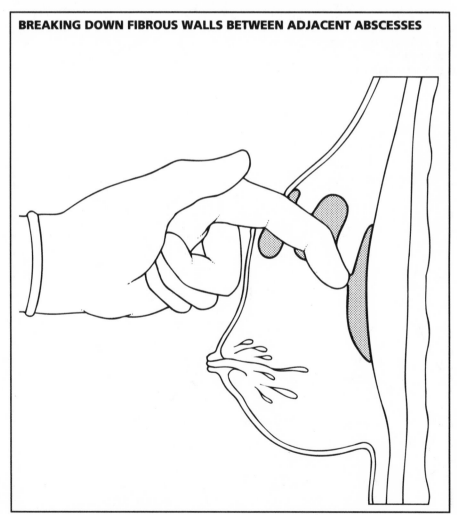

BREAKING DOWN FIBROUS WALLS BETWEEN ADJACENT ABSCESSES

© DIAGRAM

tumor, a sample of tissue and of pus from the operation site are sent to a laboratory to identify the infective organism and determine which antibiotic to use.

When the precise location of the abscess cannot be determined, the incision is made over the area of maximum tenderness.

Most incisions are made in a radial direction from the nipple because the milk ducts also radiate from the nipple: incisions like this therefore cut through fewer ducts. The surgeon's incision also varies in length according to how quickly the pus is encountered. An incision once begun is deepened until pus is reached. Next, the surgeon inserts a gloved finger into the incision in order to break down any internal compartments that might limit full drainage.

The surgeon then makes a second incision—a much smaller "stab" incision—in a lower part of the breast, perhaps even in the crease

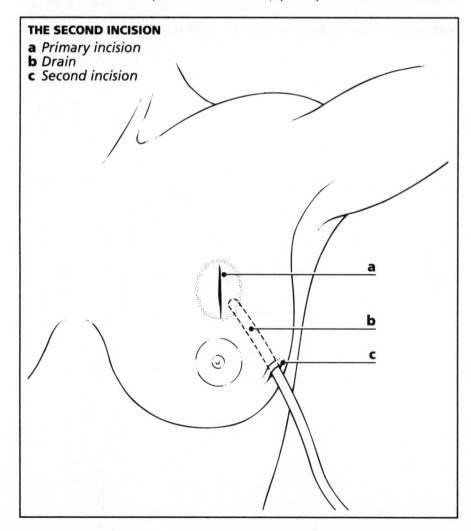

THE SECOND INCISION
a *Primary incision*
b *Drain*
c *Second incision*

a
b
c

between breast and chest wall, so that a drain tube can be pushed carefully up into the abscess cavity at an angle likely to promote drainage and without having to emerge through the infected area revealed by the first incision.

Once the abscess is cleaned out and the drain tube is in place, the surgeon closes the initial incision with simple stitches. Sterile dressings are applied, and the breast is supported in a binder (a firm, supporting breast bandage through which the drainage tube emerges). Drainage is maintained usually for two to three days and helps prevent the abscess from reforming. Widely separated abscesses will have to be drained separately.

What is it like immediately after the operation?

Much of the pain and tension that were present before the operation will have gone when you wake up. But be prepared to see the drainage tube still emerging from a lower area of your breast. Healing is rapid: you should be able to get out of bed the day after the operation. The drainage tube may be taken out after 48 hours, or when no further discharge is evident, although treatment with antibiotic drugs may be continued for five days or more. It may be only then that you are allowed to return home. It will not be possible for you to go back to nursing the baby after this operation for several reasons. First, lactation has already been suppressed and may not start again. Because it is a two-sided phenomenon, lactation will have stopped in both breasts.

In some hospitals, infrared radiation is used to promote rapid healing of breast tissue.

What are the longterm effects?

There should be no longterm effects. If there is scarring, it is likely to become far less conspicuous over the following months and may become almost invisible within years. Depressed (sunken) scars often remain depressed.

Nursing future babies need not be affected, although care should be taken when nursing so as to help prevent subsequent abscesses. For example, if your abscess was caused by a cracked nipple, you should allow the crack to heal before resuming nursing from this breast.

Radical mastectomy

Why have the operation?

Complete breast removal (radical mastectomy) is necessary to treat breast cancer that has spread inward to involve the muscles behind the breast (the pectoral muscles) that lie over the ribs.

What is the physical cause of the problem?

Radical mastectomy becomes necessary to treat breast cancer that has not been detected at a sufficiently early stage to allow less radical surgery, such as lumpectomy (see p.364). In such a case, there is no chance of eradicating the tumor unless the pectoral muscles are removed as well as the breast tissue.

A radical mastectomy may be advised when the malignant growth is extensive, even if there is evidence that the cancer has spread to parts of the body remote from the breast.

What is the goal of surgery?

Surgery is designed to rid the body of all malignant tissue by the total removal of the breast together with associated underlying muscles, lymph nodes, and other tissues. The operation may be followed by radiotherapy and chemotherapy with anticancer drugs.

Exactly what is involved in the surgical operation?

Preliminary steps. The night before the operation, your armpits will be shaved and the skin of your chest prepared by gentle swabbing with an antiseptic solution. As with any operation involving general anesthesia, you will be given a preoperative injection about an hour before surgery to dry up internal fluids and to encourage drowsiness.

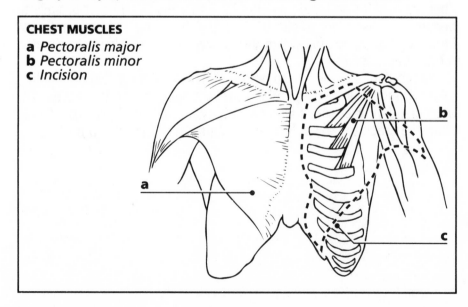

CHEST MUSCLES
a *Pectoralis major*
b *Pectoralis minor*
c *Incision*

OPERATIONS PERFORMED TO TREAT BREAST CANCER
The area of tissue to be removed is shaded.

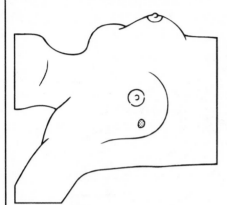

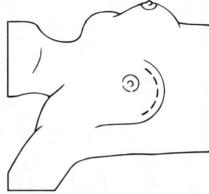

Lumpectomy *(see p.364)*
involves the removal of the
breast tumor and only a small
amount of breast tissue. It is a
method preferred by many
surgeons in cases of early
diagnosis.

Subcutaneous mastectomy
involves the removal of breast
tissue although the overlying
skin is preserved virtually intact.
It is performed in cases where
breast cancer has been
diagnosed at an early stage.

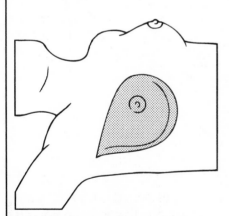

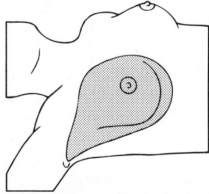

Total mastectomy *is the*
standard treatment for large
growths. It involves removal of
the affected breast, leaving the
pectoral muscles where they
are.

Radical mastectomy *is*
performed if the tumor mass
adheres to or has invaded the
muscles. This operation was the
only form of surgical treatment
for breast cancer for many
years.

© DIAGRAM

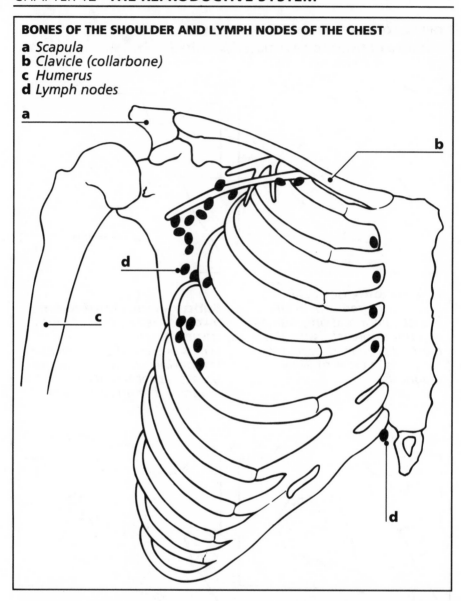

BONES OF THE SHOULDER AND LYMPH NODES OF THE CHEST

a *Scapula*
b *Clavicle (collarbone)*
c *Humerus*
d *Lymph nodes*

Once you are anesthetized, you will be positioned on the operating table lying on your back with the side of the body that is to be operated on near the edge. Your arm on that side will rest on a board well away from the body. The skin of the chest and armpit area is again gently swabbed with antiseptic cleansing solution, and sterile drapes and towels are fixed in place around the rest of the body with clips or stitches. Both clips and stitches are attached to the skin but cause no harm.

Radical mastectomy is a major procedure that can involve considerable loss of blood. It is therefore usual to have supplies of tissue-matched blood ready for transfusion should it prove necessary.

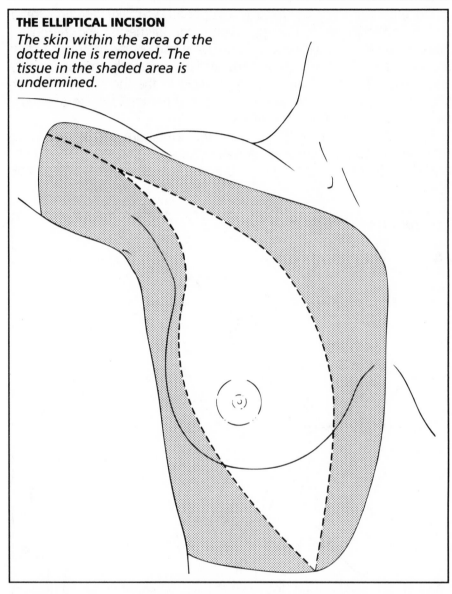

THE ELLIPTICAL INCISION
The skin within the area of the dotted line is removed. The tissue in the shaded area is undermined.

Step-by-step surgical procedure. It is common for the surgeon to make an elliptical incision as shown in the diagram. A sample of tissue (biopsy) from inside the breast may be taken for cell analysis to check on the extent of the cancer (and to confirm the diagnosis). All the skin within the incision area, including the nipple, is now removed and discarded, and the edges of this raw area are undermined for some distance in every direction and dissected free from the underlying tissue. Undermining is done with blunt-ended scissors that are pushed closed into the tissues under the skin and then opened. The margins of the flap are protected with gauze soaked in a saline solution.

© DIAGRAM

The edges of the outer muscle, the pectoralis major, are now freed and the attachments to the upper arm bone (humerus) and the collarbone (clavicle) are cut through. The muscle and overlying breast tissue are now pulled downward to expose the pectoralis minor muscle underneath. The attachment of this muscle to the top of the shoulder blade is cut through. The blood vessels and nerves to these two muscles are now tied off and cut through.

The fatty tissue and lymph nodes in the armpit are now exposed and removed as fully as possible. A moist pack of gauze is placed temporarily in the cavity. Lymph nodes are sent for cell analysis by a pathologist.

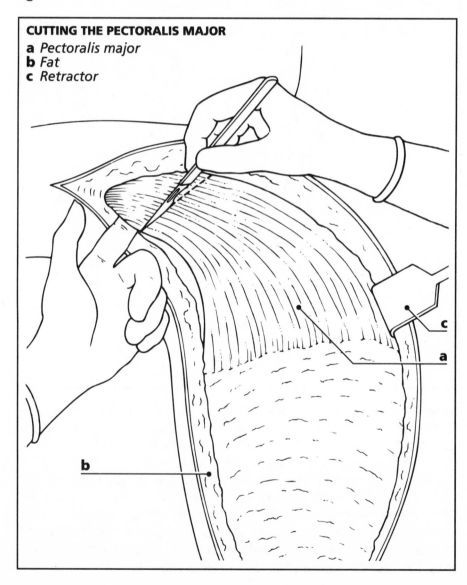

CUTTING THE PECTORALIS MAJOR
a *Pectoralis major*
b *Fat*
c *Retractor*

The muscles are now pulled downward to allow the attachments of the muscles to the ribs behind to be systematically severed. Blood vessels are clamped, tied, and cut. The whole mass of tissue, consisting of the breast and muscles, can now be removed, exposing the ribs.

The surgeon checks for any signs that cancer may have spread even further and, if there is none, brings together the flaps of loose skin created by the earlier undermining process. If the tension is too great when the surgeon tries to stitch the two sides together, further separation of underlying tissues is necessary. Occasionally, too much skin has been removed to permit closure of the wound in this way, and a skin graft is required. This can be taken from the abdomen, buttock, thigh,

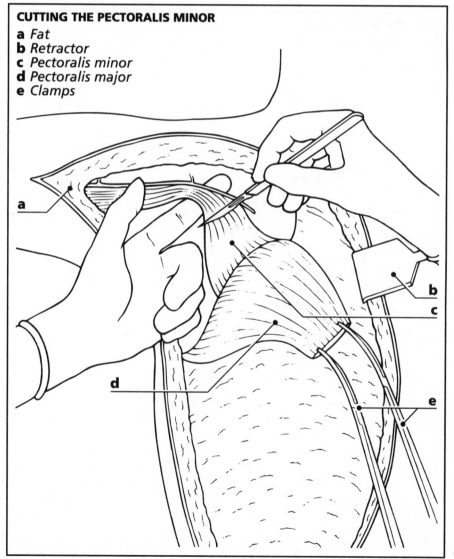

CUTTING THE PECTORALIS MINOR
a Fat
b Retractor
c Pectoralis minor
d Pectoralis major
e Clamps

© DIAGRAM

or elsewhere. Once the incision has been stitched up, a drainage tube is inserted through a separate incision in the skin.

The stitched incision is well padded and covered with a large gauze dressing held in place with adhesive tape. Your arm is likely to swell through the accumulation of lymphatic fluids (lymphedema) following the removal of the lymph nodes and is likely to be swathed in an elastic net-bandage that should help to reduce the swelling.

What is it like immediately after the operation?

You will wake up feeling rather sore and stiff, and with the arm nearest the scar in a sling. Nonetheless, you will probably be encouraged to get out of bed even on the first day after surgery, to move around a little.

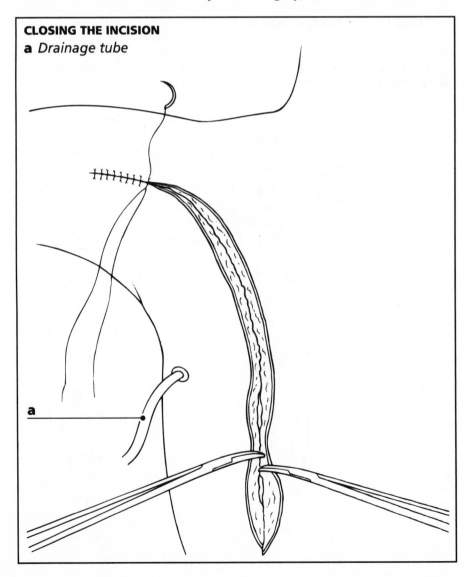

CLOSING THE INCISION

a *Drainage tube*

There may be persistent pain over the first seven days or so, focused on the incision, but it can be dealt with using painkilling drugs administered by the medical staff. The drainage tube remains in place usually for two to three days but seldom longer than a week unless infection occurs. The drainage tube is removed when no further blood and/or serum comes out. The dressings are left in place for three to five days to allow time for the skin to adhere firmly to the newly underlying tissue and to prevent pockets of accumulated blood or serum from forming under the skin. If fluid does accumulate there, it is usually sucked out with an aspirating needle.

Once the bandages are removed, you will see the scar where your breast used to be. Be prepared to be shocked and distressed—and if it helps, remember the following:

- There are ways in which your appearance can be made quite normal, with or without further surgery.
- You are likely to be more shocked and distressed than anybody else who sees the scar.
- After a time even you will not find it shocking or distressing, simply part of your own life history.

You will also be encouraged to exercise the arm, which will be difficult and painful at first. But within a week you should be able to reach well behind your head with your hand.

What are the longterm effects?

Arm swelling and stiffness may persist for months. Muscles removed during the operation do not grow back and weakness in the ability to move the arm is permanent. However, patients who keep active after their operation can achieve some improvement in the function of the assisting arm muscles and are likely to find their weakness becomes less troublesome with the passage of time. To disguise the lack of a breast, most women use a padded bra or some external prosthesis. Others prefer to undergo further major surgery for breast reconstruction (see p.424). This is a major procedure involving general anesthesia and the insertion of a silicone implant. Note that research into the safety of silicone breast implants is ongoing in light of questions concerning dangerous longterm side effects. Patients considering having such implants must confer with their surgeons to determine whether the procedure is possible and appropriate in their case and whether the potential dangers outweigh the possible benefits. The implant operation may be performed at the time of the mastectomy or, more commonly, at a later date.

If the cancer has been completely removed, longterm prospects are excellent.

Lumpectomy

Why have the operation?

Breast cancer is very dangerous and the longer it is left the greater the danger. Delay in effective treatment is the largest single factor in determining the outcome. When cancer is suspected or has already been confirmed by open tissue sampling (biopsy) or by needle biopsy, and when the cancer is believed to be small and probably limited to the breast, it may be possible to treat it by performing a minimal operation (lumpectomy) in which only the obvious tumor and some tissue around

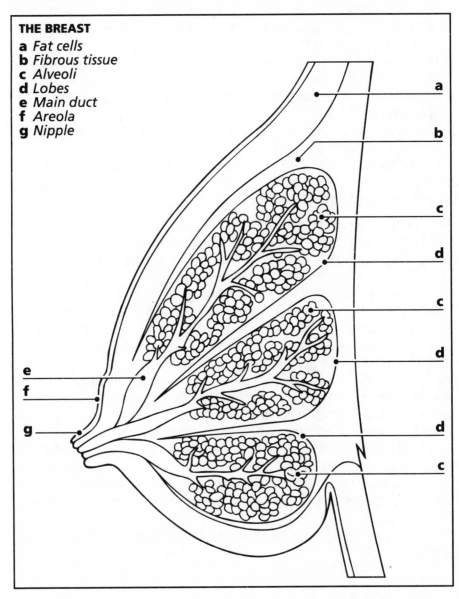

THE BREAST

a Fat cells
b Fibrous tissue
c Alveoli
d Lobes
e Main duct
f Areola
g Nipple

it are removed. This is much less disfiguring than a complete or radical mastectomy (see p.356) and, if combined with radiation therapy, can give results as effective as more radical procedures.

What is the physical cause of the problem?
Like all malignant tumors, cancer of the breast is the abnormal and uncontrolled reproduction of cells, forming a mass of tissue that grows, invades, and spreads into adjacent areas and is able to seed itself off via the bloodstream or similar channels to remote parts of the body, resulting in secondary tumors (metastasis). Breast cancer seems to originate mainly in cells of the upper, outer part of the breast, in ducts within the glandular tissue. The actual cause remains unknown, although the types of cells involved would seem to suggest a hormonal association; diet appears also to be a factor, particularly consumption of high levels of fat.

Because tumors grow steadily (and, in the breast, fairly rapidly), a large lump implies that the tumor has been present for a long period and is more likely to have spread.

What is the goal of surgery?
The aim of surgery is to remove the tumor and cells around it to an extent that the body's natural defenses, together with additional thera-peutic measures (such as radiation therapy and anticancer drugs), can deal with any remaining cancerous cells.

But there is still a wide spectrum of opinion on the optimum method of breast cancer surgery.

It is very important that you discuss with your surgeon the question of what type of surgery is best for your particular situation. You should be quite clear about what the surgeon proposes to do, why, and what the effects will be. At the same time, you should be aware that it is sometimes necessary to diverge from the planned procedure during the operation if the condition is discovered to be worse than was sus-pected.

Exactly what is involved in the surgical operation?
Before the operation, exhaustive investigation will suggest a specific diagnosis on which the surgeon will base the decision as to what form of surgery to perform. In many cases that diagnosis will also already have been confirmed by a procedure known as fine-needle aspiration biopsy-cytology. This common diagnostic method involves the insertion into the tumor mass of a narrow and very sharp needle attached to a syringe; a number of tumor cells are drawn out through the needle, blown onto a microscope slide, dried, fixed, and stained for examina-tion by an expert pathologist. The procedure causes minimal distur-bance and is thought not to risk the spread of cancer cells into the bloodstream.

Preliminary steps. As with all operations involving general anesthesia, you will be given a preoperative injection about an hour before surgery to dry up internal fluids and to encourage drowsiness.

Step-by-step surgical procedure. Once you have been anesthetized, you will be positioned on the operating table lying on your back. The skin over the whole of the affected breast is thoroughly swabbed with an antiseptic solution. All but the operating site is then covered with sterile towels and drapes fixed in place by clips.

The surgeon's first incision is a short, curved stroke over the area of the lump. The underlying layer of fatty tissue is then cut through in order to reveal the glandular tissue of the breast. This tissue is of a soft consistency, amidst which the lump can now more easily be felt and its extent assessed. The surgeon will take care not to cut into the lump; the dissection is confined to areas well clear of it. Using surgical scissors to pry the tissues apart, and with minimal actual cutting, the surgeon removes the lump, together with a considerable quantity of apparently normal surrounding breast tissue. The material removed is put into a specimen jar (with preservative) and sent to the pathology laboratory for analysis.

Finally, the surgeon closes the skin incision with a continuous stitch tied only at each end, or with separate stitches, each separately tied.

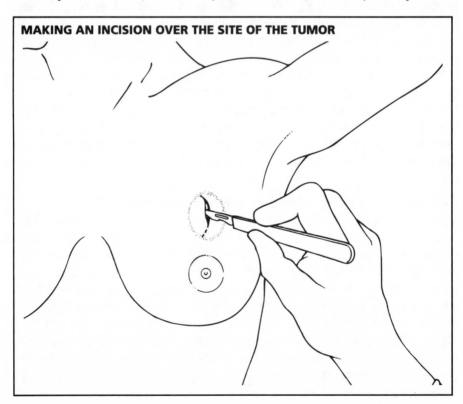

MAKING AN INCISION OVER THE SITE OF THE TUMOR

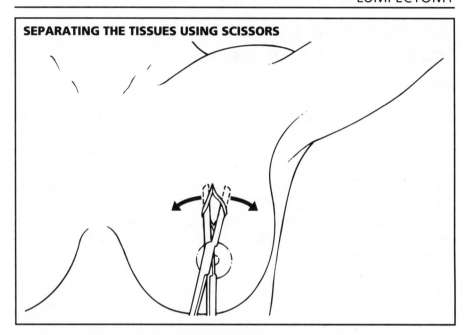

SEPARATING THE TISSUES USING SCISSORS

What is it like immediately after the operation?

Lumpectomy is a minor procedure. You should feel little discomfort after the operation and be able to leave the hospital almost at once. The stitches can usually be removed in your own physician's office in less than a week. Some temporary swelling within the breast will partly make up for loss of breast bulk, but the loss may become apparent (though possibly only to yourself) when the swelling has subsided. If you are at all concerned about this, discuss with your surgeon the possibility of breast augmentation (see p.428) at some later date. Note that research into the safety of silicone breast implants is ongoing in light of questions concerning dangerous longterm side effects. Patients considering having such implants must confer with their surgeons to determine whether the procedure is possible and appropriate in their case and whether the potential dangers outweigh the possible benefits.

What are the longterm effects?

Lumpectomy is not a complete therapy by itself—additional measures, such as radiation therapy, are essential. Further options include chemotherapy and hormone therapy. In the case of tumors less than about 1 inch (2.4cm) in diameter, 60 percent of women have no recurrence within five years. This is considered a cure. Larger tumors are subject to a lower cure rate. Even then, recurrent cancer may not require further surgery if caught early enough: radiation therapy and chemotherapy may be sufficient to halt the growth process. In any event, every lumpectomy patient should have regular medical check-ups, including periodic mammography (breast X-ray photography).

Circumcision: removal of the foreskin of the penis

Why have the operation?

Medical reasons for this operation are few—there is no medical point in cutting off the foreskin of the penis (the prepuce) unless it is physically malformed and so causing difficulty in urinating, interfering with ordinary hygiene, or hindering sexual intercourse. Only the first of these possibilities is evident in early infancy and represents a genuine medical indication for this type of surgery at that age. There is no truth at all in the surprisingly common belief that an uncircumcised boy is more likely to develop urinary tract infection than a circumcised boy (if they are both taught to adopt the normal standards of personal hygiene) or that in adult life somehow a circumcised penis is more sensitive during sexual congress than an uncircumcised one (when in fact the glans penis is normally unsheathed in both cases anyway). The American Academy of Pediatrics has confirmed that routine circumcision of male infants is unnecessary—and yet, rather strangely, most male infants in the United States undergo circumcision.

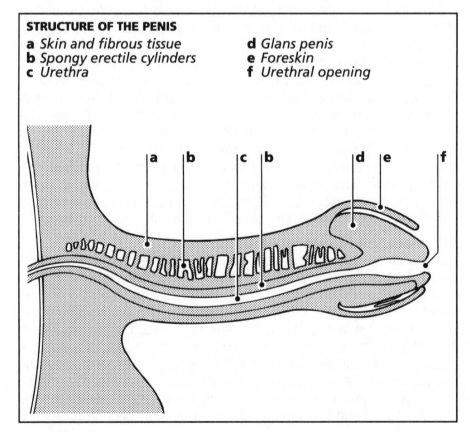

STRUCTURE OF THE PENIS

a *Skin and fibrous tissue*
b *Spongy erectile cylinders*
c *Urethra*
d *Glans penis*
e *Foreskin*
f *Urethral opening*

At the same time there is little medical harm in the operation, performed at any stage of life—although psychological associations may cause qualms in adult patients. Traditions and religious beliefs in many families are the reason for the operation in adulthood.

What is the physical cause of the problem?
Circumcision may be used to remedy several physical problems.

Phimosis. The most common medical problem is phimosis, a condition in which the urethral opening is so small that urine is impeded from escaping. The result is that the foreskin balloons out while urination is in progress. If left untreated, this can cause potentially damaging back-pressure of urine right up as far as the kidneys and can also encourage infection of the urinary tract.

Paraphimosis. When erections become common from initial puberty onward, a tight foreskin can constrict blood vessels at the base of the glans and so cause acute and painful swelling of the penile bulb. This condition is called paraphimosis, and also requires circumcision.

Cancer of the penis is extremely uncommon, but usually begins in the foreskin; circumcision thus virtually eliminates the risk. It is, however, a condition restricted almost exclusively to men who do not wash thoroughly (or) enough.

Retraction of the foreskin. It is quite normal for the foreskin to be attached to the underlying tissue by fine strands for the first few months of life, so that it cannot be pulled back. In about 50 percent of boys it can be retracted manually by the end of the first year (although parents are strongly advised not to try). But it is just as common that it cannot be retracted until at least age five. Only after this age should there be any suggestion of medical attention. And even then—or later—any restricting strands ("tied parts") that remain can most likely be surgically severed without the need for a total circumcision.

What is the goal of surgery?
The aim of circumcision—whatever the reason for it being performed—is to remove the foreskin covering the glans penis.

Exactly what is involved in the surgical operation?
Circumcision of a newborn boy is performed using either a local anesthetic or no anesthetic at all; older children and adults are much more commonly operated on under general anesthesia, as described below. In every case, however, surgery follows the same basic outline.

Preliminary steps. As in all operations involving general anesthesia, you will be given a preoperative injection about an hour before surgery to dry up internal fluids and to encourage drowsiness. (In the rare event of an adult's being operated on under a local anesthetic, two injections will be administered: one at the root of the penis and another in the foreskin at the base of the glans.)

Step-by-step surgical procedure. Once sensation has been numbed, the surgeon makes the first incision around the foreskin at the base of the glans, taking great care to avoid cutting through into the glans itself. The foreskin, freed from the skin that covers the penile shaft, then remains attached only by the mucous membrane that lines the foreskin and by the thin layer of connective tissue that forms the attachment between them. The skin covering the shaft of the penis naturally retracts a little, leaving a short length of raw area. The surgeon now cuts from the top of the foreskin directly toward the base of the glans through all layers of the foreskin to the initial line of incision, where just a little further easing with a blade all around (so, in effect, "circum-cising") lifts the foreskin off altogether. Any bleeding points are nipped by forceps and tied off with a catgut suture. All that remains to be done is to stitch together the raw top edges of the skin that covers the penile shaft and the mucous membrane that lines it, at the site of the initial incision, using fine catgut. At the same time, control of bleeding is important, in order to avoid the formation of hematomas (localized accumulations of clotting blood) in the tissues which might in turn lead to infection and subsequent poor healing and possible scarring.

What is it like immediately after the operation?

If you have just been circumcised, it is probable that no dressing will have been applied and you will wake up to find that the appearance of your penis has changed considerably. Until healing is complete there will be some pain, but this can be controlled by painkillers. Urination may also be painful and you should try to keep the urine away from the incision.

For some days you will try to avoid walking or any movement that may cause penile contact with clothes or thighs while the previously very sensitive glans loses some of its sensitivity through constant exposure to air. At the end of that time, however, there should be no pain, the stitches should be removable or fading, and your interest in sexual intercourse may well have been re-established.

While healing is taking place, there is little risk of the stitches splitting or pulling out because of an erection. The good blood supply to the area also means the chance of infection is rare.

What are the longterm effects?

The longterm effects reflect the specific aim of surgery, as outlined earlier.

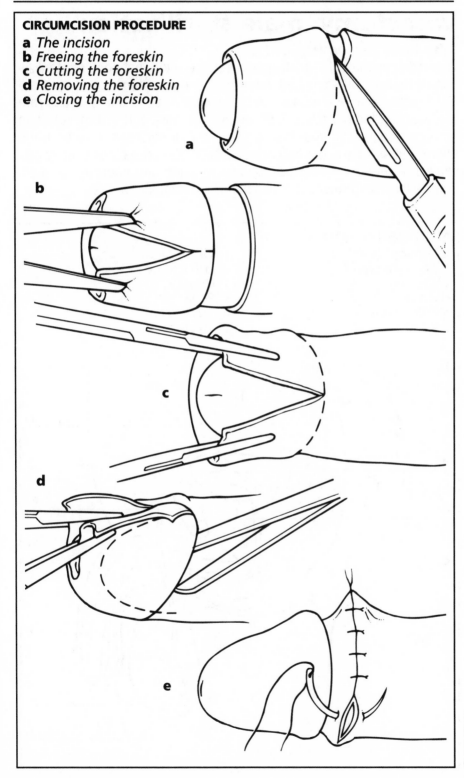

CIRCUMCISION PROCEDURE
a *The incision*
b *Freeing the foreskin*
c *Cutting the foreskin*
d *Removing the foreskin*
e *Closing the incision*

© DIAGRAM

Vasectomy: male sterilization

Why have the operation?

Vasectomy is the only widely employed operation that confers sterilization on males. You should not even consider vasectomy unless you are quite certain that you wish to be permanently sterile (the success rate for reversing the operation is 50 percent or less), and that there will be no regrets either on your part or your sexual partner's, now or in the future. But sterility is the only consideration: the operation is purely preventive, a means of contraception. Your libido and capacity for erection, sexual excitement, and climax remain unimpaired.

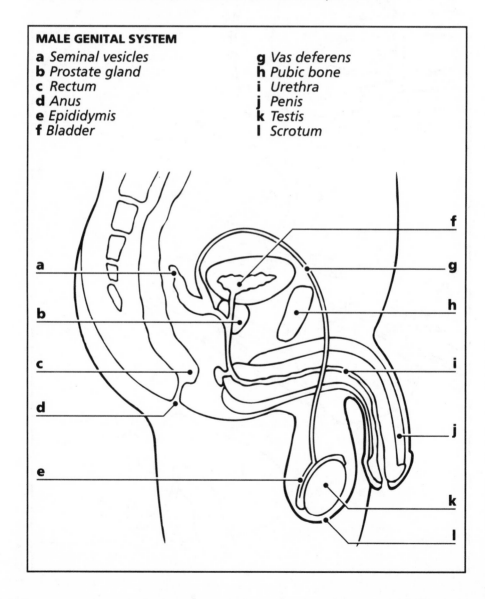

MALE GENITAL SYSTEM

a Seminal vesicles
b Prostate gland
c Rectum
d Anus
e Epididymis
f Bladder

g Vas deferens
h Pubic bone
i Urethra
j Penis
k Testis
l Scrotum

What is the physical cause of the problem?

This operation is entirely voluntary: even the timing of the operation is largely up to the patient.

What is the goal of surgery?

The surgeon's aim is to disconnect the two tubes that allow sperm produced in each testis to be transferred for storage to special sacs (seminal vesicles) lying just under the bladder. Each tube is called a vas deferens (plural: vasa deferentia), and the operation comprises cutting them and ensuring that they can't join up again.

Prior consultation is particularly important between surgeon and patient before this operation, not because surgery is in any way diffi-

AFTER THE OPERATION

Once the vasa deferentia are cut and tied, sperm cannot reach the seminal vesicles and so be included in the seminal fluid ejaculated at climax.

a *Seminal vesicles*
b *Vas deferens*
c *Urethra*
d *Penis*
e *Testis*
f *Scrotum*
g *Bladder*

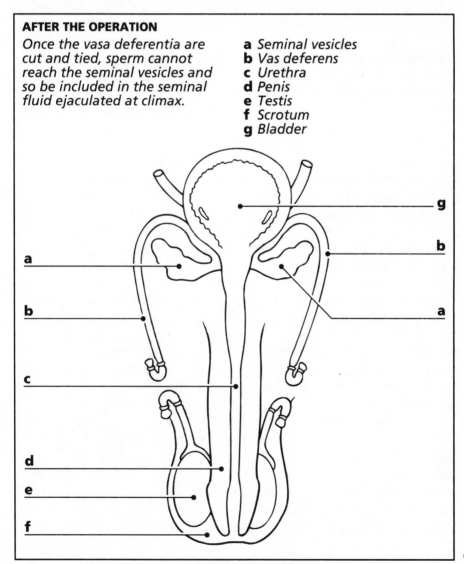

© DIAGRAM

cult—it is in fact a simple operation usually performed under only local anesthesia—but because many patients tend to confuse sterility (which is the aim) with an inability to achieve and maintain an erection or to reach a climax (although those aspects should be unaffected). An additional aim for the surgeon is thus to dispel any lingering doubts about capacity for future sexual enjoyment: after a vasectomy you will continue to ejaculate at climax exactly as before. The semen ejaculated will look the same, but it will not contain sperm, which were only a small part of the ejaculate. Everything will feel the same as it always did.

Exactly what is involved in the surgical operation?

One thing that is not normally involved is hospitalization. The entire operation is very simple, takes about 20 minutes or less, and can be quite comfortably performed in a surgeon's office or an outpatient clinic.

Preliminary steps. You will be asked to undress and get into a gown; you will then be taken into a small operating room and asked to lie on the operating table. The surgeon will then swab the whole of your genital area with a cleaning fluid that may leave you temporarily painted a bright yellow-brown (or other) color, but will drastically reduce the number of bacteria on your skin. The surgeon will then apply aseptic towels, leaving only your penis and scrotum exposed.

Step-by-step surgical procedure. First the surgeon will inject local anesthetic on each side of the scrotum in order to take away all sensation: in itself this is practically painless. (Once the anesthetic has taken effect you will feel no pain, but there may be an odd grating sensation from time to time: the anesthetic does not necessarily remove all sense of vibration, and this may be transmitted to nearby areas that are not anesthetized.)

The two vasa deferentia lie within the vessels called the spermatic cords just under the skin of the scrotum. The surgeon will approach each of them through a single short vertical incision made just below the root of the penis. When the skin on the first side has been opened, the surgeon will use an instrument to draw out the spermatic cord on that side and, after injecting further anesthetic as necessary, carefully cut into the spermatic cord to get to the vas deferens.

The spermatic cord also contains numerous blood vessels, and the surgeon will try to avoid severing these so as to minimize bruising. A loop of the vas deferens is pulled through the wound and, usually, a piece about one-half inch (1cm) long is cut out with scissors. Most surgeons fold back each cut end and tie it tight. The free ends are then put back through the wound, and the skin edges of the vas deferens are brought together and sealed with a few fine stitches.

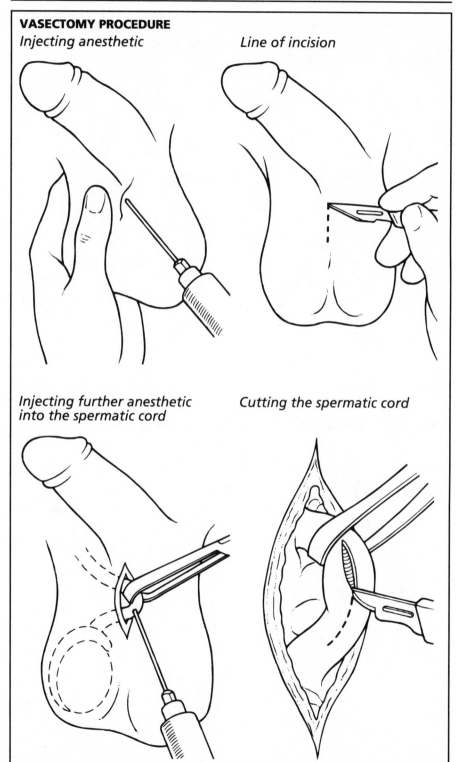

VASECTOMY PROCEDURE

Injecting anesthetic

Line of incision

*Injecting further anesthetic
into the spermatic cord*

Cutting the spermatic cord

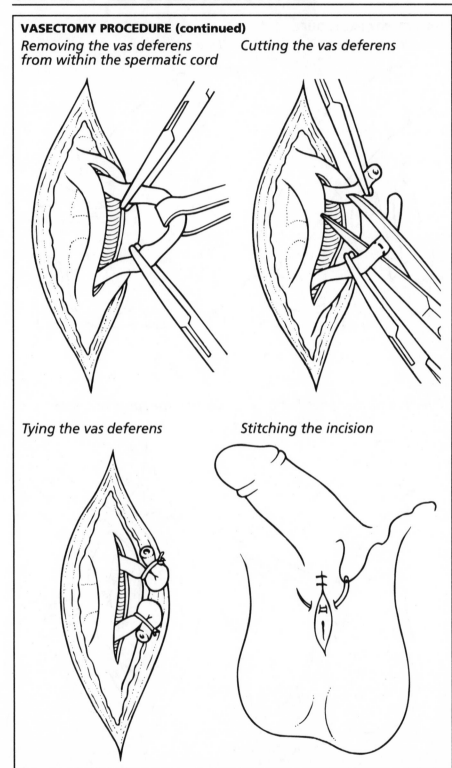

VASECTOMY PROCEDURE (continued)

Removing the vas deferens from within the spermatic cord

Cutting the vas deferens

Tying the vas deferens

Stitching the incision

The surgeon then carries out the identical procedure on the vas def-erens on the other side.

What is it like immediately after the operation?

When the anesthetic wears off you will probably experience a dull ache in the area for a few hours—unless you take a couple of ordinary acetaminophen tablets (but not aspirin, which may encourage bleeding) to relieve it. Local bruising—in effect, blood escaping into the skin tis-sues where it can in the next four to seven days be reabsorbed—is also common. You may feel tired and in need of sympathy. For the first week or two it might be more comfortable for you to wear tight jockey shorts or an athletic support. And during that time, sexual intercourse is better avoided altogether.

What are the longterm effects?

Healing is almost always excellent, and the operation scars remain vir-tually invisible. Some internal bleeding, with conspicuous bruising, is very common and usually causes no trouble, but the rare development of a hematoma will require further surgery. In a few cases, long-term inflammation in the area of the testicles can occur, causing persistent discomfort. Most men return to work after four or five days. Sexual intercourse may be resumed as soon as you feel capable of it, gener-ally about a week after the operation.

However, don't forget that sterilization is not immediate. You will still be able to father children until all the sperm already stored in your sem-inal vesicles have been ejaculated. The safest thing to do is to use other forms of contraception for two or three months, and then to ask your own physician to make a sperm count.

Most serious complications following vasectomy are psychosexual, in people who have not understood from the beginning that sterility need have no effect on sexual excitement and enjoyment. Special coun-seling, and a loving relationship with a patient partner, are the most suc-cessful remedies in such cases.

Prostatectomy: removal of part or all of the prostate gland

Why have the operation?
The symptoms of prostate enlargement—a normal feature of aging in men—only gradually impinge upon the consciousness, but may eventually become troublesome and finally even painful and potentially health threatening. This process is generally slow, and in many men never amounts to a serious problem, but in others the process may be more rapid and require surgery to correct it and to prevent the worst symptoms from occurring.

What is the physical cause of the problem?
The prostate gland lies under the bladder and surrounds the first part of the tube (the urethra) that carries urine to the penis. When the prostate becomes enlarged, it tends to obstruct the urethra. This makes urination difficult: no matter how urgent the necessity, the urine stream becomes progressively less forceful. Eventually initiating urination

LOCATION OF THE PROSTATE GLAND
a *Bladder*
b *Urethra*
c *Rectum*
d *Prostate gland*

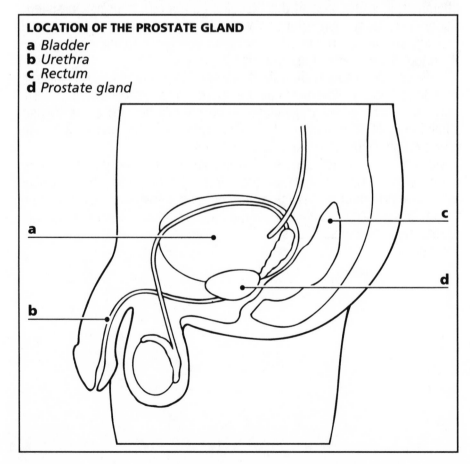

becomes a physical and mental effort, it is impossible to empty the bladder completely, and the intervals between wanting to urinate become progressively shorter. Moreover, during the early stages of obstruction the muscular wall of the bladder is strong enough to force urine down and through the urethra, but applying such pressure finally causes the bladder to distend—sometimes resulting in a visible bloating of the abdomen—and there may be incontinence: small quantities of urine may "overflow." Bladder stones may form. Infection of the bladder is common. In the end, the bladder may fail altogether, causing severe pain and an inability to pass more than a few drops of urine. This is an emergency situation and requires urgent surgical drainage of urine: if the pressure is not relieved, serious damage may be done to the kidneys because of the pressure of urine unable to escape through the already filled ureters.

The condition of the prostate is assessed by a rectal examination, in which the surgeon probes through the anal opening into the rectum and physically feels the size and shape of your prostate.

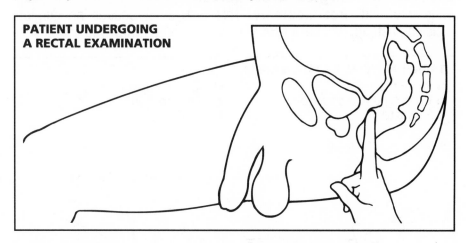

**PATIENT UNDERGOING
A RECTAL EXAMINATION**

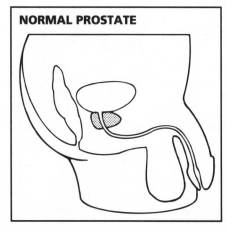

NORMAL PROSTATE

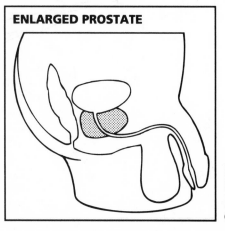

ENLARGED PROSTATE

© DIAGRAM

What is the goal of surgery?

The aim is to remove the prostate gland, and so relieve the symptoms. There are three common methods of prostatectomy, each involving a different means of approach to the gland: transurethral (the most common method), retropubic, and perineal. The choice of method depends mostly on how the prostate gland has enlarged (although other physical factors may also be significant).

Exactly what is involved in the surgical operation?

Each of the three ordinary methods of prostatectomy requires general or spinal anesthesia. Before the operation the anesthetist will investigate your overall health and medical record to ensure that you receive the correct amount of anesthetic and one with which you are comfortable.

Preliminary steps. As with all operations involving general anesthesia, you will be given a preoperative injection about an hour before surgery to dry up internal fluids and to encourage drowsiness.

Step-by-step surgical procedures

Transurethral prostatectomy. This operation requires no surgical incision. Instead, it is performed using a straight, narrow, tubular instru-

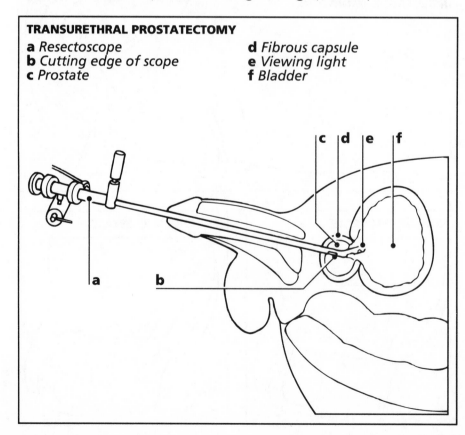

TRANSURETHRAL PROSTATECTOMY

a *Resectoscope*   **d** *Fibrous capsule*
b *Cutting edge of scope*   **e** *Viewing light*
c *Prostate*   **f** *Bladder*

ment called a resectoscope that is passed through the opening at the tip of the penis and on inside the urethra. The surgeon uses an edge of the resectoscope to cut away the urethra wall in order to reach the interior of the prostate gland. For this approach you will be positioned on your back, your knees and feet high (often in stirrups), and your legs wide apart (the lithotomy position). Most resectoscopes use a small loop of tungsten wire that can be made red hot by electric current to cut away the redundant prostate tissue piece by piece; others may use laser beams in the same way. The operation is performed under the surgeon's direct vision, facilitated by fiberoptic channels within the resectoscope. One advantage of using heat to cut or destroy prostate tissue is that it minimizes bleeding, which is occasionally a hazard of prostate surgery; additional control may be achieved by a high-frequency coagulating current. After as much as possible of the prostate tissue has been cut away and flushed out through the resectoscope, the instrument is slid gently out and a catheter is equally gently pushed inside the urethra into the bladder, where it will temporarily facilitate urination and bladder irrigation.

INSERTING A URINARY CATHETER AFTER PROSTATECTOMY
a *Catheter*
b *Urethra*
c *Bladder*
d *Drainage tube*

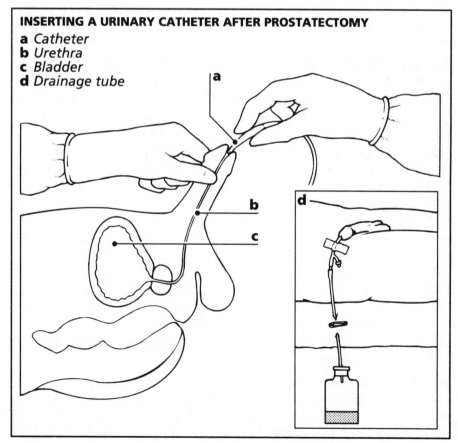

© DIAGRAM

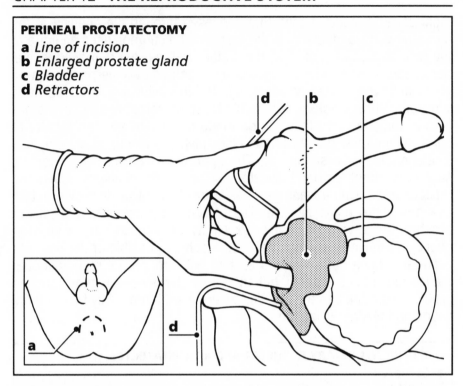

PERINEAL PROSTATECTOMY
a *Line of incision*
b *Enlarged prostate gland*
c *Bladder*
d *Retractors*

Perineal prostatectomy. For this approach the patient is also placed in the lithotomy position. The surgeon then makes a curved incision between the back of the scrotum and the anus, and cuts straight down to the underlying prostate. The surgeon then cuts through the fibrous capsule that encloses the prostate and, using his or her fingers or a blunt-edged blade, can often simply shell out the entire prostate. The incision is then closed with stitches and a catheter is passed into the bladder through the penis, where it will temporarily facilitate urination and bladder irrigation.

Retropubic prostatectomy. For this approach the patient is positioned flat on his back, so that the surgeon can make an incision in the front wall of the abdomen, just above the pubic bone, and thereby reach directly to the prostate. Again, the surgeon cuts through the fibrous capsule that encloses the prostate and, using a blunt-edged blade or his or her fingers, can often simply shell out the entire prostate. The incision is then closed with stitches and a catheter is passed into the bladder through the penis, where it will temporarily facilitate urination and bladder irrigation.

What is it like immediately after the operation?
The catheter is left in place for a few days while you remain in the hospital. Bladder drainage is not painful, and bladder irrigation—if necessary to clear small blood clots from within the bladder—is no more than

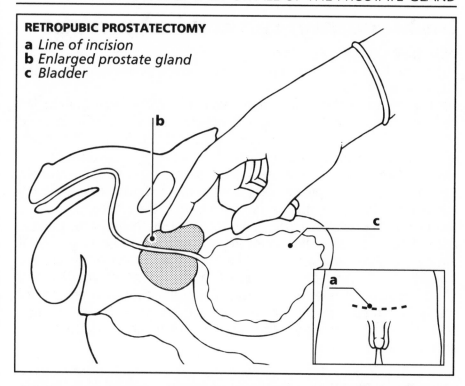

RETROPUBIC PROSTATECTOMY
a *Line of incision*
b *Enlarged prostate gland*
c *Bladder*

slightly uncomfortable. However, patients treated surgically by the increasingly rare perineal approach may feel considerable local discomfort for a week or more and require special sympathy and support from the family. Local bruising, sometimes spectacular, may also last for four to seven days. Total hospitalization may be for between two and four days depending on which surgical method was employed. Once the catheter has been withdrawn, urination may be painful for a time.

The most common complication in the short term is continued bleeding which, in rare cases, may eventually demand transfusion.

What are the longterm effects?
The main effect is an increased sense of well-being. However, frequency of urination and slight incontinence may still be troublesome after a few weeks. Sexual intercourse may be resumed after two or three months, but even if sexual performance and enjoyment are not affected—and in many cases, especially for those who have undergone transurethral prostatectomy, sexual performance is undiminished—the likelihood of fathering children is reduced to a virtual impossibility because on ejaculation the semen travels (harmlessly) back down into the bladder, rather than out via the urethra, and is passed with the next urination.

Orchiectomy: removal of a testis

Why have the operation?

There are three major reasons for a surgeon to advise removal of the testis (orchiectomy):

Torsion of the testis. If the spermatic cord within one or both testes becomes twisted so that the blood supply to the testis (carried in blood vessels through the spermatic cord) is cut off, the testis will become gangrenous and should be removed.

Tumor of the testis. These are virtually always malignant, but modern treatment now offers an excellent outlook on the basis of orchiectomy followed by chemotherapy and (sometimes) radiation therapy.

Cancer of the prostate gland. A tumor in or on the prostate gland is dependent on male sex hormones for its continued abnormal growth. If the cancer spreads elsewhere in the body, the secondary tumors are similarly reliant on male sex hormones for their development. Removal of both testes (bilateral orchiectomy) is the most effective method of halting the production of male sex hormones in the body. This method controls both the primary tumor and the secondary prostate cancer growth, especially in the bones.

TORSION OF THE TESTIS

A *Normal testis*
B *Normal testis exposed*
C *Torsion of the testis exposed, showing twisted right spermatic cord*
a *Spermatic cord*
b *Epididymis*
c *Testis*

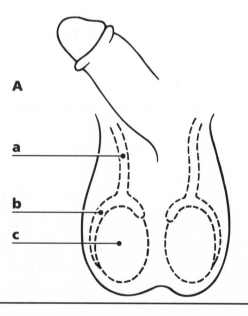

What is the physical cause of the problem?

Torsion of the testis is caused by a slight congenital defect in the covering of the spermatic cord. It causes severe pain, swelling, nausea, vomiting, and sometimes fever. The affected testis rides higher than normal, and lies more horizontally. Unless surgery to untwist the cord and restore the blood supply to the testis is performed within a few hours, the organ will atrophy and die, and must be removed.

A testicular tumor appears as a stony swelling on the side of one testis. These represent about two percent of all malignant growths and occur at any age, but are most common between the ages of 20 and 35. The usual type—a seminoma—generally grows slowly and spreads at a late stage: most are detected while still restricted to the testis, although detection may not occur until a dull, aching, dragging pain develops. A tumor of this sort occasionally causes the production in the body of female sex hormones, resulting in enlargement of the breasts (gynecomastia).

Cancer of the prostate causes frequency of urination, difficulty while urinating, discomfort, and acute retention of urine. These symptoms are also those of benign prostate enlargement, but rectal examination—mandatory in all such cases—may confirm the diagnosis.

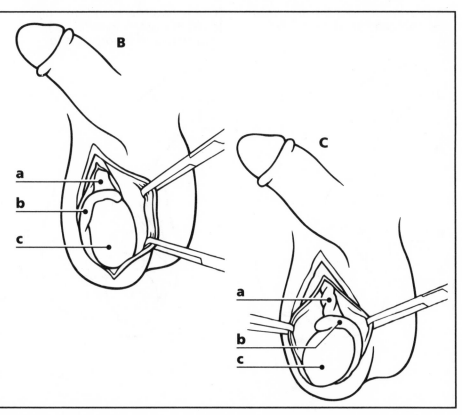

© DIAGRAM

What is the goal of surgery?

Torsion of the testis. The aim is to remove dead tissue. The loss of one testis has no effect on overall sexual function, hormonal balance, or fertility. A plastic prosthesis can be inserted in the scrotum at the time of surgery to make up the loss if so desired.

Testicular cancer. The aim is to remove all malignant tissue and save life.

Prostate gland cancer. The aim is to assist in the management of the condition and, by reducing the effects especially of secondary growths, to prolong life and improve its quality.

Exactly what is involved in the surgical operation?

Before surgery, you should expect to undergo a number of tests to confirm the diagnosis. These might include clinical confirmation of torsion, needle biopsy to confirm cancer, cystoscopy and biopsy to confirm prostate cancer, scanning to confirm secondaries, and so on.

Preliminary steps. The operation can be performed under local anesthesia or spinal anesthesia (by which sensation is numbed from the waist down following the injection of anesthetic into the cerebrospinal

---

ORCHIECTOMY FOR TESTICULAR TORSION AND PROSTATE CANCER

A *Incisions through the scrotum (**a**) and testical covering (**b**)*

B *Exposing the spermatic cord (twisted in torsion cases) (**c**), testis (**d**), and epididymis (**e**)*

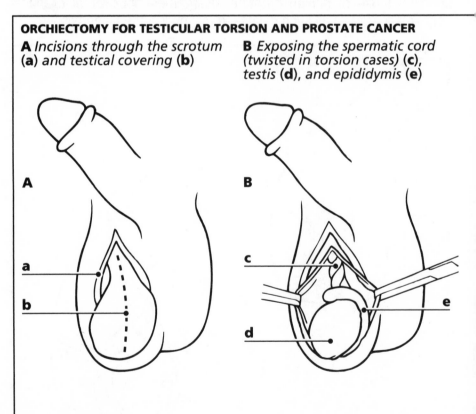

fluid within the lower part of the spinal column), but many patients pre-fer general anesthesia. If you are to have general anesthesia, you will be given a preoperative injection about an hour before surgery to dry up internal fluids and to encourage drowsiness. You may or may not be given a preoperative injection before spinal anesthesia.

Step-by-step surgical procedure

Testicular torsion and **prostate cancer.** The procedure in these cases is identical. After painting your genital area with antibacterial solution and administering a local anesthetic if no other form of anes-thesia is to be used, the surgeon makes a small incision in the skin of the scrotum. Another incision is made through the testical covering to expose the twisted spermatic cord and testis, which are then brought out through the incision. The spermatic cord is then tied off and sev-ered. Similarly the blood vessels and nerves associated with the testis are tied and severed. The testis is removed and the skin is closed with a few stitches. (If the aim is to eliminate sex hormones, the procedure is repeated on the second testis.) Healing is rapid.

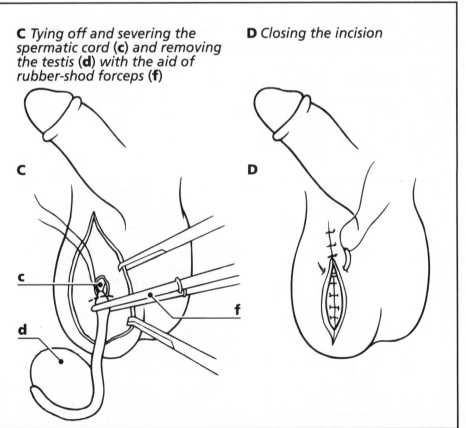

C *Tying off and severing the spermatic cord (**c**) and removing the testis (**d**) with the aid of rubber-shod forceps (**f**)*

D *Closing the incision*

C

c

d

D

f

© DIAGRAM

Testicular cancer. Special precautions must be taken to prevent the spread of cancerous material during the operation. The surgeon's incision is made not in the scrotum but in the crease of the groin. From here it is still possible to bring out the upper portion of the spermatic cord, which the surgeon then clamps with rubber-shod forceps. The testicle is freed from its bed in the scrotum and pulled up through the groin incision for inspection. If cancer is confirmed visually (it is usually readily apparent if present), further, tighter clamps are applied to the spermatic cord, which is firmly tied off and severed. The stump of the cord is replaced in the abdomen, and the testis is removed for examination in a pathology laboratory. The surgeon then closes the groin incision with stitches. Healing is rapid.

What is it like immediately after the operation?

In all cases, the operation itself causes only minor discomfort afterward, and for only a short time; you should expect to be up and about within a day or two.

Effects are more likely to be psychological. The loss of one testicle should be regarded as having little or no effect on your life and your relationships. But the loss of both has considerable bearing on your potency and fertility.

In the case of testicular cancer, you should expect to undergo further treatment with chemotherapy and radiation therapy. If your other testis

ORCHIECTOMY FOR TESTICULAR CANCER
A *Incision (***a***) in crease of groin*
B *Bringing spermatic cord (***b***) out through incision using forceps (***c***)*
C *Inspecting the testis (***d***) and tying off spermatic cord*

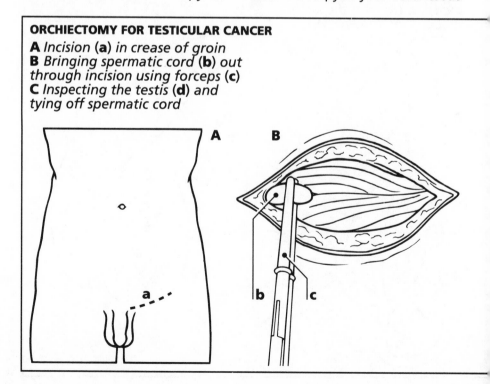

is healthy, such treatment should cause it no harm and fertility is normally retained. Radiation therapy, however, immediately increases the likelihood of genetic disorders. If conception occurs, discuss with the physician the advisability of amniocentesis or chorionic villus sampling to detect genetic disorders.

What are the longterm effects?
Effects depend on the condition for which the operation was performed. Testis removal following testicular torsion has no significant effects. The outlook after orchiectomy and associated treatment for testicular cancer is excellent: more than 90 percent of affected men recover fully, and the success rate is much higher still if the initial detection of the cancer was early. Men with prostate cancer and secondary growths have about a 50 percent chance of surviving for three years following bilateral orchiectomy.

The loss of one testis will not affect potency or fertility. Sex hormones and sperm continue to be produced. Removal of both testes, however, renders a patient sterile and causes loss of libido and of the masculinizing effect of the androgens. Sex hormone replacements cannot be used, as the point of surgery was to remove such hormones. The power of erection and ejaculation are likely to be lost. Personality changes—secondary to loss of male sex hormones—are also likely.

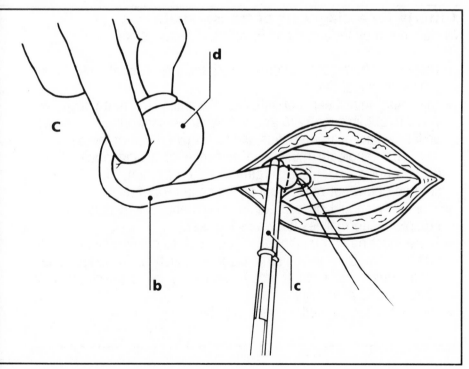

© DIAGRAM

Sex-change surgery

Why have the operation?

This operation is performed to make the patient's anatomical sex conform fully with the patient's own conviction of his or her gender.

There are two main ways in which such a difference between the patient's body and the patient's own sense of gender arises: either as a result of the presence of ambiguous genitalia at birth and external pressures from family thereafter, or because of transsexualism—the utter certainty on the part of the patient that he or she is somehow in a body of the wrong sex, and has always been, even though the body he or she has is anatomically normal.

Babies who have ambiguous genitalia at birth in the United States are more commonly operated on within a short time after birth, following chromosomal analysis. Almost all sex-change operations today are on adult transsexuals.

What is the physical cause of the problem?

Sex (or gender) is a complex characteristic that involves identification of the self from early childhood as either female or male and that cannot thereafter simply be established by checking whether the chromosomes in the body's cells are of the female configuration (XX) or of the male pattern (XY).

Criteria for a diagnosis of transsexualism
(as laid down by the American Psychiatric Association)

- There must be a sense of discomfort and inappropriateness about your anatomical sex.
- You must have been persistently attempting for more than two years to obtain surgery to get rid of your present primary and secondary sexual characteristics and to acquire those of the opposite sex. The candidate must give evidence of having made determined efforts to achieve surgery in spite of rebuff. The matter is not one of law but of medical caution and propriety.
- Your body should be subject to no genetic defect (such as the group of abnormalities known as intersex).
- There must be no question that your wish to change sex might in fact be due to a psychiatric disorder (such as schizophrenia). Candidates must have thorough screening by a psychiatrist to eliminate this possibility.
- You must have passed the age of puberty.

In the case of children born with ambiguous genitalia and for one reason or another not surgically treated soon after birth, the gender assumed to be correct (and probably most desired) by parents or guardians, and in which they are reared, is virtually always the one they accept and wish to retain. Physical development—and the effects of puberty on sexual characteristics—may later cause serious internal conflict.

In the case of transsexuals, the conviction that they are somehow in an alien body is often so strong that they will go to almost any lengths to change it. This has nothing whatever to do with homosexuality or transvestism, although transsexuals often wish to wear the clothes of the opposite anatomical sex (cross-dressing). The cause of transsexuality is unknown. There is no evidence that it arises as a result of inappropriate levels of the opposite sex hormones before birth, as has been suggested. One suggested cause is—as in those allowed to grow up with ambiguous genitalia—the conscious or unconscious imposition on the patient as an infant of the desire of one or both parents for a child of the other sex.

The American Psychiatric Association has produced some guidelines for diagnosing transsexualism (see box). These criteria are not in themselves sufficient justification for surgery. In some cases in the past the transformation has proved to be a disastrous error, exposing a patient to such social, sexual, legal, and psychological trauma as to lead to suicide. The decision to undergo surgery is not to be taken lightly. But with proper preparation, counseling, and encouragement, and with efficient psychiatric selection and surgical advice, many sex-change patients have become well integrated into their new gender role, are confident in their new persona, and enjoy a novel sense of well-being.

© DIAGRAM

MALE TO FEMALE
What is the goal of surgery?

As far as is medically possible, surgery aims to remove the secondary sexual characteristics of a male, and to replace them with at least the outward secondary sexual characteristics of a female, including labia and a vagina. But it is important that you do not permit yourself to entertain any unrealistic ambitions: your new genitalia will not include a uterus or ovaries; you will not be able to menstruate; and there is no possibility ever of conception. Even the provision of an artificial vagina bears some risk of injury to the bladder or to the rectum (although such injury could be repaired surgically afterward).

Exactly what is involved in the surgical operation?

Preliminary steps. Before any part of a sex-change operation, the surgeon must be totally satisfied that you are genuinely transsexual, and that you are aware that male-to-female sex-change surgery is irreversible. You will already have undergone a lengthy and rigorous program of investigation by an experienced psychiatrist to establish this, and will have successfully undertaken a careful gender reassignment program during which you will have received instruction on adopting female behavioral patterns. The latter program is supplemented by the administration over at least one year of female sex hormones, which has the effect of improving skin texture and laying down deposits of fat at the hips and in the breasts.

The most significant part of the process for anatomical men accepted for sex-change surgery is the operation to remove the penis, testicles, and scrotum, and to create a vagina, labia, and, from the base of the penis, a platform to support the truncated urethra (the urine outlet).

Step-by-step surgical procedure. For this crucial operation, you will be placed on the operating table lying on your back, with your feet in stirrups, knees bent and held wide apart (the lithotomy position).

The surgeon then makes a V-shaped incision in the skin on the underside of the base of the penis, drawing back the flap of skin created so that the base of the penile shaft is exposed. Working through this opening, the surgeon dissects out each testicle in turn, with its spermatic cord. The cords are clamped, tied off with strong linen or silk threads, and severed. In this way the testicles and most of both spermatic cords are removed. The skin is then completely stripped from the penis but left attached to the body; the penis, including the urethra, is partly cut through. The shorter urethra needed is separated from the penis, and a catheter is passed along the urethra and into the bladder. A tunnel for the vagina is now created by blunt dissection of the tissue that lies at the base of the urethra immediately under the bladder. The tunnel extends from the prostate gland (which lies in this tissue at the base of

THE V-SHAPED INCISION

a *Penis*
b *Incision*
c *Anus*

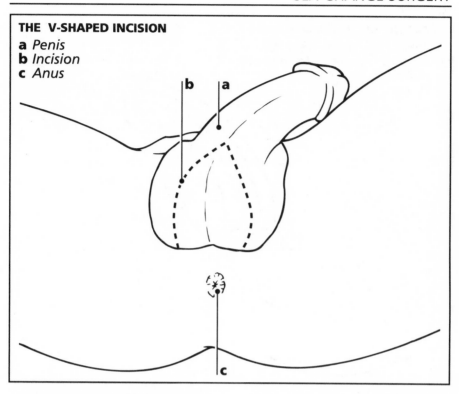

EXPOSING THE PENILE SHAFT

a *Right testicle*
b *Penile shaft*
c *Urethra*
d *Spermatic cord*
e *Left testicle*

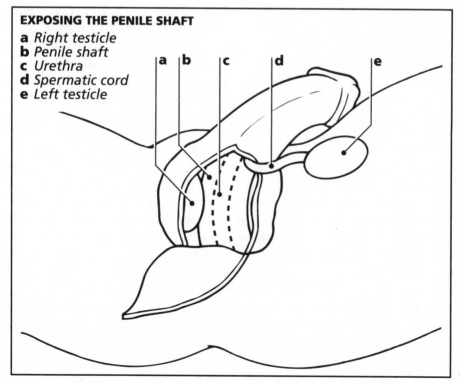

© DIAGRAM

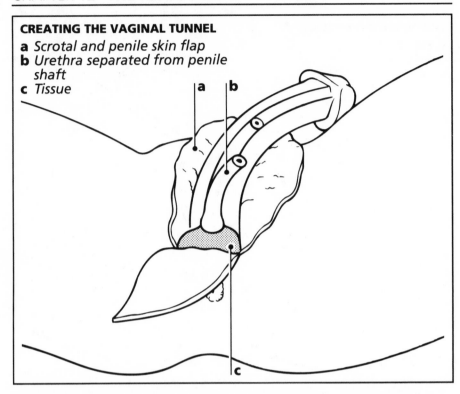

CREATING THE VAGINAL TUNNEL
a *Scrotal and penile skin flap*
b *Urethra separated from penile shaft*
c *Tissue*

the urethra) to the rectum behind. Although the prostate gland is not needed after surgery, removal would unnecessarily complicate the procedure; the surgeon takes great care to avoid damage to the prostate gland itself (which would cause profuse bleeding) or to the wall of the rectum (which would cause problems in defecating afterward).

The base of the penis is now detached from the pubic bone, using a scalpel. Most of it is cut off, but a small stump is left to provide support for the new urethral opening. Layers of the skin of the lower part of the abdomen—to which the skin of the penis remains attached—are now separated and mobilized so that the skin as a whole can be pulled well downward between the legs. A central stitch is passed through it and secured to the membranous covering (periosteum) of the pubic bone: this not only relieves the tension on the lower part of this flap of skin but also helps to create a natural-looking cleft. A little below the stitch, in the middle of the flap, the surgeon creates a small hole through which the urethra can be brought out. The lower part of the same flap together with the skin freed from the penis become the front and side walls of the new vagina; the back of the vagina is created from the triangular flap from the back of the penis. All these flaps are stitched together to form a tube before being pushed into the cavity between the prostate gland and the rectum. This cavity can be made as deep as desired, providing there is enough penile skin to line it. Skin from the

REMOVING THE PENIS

a *Skin flap*
b *Penis*
c *Scalpel*

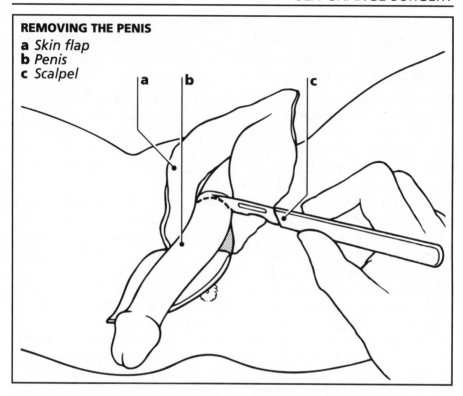

CREATING THE GENITAL AREA

a *Urethra brought out through a small incision*
b *Scrotal skin trimmed to form labia (vaginal skin flaps)*
c *Vagina*

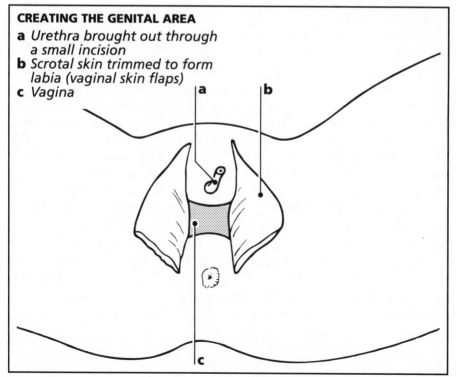

© DIAGRAM

scrotum is used to form the labia. Finally, a lubricated glass mold is pushed into the vagina and held in place with a sanitary pad: this prevents shrinkage of the vagina and holds it in place until it heals onto the internal tissues that then support it.

What is it like immediately after the operation?

Swelling may be considerable, and the catheter must be left in position for four or five days. The mold must be removed from time to time to check that the vaginal skin is healing satisfactorily. Healing is normally rapid, and you should be able to leave the hospital about seven days after this part of the surgical process.

Other operations in the process include breast augmentation, if the female sex hormones do not give rise to breasts of a size you deem sufficient (see *Breast enlargement*, p.428), and cosmetic surgery to feminize certain features, such as nose reshaping (see *Rhinoplasty*, p.406), ear remodeling, and surgery to reduce baggy eyelids (see *Blepharoplasty*, p.410). Note that research into the safety of silicone breast implants is ongoing in light of questions concerning dangerous longterm side effects. Patients considering having such implants must confer with their surgeons to determine whether the procedure is possible and appropriate in their case and whether the potential dangers outweigh the possible benefits (see *Breast enlargement*, p.428).

What are the longterm effects?

If you were genuinely transsexual and are fairly resilient psychologically, and have taken these steps in full and realistic awareness of all the implications, the longterm results are likely to be excellent.

The artificial vagina will remain constantly dry: it will require lubrication to allow sexual intercourse and the longterm presence of the mold to prevent it from shrinking or closing. The mold need not be worn continuously, but shrinkage of the artificial vagina is one of the commonest and most serious problems and—unless the mold is worn much of the time—is likely to occur. You should not expect to experience the vaginal or clitoral sensation that in ordinary women leads to orgasm although massage of the prostate may help. Yet you can have orgasms based on mental stimulation. Although you may have to continue taking hormonal supplements for the rest of your life, it is a life that you are now free to embark on in the gender role that is, for you, normal.

Possible complications include closure of the urethral opening, infection of any of the incisions (perhaps with an abscess at the site), and the formation of an abnormal connection between the vagina and the rectum. All these can be dealt with surgically if they occur.

FEMALE TO MALE
What is the goal of surgery?
As far as is medically possible, surgery aims to remove the secondary sexual characteristics of a female—breasts and other reproductive organs, including those that secrete female sex hormones—and to replace them with at least the outward secondary sexual characteristics of a male. In some cases this includes the construction of a simulated penis, although this is rarely satisfactory and most transsexuals choose to use a dildo or penile prosthesis.

Exactly what is involved in the surgical operation?
Preliminary steps. Before any part of a sex-change operation, the surgeon must be totally satisfied that you are genuinely transsexual. You will already have undergone a lengthy and rigorous program of investigation by an experienced psychiatrist to establish this, and will have successfully undertaken a careful gender reassignment program during which you will have received instruction on adopting male behavioral patterns. The latter program is supplemented by a schedule of body-building exercises and the administration of male sex hormones (such as testosterone). The hormones have anabolic effects and encourage the growth of body and facial hair and suppress menstruation. Testosterone alone may have a remarkable impact, bringing about an apparent and convincing change to maleness in the parts of the body normally visible.

Surgery to change a female body into a male one is undertaken in a number of stages, many of which are operations described separately within this book. The whole process may be performed over the course of several months or even longer, depending on the success of each individual stage and on your physical and mental recovery from it.

Step-by-step surgical procedure. Anatomical women accepted for sex-change surgery generally first undergo surgery to remove the tissues within the breasts, together with any redundant surface skin. The procedure is similar to that described in the operation for breast reduction (see *Breast reduction*, p.432), appropriately modified to result in a male configuration.

The next stage involves removal of the uterus together with the Fallopian tubes and ovaries—a major procedure (see *Hysterectomy*, p.314).

Having come this far, and with a body now quite unlike that with which they started, most female-to-male sex-change patients go no further. From a social point of view they look, and may well also sound, male. If a manly contour in the groin is desired, various penile prostheses are available. Only a minority of patients opt for the difficult—and seldom wholly satisfactory—process of surgical penis construction.

© DIAGRAM

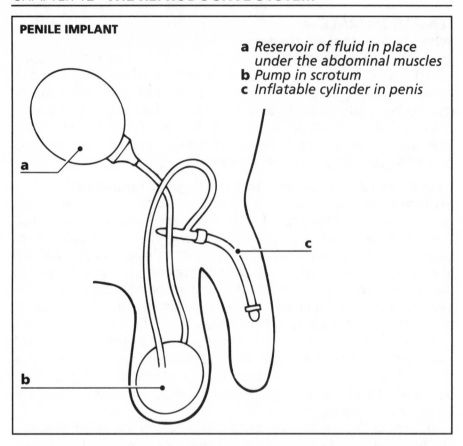

PENILE IMPLANT

a *Reservoir of fluid in place under the abdominal muscles*
b *Pump in scrotum*
c *Inflatable cylinder in penis*

Construction of a penis requires a further group of surgical proce-dures—mostly to create the outward form of the organ, together with a scrotum, but also to ensure that urination is not affected and to pro-duce the ability to simulate an erection (for some patients an important factor). The penis itself can be created from nearby tissues (for exam-ple, from the abdominal wall), with or without a skin graft from else-where on the body, but is generally comparatively small and, even with an implant, is unlikely to achieve the 5–6 inches (12–15cm) of the aver-age erect organ. Membrane from the vaginal lining (or elsewhere) can be used to extend the urethra (the urine outlet) within the new penis to its end. The scrotum can be formed from the skin of the labia majora—a relatively easy surgical exercise—and plastic testicles may be inserted for realism. But in this constructed penis there can be no sex-ual sensation, no excitement leading to ejaculation, and erection must be effected by means of a device implanted down the length of the penis, controlled by a fluid pump with a release valve probably also based in the new scrotum. Once pumped up, the erection is maintained until the release valve is pressed to allow the erection to subside and the fluid to return to the reservoir.

SIMULATING AN ERECTION

Squeezing the pump with the fingers fills the cylinder with fluid to simulate an erection.

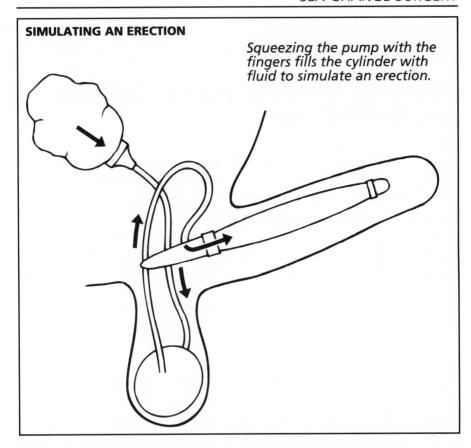

What is it like immediately after the operation?

How you feel after each of the contributory operations depends on what has been done and on how relieved you are to observe the effects of the procedure. You are likely to be much more concerned with such matters than with any temporary discomfort (or even pain) from operative interference. Without doubt, the most physically weakening and severe effects of surgery will follow the operation to remove the uterus, Fallopian tubes, and ovaries. It is possible that even if you had intended to go on to have a penis and scrotum created, the very major nature of this prior surgery and the associated debility (even if only temporary) may dissuade you.

What are the longterm effects?

If you were genuinely transsexual, are fairly resilient psychologically, and have taken these steps in full and realistic awareness of all the implications, the longterm results are likely to be excellent. Although you may have to continue taking hormonal supplements for the rest of your life, it is a life that you are now free to embark on in the gender role that is, for you, normal.

© DIAGRAM

CHAPTER 13
COSMETIC SURGERY

Removal of birthmarks, tattoos, and keloid scars

Why have the operation?
As with all cosmetic surgery, the major intention behind the operation is to enhance appearance, and by so doing to increase morale and self-image, leading to an overall improvement in lifestyle.

What is the goal of surgery?
The aim of surgery is to do whatever can be done to remove the blemish on the skin. After a successful operation, no sign of the blemish should remain, but this is not always possible. After removal of some of the smaller lesions—which can be cut out entirely—a faint, nondisfiguring scar sometimes remains. It is impossible to remove larger lesions and large tattoos completely (even using a full-thickness skin graft) and it is usually impossible to obtain a perfect skin match in color, texture, skin markings, or thickness.

Exactly what is involved in the surgical operation?
Most skin blemishes that are small can be simply cut out and the opening closed with stitches. This applies to many birthmarks (including small portwine stains), most moles, a few tattoos, and some very small keloid scars, and in the majority of cases leaves only a minor scar afterward. The method is described fully in the section on wart removal in this chapter (see *Removal of warts*, p.403).

BIRTHMARKS
Localized skin blemishes (nevi) that have been present from birth are seldom dangerous; removal is usually of cosmetic importance only. Many of them represent benign abnormalities of blood vessels in the skin; these are technically called cavernous hemangiomas and are of two main forms: strawberry nevi and portwine stains.

Strawberry nevi (singular: nevus) are raised, red-purple marks on the face or body of a newborn baby. They tend to become smaller as the child grows, and may disappear altogether by the age of five. Accordingly, they are not regarded as suitable for surgical removal.

Portwine stains are flat, red-purple, and often large areas. They do not disappear gradually over time; instead they tend to remain highly visible (often appearing on the face) and may even darken and become warty. Those that affect a large area of skin may be difficult to deal with.

TYPES OF BIRTHMARK
a *Strawberry nevus*
b *Spider nevus*
c *Portwine stain*
d *Mole*

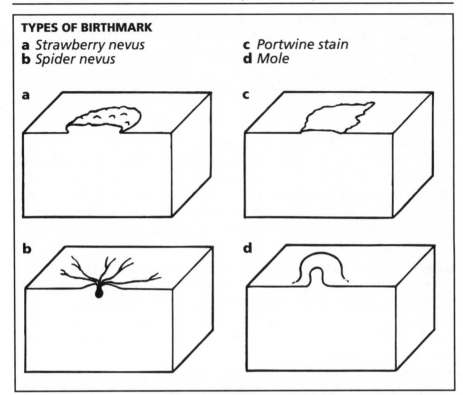

Treatment for portwine stains. A large stain can be reduced in size by partial removal, in which an area is cut out and the opening closed with stitches. Other methods of improving the appearance of large stains include:

- freezing: commonly done with a cotton swab dipped into liquid nitrogen and applied directly to the nevus, a little at a time. It flattens and lightens the lumpy type of portwine stain in about one-third of cases.
- electrocoagulation: gentle application of a red-hot loop of wire burns and destroys the tissue. This method is more often used to treat the blotchy birthmarks known as spider nevi.
- laser therapy: lasers produce intense, but localized, heat that vaporizes tissue.
- cosmetic surgery: finding an exact match elsewhere on the body for facial skin over a large area is seldom possible.
- cosmetic preparations: for many patients, cosmetics may be the best, most convenient, and most permanently reliable solution.

Other types of birthmarks include spider nevi and moles.

Spider nevi appear as spidery lines radiating from a tiny raised, red dot. They occur in children and pregnant women and are generally not serious.

13

© DIAGRAM

Moles, present from birth and pigmented brown or black, are also called nevi. There are many different types, some hairy. One that changes color over a few weeks should be investigated by a physician in case surgical removal is of more than merely cosmetic importance: such a color change can indicate a small cancerous tumor.

TATTOOS

As a medical term, tattooing refers not only to "decorative" tattoos but also to the effect of virtually any foreign material more or less permanently embedded in the skin. This most often occurs in traffic accidents and in exposure to explosive blasts of fireworks, shotguns, and bombs. Buried particles of fine gravel, gunpowder, vaporized plastic, and other material can cause disfiguring black or blue scars, and may also cover a wide area of skin.

Treatment for tattoos. Most accidental tattooing can be treated by scrubbing the skin surface under local anesthesia with a stiff bristle brush and surgical skin-cleaning solution; individual particles may be picked out with a sharp needle or a scalpel and fine forceps. For deeper and decorative tattoos, methods of improving the appearance under local anesthesia include:

- abrading the skin with sandpaper or with a wire brush (dermabrasion) under local anesthetic; this method works well with particles or pigments that remain in the upper layers of the skin
- laser therapy: this must be used with care because it involves the vaporization of the pigments or particles while they are still in the skin—they melt and, as vapor, burn their way out of the skin; there is a great possibility of scarring with this method
- cosmetic surgery involving a skin graft

Methods of treating larger blemishes and tattoos include:

- cryotherapy/cryosurgery (a technique of freezing areas of skin)
- electrocoagulation (use of a high-frequency electric current to destroy and seal abnormal blood vessel formations)

KELOID SCARS

Keloid tissue results from a defect in the usual healing process. Instead of normal skin gradually forming over a wound, for some reason an excess of the connective tissue collagen at the site creates a raised, hardened, fibrous area that may initially be itchy and may in later months actually enlarge its surface. Drug therapy may include injections of corticosteroids. The surgical removal of all but the smallest keloid scars is usually pointless: the scar is almost always replaced by a new keloid scar.

Removal of warts

Why have the operation?

As with all cosmetic surgery, the major intention behind the operation is to enhance appearance, and by so doing to increase morale and self-image, leading to an overall improvement in lifestyle. Small warts—as most are—need no surgery; they can be removed by a physician in any of a variety of ways, including:

- softening with salicylic acid
- soaking in a very mild solution of formaldehyde (formalin)
- applying podophyllin resin
- highly localized freezing with liquid nitrogen
- spot-burning with an electric cautery under local anesthetic

Most warts eventually disappear without treatment. About one-third of them are present for less than six months altogether; others, however, may persist for years.

What is the physical cause of the problem?

Warts—known medically as verrucas—are caused by viruses that prompt a local overgrowth of the epidermis of the skin. They take different forms depending on the type and thickness of the skin affected. Nearly everybody harbors the wart virus. The appearance and disappearance of warts is the result of changes in our immune systems. People who suffer from immune deficiency from any cause are more liable to develop warts. But warts are in no sense cancers, nor do they turn into malignant tumors. Certain rarer forms of skin cancer can loosely resemble warts, however, so anything that looks unusual should be reported to a physician without delay.

Because the behavior of warts is unpredictable, many superstitions have grown up about them. There is a widely held belief that warts can be removed by "charming" them away; indeed, many physicians believe the power of suggestion may be of value in removing warts.

What is the goal of surgery?

Cosmetic surgery is performed mainly to remove warts that are unusually large (and prominently sited) or located in such areas of the body as actually to cause some physical problem. The methods of treatment used to remove smaller warts may prove difficult and potentially painful when applied to larger warts. Surgery in any case effects a much more rapid result than other treatments.

Exactly what is involved in the surgical operation?

The operation is usually so minor that it can be performed in the surgeon's office and a general anesthetic is not called for.

Preliminary steps. The affected area is thoroughly cleaned with an antibacterial solution, and sterile towels are applied to cover the sur-

© DIAGRAM

rounding skin, leaving the wart exposed. A local anesthetic is then injected through a fine needle. Usually the needle is inserted only once, for the small area concerned can be more widely infiltrated with the anesthetic drug by moving the point of the needle around under the skin. There should be no pain at all if the injection is administered slowly. The surgeon can then proceed.

Types of warts

There are various types of warts, some of which require individual methods of treatment.

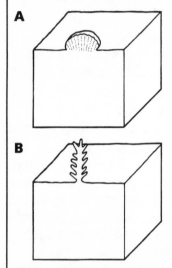

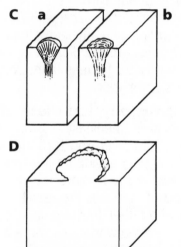

A Rough-topped warts
Can occur on most parts of the body, especially the hands.

B Filiform warts
Resemble little fir trees, and can affect the thin skin of the eyelid, neck, and armpits. One on an eyelid may become large—an eyelash may even grow through it, causing considerable discomfort—and require ophthalmic surgery under local anesthetic. In that case, the surgeon removes the wart and the underlying skin, taking out a full-thickness segment of the eyelid and bringing the edges together with stitches.

C Plantar warts
*Occur on the sole of the foot. They are essentially the same as other warts (**a**), but the weight of the body on top of them forces them deeply into the thick skin of the sole (**b**). Walking on them can become painful, relieved only by the use of ring-pads around them to absorb the pressure. The usual treatment for plantar warts is to scoop them out with a strong, sharp-edged "spoon," known as a curette, under local anesthesia.*

D Venereal warts
Occur when the wart virus has been transmitted sexually, and appear as pink, cauliflower-like masses on the penis or vulva.

Step-by-step surgical procedure. In making the incision, especially if the wart is in a conspicuous area, the surgeon most commonly arranges it so that the fine, hairlike scar left afterward will lie in a natural skin crease. The intention is to remove the wart and its underlying skin, leaving a hole that can be simply converted into a thin line. For this reason, the usual shape of incision is a narrow ellipse with pointed ends. The cut has to be made quite deeply, for some warts occupy a surprising number of skin layers. When the incision is complete, the surgeon pulls up the wart with forceps and cuts underneath it. The edges of the skin generally come together easily enough to be joined with a few stitches, but if there is too much tension when the skin edges are brought together, the surgeon may first loosen the upper layers of skin from deeper layers on both sides before again positioning the edges together and closing the wound.

When warts are removed surgically, the tissue is never thrown away but is always sent to a laboratory for histological examination, just in case there is something unusual either in the virus giving rise to the condition or in the nature of the cells removed.

What is it like immediately after the operation?
There may be a few stitches over a small wound—depending on the site—which may cause minor inconvenience. Removal of a plantar wart may require temporary use of a ring-pad to avoid putting pressure on stitches or wound. You may possibly be given antibiotic drugs to deter infection. You will be able to walk right away, although it will be painful.

What are the longterm effects?
There are no longterm adverse effects of the operation. Recurrence is a possibility, as with any virus; one precaution is to avoid going barefoot in public swimming pool/shower areas.

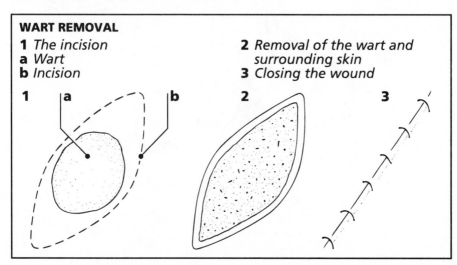

WART REMOVAL
1 *The incision*
a *Wart*
b *Incision*

2 *Removal of the wart and surrounding skin*
3 *Closing the wound*

© DIAGRAM

Rhinoplasty: reshaping the nose

Why have the operation?

As with all cosmetic surgery, the major intention behind the operation is to enhance appearance, and by so doing to increase morale and self-image, leading to an overall improvement in lifestyle. Occasionally the operation is performed for medical reasons such as deformity by injury, disease, or birth defect.

What is the physical cause of the problem?

The framework of the nose is made up of four thin bones at the top, forming the bridge and upper sides of the nose, and about ten small pieces of cartilage, arranged in pairs and joined edge-to-edge by fibrous tissue. All the bones and cartilages may vary considerably in size, shape, and position. Before the operation, you must be sure to explain why you are dissatisfied with the shape of your nose so that the surgeon can decide exactly which of these components is responsible and how to remedy the situation.

What is the goal of surgery?

The aim is to provide you with a nose that conforms to a shape you will be much happier with, and that has lost nothing in natural efficiency and sensitivity. Almost all operations to reshape the nose are performed

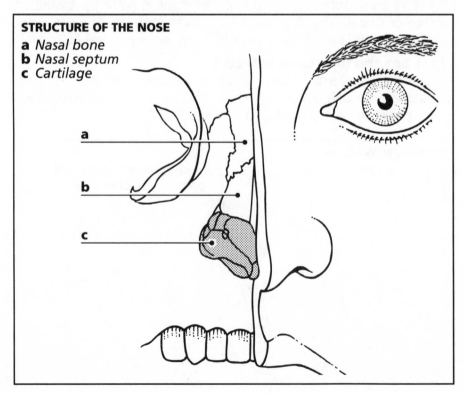

STRUCTURE OF THE NOSE
a *Nasal bone*
b *Nasal septum*
c *Cartilage*

a

b

c

through the nostrils and require no cuts at all in the external skin. The results of rhinoplasty are usually excellent—but the operation will change the way you look, and you must be prepared for the permanently altered face that will gaze back at you from the mirror for the rest of your life.

Exactly what is involved in the surgical operation?

The operation can be performed easily, painlessly, and safely under local anesthesia, but some surgeons may prefer general anesthesia.

Preliminary steps. If you are to be operated on under general anesthesia, you will be given a preoperative injection about an hour before surgery to dry up internal fluids and to encourage drowsiness.

Step-by-step surgical procedure. Once you are comfortably anesthetized, the surgeon will probably also inject an anesthetic solution containing epinephrine into the nasal tissues. This constricts the blood vessels, with which the nose is well supplied, and so avoids excessive bleeding, which would also make the operation difficult to perform. The effect may be enhanced by the use of small nasal packs soaked in a strong solution of cocaine. Finally, especially if you are being operated on under local anesthesia, the drug diazepam may also be injected into a vein in order to reduce tension.

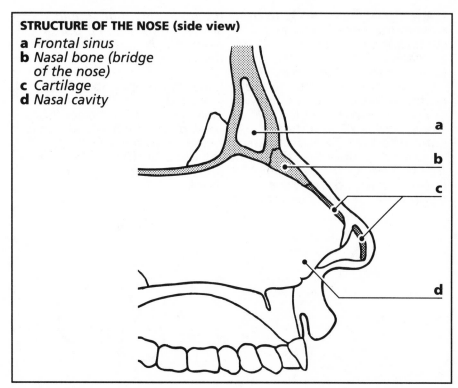

STRUCTURE OF THE NOSE (side view)

a *Frontal sinus*
b *Nasal bone (bridge of the nose)*
c *Cartilage*
d *Nasal cavity*

a
b
c
d

© DIAGRAM

When the operation is finished, all blood clots are sucked out by machine and the inside of the nose is packed with special gauze. The outside is now strapped and the nose is splinted either with plaster of paris or with a plastic compound that hardens soon after application, in order to minimize swelling and to ensure that all parts remain in their proper relationship while healing takes place. Retaining bandages complete the dressings.

What is it like immediately after the operation?

Surgery of this kind produces considerable swelling and bruising. You may wake up with a couple of impressive black eyes and have some difficulty seeing past your nose. But the condition is only temporary, and not particularly painful. You will have to breathe through your mouth until the bandages and nostril-packs come off, which is usually after

---

Altering the shape of the tip of the nose

This is achieved by sculpting the curved wing cartilages at the tip. It is often necessary to remove a part of the upper edge of both wing cartilages to create the required shape. Such cartilage sculpting must be done very carefully through an incision in the skin inside the nostrils: when making this incision, the surgeon avoids cutting right through to the outside, which might leave a permanent mark.

If the tip of the nose is to be raised, *the surgeon makes a cut through the central cartilage that separates the two internal halves of the nose. The surgeon must avoid causing the nostrils to become too vertically oriented, viewed from the front, resulting in a sort of piggy effect (**a**). Care must also be taken to ensure that the free skin edge—the overhang between and in front of the nostrils—is not pulled up into* the nose. This edge should always be visible, in profile, below the line of the edges of the wings of the nostrils.

If the tip of the nose is to be lowered, *the nostrils tend to flare outward. To correct this, a small piece of nostril rim skin is removed from each side (**b**), at the back, to take up the slack until each nostril is taut once more.*

about a week, when much of the bruising has also absorbed away. Only then will you be able to inspect your new profile—and even then the nose is subject to continued gradual shrinkage for at least a month and maybe several months more, so that the final result may not be apparent for as long as half a year.

What are the longterm effects?

Ideally, the effects are precisely those you desired, and for which the surgeon was striving. Very occasionally there are complications, however, such as a recurrent nosebleed through inadequate healing of incision sites within constantly moist nostrils, or an awkward imbalance in the quantity of air breathed in by one nostril in comparison with the other due to a difference in volume of the surgically altered passages.

Altering the bridge of the nose

An incision is made—again inside the nose—so that a small rasp (a type of rough file) can be slipped up through the nostril to lie between the bone and the skin. The edge of the rasp is effective in one direction only, and in this case is used so that it files as the surgeon pulls it toward him- or herself, abrading the bony hump with each stroke. In this way the hump is gradually eroded until the outline is in line with the tip. The central cartilage below the bone is also likely to be humped, and must be carved into shape with a small scalpel. Eventually, the line from the bridge of the nose to the tip is perfectly straight. If the two side pieces of bridge bone are also prominent and make the nose unacceptably broad, the bones can be gently broken and pressed inward after some preliminary work with a small chisel.

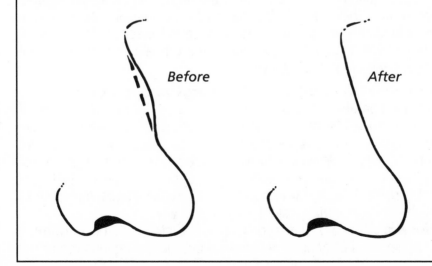

Before   *After*

© DIAGRAM

Blepharoplasty: removal of bags around the eyes

Why have the operation?

Bagginess of the upper and lower eyelids is one of the most conspicuous signs of aging, although it may affect people of any adult age group. The major intention behind the operation is to enhance appearance, and by so doing to increase morale and self-image, leading to an overall improvement in lifestyle. Blepharoplasty is one of the most common and least problematic of cosmetic procedures.

What is the physical cause of the problem?

As the skin ages, especially in warm climates where it is subject to the effects of relatively high amounts of ultraviolet light, it stretches and loses elasticity. Eventually, the skin begins to hang in slack pouches.
Dermochalasia (or dermatochalasia) means slack skin and is the simplest cause of bagginess around the eyes.
Blepharochalasia is a slightly more complex case in which a layer of fat lies under the skin. This layer of fat derives ultimately from the collection of loose fat normally contained within the eye socket (the orbit of the skull), which acts as a cushion for the eye and permits its free movement. An escape of this fat from the eye socket can cause baggy eyelids even in fairly young people whose skin is by no means stretched and lax. Older people may suffer from both dermochalasia and blepharochalasia.

What is the goal of surgery?

To remedy **dermochalasia** requires removal of just enough redundant skin to take up the slack. To repair **blepharochalasia** requires a more difficult operation involving removal of the fat beneath the skin—generally present in the form of little pads of fat—possibly together with some redundant skin, and may also require the surgical shoring up of the fibrous wall around the eye socket (the orbital septum) to prevent further escape of fat into the eyelids.

Exactly what is involved in the surgical operation?

Before the operation, the surgeon will have performed a number of tests on your eyelids, both to establish whether dermochalasia, or blepharochalasia, or both, is the problem, and to assess whether you are one of the few people with naturally reduced tear secretion and a tendency to dry eyes. The latter condition renders the surgeon's task considerably more difficult, for in such cases a repair that is imprecise to the slightest degree may make the condition worse.
Preliminary steps. Operations on the eyelids can be performed under either local or general anesthesia, but many surgeons prefer not

CROSS-SECTION OF A NON-BAGGY LOWER EYELID

a *Orbital septum*

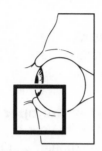

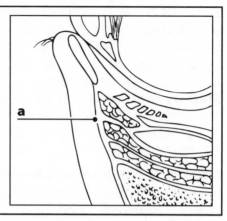

CROSS-SECTION OF A LOWER EYELID WITH DERMOCHALASIA

a *Slack skin*
b *Outline of original eyelid*

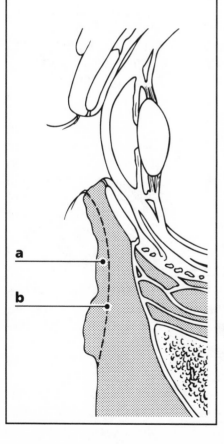

CROSS-SECTION OF A LOWER EYELID WITH BLEPHAROCHALASIA

a *Slack skin*
b *Outline of original eyelid*
c *Orbital septum through which fat has escaped into adjacent eyelid (**d**)*

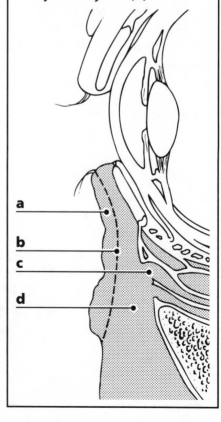

© DIAGRAM

to use local anesthetic because it tends to balloon out the lids, temporarily altering their appearance and making it more difficult to judge the final effect. If you are to have a general anesthetic you will be given a preoperative injection about an hour before surgery to dry up internal fluids and to encourage drowsiness.

Step-by-step surgical procedure. The surgical procedures for dermochalasia and for blepharochalasia are different but equally straightforward. If it is appropriate to your condition, once you are anesthetized one procedure may be performed in conjunction with the other.

What is it like immediately after the operation?

You may wake up to find you cannot open your eyes at all. Swelling is usually considerable, as is bruising—although you may not be able to

---

To operate for dermochalasia

The surgeon pinches the redundant skin with his or her fingers until the skin above and below the eye lies flat and the upper and lower lids are not pulled apart. The pinched-up excess skin is then cut off with scissors in such a way as to form an elliptical wound lying exactly along the natural skin creases of the lid. Both upper and lower eyelids are treated in this fashion, the size of each elliptical wound just sufficient to leave the remaining skin even and flat once the edges of the wound are brought together. The wound edges are stitched together with very fine sutures—the skin of the lid is so thin that stitches as fine as a human hair are quite strong enough.

1 *Pinching the redundant skin*
2 *Cutting the skin off*
3 *Closing the incisions*

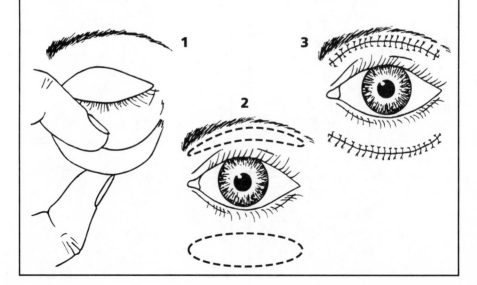

see it at first. Icepacks and various other forms of therapy may be used to reduce the swelling, and there may be a fair measure of discomfort. Nonetheless, you may be encouraged to leave the hospital well within 24 hours of surgery. Much of the swelling should have vanished by about the fourth day, when some of the stitches may be removed. Other stitches may come out after a week. The bruising may take a couple of weeks to subside, however.

What are the longterm effects?
Only after a month or so will the final effect be truly visible, and the hairline-thin scars may take up to twelve months to become totally invisible. Results are generally excellent, although there is a chance of recurrence.

To operate for blepharochalasia
Your surgeon will already have assessed whether it will be necessary to remove any excess skin in addition to removing the redundant fat. Skin may be removed as described for dermochalasia. In order to remove fat, the surgeon makes a carefully curved incision following exactly along one of the crease lines of your eyelid. The eyeball is then gently pressed back a little into the eye socket, to reveal the pads of fat hanging within the lid. These pads can be grasped in forceps, pulled out farther, and severed. The gaps in the lid tissue through which the pads have passed are then tightly closed with catgut or other absorbable sutures, and the skin is closed with fine stitches. The procedure is performed on both lower eyelids.

1 *Making the incision in crease line*
2 *Exposing the fat pads*
3 *Closing the incision*

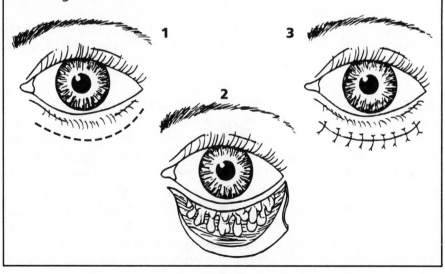

© DIAGRAM

Rhytidectomy: facelift

Why have the operation?

The operation is intended to rid the skin of wrinkles and folds around the face and under the chin, many of which may be the natural effects of aging. To some extent it thus represents a form of rejuvenation for many patients, and in addition to enhancing the appearance should also increase morale and self-image, leading to an overall improvement in lifestyle.

What is the physical cause of the problem?

Sagging, wrinkled facial skin is caused by overexposure to sunlight and other ultraviolet light. This type of radiation affects the structural collagen in the skin, causing it to lose elasticity. The skin is further stretched by the layer of subcutaneous fat beneath it, a layer that may increase in thickness as the skin loses elasticity and takes on the characteristic sag patterns represented by folds of skin that progressively hang downward, eventually falling over the angle of the jaw and forming jowls. Subcutaneous fat is responsible also for the loss of the contour around the cheekbone, a feature of the youthful face. Conversely, loss of subcutaneous tissue together with natural stretch eventually give rise to short, deep, vertical lines in the upper lip which tend to become progressively more marked.

What is the goal of surgery?

The major principle behind the "facelift" is simple. To be tautened the skin must be freed from its underlying tissue ("undermined"), and pulled backward and upward. Redundant skin can then be snipped off and discarded.

Before surgery, the surgeon will ask you exactly what you are hoping for from the operation, and may tell you what can and cannot be done. The surgeon may, for instance, be unable to correct severe skin and fat redundancy in the neck during the rhytidectomy—an operation that can itself last for up to three hours. A separate operation may be performed at a later stage to alter the appearance of the neck.

Exactly what is involved in the surgical operation?

Before deciding on how to undertake the operation, the surgeon will have studied your face extremely carefully. Close attention will be paid to the position of your eyebrows and to the degree of bagginess in your upper eyelids, from which the surgeon will determine whether simple brow elevation would deal adequately with the lid skin redundancy, or whether separate lid surgery is indicated. If appropriate, the surgeon will also decide whether anything can be done during the same overall operation to remove a double chin (usually caused by subcutaneous fat filling the pocket of skin between the point of the chin and the hyoid bone in the center of the upper part of the neck). Part of the surgeon's examination will also be to discover if you have had any unexplained bruising or bleeding around the facial tissues, or if you have any keloid scars (raised scars formed of fibrous tissue and that may recur if removed); if you have, the surgeon may decide against operating.

Preliminary steps. To expose the site of the upper part of the surgeon's incision on each side of the head, your hair will have to be shaved along a narrow channel above and behind each ear. This part will be concealed by your hair as it grows back; the rest of the incision will be invisible by its proximity to the ear itself.

Rhytidectomy can be performed under local or general anesthesia, but it is a lengthy procedure and most surgeons prefer to administer a general anesthetic—in which case you will be given a preoperative injection about an hour before surgery to dry up internal fluids and to encourage drowsiness.

Step-by-step surgical procedure. Once you are anesthetized, the surgeon makes an incision on each side of the head above and behind the ear. Undermining can then begin. The major tool for undermining is a sort of blunt-pointed pair of scissors, used not by closing them to cut but by opening them wide between tissue layers in order to separate them (the process is known technically as "blunt dissection"). Very carefully the surgeon separates the soft skin tissue from its underlying base, avoiding injury to all but the most minute nerves and blood vessels and trying to remain at a constant optimum level beneath the skin surface, especially close to the incision line where damage to hair roots could cause a loss of hair and thus exposure of the scar. Conversely, to delve too deeply might touch nerves that control facial mobility and cause partial facial paralysis.

Once undermining is completed, the amount of overlap when the skin on each side is drawn backward and upward may be anything from half

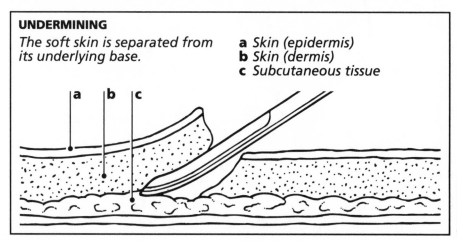

UNDERMINING

The soft skin is separated from its underlying base.

a *Skin (epidermis)*
b *Skin (dermis)*
c *Subcutaneous tissue*

© DIAGRAM

an inch to two inches. Excess fat is then removed, and the drawn-up skin is secured in place with two or three stitches. The excess skin is cut free, fine rubber drainage tubes are inserted, and the incision is closed.

Your surgeon may have decided also to remove forehead wrinkles and severely sagging eyebrows. To do this, the surgeon makes an incision in the scalp behind the hairline and undermines the skin from there down almost to the bony ridges of the eyes. The vertically acting muscles that permit frowning—as opposed to those that act horizontally to form the same facial expression—are weakened by removing muscle tissue from them in strips. The skin is then pulled up taut, any overlap is removed, and the free edges are stitched together.

Finally, your surgeon may inject small quantities of the protein collagen under the skin to fill up any minor creases. (Collagen is very good for getting rid of crow's-feet.) Normally enough collagen is put in to leave you looking a little swollen, for some of the protein will in due course be absorbed.

What is it like immediately after the operation?

You will wake up to find your face rather puffy and becoming discolored with bruising; there may also be stitches visible where the hair has been shaved away; the drainage tubes inserted through the main incisions to guard against the possibility of blood accumulations within the tissues (hematomas) may even still be in place. Altogether, a look in the mirror might give you something of a shock—not at all the instant improve-

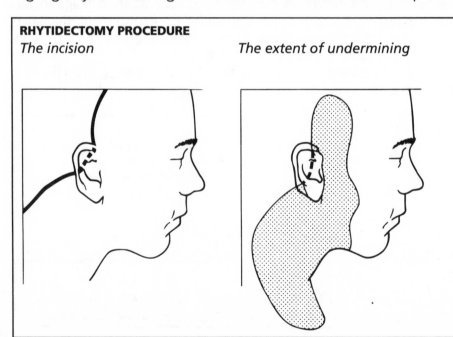

RHYTIDECTOMY PROCEDURE

The incision   *The extent of undermining*

ment in appearance that you were perhaps hoping for. But be patient. Provided that there is no further danger of hematomas, the drainage tubes can come out within two days or so; and a temporary change of hairstyle can probably disguise the line of stitches until the hair grows back.

Some surgeons prevent such shock by bandaging their patients fairly comprehensively—and you may wake up instead unable to see anything of your new face for several days.

The bruising may last for ten days to two weeks. Much more quickly you will feel comfortable with the unaccustomed tautness of your facial skin, and feel free then to smile and frown and jut your chin at will.

What are the longterm effects?
There are few possible complications following a rhytidectomy. The most serious is a hematoma, which may prevent the skin from reattaching itself properly to the subcutaneous tissue and may require drainage and possibly further surgical attention.

On the other hand, skin sagging tends to be an accelerating natural process. The older you are, the briefer your period of "rejuvenation" is likely to be, as once more your skin ages and loses elasticity. The length of time the effect of the rhytidectomy endures will depend both on the state of your skin before the operation and on the way you treat it afterward. But over ten years or less, your appearance will inevitably progress again to something like it was before you underwent surgery. This too is something you should be aware of before you start.

The skin is freed.

The skin is pulled upward and the overlapping skin removed.

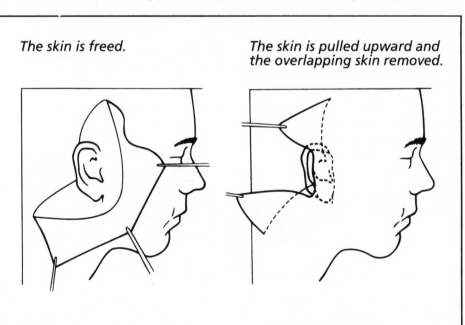

© DIAGRAM

Hair transplants and implants

Why have the operation?

Hair loss can represent a source of considerable embarrassment and sensitivity to a man—and even more to a woman, although the condition is much rarer in females. As with all cosmetic surgery, the major intention of the operation is to enhance appearance, and thus increase morale and self-image, leading to an overall improvement in lifestyle.

What is the physical cause of the problem?

In men, baldness virtually always follows a genetic pattern—the way a son goes bald echoes the way his father or grandfather went bald—unless it is caused by disease. In women, disease is the usual cause, although women too are subject to natural hair loss through aging. Hair implantation is nonetheless performed almost exclusively on men.

What is the goal of surgery?

The purpose of hair implantation is to correct markedly receding hairlines or large bald patches. Both types of baldness can be treated by relocating hairbearing skin from the back to the front—and there are several methods for effecting this. But the only hairbearing skin that can successfully be implanted is your own skin. People without *any* hair, therefore, cannot be treated.

Exactly what is involved in the surgical operation?

Before the operation, the surgeon will have examined your scalp in order to assess the best way to proceed. The method the surgeon adopts will depend on the degree and location of the baldness. The main methods of hair implantation are:

Full-thickness grafts. Short strips of full-thickness, hairbearing skin are transplanted from hairbearing areas at the back of the head to the hair loss areas at the front.

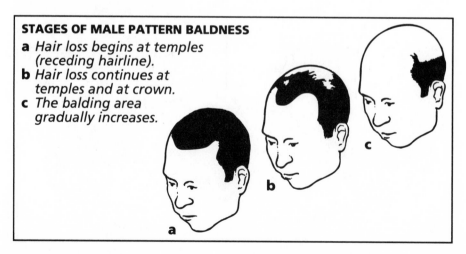

STAGES OF MALE PATTERN BALDNESS
a *Hair loss begins at temples (receding hairline).*
b *Hair loss continues at temples and at crown.*
c *The balding area gradually increases.*

Punch grafting. Multiple tiny cylinders of hairbearing skin are transplanted.

Flap grafting. Strips of hairbearing skin are rotated from their original position into a new location, together with their underlying blood vessels, all still fully connected at one end.

Scalp reduction. A bald gap is progressively closed by excising areas of bald skin and drawing the hair-containing skin close together through a series of operations.

Most hair transplantation operations are performed under general anesthesia.

Preliminary steps. As with all operations involving general anesthesia, you will be given a preoperative injection about an hour before surgery to dry up internal fluids and to encourage drowsiness.

Step-by-step surgical procedure. Once you are anesthetized, the surgeon begins to operate according to the method selected as most appropriate.

Full-thickness graft method

The surgeon carefully uses a surgical knife to make a number of incisions at the back of the scalp, cutting out strips about ¼ inch in width (**1**), and of a depth sufficient to ensure the inclusion of the tissue beneath the skin that contains the hair roots (follicles). Similar strips are cut from the bald area (**2**), the surgeon meanwhile ensuring that when the hairbearing strips are positioned and stitched in the slots from which the bald strips have been removed (**3**), the result still looks natural. Between 40 and 60 strips can be transplanted in this way. The slots at the back of the scalp from which the hairbearing strips have been taken are then also sewn up with fine stitches.

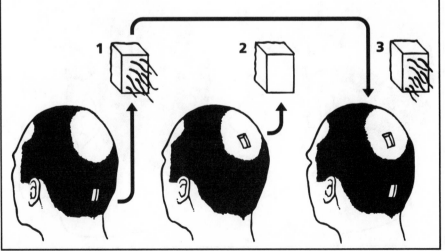

© DIAGRAM

The punch grafting method

The surgeon uses a device known as a trephine to cut tiny cylinders of hairbearing tissue from the donor site. These are then inserted in cylindrical holes cut by the same device in the bald area. No stitching is required: the hairbearing cylinders are simply pressed into position and soon heal securely. In general, only small bald patches are treated using this method.

a Cylinder of hairbearing tissue
b Common location for punch grafting
c Common donor site
d The grafts in place

The flap grafting method

The surgeon creates flaps of hairbearing skin that slot across into adjacent bald areas (from which surface tissue is removed appropriately), leaving an edge still connected. This most successful method is often unsuitable: it is not common for an area containing enough hair to be immediately adjacent to a completely bald area. In another, similar method, the entire scalp may be shifted forward after a large ellipse of tissue at the front has been removed. This somewhat radical procedure is usually restricted to injury cases.

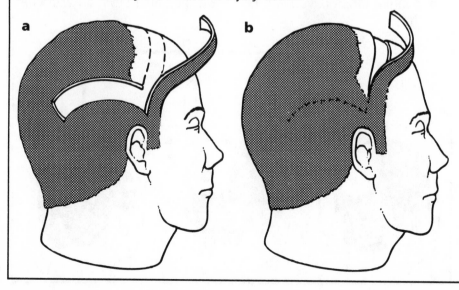

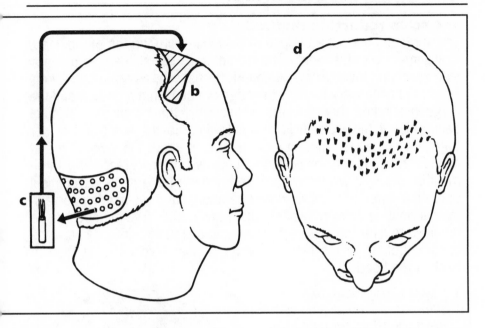

a First flap is lifted and rotated.
b First flap is sewn in position.
c Second flap is lifted and rotated.
d Second flap is sewn in position.

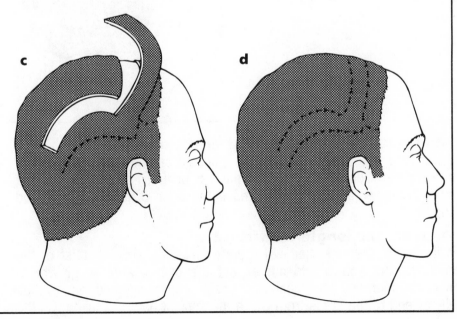

© DIAGRAM

The scalp reduction method

The surgeon cuts out an ellipse of bald skin from the top of the head, in alignment with the length of the bald area. The skin edges on each side are then closed from the underlying tissues, as far in both directions as is necessary to allow the edges to be pulled together, and the surgeon stitches them closed. In this way, the hairbearing skin on each side of the incision is drawn farther up the head and closer together. The ellipse must not be more than about 1.5 inches wide at its center, or the tension on the stitches will be too great. After three months, the skin will have stretched enough for a second, identical operation. After one or two more operations, at three-month intervals, the hairbearing sides may finally meet each other. The method can be modified to alter the shape of the removed area of skin; it can also be used to get rid of the fairly common circular bald patch at the top back of the head.

1 *Ellipse of skin removed*
2 *Ellipse removed and edges sewn together, reducing the size of the bald area*
3 *Eventual result after several operations*

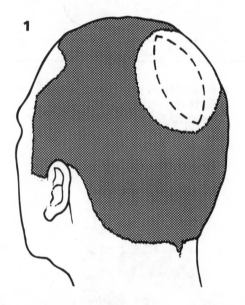

What is it like immediately after the operation?
You may wake up with a headache; it should pass, but may turn into a more general discomfort around the top of the head. In general the scalp heals remarkably quickly, mainly because of its excellent blood supply.

What are the longterm effects?
With reasonable luck, hair will grow from all or at least most of the implants, but you should not expect the overall area of growth to increase. Moreover, baldness is normally progressive and may eventually extend to the areas from which the implant hair was taken. On the

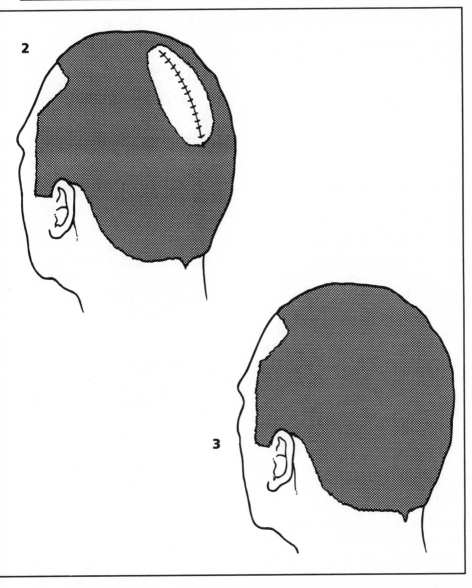

other hand, it is quite common with advancing age for hair to start to grow more enthusiastically in areas of the body remote from the top of the head—so if those are the areas used for grafting, the implants may actually grow more quickly than expected.

Breast reconstruction

Why have the operation?

It is common for women who have had a breast removed to suffer at least some degree of depression and anxiety and to experience some sexual difficulties. Breast reconstruction may in many cases represent a means of overcoming these problems. As with all cosmetic surgery, the major intention behind the operation is to enhance appearance, and by so doing to increase morale and self-image, leading to an overall improvement in lifestyle.

What is the physical cause of the problem?

Most patients who request breast reconstruction have had cancer of the breast and for that reason have had the breast removed. It is uncommon to undertake breast reconstruction until at least three months to one year after the breast removal operation. The longer period is advisable for patients who have undergone radiotherapy, which may interfere with healing and increase the chances of graft rejection. A few surgeons, however, prefer to undertake reconstruction at the time of the original mastectomy operation.

Patients most suitable for breast reconstruction are those who have undergone radical mastectomy, involving the removal of both the skin and the underlying tissue bulk of the breast. However, even in the most suitable case there remains one particularly thorny problem for the surgeon: to achieve adequate symmetry in relation to the size and shape of the other breast. (If the other breast is large, for example, the question might even arise of whether to undertake a reduction operation on it, notwithstanding the resultant additional scarring.) There is also the question of creating a nipple for the reconstructed breast. A perfect result is uncommon, and you should be aware of this.

What is the goal of surgery?

The surgeon's aim is to use tissues from elsewhere in your body to provide a breast of sufficient size and shape to match the one still present.

Exactly what is involved in the surgical operation?

Preliminary steps. As with all operations involving general anesthesia, you will be given a preoperative injection about an hour before surgery to dry up internal fluids and to encourage drowsiness.

Step-by-step surgical procedure. Once you are anesthetized, the surgeon has a choice of two sites from which to take the tissues that will make up the new breast: the back or the abdomen.

In both cases once the donor tissue has been prepared, the surgeon cuts along the line of the old mastectomy scar and stitches the new elliptical area of transferred skin to its edges. The underlying muscle of the transferred tissue creates most of the bulk of the new breast

Using muscles of the back as the donor site

Just under the skin is a thick, broad muscle called the *latissimus dorsi*. By making an incision parallel with the fibers of the muscle— obliquely toward the shoulder from the midline—the surgeon can transfer a fairly large, elliptical piece of skin together with its attached underlying muscle and supplying blood vessels all from the back wall of the armpit around to the front. If the blood supply can be transferred in full, the chances of total success are high. The edges of muscle where the tissue has been removed are brought together with catgut sutures and the skin incision at that point is closed with stitches of nylon (or other material) or with clips.

A *Donor site*
a Latissimus dorsi *muscle*

B *Post-graft scar*
b *Site for nipple to come*

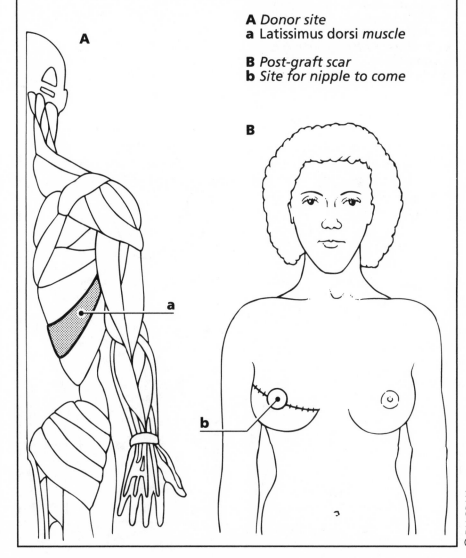

© DIAGRAM

Using muscles of the abdomen as the donor site

Using this donor site allows a more extensive area of skin and muscle to be taken and there is nearly always an abundance of fat under the skin that can also be transferred, which will help to bulk up the new breast. The main disadvantages are that loss of muscle from the abdominal wall may occasionally lead to the development of a hernia later in life, and that there is a slightly greater risk of tissue rejection than if the graft had been taken from the back. The incision is usually made as a wide ellipse across the body, its widest point just approaching the navel. Afterward, the wound is closed with stitches of nylon (or other material) or with clips.

a *Line of incision to remove skin and muscle for graft*
b *Mastectomy scar*
c *Final scars after grafting is complete*
d *Site for nipple to come*

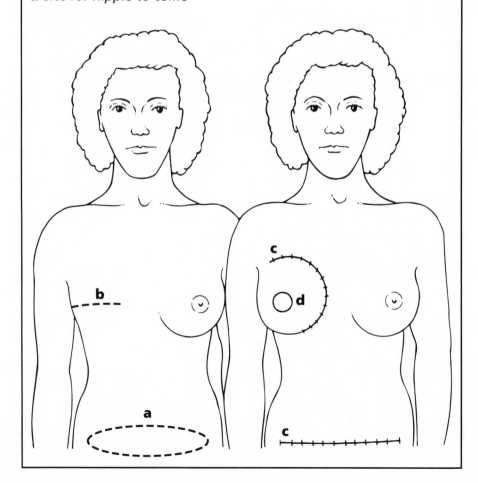

although, with tissue taken from the back, the surgeon may suggest including a silicone implant in the new breast. A silicone implant is less commonly inserted with tissue from the abdomen because abdominal tissue comes with additional fat.

The addition of a nipple, if performed surgically, is generally left for another operation after about three months.

What is it like immediately after the operation?
There will be initial discomfort arising in the area from which the surgeon took the tissue to create the breast, and the rows of stitches and the lack of a nipple may be something of an unwelcome sight. You will be encouraged to remain fairly motionless for several days—you won't feel like doing much anyway—before mild and careful exercise is undertaken, with precautions against the possibility of pulling stitches. Breast reconstruction is a major surgical procedure, and requires hospitalization for at least one week after the operation.

What are the longterm effects?
You should recover full use of the shoulder or abdominal muscles in a few weeks. If a nipple is required, an adhesive prosthetic nipple can be provided—many patients decide not to undergo further surgery and use this on a longterm basis instead. After three months, however, if a surgical operation is decided upon, an areola can be created out of a disk of skin taken from the inside of the thigh, and with luck the remaining nipple can be split to provide nipple tissue, or that too can be created from skin taken from an earlobe or elsewhere.

Complications of breast reconstruction surgery are rare, but they do occur. They include tissue rejection, resulting in the death and shrinkage of the grafted tissue (the skin or the fat, or both), which usually requires reoperating. Also, note that research into the safety of silicone breast implants is ongoing in light of questions concerning dangerous longterm side effects. Patients considering having such implants must confer with their surgeons to determine whether the procedure is possible and appropriate in their case and whether the potential dangers outweigh the possible benefits. If you meet the required qualifications, you must agree to take part in a clinical study of the longterm effects of the implants. (For more information about silicone implants and implantation, see *Breast enlargement*, p.428.) And, quite independently, the cancer for which the original operation was undertaken may reappear.

Breast enlargement

Why have the operation?

The size and shape of the breasts is very much a matter of genetic inheritance, influenced to a minor degree by such factors as racial characteristics, diet, and individual glandular secretions. Nonetheless, breasts that are considered undersized by their "owner" can represent a source of fierce resentment and intense unhappiness. As with all cosmetic surgery, the major intention behind the operation is to enhance appearance, and by so doing to increase morale and self-image, leading to an overall improvement in lifestyle.

Surgically enlarging the breasts involves implanting a rubber silicone capsule loosely filled with a soft silicone gel behind the glandular tissue of each breast. (Very occasionally, the implant is of some other material.) The technique is called augmentation mammoplasty. It is not a

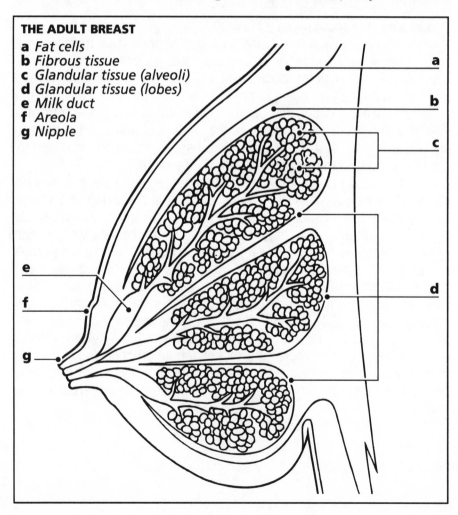

THE ADULT BREAST

a *Fat cells*
b *Fibrous tissue*
c *Glandular tissue (alveoli)*
d *Glandular tissue (lobes)*
e *Milk duct*
f *Areola*
g *Nipple*

major operation and can be performed as well under local anesthesia as under general.

Large breasts are not suitable for every woman who wants them. If your breasts were once of satisfactory size and shape but have since become flat and drooping as a result of a loss of fat, for example, the appropriate operation is not augmentation mammoplasty but masto-pexy, in which no implant is involved but the appearance is improved by the removal of an area of redundant skin tissue from each breast. The general rule is that if, when you are sitting upright, your nipples lie at a level below the crease at which the breasts join your chest, augmenta-tion should not be performed—unless combined with a mastopexy. If your nipples lie above this line, you may be a suitable candidate.

Research into the safety of silicone breast implants is ongoing in light of questions concerning dangerous longterm side effects. You may experience changes in sensation afterward: you have about a one in six chance of discovering that the sensitivity of your nipples has altered in some way after surgery, and in rare cases there is total and permanent loss of nipple sensation. Other possible side effects caused by the sili-cone implant are hardening of the breast, leakage of the implant into the body's tissues, recurrent infection in the breast, and difficulty in get-ting an accurate mammogram. Links between silicone implants and immune disorders are currently being explored. Patients considering having such implants must confer with their surgeons to determine whether the procedure is possible and appropriate in their case and whether the potential dangers outweigh the possible benefits. If you meet the required qualifications, you must agree to take part in a clini-cal study of the longterm effects of the implants.

Keep in mind also that augmentation mammoplasty will change the way your body looks to you in the mirror; you must be prepared for that change.

WHICH PROCEDURE?

Breast shape suitable for augmentation mammoplasty

Breast shape not suitable for augmentation mammoplasty unless combined with mastopexy

© DIAGRAM

What is the goal of surgery?

The aim of the surgeon is to enlarge the breasts in a way and by a factor that will still look natural, with invisible or minimal scarring.

Exactly what is involved in the surgical operation?

Preliminary steps. If the operation is to be performed under general anesthesia, you will be given a preoperative injection about an hour before surgery to dry up internal fluids and to encourage drowsiness.

Step-by-step surgical procedure. Once you are anesthetized, the surgeon makes an incision about 1.5 inches long on the underside of one breast, just a little in front of the crease. The surgeon then carefully reaches into the tissues and separates the layers, creating a flat pocket or pouch in the tissues behind the breast. If necessary, the surgeon widens the pocket with his or her fingers to ensure that it will accommodate the chosen implant. The reason for this is that the implant should be buried as deeply within the breast as possible—certainly behind the milk-secreting breast tissue and, in the view of some surgeons, preferably even behind the flat pectoral muscles that lie under the breast. If there is any bleeding, the surgeon checks it firmly and at once; any collection of blood forming a clot (hematoma) must at all costs be avoided. The flexible implant is slipped into the pocket, and the short incision is closed with a few fine stitches.

The procedure is then repeated with the other breast.

What is it like immediately after the operation?

There should be little discomfort and virtually no pain. Assuming no

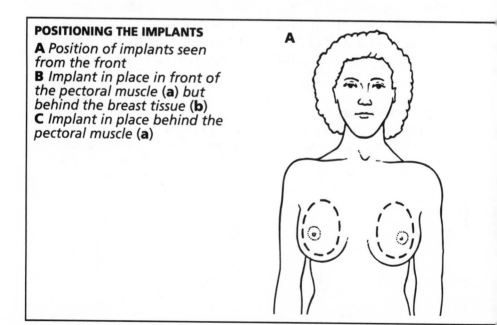

POSITIONING THE IMPLANTS

A *Position of implants seen from the front*
B *Implant in place in front of the pectoral muscle (**a**) but behind the breast tissue (**b**)*
C *Implant in place behind the pectoral muscle (**a**)*

complications occur, you can go home a day or two after the operation. However, there is on rare occasions a potential complication even at this early stage. If bleeding continues around the implant for any reason, a hematoma may form, causing the breast to become swollen and painful. Hematomas must be removed without delay for they can lead to an abscess and later scar formation with consequent contractures and distortion of the breast. In the unlikely event of a hematoma developing, you will have to go back to the operating room for drainage and control of further hemorrhage.

While you are in the hospital, the medical staff will instruct you on how to keep the implants flexible by daily massage of each breast. This also helps to avert—or at least greatly delay—the formation of a fibrous capsule around each implant (fibrosis).

What are the longterm effects?

In spite of research into possible links between silicone implants and serious health risks (as described on p.429), most women experience no adverse side effects. The effects of the operation are generally excellent and permanently satisfactory. That said, as many as one in four patients does eventually (after six months though sometimes not for a number of years) experience the development of a fibrous capsule around one or both implants, which may give the breasts an unnatural feel and may even distort their shape. The treatment for it is forceful external manipulation by a physician to break up the capsule or, in a few cases, another operation to remove and, if appropriate, to replace the first implant.

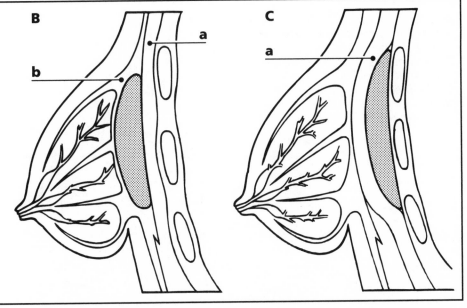

Breast reduction

Why have the operation?

The size and shape of the breasts is determined by several factors, including genetic inheritance, diet, and individual glandular secretions. Breasts that are considered oversized by their "owners" can be a source of unhappiness and discomfort; many women adopt a stooping posture to minimize the size of their breasts. One major intention behind the operation is to enhance appearance, and by so doing to increase morale and self-image, leading to an overall improvement in lifestyle.

What physical problems arise from having overlarge breasts?

Large, heavy breasts may cause difficulty in running, skin rashes from skin-to-skin contact, and even orthopedic problems such as arthritis at the neck from the constant need to brace back the spine.

What is the goal of surgery?

The major consideration in this operation is that surgery must be above all cosmetic: visible scarring must be minimal or nonexistent. In effect, this limitation transforms the operation from potentially minor (for it would be quite easy simply to remove a strip of tissue from the upper breast—and so leave conspicuous scars) into a relatively extensive and complex undertaking.

At the same time, the surgeon's goal is to fashion for you the breasts

---

THE OPERATION

A *Line of incision*
a *Keyhole-shaped new site for nipple and areola*
B *Area of tissue to be removed (shaded)*
C *The incision*
b *Skin*
c *Breast tissue*

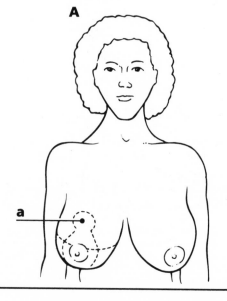

that you want. All preliminary investigatory examinations are geared to fulfilling your stated requirements.

Exactly what is involved in the surgical operation?

Reducing the overall bulk of each breast inevitably involves repositioning the nipple (and its surrounding areola). If your breasts are initially very large, one result is that after the operation you may have no sensation in your nipples, and later nursing (breastfeeding) may likewise be impossible.

Preliminary steps. As with all operations involving general anesthesia, you will be given a preoperative injection about an hour before surgery to dry up internal fluids and to encourage drowsiness. Once you are anesthetized in the OR, the surgeon will begin by marking out with a felt pen on each of your breasts the area of skin tissue to be removed (as shown by the shaded zone in the illustration).

The placing of these lines requires fine judgment: the final size of your breasts will be entirely determined by the surgeon's marks, so great care must be taken to get the two sides exactly symmetrical.

Step-by-step surgical procedure. The surgeon now makes the incisions, cutting out a carefully measured keyhole-shaped area above the nipple and a horizontal line across the breast. An incision is also made completely around the nipple and areola.

The surgeon now removes the skin and a certain amount of the underlying breast tissue on either side of the breast. The surgeon must judge carefully that an equal amount of the internal tissue is removed

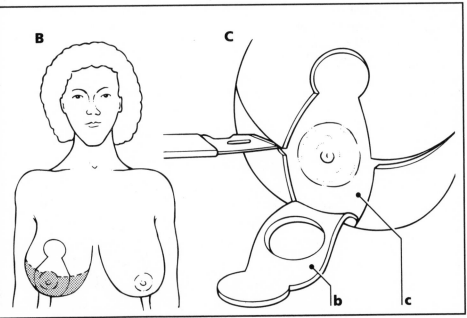

© DIAGRAM

from both sides. Anything from a few ounces to several pounds in weight of tissue may be removed, depending on the preoperative size of the breasts.

It is then time for reconstruction. The nipple and areola are to fit within the circle of the keyhole-shaped area. The surgeon will prefer it if they can be bodily moved up to their new site still attached to their underlying tissues (which include the milk ducts and the nerves that supply sensation). However, in the case of very large breasts, the nipple and areola may have to be completely separated from the underlying tissues and be replaced in the new site as a free graft. (It is only in these circumstances that there will later be no sensation in your nipples and no possibility of breastfeeding later.)

The nipple and areola are stitched into place: the stitches are virtually invisible in the pigmented tissue of the areola. The rest of the keyhole shape is brought together beneath the new nipple and stitched together as a short vertical line beneath the nipple. The horizontal cut becomes the new crease that joins the breast to the chest wall, and is invisible under the bulk of the breast.

What is it like immediately after the operation?

You will feel some pain, which can be controlled with painkilling drugs. Some hours after surgery, your surgeon may remove the dressings. Many surgeons check at this point that the healing process has started and is progressing correctly. If a large mass of clotted blood (a hematoma) is accumulating anywhere—as sometimes happens—a sur-

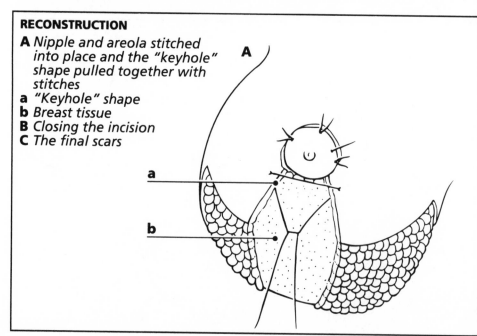

RECONSTRUCTION
A *Nipple and areola stitched into place and the "keyhole" shape pulled together with stitches*
a *"Keyhole" shape*
b *Breast tissue*
B *Closing the incision*
C *The final scars*

A

a

b

gical drain must be inserted in order to avoid infection and the development of an abscess. The surgeon may also check that the stitches are holding (if they pull loose, scarring will be much more visible) and that the blood supply to the resited nipples remains adequate.

Because both the incisions and the stitching are extensive, your first reaction to your breasts' appearance may be shock at how much has been done. Your surgeon should also inform you at this time whether or not your nipples are still attached to their original underlying tissues (and whether or not you will have sensation in them). All being well, you should be able to leave the hospital about a week after the operation.

What are the longterm effects?
Ideally, the longterm effects are that your breasts are exactly the size and shape you wanted, and that there are no visible scars. If the surgery has been performed well, and the stitching is regular and neat, then the only scar that might remain visible—the vertical line down from each nipple to the crease—should virtually disappear after a few months.

A subsequent pregnancy will naturally again alter the shape of your breasts. They will increase in size during the months of gestation, and the skin will expand to allow them to do so. If your nipples have been resited by free graft and you have no sensation in them, however, milk production (lactation) will have to be prevented with hormone treatment after the baby is born, because the internal milk ducts have been severed and are no longer continuous with the ducts in the nipples.

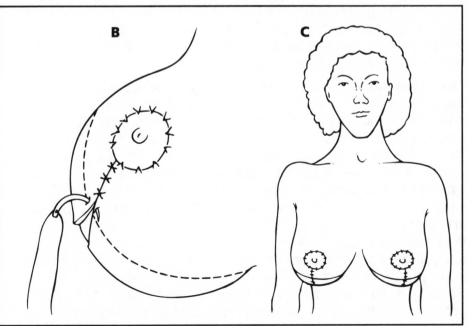

© DIAGRAM

Removing excess tissue and fat from the abdomen

Why have the operation?

As with all cosmetic surgery, the major intention behind the operation is to enhance appearance, and by so doing to increase morale and self-image, leading to an overall improvement in lifestyle.

What are the physical facts that relate to the operation?

A fold of tissue, especially fatty tissue, around the abdomen implies serious obesity, although advancing years and skin laxity undoubtedly tend to compound the problem. Obesity, however, presents its own health risks—notably that of heart disease—and is a complex condition for which cosmetic surgery is not necessarily the correct answer. Once you and your surgeon decide cosmetic surgery is right for you, the surgeon must still ascertain whether in your particular case it is necessary to deal with just an excess of skin in folds, or with an excess of skin plus fat deposits beneath. Most of the fat forms a thick yellow, oily layer that separates the skin from the abdominal muscles and may be many inches deep. Removal may demand extensive surgery, making conceal-ment of surgical scars more difficult and increasing the chances of such complications as blood loss, which may temporarily affect your overall health, bleeding into the tissues (hematoma) causing conspicu-ous marks, or infection.

What is the goal of surgery?

The surgeon's goal is to remove a section of skin, or of skin-plus-fat, in such a way as to be able to pull together the remaining outside edges and stitch them together without undue tension, while still preserving normal bodily features as much as possible.

Exactly what is involved in the surgical operation?

The surgeon must first determine precisely what to remove and what to leave. To do this he or she may use a felt pen and, while you stand upright, may draw on your abdomen an outline of the area for removal. There are two main designs, depending on whether (**A**) you have been dieting, or have been pregnant, and now have an "apron" of loose, sag-ging skin in folds over your lower abdomen, or (**B**) fat has accumulated under the skin of the central abdomen. Both designs attempt to leave the navel alone.

Preliminary steps. As with all operations involving general anesthe-sia, you will be given a preoperative injection about an hour before surgery to dry up internal fluids and to encourage drowsiness.

Step-by-step surgical procedure. Following design **A**, your sur-geon removes the excess skin from the shaded area, avoiding the mus-

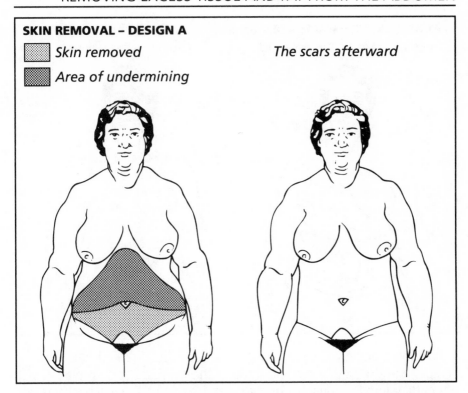

SKIN REMOVAL – DESIGN A

Skin removed

Area of undermining

The scars afterward

cles beneath and leaving the navel intact. The darker-shaded area is then "undermined," separating the top layers of skin from their base of subcutaneous tissue. This allows those layers of skin to be pulled down tautly to meet the lower edges of the initial area removed. The navel is thereby covered—but the surgeon simply feels for it through the skin, makes a short horizontal cut, and stitches it back in place.

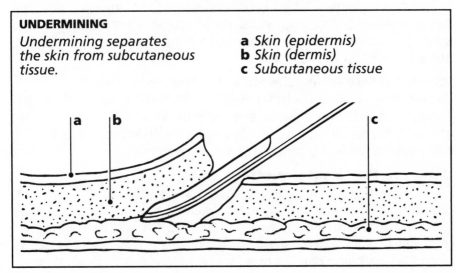

UNDERMINING

Undermining separates the skin from subcutaneous tissue.

a Skin (epidermis)
b Skin (dermis)
c Subcutaneous tissue

FAT AND SKIN REMOVAL – DESIGN B

Fat and skin to be removed   *The scar afterward*

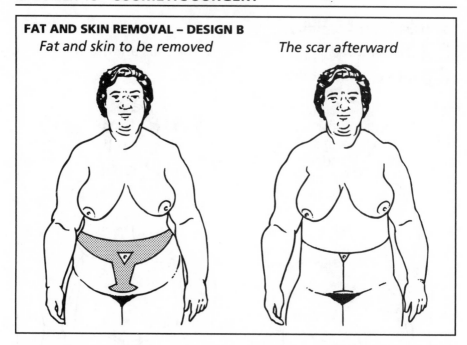

Following design **B**, your surgeon traces the marked lines with a scalpel, carefully cutting down through the skin and underlying fat, but not cutting into the muscles beneath, and leaving the navel intact. He or she then removes the skin together with its underlying fat from the shaded area. Fat layers left at the edges are pulled together so that they join in the center, and are stitched. Finally the surgeon pulls the edges of skin together at the center, and secures them with stitches.

The amount of bleeding depends both on the surgeon's methods and on the individual's response.

Tension on stitches is high in both operations. To prevent them from being pulled out, many surgeons reinforce them with adhesive tape applied criss-cross over the entire abdomen and around the buttocks; this is left for two weeks or more.

What is it like immediately after the operation?
You will feel some pain, which can be controlled with painkilling drugs. To reduce tension on stitches and minimize strain on abdominal skin you will probably be kept in bed, lying with your knees up, for as long as two weeks or while the adhesive tape is in position.

What are the longterm effects?
The longterm effect is, ideally, that with the excess fat and skin removed, you are now the shape you want to be. The scars should be virtually invisible. If obesity was the cause of the problem, however, returning to your former size and weight might cause your scars to stretch and become obvious or your skin to stretch to its former size.

SUCKING AWAY THE FAT

Liposuction, or suction lipectomy, is a method of fat removal that requires only a very small incision and that is effective in people with excess fat but reasonably elastic skin. The process makes use of the fact that at body temperature human fat is liquid, effectively a kind of oil held within thin-walled fat cells.

A small incision is made in the skin, and an instrument (about one foot long and ¾ inch in diameter) with a long, thin, hollow shaft ending in a small, sharp-edged spoon is pushed through the incision and moved along under the skin to the area of excess fat. The "spoon" is then used to scrape the fat free from its natural location between the skin layers and the deeper subcutaneous tissue, after which it can be sucked out through a metal tube connected to an ordinary operating room suction pump.

The procedure carries possible complications and risks. In addition to fat, a considerable quantity of blood will be sucked out, which could leave you anemic. Very rarely, fat that has been freed may enter the bloodstream and be carried to the heart, and then to the lungs where it can block arteries. This is called fat embolism and it can be fatal. Discuss all possible complications with your surgeon.

LIPOSUCTION
a *Sharp-edged "spoon"*
b *Suction pump*

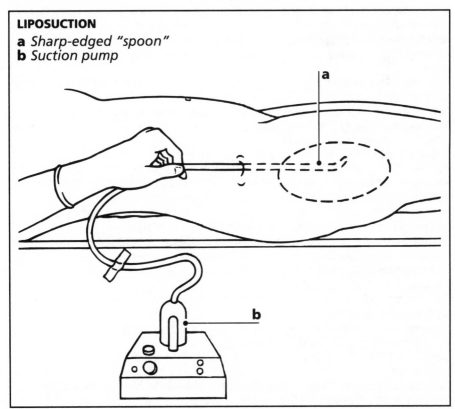

© DIAGRAM

Glossary of surgery-related terms

Abduction A movement outward from the center of the body or of a limb

Abortion Ending of a pregnancy before the fetus can survive outside the uterus

Abscess Pus-filled cavity usually caused by infection

Adduction A movement inward toward the center of the body

Adhesion The abnormal joining of tissues or other surfaces within the body caused by inflammation and resulting in scars

Analgesics Painkilling drugs

Anesthesia Loss of sensation, including sensitivity to pain, induced before many surgical procedures. Types include local, general, spinal, and epidural

Angiography Diagnostic method of viewing the blood vessels after injecting a radiopaque substance

Anoxia Lack of oxygen, often caused by obstruction to blood supply

Anterior Toward or at the front

Antibiotic Drug given to prevent infection by destroying bacteria in the body

Anti-inflammatory Drug to combat inflammation and so decrease pain or discomfort

Appendectomy Removal of the appendix

Arrythmia Irregularity in the heartbeat

Artery Vessel carrying blood from the heart to the rest of the body

Arthroscopy Diagnostic method of examining the inside of a joint using an illuminating instrument, such as a fiberoptic ENDOSCOPE

Aseptic Sterile; free of dangerous microorganisms

Aspiration Using suction to draw out fluid from a body cavity, using a tube, syringe, or by mouth

Atherosclerosis Degenerative disease of the arteries featuring fatty deposits

Atrophy Wasting away and/or emaciation, caused by aging, disease, infection, or injury

Augmentation Another term for enlargement, especially relating to breast enlargement surgery

Autograft Graft made from tissue or skin of same person receiving the graft

Balloon angioplasty Surgical method of expanding narrowed arteries by inserting an inflatable fine tube, or CATHETER

Barium enema Diagnostic method of examining rectum and colon using X RAYS after inserting contrast medium of barium sulfate liquid paste

Barium meal Diagnostic method of examining internal organs of the digestive tract using X RAYS and contrast medium of liquid barium sulfate, which is swallowed

Benign Used to describe abnormal growth that will not spread to other tissues or organs and so is usually nonfatal; compare with MALIGNANT

Biopsy Surgical procedure in which sample of tissue is removed for microscopic examination in a laboratory

Blepharoplasty Removal of bags around eyes

Carcinogenic Cancer causing

Carcinoma Malignant growth of cancerous surface tissues

Cardiac Relating to the heart

Cardiac catheterization Diagnostic method of examining the heart and arteries using a fine tube, or CATHETER, passed into the heart

Carotid arteries Pair of arteries on either side of the neck that provide blood supply to the brain

Carotid arteriogram Diagnostic method of examining the blood vessels of the brain using an opaque dye and X RAYS

Carpal tunnel Passage on the front of the wrist through which nerves and tendons extend from forearm to fingers

Catgut Threadlike substance made from sheep intestine and used for absorbable ties (ligatures) and SUTURES in surgery

Catheter Fine, plastic tube used in diagnostic procedures to examine internal organs and passages or as a drain to empty organs such as the bladder

Caudal Toward the feet

Cauterization Surgical method of destroying tissue by burning with a chemical, electricity, heat, or a laser

Cerebral Relating to the brain

Cerebral angiography Diagnostic method of examining the blood vessels of the brain using X RAYS and an opaque solution passed through a CATHETER

Cerebrospinal fluid Fluid surrounding the spinal cord and brain

Cesarean section Surgical procedure of delivering a baby through an incision in the mother's abdomen

Chemotherapy Treatment of disease (including cancer) and infection by the ingestion of medications

Cholecystectomy Gallbladder removal

Circumcision Removal of the foreskin of the penis

Colonoscopy Diagnostic method of examining the colon using a flexible illuminated tube, such as a fiberoptic ENDOSCOPE

Colostomy Surgical procedure in which an opening is created in the abdominal wall, to which the colon is brought up and attached, to act as an artificial "anus" in evacuating contents of bowel when colon has had to be severed or removed

Colposcopy Diagnostic method of examining the vagina and cervix using a low-power microscope

Computerized Axial Tomography (CT) scan Diagnostic method of examining the inside of the body (especially the brain) using hundreds of X RAYS that are combined by computer to build up a detailed picture

Cone biopsy Surgical method of removing a cone-shaped piece of the cervix for analysis in a laboratory

Congenital Condition or disease that is present at birth

Congestive Heart failure affecting either the right or left sides of the heart

Contracture Shortening of a muscle or tendon because of disease or injury and resulting in distortion and discomfort

Coronal Relating to the crown of the head

Coronary Relating to a crown, as in the coronary arteries whose branches spread above the heart

Cranial Toward the head

Craniotomy Surgical method of opening the skull

Cryosurgery Surgical method of destroying tissue by freezing

CT scan See COMPUTERIZED AXIAL TOMOGRAPHY (CT) SCAN

Curettage Surgical method of scraping out a thin layer, as of the uterus, for disposal or for analysis in a laboratory

Cutaneous Relating to the skin

Cystectomy Removal of the bladder

Cystography Diagnostic method of examining the bladder using X RAYS and an opaque solution injected into the bladder

Cystoscope A type of ENDOSCOPE used to examine the inside of the bladder

Cystoscopy Diagnostic method of examining the bladder using a CYSTOSCOPE

D & C See DILATATION AND CURETTAGE

Diagnostic Used to describe a procedure or method for identifying disease or other cause of symptoms

© DIAGRAM

Dialysis Method of compensating for poorly functioning kidneys by artificially removing waste products from the blood using a machine

Diathermy Surgical method of destroying tissues using a high-frequency electric current

Dilation Widening, either using a drug or mechanically

Dilatation and curettage (D & C) Surgical method of treating abnormal bleeding or removing tissue from inside the uterus by widening the cervix and using a scraping tool to scoop out tissue

Distal Toward the extremities of the body

Drip See INTRAVENOUS DRIP

ECG See ELECTROCARDIOGRAM

Echocardiography Diagnostic method of examining the heart's structure using ultrasound (high-frequency) waves

Echography Diagnostic method of examining the chest area using ultrasound (high-frequency) waves to produce a recording, called an echogram

EEG See ELECTROENCEPHALOGRAM

Electrocardiogram (ECG) Recording of pattern of the heart's electrical impulses made using ELECTROCARDIOGRAPHY

Electrocardiography Diagnostic method of examining the electrical impulses through the heart using electrodes attached to the chest and to a recording device to make an ELECTROCARDIOGRAM

Electroencephalogram (EEG) Recording of pattern of the brain's electrical impulses made using ELECTROENCEPHALOGRAPHY

Electroencephalography Diagnostic method of examining the electrical impulses of the brain using electrodes attached to the head and to a recording device to make an ELECTROENCEPHALOGRAM

Electromyography Diagnostic method of examining the electrical activity of the muscles using metal probes

Embolectomy Emergency procedure to remove an embolus

Embolism Blockage of a blood vessel by an embolus, or blood clot

Endoscope A thin, illuminated instrument used to examine body cavities and vessels and to remove samples for analysis. Can be used with different attachments for different surgical procedures

Endoscopy Examination of internal organs (usually the esophagus and stomach) for diagnostic or surgical purposes using an ENDOSCOPE. Endoscopy for other procedures uses specific names—e.g., LAPAROSCOPY

Epidermis Outermost layer of the skin

Episiotomy Surgical cut made in the PERINEUM during childbirth to enlarge the vaginal opening

Estrogen Sex hormones responsible for female sex characteristics; produced in ovaries and, to lesser degree, in testicles

Eversion Turning outwards

Extension Straightening of a limb or other body part

Flexion Bending or being bent, as of a joint

Frontal Toward or of the front of the body or body part; relating to the forehead

Gastrectomy Removal of all or part of the stomach

GI series See UPPER GASTROINTESTINAL (GI) SERIES

Hematoma A blood-filled swelling

Hemorrhage Abnormal bleeding, inside or outside the body

Hemorrhoidectomy Removal of hemorrhoids

Hepatectomy Removal of all or part of the liver

Homograft Graft using tissue or skin taken from someone other than person receiving the graft

Hyperactive Overactive

Hysterectomy Removal of the uterus

ICU See INTENSIVE CARE UNIT

Ileostomy Creation of an opening in the wall of the abdomen to which the ileum is attached and through which the intestine is emptied

Immobilization Fixing and holding in place (using TRACTION or splints) of fractured limb or damaged joint to allow healing to take place

Inferior Below

Intensive care unit (ICU) Area of hospital for constant medical care and observation of seriously ill patients

Intravenous drip (IV) Fluid (especially medication or nourishment) introduced intravenously (into a vein) from a sterile container held upright. The rate of flow can be controlled and adjusted

Intravenous pyelography (IVP) Diagnostic method of examining the urinary system using X RAYS and an opaque solution injected into veins to produce images called pyelograms

Inversion Turning inside out

Iridectomy Removal of part of the eye's iris

Irreducible Incapable of being restored to former condition or position

Isotope scan Diagnostic method of examining interior of the body using a scanner and radioactive material injected into veins and organs

IV See INTRAVENOUS DRIP

IVP See INTRAVENOUS PYELOGRAPHY

Laparoscopy Diagnostic method of examining the abdomen (including reproductive organs) using an ENDOSCOPE

Laparotomy Incision in the abdominal wall for surgical or diagnostic procedures

Laryngectomy Removal of the larynx

Lateral Toward or at the side

Lithonephrotomy Kidney stone removal

Lumbar puncture Method of obtaining cerebrospinal fluid for diagnostic purposes by injecting a needle between two vertebrae at the base of the spine; also used for administering drugs for treatment or anesthesia

Lumpectomy Removal of a breast tumor only, and not the surrounding tissue; compare with MASTECTOMY

Lymphadenectomy Removal of a lymph node

Lymph nodes Small oval-shaped bodies grouped in certain areas of the body, including armpits, groin, neck, and abdomen, that produce antibodies to fight the spread of infection

Magnetic Resonance Imaging (MRI) Diagnostic method of examining the inside of the body using radio waves

Malignant Used to describe cancerous growth that will spread to surrounding tissues and, if not totally removed, may be fatal; compare with BENIGN

Mammography Diagnostic method of determining the presence of breast cancer using X RAYS

Mastectomy Removal of a breast

Medial Toward the midline of the body

Meninges Three layers of membrane—pia mater, arachnoid mater, and dura mater—surrounding the brain and spinal cord

Meniscectomy Surgical procedure to remove a knee cartilage

Metastasis The spread of an abnormal growth, especially cancer, from one part of the body to another

MRI See MAGNETIC RESONANCE IMAGING (MRI)

Myelography Diagnostic method of examining the space around the spinal cord (e.g., to detect prolapsed disks) using X RAYS and a contrast medium injected by LUMBAR PUNCTURE

Myringotomy Cutting of the eardrum to release trapped fluid

Narcotic Drug that induces sleep and relieves pain

Nasogastric tube Thin, flexible, rubber or plastic tube passed through the nose and into the esophagus and stomach either to draw out digestive fluid or to provide nutrition

Necrotomy Removal of a piece of dead bone

Nephrectomy Kidney removal

Neurotomy Cutting of a nerve, usually to relieve pain

Obstructed Blocked; especially refers to a passageway within the body

Omentum Part of the PERITONEUM, the membrane that suspends from the abdomen to cover the intestines

Oophorectomy Removal of one or both ovaries

Ophthalmoscope Illuminated instrument used to examine the inside of the eye

Orchiectomy Removal of one or both testicles

Osteotomy Cutting of bone

Otoscope Tool for examining the inside of the outer ear canal and eardrum

Palmar On the palm of the hand

Paracentesis Method of removing fluid from a body cavity (especially the abdomen) for diagnostic or therapeutic purposes

Perforation Hole formed by erosion in an organ or passageway of the body

Pericardectomy Removal of the PERICARDIUM

Pericardium Membranous sac surrounding the heart

Perineum Pelvic floor, especially referring to area of muscle and tissue between vaginal opening and anus that is susceptible to tearing in childbirth

Peripheral Toward the surface

Peritoneum Membrane lining the wall of the abdomen and covering organs within the abdomen

PET scan See POSITRON EMISSION TOMOGRAPHY (PET scan)

Phlebotomy Puncture of a vein, usually to withdraw blood

Plantar On the sole of the foot

Pneumonectomy Removal of a lung

Polyp Tissue growth projecting from the skin or mucous membrane, such as inside the nose

Positron Emission Tomography (PET scan) Diagnostic method of examining tissues within the brain using a radioactive isotope injected into the bloodstream

Posterior Toward or at the back

Proctoscopy Method of examining the anus and rectum using an ENDOSCOPE inserted through the anus

Prolapse Slipping of an organ or tissue into an abnormal position, as with a prolapsed uterus or prolapsed intervertebral disk

Pronation Turning to a face-down or palm-down position

Prostatectomy Removal of the prostate

Prosthesis Artificial attachment to replace a body part, such as a limb or organ

Proximal Toward the attachment of a limb

Pulmonary Relating to the lungs

Radiation therapy (also called Radiotherapy) Method of treating disease, especially cancer, using X RAYS or radioactivity to destroy malignant growths

Radioisotope scan (also called Radionuclide scan) Diagnostic method of examining an internal organ by injecting a radioactive isotope and following its progress within the body

Reduction Manipulation back into original position, as of a bone or a hernia

Respirator A machine that maintains regular breathing by pumping air in and out of the lungs

Rhinoplasty Cosmetic surgery to change the shape of the nose

Rhizotomy Cutting or dividing nerve roots from the spinal cord to relieve pain

Rhytidectomy Facelift

Sagittal Relating to the median plane or a parallel plane of the body

Salpingectomy Removal or severing of one or both Fallopian tubes

Sigmoidoscopy Diagnostic method of examining the rectum and colon using an ENDOSCOPE called a sigmoidoscope

Splenectomy Removal of the spleen

Stapedectomy Replacing a diseased stapes (stirrup bone) within the ear

Stethoscope Tool used for listening to the sounds made by the internal organs, especially the heart and lungs, from outside the body

Stoma An opening, usually formed surgically, such as in the abdomen

Superior Above

Supination Turning to a face-up or palm-up position

Suppository Tablet inserted into the anus or vagina that dissolves to administer drug treatment or anesthesia

Suture Thread used for closing surgical incisions, often with needle already attached

Synovium Membrane lining a joint or surrounding a tendon that releases fluid allowing for joint movement

Testosterone Sex hormones responsible for male sex characteristics; produced in testicles

Thermography Diagnostic method of examining the inside of the body using a heat-sensitive camera

Thoractomy Opening of the chest wall, either between ribs or by splitting the breastbone, to gain access to heart and lungs

Thorascope A special type of ENDOSCOPE used to examine the lung cavity

Thrombosis Condition involving blood clotting within an artery or vein and possibly cutting off or obstructing blood flow

Thrombus A blood clot on the lining of a blood vessel

Thyroidectomy Removal of all or part of the thyroid gland

Tonsillectomy Removal of the tonsils

Tracheostomy Procedure for creating an opening in the trachea (windpipe) to maintain breathing

Traction Method of treating broken bones by pulling apart and maintaining proper alignment

Transverse Crosswise, or at right angles to the front-back axis of the body

Ultrasound scan Diagnostic method of examining internal organs using high-frequency sound waves

Upper gastrointestinal (GI) series Diagnostic method of examining the esophagus, stomach, and intestines using X RAYS and a BARIUM MEAL

Vagotomy Surgical procedure to reduce stomach acid production

Valvotomy Procedure for separating heart valves that have become fused

Vasectomy Severing the vas deferens for the purpose of sterilization

Venography Diagnostic method of examining the inside of veins using X RAYS and an opaque solution injected into the veins

X rays Short-wavelength rays used to penetrate body tissues for diagnostic purposes (to produce an x-ray image of the inside of the body) or therapy (to destroy diseased tissue)

Index